BUSINESS MATHEMATICS

The Easy Way

Third Edition

Calman Goozner

BARRON'S

All inquiries should be addressed to:
Barron's Educational Series, Inc.
250 Wireless Boulevard
Hauppauge, New York 11788
http://www.barronseduc.com

Library of Congress Catalog Card No. 00-031244

ISBN-13: 978-0-7641-1359-8
ISBN-10: 0-7641-1359-3

Library of Congress Cataloging-in-Publication Data
Goozner, Calman.
   Business mathematics the easy way / Calman Goozner.—3rd ed.
      p. cm.
   Includes index.
   ISBN 0-7641-1359-3
   1. Business mathematics. I. Title.

HF5691 .G655 2000
650'.01'513—dc21

                                                    00-031244

PRINTED IN THE UNITED STATES OF AMERICA
9 8 7

Contents

iv Contents

II   MATHEMATICS OF PERSONAL FINANCE   201

III APPLICATIONS OF MATHEMATICS TO BUSINESS 289

Preface to the Third Edition

Business Mathematics the Easy Way was written with two purposes in mind: to provide a review of mathematics skills for people who will soon need to use such skills, and to provide a realistic survey of applications to the business world. This edition includes lessons on using a calculator to check your work.

This work will have relevance to students who need to brush up on mathematics skills before entering the job market. Equally, people already in the business world can use this book to prepare themselves for broader responsibilities.

Because the reader is assumed to already have basic math competency, I have kept mathematical explanations as brief as possible. Most such content is handled in outline format as "procedures" or "hints."

Each unit contains examples with step-by-step explanations, as well as numerous exercises so that skills are reinforced adequately. I have also included a large number of realistic problems based on forms used in business and word problems drawn from actual business situations.

In addition, the reader will find notes regarding common business practice.

It is hoped that these procedures, hints, examples, exercises, and notes will provide the framework for the reader's successful transition into a chosen career.

Basic mathematics skills are reviewed in the first six chapters and are applied directly to business practices and business forms. Accuracy and checking methods, as well as shortcuts in business computations, are emphasized. Chapters 7 and 8 cover selected mathematical topics that have high relevance to the business situation—statistics and graphing, and measurement (including metric/English conversions).

Part II is devoted to topics of personal finance—banking, investments, loans and credit, and major expenditures (houses, cars, insurance). These chapters provide realistic uses for the mathematics skills of Part I in a highly motivational setting.

Similarly, Part III presents case problems from retailing, purchasing, and management and finance that will be directly transferable to the job situation.

I hope that this work is as satisfying to you, the reader, as it has been to me, the author and teacher. Please let me know of your suggestions or corrections through the publisher: Barron's Educational Series, Inc., 250 Wireless Boulevard, Hauppauge, NY 11788, or *www.barronseduc.com*.

Calman Goozner

PART

MATHEMATICS SKILLS

CHAPTER ONE

Addition in Business

UNIT **1** Addition Skills

Addition is the most frequently used mathematical operation in business. In the course of maintaining business records and carrying out business transactions, you will have to use addition and be accurate in such calculations.

Invoices, purchase orders, stock records, and time cards require the use of addition. Moreover, most business transactions involve money, so you will be doing many calculations involving the addition of dollars and cents.

Review of Addition

Addition involves combining two or more numbers called **addends** to obtain the **sum,** or **total,** of the group. Note that you will always be adding numbers with the same unit of measure—dollars and dollars, hours and hours, gallons and gallons. You *cannot* add dollars to hours or gallons to miles or minutes to pounds.

$$\left.\begin{array}{r}\$45.75 \\ 8.35 \\ +\ 1.58\end{array}\right\} \leftarrow \text{Addends}$$
$$\overline{\$55.68} \leftarrow \text{Sum (Total)}$$

PROCEDURE: To find the sum of two or more decimal numbers:

1. Arrange the numbers in column form so that digits with the same place value are directly under each other. The numbers should be written so that the decimal points line up vertically.

2. Always add from right to left. The right-hand column of digits is added first to get the first partial sum. The right-hand digit of this partial sum is written under the right-hand column, and the remaining digit (or digits) is carried to the next column.
3. Continue this procedure for each column.
4. Place the decimal point in the answer under the column of decimal points in the addends.

Example 1   Find the total of $23.45 and $38.28.

STEP 1.
$$\begin{array}{r} \$23.45 \\ +38.28 \\ \hline \end{array}$$

Write the numbers in columns with the decimal points aligned.

STEP 2.
$$\begin{array}{r} \overset{1}{\$23.}45 \\ +38.28 \\ \hline 3 \end{array}$$

Starting with the ones column, add the digits in each column, and write each *partial* sum that is 9 or less directly *under the column being added.*

STEP 3.
$$\begin{array}{r} \overset{1}{\$2}\overset{1}{3}.45 \\ +38.28 \\ \hline 61\ 73 \end{array}$$

If the *sum* of the digits in *any column* is greater than 9, write the *right-hand digit* under the column being added, and carry the *left-hand digit* to the *column to the left.*

STEP 4.
$$\begin{array}{r} \$23.45 \\ +38.28 \\ \hline \$61.73\ \textit{Answer} \end{array}$$

Insert the decimal point in the answer under the decimal points of the addends. Place the $ sign with the total, and label your answer.

Note: Whole numbers are a special case, as the decimal point does not appear. With whole numbers, the decimal point is always understood to be to the right of the digits. For example:

$$\left. \begin{array}{r} 234 = 234. \\ 1,386,934 = 1,386,934. \\ 3 = 3 \end{array} \right\} \text{(The decimal point is understood).}$$

Example 2   Add $234 and $3.78.

STEP 1.
$$\begin{array}{r} \$234.00 \\ +\ \ \ 3.78 \\ \hline \end{array}$$

Place the decimal point to the right of the whole number, and align the decimal points. Note that $234 has .00 cent.

STEP 2.
$$\begin{array}{r} \$234.00 \\ +\ \ \ 3.78 \\ \hline \$237.78 \end{array}$$

Add the numbers according to the procedure given.

Note: Many forms use a line instead of a decimal point to separate dollars and cents. For example:

$$\$237.78 = \boxed{\$237\ |\ 78}$$

Checking Addition

Accuracy is very important in business, because a mistake may cost a business concern thousands of dollars. It is good practice *always* to check the accuracy of your arithmetic in order to avoid mistakes.

You can define *addition* in terms of *subtraction*. Every addition problem has its related subtraction problem that will *undo* the addition.

For the *sum* 5 + 3 = 8, start with the number 5 and add 3 to get 8. Now, if you *subtract* (take away) 3 from 8, you have 5, the number you started with.

To check the solution to an addition problem, use subtraction to undo the addition:

If 20 + 3 = 23, then 23 − 3 = 20.

PROCEDURE: To check the addition of two or more numbers:

1. For problems with *two addends,* subtract *one addend from the sum.* The answer should be the other addend.
2. For problems with *more than two addends,* subtract all the addends from the sum. The answer should be zero.

Unless instructed otherwise, solve all calculations *by hand, showing all of your work, and use a calculator only to check your solutions.*

Example 3   Add: 485 + 337.

Solution: Add, and use a calculator to check the answer.

$$
\begin{array}{r}
^{1\,1} \\
485 \\
+\ 337 \\
\hline
822
\end{array}
$$

Check: Sum − Addend = Other addend
Keystrokes: 822 ⊟ 337 ⊜ 485 √
Answer: 485 + 337 = 822

As each keystroke is entered, check the display to make sure the entry is correct.

Example 4   Add: 495 + 702 + 689.

Solution: Add, and use a calculator to check the solution.

$$
\begin{array}{r}
^{1\,1} \\
495 \\
702 \\
+\ 689 \\
\hline
1,886
\end{array}
$$

Check: Sum − Addends = Zero
Keystrokes: 1886 ⊟ 689 ⊟ 702 ⊟ 495 ⊜ 0 √
Answer: 495 + 702 + 689 = 1,886

Exercises

Exercise A   Solve the following problems, indicating zero cent where necessary, and check your answers:

1. $63.75 + $28.15 + $35.82 + $73.47

2. $472 + $3,428.75 + $35.60 + $25

3. $232.43 + $364 + $472.10 + $527

4. $4,620 + $28.75 + $473.58 + $39

5. $607.75 + $28 + $327.85 + $215

6. $78 + $3,420.75 + $215.05 + $325

7. $48.73 + $2,070 + $628.47 + $372

8. $2,105.80 + $63 + $472.98 + $65.75

9. $35 + $347.80 + $8,923

10. $68 + $5,255 + $347.75 + $78.63

11. $4,623.49 + $793.78 + $93 + $78.50

12. $415.09 + $5,168.35 + $368 + $3.68

13. $649.57 + $84 + $5,627.26 + $10,738.47

14. $4,628.63 + $8,418.97 + $12,657.35 + $18,721.62

15. $6,327.56 + $14,246.76 + $976 + $18,648.95

16. $17,984 + $864.77 + $9,458.67 + $25,638.29

17. $6,456.36 + $49,275.49 + $876 + $9,786.68

18. $19,753.68 + $8,372.56 + $27,419 + $678.55

19. $5,458.63 + $7,568 + $43,786.17 + $596.56

20. $28,705 + $827 + $5,947.66 + $18,572.98

Exercise B   Find the total for each of the following forms, and check your answers:

Sample Problem

21.

Expense Records Week of 9/19		Check
Salesperson	**Amount**	
Anderson, B.	$63 50	63￼5
Bates, G.	71 68	⊞ 71￼68
Berger, M.	94 32	⊞ 94￼32
Carter, J.	87 55	⊞ 87￼55
Chambers, V.	74 19	⊞ 74￼19
Total	**$391 24**	⊟ √391.24

22.

Expense Records Week of 9/26	
Salesperson	**Amount**
Anderson, B.	$72 61
Bates, G.	68 24
Berger, M.	87 57
Carter, J.	76 42
Chambers, V.	83 81
Total	

23.

Expense Records Week of 10/3		
Salesperson	Amount	
Anderson, B.	$88	50
Bates, G.	91	50
Berger, M.	84	82
Carter, J.	77	44
Chambers, V.	64	29
Total		

24.

Expense Records Week of 10/10		
Salesperson	Amount	
Anderson, B.	$82	31
Bates, G.	78	45
Berger, M.	67	70
Carter, J.	76	36
Chambers, V.	83	87
Total		

25.

	Date: September 3			
Salesperson	Sales		Commission	
Anderson, B.	$15,685	75	$1,568	58
Bates, G.	13,856	80	1,385	68
Berger, M.	18,560	44	1,856	04
Carter, J.	14,375	86	1,437	59
Chambers, V.	15,963	45	1,596	35
Totals				

26.

	Date: October 3			
Salesperson	Sales		Commission	
Anderson, B.	$14,888	93	$1,488	89
Bates, G.	15,958	55	1,595	86
Berger, M.	21,060	66	2,106	07
Carter, J.	24,395	89	2,439	59
Chambers, V.	45,964	45	4,596	45
Totals				

27.

Inventory	
Item	Quantity
25-Watt Bulbs	75
40-Watt Bulbs	123
60-Watt Bulbs	115
75-Watt Bulbs	98
100-Watt Bulbs	135
Total	

28.

Inventory	
Item	Quantity
8 × 10 Frames	1,327
11 × 14 Frames	864
12 × 16 Frames	649
16 × 20 Frames	2,115
18 × 24 Frames	1,923
Total	

29.

Inventory	
Item	Quantity
Men's Ties #62	2,478
Men's Ties #68	987
Men's Ties #71	3,628
Men's Ties #74	5,870
Men's Ties #78	697
Men's Ties #81	874
Men's Ties #85	1,320
Men's Ties #90	2,054
Total	

30.

Inventory	
Item	Quantity
Vinyl Tiles #608	648
Vinyl Tiles #715	8,627
Vinyl Tiles #312	963
Vinyl Tiles #077	4,738
Vinyl Tiles #347	763
Vinyl Tiles #920	817
Vinyl Tiles #516	5,078
Total	

Find the subtotal and the total for each of the following forms:

31.

HANDY & SONS		
March 28 20--		
SOLD TO *P. Griffiths*		
ADDRESS *1031 Brookfield Ave.*		
CLERK *M.W.*	DEPT *33*	AMT REC'D $*105*

QUAN.	DESCRIPTION	AMOUNT	
3	Sport Shirts	$26	85
6	Pair of Socks	11	70
2	Ties	18	00
1	Pair of Shoes	36	95
	Subtotal		
	8% Sales tax	7	48
	Total		

POSITIVELY NO EXCHANGES MADE UNLESS
THIS SLIP IS PRESENTED WITHIN 3 DAYS.

32.

OFFICE SUPPLIES, INC.		
March 30 20--		

SOLD TO _J. Mendez_

ADDRESS _628 Amboy Road_

CLERK *J.R.*	DEPT *6*	AMT REC'D *$120*

QUAN.	DESCRIPTION	AMOUNT	
6 reams	Typing Paper	$29	10
12	Ribbons	33	75
12	Ko-rec-type	22	20
5 doz.	#2 Pencils	19	75
	Subtotal		
	8% Sales tax	6	29
	Total		

POSITIVELY NO EXCHANGES MADE UNLESS
THIS SLIP IS PRESENTED WITHIN 3 DAYS.

Word Problems

Word problems are easier to solve if you watch for key phrases. For instance, key phrases indicating addition are:

"Find the total."
"What is the cost of …?"

Use addition if you are given a set of numbers in the same units (money, hours, parts, etc.) and are asked for the *total*, the *sum*, or the *(total) cost*.

Exercise C   Solve the following problems:

33. A company bought two typewriters for $1,525 each, a desk for $785.90, a chair for $124.75, and an adding machine for $1,250.95. Find the total amount of the purchases.

34. Last week you made the following sales: Monday, $529.50; Tuesday, $327.85; Wednesday, $98.25; Thursday, $705.80; Friday, $615.75. What were your total sales for the week?

35. The Taylor Building Company deposited the following checks: $315.80, $475.60, $115.28, $287.60, $330.50, and $98.15. What was the total amount of the deposit?

36. The Ace Real Estate Company estimates the monthly cost of maintaining its office as follows: rent, $1,325; electricity, $175; telephone, $165; supplies, $145; miscellaneous expenses, $170. Find the estimated total cost of running the office for a month.

37. Sam Steinfeld has the following deductions from his weekly paycheck: federal withholding tax, $42.50, Social Security, $12.75; state tax, $14.10; city tax, $8.75; medical insurance, $2.40. Find the total of his payroll deductions.

38. Marcia Rice had the following travel expenses for the week of June 14: hotel, $301; food, $117.25; entertainment, $63.85; car rental, $289.68; and telephone, $38.90. What were her total expenses for that week?

39. The breakdown of the Alvarez family's monthly mortgage payment is as follows: reduction of principal, $98.75; interest charges, $138.63; escrow for real estate tax, $113.78; and mortgage insurance premium, $13.52. How much is the total monthly payment?

40. The sales by department for the Buy-Rite Supermarket for November 8 were as follows: grocery, $9,468.75; meat, $5,627.93; deli, $4,193.43; produce, $4,248.65; and nonfood, $6,374.60. What were the total sales for that day?

41. Sharon earns part of her salary from commissions based on sales. Last week she earned the following commissions: $35.63, $41.50, $23.78, $47.83, and $38.35. She also earns a base salary of $125, to which the commissions are added. What was Sharon's total salary last week?

42. Frank made the following credit card purchases for the month of June: $28.95, $15.63, $89.78, and $53.27. Find his total credit card purchases for the month.

UNIT **2** Horizontal and Vertical Addition

Many business forms are designed with sums to be added *horizontally* (across the page) and totaled in the right-hand column. Very often, these forms also require *vertical* addition, totaled under each column. This is an automatic check on your accuracy. If the two totals do not agree, you have made a mistake in addition.

Checking Horizontal Addition

As in vertical addition, you should check your accuracy by adding the numbers in the reverse direction.

Example Find the weekly sales by department and the grand total for the week of 1/15.

Weekly Sales by Department																Date: 1/15
Dept.	Mon.		Tues.		Wed.		Thurs.		Fri.		Sat.		Sun.		Total	
Grocery	$1,821	72	$1,763	15	$1,948	65	$2,163	47	$2,065	38	$1,918	42	$1,621	40	$13,302	19
Produce	963	54	907	43	1,163	70	1,485	72	1,391	72	1,268	34	1,020	65	8,201	10
Dairy	1,461	70	1,368	50	1,485	61	1,538	45	1,465	68	1,371	52	1,169	37	9,869	83
Meat	1,235	85	1,173	85	1,345	57	1,478	45	1,315	10	1,219	05	1,129	15	8,897	02
Deli	863	50	743	78	968	43	1,019	25	982	15	872	38	784	19	6,233	68
Nonfood	734	68	715	93	853	19	916	42	868	58	753	62	642	35	5,484	77
Totals	$7,080	99	6,672	64	7,765	15	8,601	76	8,088	61	7,403	33	6,367	11	51,979.59	

Grand Total

STEP 1. Using a calculator
    a. Add the daily sales and write each total in the total column on the right.
    b. Add each column and write the total under the column being added.
Note   c. Enter all decimal points.

STEP 2. As a check on accuracy, the two totals should be the same.

Check: $51,979.59 = $51,979.59 √

Exercises

Exercise A Using a calculator, find the sum of each set of numbers by adding horizontally.

1. $8 + 5 + 3 + 2 + 8 + 9 =$

2. $6 + 8 + 9 + 5 + 3 =$

3. $32 + 45 + 13 + 72 + 63 =$

4. $68 + 75 + 93 + 84 + 48 =$

5. $53 + 61 + 94 + 68 + 47 =$

6. $372 + 593 + 625 + 853 + 729 =$

7. $3,427 + 5,628 + 7,964 + 4,943 =$

8. $5,925 + 8,615 + 4,457 + 2,815 =$

9. $23,472 + 47,065 + 17,528 =$

10. $63,067 + 42,971 + 33,461 =$

11. $94,128 + 21,072 + 15,735 =$

12. $72,361 + 54,135 + 24,715 =$

13. $96,725 + 63,420 + 15,823 =$

14. $37,621 + 49,268 + 10,674 =$

15. $19,432 + 27,419 + 31,620 =$

16. $73,128 + 25,625 + 43,119 =$

17. $50,623 + 18,972 + 21,682 =$

18. $46,721 + 27,632 + 58,119 =$

19. $23,125 + 48,575 + 63,945 + 15,075 =$

20. $68,475 + 73,243 + 54,972 + 85,925 =$

Exercise B   Find the totals on the following forms, and check your answers:

21.

	Hours Worked Week of 10/17					
Employee	Mon.	Tues.	Wed.	Thurs.	Fri.	Total Hours
Adams, C.	8	8	12	12	10	_____
Adman, M.	9	9	13	4	10	_____
Burke, W.	8	8	10	8	7	_____
Curtis, A.	8	6	12	8	10	_____
Dellman, A.	12	8	6	12	6	_____
Evans, P.	8	10	8	8	12	_____
Totals	+	+	+	+	=	**Grand Total**

22.

	Hours Worked Week of 10/24					
Employee	Mon.	Tues.	Wed.	Thurs.	Fri.	Total Hours
Adams, C.	8	7	11	9	12	_____
Adman, M.	9	8	12	7	10	_____
Burke, W.	10	8	7	12	9	_____
Curtis, A.	8	7	11	9	10	_____
Dellman, A.	11	8	9	12	7	_____
Evans, P.	9	11	7	8	12	_____
Totals	+	+	+	+	=	**Grand Total**

23.

Payroll Deductions											Week of 3/23	
Employee Card No.	Federal Tax		FICA Tax		State Tax		City Tax		Pension		Health Plan		Total	
01	$35	15	$12	25	$ 8	79	$ 5	18	$7	35	$2	15	_____	___
02	43	70	13	47	9	16	5	78	8	38	3	21	_____	___
03	42	61	14	18	9	83	6	10	8	74	3	47	_____	___
04	38	61	13	17	8	91	5	83	7	84	2	65	_____	___
05	53	26	19	25	12	42	7	86	9	24	3	81	_____	___
06	51	80	18	72	12	39	7	47	9	18	3	34	_____	___
07	45	73	16	37	9	72	6	19	7	49	2	73	_____	___
08	57	20	19	38	13	24	8	86	9	42	3	68	_____	___
09	38	90	13	41	8	64	5	93	7	92	2	71	_____	___
10	55	30	18	15	13	05	8	74	8	19	3	42	_____	___
Totals		+		+		+		+		+		=		Grand Total

24.

Articles Sold						Stock # 6178
						Week Ending 4/13
Salesclerk	Mon.	Tues.	Wed.	Thurs.	Fri.	Total
Bohlen, D.	417	378	392	365	453	_____
Brown, C.	325	465	353	328	437	_____
Cortez, A.	364	405	428	429	349	_____
DeMato, J.	378	372	364	347	391	_____
Keelman, W.	427	437	415	328	467	_____
Gonzalez, J.	394	364	371	412	368	_____
Totals	+	+	+	+	=	Grand Total

25.

Weekly Sales by Department														Date: 1/8
Dept.	Mon.		Tues.		Wed.		Thurs.		Fri.		Sat.		Sun.		Total	
Grocery	$1,943	16	$1,948	65	$1,863	41	$2,158	17	$1,984	53	$1,928	31	$1,730	09	_____	___
Produce	983	75	973	18	867	38	968	38	828	16	793	82	834	15	_____	___
Dairy	1,575	68	1,562	84	1,471	35	1,420	93	1,420	93	1,341	72	1,286	94	_____	___
Meat	1,316	37	1,347	19	1,285	64	1,241	63	1,241	63	1,163	58	1,092	66	_____	___
Deli	965	53	860	93	763	28	738	40	738	40	629	40	643	19	_____	___
Nonfood	847	19	784	52	654	32	635	19	635	19	515	15	553	55	_____	___
Totals		+		+		+		+		+		+		=		Grand Total

26.

Weekly Sales by Department														Date: 1/15
Dept.	Mon.		Tues.		Wed.		Thurs.		Fri.		Sat.		Sun.		Total	
Grocery	$1,743	87	$1,901	94	$1,941	28	$1,876	70	$2,132	13	$1,970	66	$1,740	89	_____	___
Produce	985	86	970	52	847	24	920	40	943	09	794	77	818	18	_____	___
Dairy	1,427	93	1,518	18	1,459	64	1,347	58	1,496	75	1,581	29	1,362	74	_____	___
Meat	1,508	10	1,484	53	1,389	99	1,475	33	1,397	16	1,284	43	1,171	88	_____	___
Deli	813	27	875	06	773	26	798	18	852	28	806	11	723	35	_____	___
Nonfood	641	32	799	17	683	38	661	65	647	03	539	12	528	05	_____	___
Totals		+		+		+		+		+		+		=		Grand Total

27.

Department Sales							Week of 6/17
Department	Cash		Charge		C.O.D.		Total	
Ladies' Wear	$3,425	65	$2,315	78	$3,478	58	_____	___
Men's Wear	2,975	40	1,848	37	2,264	37	_____	___
Children's Wear	1,563	90	987	35	1,287	50	_____	___
Appliances	2,562	76	4,628	74	3,768	87	_____	___
Furniture	3,728	35	5,947	39	4,215	95	_____	___
Toys	1,584	72	867	48	1,367	58	_____	___
Totals		+		+		=		Grand Total

Exercise C Find the totals on the following forms:

28.

Please endorse all checks and list below singly

DATE , 20		DOLLARS	CENTS
	BILLS	872	00
	COINS	29	36
	CHECKS	536	63
		298	74
		974	97
		512	37
		839	16
		138	73
	TOTAL		

29.

Please endorse all checks and list below singly

DATE , 20		DOLLARS	CENTS
	BILLS	394	00
	COINS	19	59
	CHECKS	296	42
		358	47
		963	98
		152	63
	TOTAL		

30.

Please endorse all checks and list below singly

DATE , 20		DOLLARS	CENTS
	BILLS	374	00
	COINS	93	69
	CHECKS	947	41
		517	93
		493	69
		53	65
		8	15
		324	00
		173	75
	TOTAL		

31.

Please endorse all checks and list below singly

DATE , 20		DOLLARS	CENTS
	BILLS	474	00
	COINS	48	54
	CHECKS	939	75
		362	59
		691	35
		543	91
		478	79
		369	75
		592	34
	TOTAL		

32.

Please endorse all checks and list below singly

DATE , 20		DOLLARS	CENTS
	BILLS	63	00
	COINS	3	98
	CHECKS	89	61
		45	56
		78	49
		51	92
		39	88
		53	14
	TOTAL		

33.

Please endorse all checks and list below singly

DATE , 20		DOLLARS	CENTS
	BILLS	893	00
	COINS	5	98
	CHECKS	692	65
		473	95
		230	77
		149	02
	TOTAL		

34.

Please endorse all checks and list below singly

DATE	, 20	DOLLARS	CENTS
BILLS		245	00
COINS		1	58
CHECKS		3	99
		4	59
		3	99
		1	92
		6	45
TOTAL			

35.

Please endorse all checks and list below singly

DATE	, 20	DOLLARS	CENTS
BILLS		190	00
COINS		4	55
CHECKS		39	98
		99	59
		46	22
		70	95
		68	87
		27	77
TOTAL			

36.

Petty Cash Expenditures

Date	Amount	
2/3	$35	60
2/4	15	75
2/5	8	25
2/6	23	50
2/7	19	65
2/9	32	06
2/10	6	28
2/11	25	65
2/12	11	15
Total		

37.

Petty Cash Expenditures

Date	Amount	
1/3	$22	50
1/4	39	68
1/5	34	99
1/6	8	77
1/7	28	66
1/10	43	42
1/11	3	19
1/12	17	50
1/13	21	63
Total		

38.

Petty Cash Expenditures

Date	Amount	
4/12	$29	06
4/13	40	62
4/14	8	95
4/15	35	74
4/16		18
4/18	18	64
4/19	24	72
4/20	15	00
4/21	19	82
Total		

39.

Petty Cash Expenditures

Date	Amount	
3/13	$28	50
3/14	19	68
3/15	34	79
3/16	8	18
3/17	43	65
3/19	22	42
3/20	3	17
3/21	17	50
3/22	21	63
Total		

40.

Petty Cash Expenditures

Date	Amount	
5/12	$29	05
5/13	10	62
5/14	8	15
5/15	33	75
5/16		98
5/18	17	63
5/19	25	84
5/20	15	09
5/21	18	83
Total		

41.

Petty Cash Expenditures

Date	Amount	
5/1	$20	65
5/2	31	19
5/3	5	78
5/4	14	60
5/5	37	92
5/7	28	43
5/8	12	21
5/9	19	46
5/10	25	28
Total		

UNIT 3 Review of Chapter One

TERMS:	• Addends
	• Sum or Total
KEY PHRASES:	• "What is the total?"
	• "Find the (total) cost of . . . ."
HINTS:	• Line up the decimal points in vertical addition.
	• Check your totals.

Find the totals on the following forms:

1. Please endorse all checks and list below singly

DATE	, 20	DOLLARS	CENTS
BILLS		428	00
COINS		23	86
CHECKS		73	68
		110	52
		93	87
		47	58
		242	34
TOTAL			

2. Please endorse all checks and list below singly

DATE	, 20	DOLLARS	CENTS
BILLS		738	00
COINS		2	64
CHECKS		388	40
		169	92
		148	98
		65	79
		145	76
TOTAL			

3.

Please endorse all checks and list below singly

DATE	, 20	DOLLARS	CENTS
BILLS		928	00
COINS		123	86
CHECKS		93	69
		128	82
		95	04
		69	58
		193	94
TOTAL			

4.

Please endorse all checks and list below singly

DATE	, 20	DOLLARS	CENTS
BILLS		839	00
COINS		51	64
CHECKS		368	46
		59	72
		142	98
		65	34
		145	76
TOTAL			

5.

Sales for June				
Department	Cash Sales		Charge Sales	
A	$14,728	63	$15,628	47
B	8,649	47	9,473	64
C	29,382	69	32,592	63
D	17,461	63	19,637	46
E	31,728	41	34,528	47
F	20,649	47	21,473	64
G	15,349	72	16,593	75
Totals				

6.

Sales for May				
Department	Cash Sales		Charge Sales	
A	$13,468	72	$17,347	83
B	9,349	85	11,463	92
C	27,632	34	18,634	27
D	15,761	28	19,374	68
E	33,498	75	47,268	83
F	18,349	63	22,731	42
G	12,528	17	15,842	27
Totals				

7.

Salesperson	Sales		Commissions	
A	$23,575	85	$1,650	31
B	21,728	60	1,521	00
C	19,535	25	1,367	47
D	27,382	49	1,916	77
E	24,628	35	1,723	98
Totals				

8.

Petty Cash Expenditures		
Date	Amount	
9/2	$43	25
9/3	18	47
9/4	7	85
9/5	22	63
9/6	19	28
9/9	27	39
9/10	21	81
9/11	13	75
9/12	9	65
Total		

9.

Petty Cash Expenditures		
Date	Amount	
9/13	$15	83
9/16	19	65
9/17	25	27
9/18	11	45
9/19	27	78
9/20	39	57
9/23	23	35
9/24	16	42
9/25	27	35
Total		

Solve the following problems:

10. A company bought a file cabinet for $342.80, a copier for $1,528.95, an electric typewriter for $2,639.95, and paper supplies for $128.40. Find the total of all the purchases.

11. James Washington earned the following commissions: $1,463.75; $1,634.80; $1,678.65; and $1,273.32. What was the sum of all his commissions?

12. A traveling salesperson had the following expenses for 1 week: gasoline and oil, $195.75; hotel rooms, $350.35; food, $280.95; and entertainment, $174.25. Find the total expenses for the week.

CHAPTER **TWO**

Subtraction in Business

UNIT **1** Subtraction Skills

Many business forms require subtraction skills of the user. For example, companies are often permitted to subtract a *cash discount* from the amount of an invoice in return for prompt payment. Invoices may also show other types of discounts or special terms that must be calculated upon payment.

The number of articles sold has to be subtracted from the original stock for inventory records, and deductions must be subtracted from gross pay to find the take-home pay for each employee.

Many other records—bank statements, checkbooks, charge accounts, and financial statements—also require the use of subtraction.

Review of Subtraction

Subtracting involves finding the **difference** by taking a smaller number (the **subtrahend**) from a larger number (the **minuend**).

$8.65 ← Minuend
−3.67 ← Subtrahend
$4.98 ← Difference

PROCEDURE: The rules for subtraction of numbers with decimals are similar to the rules for addition:

1. Write the numbers with the decimal points lined up under each other. If this is done correctly, the digits will be in the proper columns according to place values.
2. Starting with the ones column, subtract *each lower digit* from *each upper digit* and write each *partial* difference *directly* under the digits you are subtracting.

3. When the *lower digit* in any column is *larger* than the digit above it, *borrow* 1 from the *digit to the left,* subtract 1 from that digit, and place the borrowed 1 to the left of the digit for which you borrowed it.
4. Continue this process for each column in the problem.
5. Place the decimal in the answer directly under the decimal points in the problem.

Example 1   Subtract $47.83 from $68.37.

STEP 1. $68.37
           −47.83

Write the numbers in columns with the decimal points aligned.

STEP 2. $68.37
           −47.83
               4

Subtract the digits in the first column (3 from 7). Place the answer, 4, under that column.

STEP 3. $6⁷8.¹37
           −47. 83
               54

Subtract the digits in the second column. Since the lower digit, 8, is *larger* than 3, the digit above it, borrow 1 from the 8 to the left of the 3. Change that 8 to 7, place the borrowed 1 to the left of the 3, and subtract 8 from 13 (13 − 8 = 5).

STEP 4. $6⁷8.¹37
           −47. 83
           20 54 STEP 5.

Subtract the digits in the remaining columns.

$ 6⁷8.¹37
− 47. 83
  20. 54 *Answer*

Place the decimal point in the answer *directly* under the decimal points in the problem.

Example 2   Subtract $2,448 from $3,795.75.

STEP 1. $3,795.75
           −2,448.00

Note that a decimal point and zeros are inserted to the right of the whole number (2,448) as placeholders.

STEP 2. $3,79⁸¹5.75
           −2,44 8.00
            1,34 7 75

Subtract in the normal manner.

STEP 3. $1,347.75 *Answer*

Insert the decimal point and label your answer.

Caution: When a digit in the minuend is smaller than the corresponding digit in the subtrahend, you will have to borrow. One common cause of errors in subtraction is the failure to borrow correctly from a zero in the minuend.

Example 3   Subtract 357 from 603.

STEP 1.
$$
\begin{array}{r}
603 \\
-357 \\
\end{array}
$$

Because 7 is larger than 3, you must borrow from the tens-place digit of the minuend. Since this digit is 0, you must go to 6, the hundreds-place digit.

STEP 2.
$$
\begin{array}{r}
^{5\ 9}\!\!\boxed{60}^{\,1}3 \\
-35\ 7 \\
\end{array}
$$

So that you don't forget the 0, borrow 1 from the number 60, leaving 59. *Do not borrow* 1 from 6 and then 1 from 10.

STEP 3.
$$
\begin{array}{r}
^{5\ 9}\!\!\boxed{60}^{\,1}3 \\
-35\ 7 \\
\hline
24\ 6 \\
\end{array}
$$

Complete the subtraction as before.

Example 4   Subtract 519 from 3,000.

STEP 1.
$$
\begin{array}{r}
^{2\ 99}\!\!\boxed{3,00}^{\,1}0 \\
-\ 51\ 9 \\
\end{array}
$$

Borrow 1 from the 300, leaving 299.

STEP 1.
$$
\begin{array}{r}
^{2\ 99}\!\!\boxed{3,00}^{\,1}0 \\
-\ 51\ 9 \\
\hline
2,48\ 1 \\
\end{array}
$$

Subtract as before.

Checking Subtraction

The rule in business is to check all arithmetic computations. Checking a problem does not mean doing the problem over in the same way, however. In working out the problem a second time by the same method, the chances are that you will make the same error again.

To check the solution to a subtraction problem, use addition to undo the subtraction:

If 15 – 10 = 5, then 5 + 10 = 15, the number you started with.
Add the *difference* and the *subtrahend*. The *total* should equal the *minuend*.

Example 5   Subtract: $86.28 – $34.53.

Solution: Subtract, and use a calculator to check the solution.

STEP 2.
$$
\begin{array}{r}
\$8\overset{5}{\cancel{6}}.^{1}28 \\
-34.\ 53 \\
\hline
\$51.\ 75 \\
\end{array}
$$

Check: Difference + Subtrahend = Minuend
51 ▣ 75 +   34 ▣ 53 ▤ 86.28 √

Answer: $86.28 – $34.53 = $51.75

Exercises

Exercise A Find the difference in each of the following problems, and check your answers:

1. 65
    −23

2. 87
    −61

3. 96
    −53

4. 48
    −33

5. 76
    −56

6. 84
    −36

7. 98
    −49

8. 628
    −437

9. 825
    −768

10. 953
    −638

11. 328
    −249

12. 519
    −326

13. 738
    −649

14. 547
    −458

15. $537.54
    −309.19

16. $419.28
    −280.36

17. $815.85
    −748.66

18. $635.42
    −347.51

19. $543.72
    −265.65

20. $714.38
    −308.72

21. $436.47
    −357.68

22. 6,528
    −3,079

23. 8,628
    −7,645

24. 5,423
    −3,856

25. 7,487
    −2,563

26. 4,573
    −3,585

27. $4,319.53
    −2,428.65

28. $23,576.36
    − 8,548.56

29. $47,475.76
    −28,258.68

30. $34,863.85
    − 9,657.97

31. $14,372.73
    − 5,453.80

32. 15,424
    − 6,948

33. 28,364
    − 9,647

34. 13,573
    − 5,646

35. 35,268
    −27,342

36. 23,538
    − 8,452

37. 24,834
    −15,748

38. 53,472
    −12,568

39. 47,628
    − 8,563

40. 32,127
    −23,053

41. 17,485
    −16,527

42. 605
    − 57

43. 403
    −168

44. 500
    −225

45. 104
    − 36

46. 3,000
    −1,453

47. 2,100
    − 834

48. 60,400
    − 3,565

49. 50,304
    − 7,347

50. 700,304
    − 57,526

51. 50,300
    −32,462

Exercise B Find the net amount or balance in each of the following problems:

52.

| Gross Pay | $261 | 63 |
Deductions	58	35
Net Pay		

53.

| Gross Pay | $223 | 15 |
Deductions	50	17
Net Pay		

54.

Gross Pay	$197	62
Deductions	36	93
Net Pay		

55.

Gross Pay	$235	27
Deductions	40	32
Net Pay		

56.

Gross Pay	$248	90
Deductions	53	15
Net Pay		

57.

Gross Pay	$265	75
Deductions	46	68
Net Pay		

58.

No. 28 $56.85

Date: 6/18

To: Transtelephone Co

For: May bill

	Dollars	Cents
Balance Brought Forward	275	63
Amount Deposited	—	—
Total	275	63
Amount This Check	56	85
Balance Carried Forward		

59.

No. 43 $247.50

Date: 6/29

To: AD Ross, D.D.S.

For: Dental work

	Dollars	Cents
Balance Brought Forward	463	57
Amount Deposited	—	—
Total	463	57
Amount This Check	247	50
Balance Carried Forward		

60.

No. 55 $143.75

Date: 8/9

To: Main Power & Light Co.

For: July bill

	Dollars	Cents
Balance Brought Forward	523	07
Amount Deposited	123	35
Total	646	42
Amount This Check	143	75
Balance Carried Forward		

61.

No. 63 $138.72

Date: 8/17

To: ABC Dept. Store

For: July bill

	Dollars	Cents
Balance Brought Forward	472	85
Amount Deposited	—	—
Total	472	85
Amount This Check	138	72
Balance Carried Forward		

62.

No. 68		$134 63
Date: _9/8_		
To: _Niel's Servistation_		
For: _Car Repair_		

	Dollars	Cents
Balance Brought Forward	325	70
Amount Deposited	—	—
Total	325	70
Amount This Check	134	63
Balance Carried Forward		

63.

No. 72		$257 92
Date: _11/7_		
To: _Winters Oil Co_		
For: _Oil delivery 10/31_		

	Dollars	Cents
Balance Brought Forward	538	67
Amount Deposited	—	—
Total	538	67
Amount This Check	257	92
Balance Carried Forward		

64.

Original Price	$703	05
Sale Price	524	38
Amount of Reduction		

65.

Original Price	$830	00
Sale Price	628	72
Amount of Reduction		

66.

Original Price	$4,005	00
Amount of Reduction	1,347	65
Sale Price		

67.

Original Price	$510	00
Amount of Reduction	193	75
Sale Price		

68.

Total Due	$5,719	63
Amount Paid	5,218	74
Balance		

69.

Total Due	$3,428	63
Amount Paid	1,463	74
Balance		

70.

Total Due	$4,627	38
Amount Paid	3,815	43
Balance		

71.

Total Due	$4,216	47
Amount Paid	3,407	63
Balance		

72.

Total Due	$8,963	47
Amount Paid	7,874	34
Balance		

73.

Total Due	$3,427	35
Amount Paid	2,473	64
Balance		

74.

Total Due	$5,264	17
Amount Paid	3,478	34
Balance		

75.

Total Due	$6,527	15
Amount Paid	4,432	63
Balance		

76.

Total Due	$7,625	72
Amount Paid	5,932	65
Balance		

77.

Total Due	$4,263	19
Amount Paid	2,472	49
Balance		

78.

Gross Pay	$238	57
Deductions	53	68
Net Pay		

79.

Gross Pay	$263	53
Deductions	47	68
Net Pay		

80.

Gross Pay	$178	58
Deductions	38	69
Net Pay		

81.

Gross Pay	$273	45
Deductions	65	53
Net Pay		

Word Problems

PROCEDURE: To solve a word problem:

1. *Read* the problem carefully to understand the *given facts* and to determine *what you have to find.*
2. *Restate* the problem in a *single sentence.*
3. *Translate* the sentence into a *single mathematical equation,* and *solve* the equation as described in the next section.
4. *Check* the solution and *label* the answer.

Solving Equations

Letter symbols called *variables* are sometimes used to represent unknown quantities whose values you have to find.

When these letter symbols include numbers and are separated by an equal sign, they form an *equation* or *formula.*

You can think of an equation as a *balanced scale* with *equal* weights on each side. Whenever you *remove* (or *add*) a weight on *one side* of the scale, you must remove (or add) the same weight on the *other side.* In other words:

> *Whatever you do on one side of an equation (add, subtract, multiply, or divide), you must also do to the other side.*

To solve the equation $n + 7 = 15$, you need to find the *numerical value* of the variable n.

You know that *subtraction* will *undo addition.* Subtracting the *same number* from each side of the equation will leave the *variable* by itself on *one side,* and its *numerical value* on the *other side,* of the equation.

Therefore, to solve the equation $n + 7 = 15$, subtract 7, the number that is added to n, from each side:

$$
\begin{array}{r}
n + 7 = 15 \\
-7 \quad -7 \\
\hline
n = 8 \ Answer
\end{array}
$$

To *check* the solution, replace n with its *numerical* value, and solve the equation:

Check:
$$
\begin{array}{r}
\underline{n + 7 = 15} \\
8 + 7 = 15 \\
15 = 15 \ \checkmark
\end{array}
$$

Example 6   Carlos has a balance of $846.75 in his checking account. If he writes checks for the following amounts: $158.50, $72.80, and $319.15, what is his new balance?

Solution: *Read* the problem carefully, *determine* what you need to find, and *outline* the given facts.

Given facts: 1.   *Starting balance* is *$846.75.*
                  2.   Carlos *wrote checks* for *$158.50, $72.80,* and *$319.15.*

Find: *The new balance.*
        Restate the problem in a single sentence.

> The *new balance* will be the *starting balance* ($846.75),
> *minus* the *sum* of the checks ($158.50 + $72.80 + $319.15).

Translate the sentence into an equation, and *solve* the equation.

Note: Since you want to *add the checks first, place parentheses around these amounts* to indicate that you are to *evaluate the amounts inside the parentheses first.*

New balance   = $846.75 − ($158.50 + $72.80 + $319.15)

                        = 846.75 − (158.50 + 72.80 + 319.15) *Add first.*

                        = 846.75 −   550.45 *Subtract.*

                        = 296.30

New balance   = $296.30

Rules for Order of Operations.

Evaluate expressions in the following order:

1. Evaluate *inside parentheses () or brackets []* first.
2. Next, perform multiplication and division in order, from left to right.
3. Finally, perform addition and subtraction in order, from left to right.

Most calculators are programmed to follow the above *order of operations.*

To check the solution to Example 6 using a calculator, enter each number (including decimal points), the symbols ⊞, ⊟, ⊠, ⊟, parentheses as they appear in the problem: ⦅ and ⦆, and finally the = sign.

Check: 846 ⊙ 75 ⊟ ⦅ 158 ⊙ 50 ⊞ 72 ⊙ 80 ⊞ 319 ⊙ 15 ⦆ ⊟ 296.30

Note: Most calculators will display the answer as 296.3 unless the decimal point has been preset at two places.

Answer: Carlos' new balance is $296.30.

Exercise C   Solve the following problems:

82. The Smith Company manufactured 12,550 transistor radios in the month of June and 11,627 radios in July. How many more radios did the company produce in June than in July?

83. A stock bin contained 375 sport shirts. If 128 shirts were removed to the display counter, how many shirts were left in the bin?

84. A color TV selling for $563.75 was on sale for $485.60. Find the difference between the original price and the sale price.

85. Yvonne earned $16,478 this year. Last year her salary was $14,625. How much more did she earn this year?

86. The list price of a refrigerator is $568.90, less a trade discount of $124.50. Find the net price of the refrigerator.

87. Albert bought a stereo on the installment plan for $1,128.50. He made a down payment of $475 and made the following monthly payments: May, $123.50; June, $142.85; July, $132.65; and August, $135.62. What is the balance owed on the stereo?

88. The gross sales of the A & R Dress Company for June amounted to $38,563.90. The expenses for the same month were as follows: cost of merchandise, $19,242.65; rent, $1,875; overhead, $947.83; and salaries, $10,563.75. Find the net profit for the month. (HINT: Net profit = Gross sales − Total expenses.)

89. Cindy's monthly take-home pay is $1,375.83. Her monthly expenses are as follows: rent, $465; food, $235.65; telephone, $56.78; travel, $23.50; clothing, $75.90; and other, $325. How much does she have left at the end of the month?

90. Henry had a balance of $347.65 in his checking account. He wrote the following checks: rent, $385; grocery, $85.78; and car payment, $265.90. He also deposited his paycheck of $583.75. What is Henry's new balance?

91. A retailer had the following sales last week: Monday, $4,628.90; Tuesday, $3,426.37; Wednesday, $5,625.22; Thursday, $4,780.65; Friday, $5,816.95; and Saturday, $8,613.50. Merchandise returned by customers for the same days amounted to the following: $368.70, $342.93, $435.65, $415.28, $462.30, and $573.92. What were the net sales for the week?

UNIT **2** Horizontal Subtraction

On many business forms where you have to do subtraction, the minuend and subtrahend may be arranged horizontally.

Invoice Number	Amount		Discount		Net Amount	
1075	$565	00	⊟ $84	75	⊜ $480	25
915	118	25	⊟ 17	70	⊜ 100	55

Check:
480 · 25 ⊞ 84 · 75 ⊜ 565 √
100 · 55 ⊞ 17 · 70 ⊜ 118.25 √

Checking Horizontal Subtraction

As in vertical subtraction, you should *add the difference to the subtrahend* to check your subtraction. This sum should equal the *minuend*.

Many business forms have a built-in check in that you must *subtract horizontally* and *add vertically*.

Example 1 Complete the following form:

STEP 1. Using a calculator, subtract the subtrahend from the minuend on each line, placing the difference in the Net Sales column.

STEP 2. Using a calculator, add the three columns, putting the totals on the bottom line.

Department	Sales		Returns		Net Sales	
Appliances →	$ 6,824	53	$ 968	65	$5,855	88
Furniture →	11,568	72	1,832	61	9,736	11
Lamps →	4,782	61	648	73	4,133	88
Totals			−		=	Grand Total

STEP 3.   Subtract horizontally on the bottom line to check your answer.

$$\$23,175.86 - \$3,449.99 = \$19,725.87$$

Department	Sales		Returns		Net Sales		
Appliances	↓ $ 6,824	53	$ 968	65	$ 5,855	88	
Furniture	↓ 11,568	72	1,832	61	9,736	11	
Lamps	↓ 4,782	61	648	73	4,133	88	
Totals	$23,175	86	☐ $3,449	99	☐ $19,725	87	**Grand Total**

$$\$19,725.87 = \$19,725.87$$

Exercises

Exercise A   Find the difference in each of the following problems, and check your answers:

1. $87.48 – $62.53
3. $59.37 – $28.50

5. $372.45 – $285.15
7. 28,963 – 14,798
9. $17.83 – $13.89
11. $68.75 – $64.37
13. 132,564 – 129,479
15. 32,865 – 4,973
17. $711.18 – $247.58
19. 3.051 – 2.069
21. 14,678,950 – 2,573,869
23. $16,483.21 – $12,689.45

2. $73.47 – $28
4. $219.68 – $147.32
6. $415.19 – $84.61
8. 56,283 – 51,937
10. 2,469 – 1,832
12. .0035 – .0005
14. $456.01 – $357.02
16. $186.93 – $86.98
18. $15,000.00 – $481.63
20. 14,360,000 – 12,158,000
22. $438.95 – $437.95
24. $4,357.80 – $2,400

Exercise B Complete the following forms by subtracting horizontally. Check your answers.

25.

Men's Apparel			Week of 9/2
Item	Stock	Sold	On Hand
Suits	578	138	_____
Slacks	363	156	_____
Sport Jackets	417	125	_____
Coats	378	115	_____
Sweaters	432	163	_____
Sport Shirts	518	235	_____
Totals	−	=	Grand Total

26.

Men's Apparel			Week of 9/9
Item	Stock	Sold	On Hand
Suits	440	108	_____
Slacks	207	206	_____
Sport Jackets	292	128	_____
Coats	263	145	_____
Sweaters	269	183	_____
Sport Shirts	283	246	_____
Totals	−	=	Grand Total

27.

Department	Sales		Returns		Net Sales	
Appliances	$ 5,824	58	$1,060	78	_____	____
Furniture	19,568	93	1,038	79	_____	____
Lamps	3,982	67	768	88	_____	____
Totals		−		=		Grand Total

28.

Item	Original Price		Sales Price		Amount of Reduction	
A	$305	50	$237	63	_____	____
B	210	65	137	70	_____	____
C	405	00	312	55	_____	____
D	200	00	173	45	_____	____
E	503	05	342	68	_____	____
F	630	00	425	50	_____	____
G	715	00	532	65	_____	____
Totals		−	=			

Grand Total

29.

Item	Original Price		Amount of Reduction		Sales Price	
A	$9,010	50	$3,420	65	_____	____
B	2,005	00	635	75	_____	____
C	1,300	50	428	64	_____	____
D	4,008	00	1,235	78	_____	____
E	5,040	50	1,836	55	_____	____
F	6,100	00	2,242	45	_____	____
G	3,050	50	943	60	_____	____
Totals		−	=			

Grand Total

30.

Dep't	Total Sales		Cash Sales		Charge Sales	
A	$28,475	80	$17,364	65	_____	____
B	23,060	45	15,679	68	_____	____
C	18,008	00	14,070	68	_____	____
D	34,130	90	23,648	75	_____	____
E	21,238	43	15,467	68	_____	____
F	25,065	07	15,627	79	_____	____
Totals		−	=			

Grand Total

31.

Employee	Gross Pay		Deductions		Net Pay	
Alan, G.	$205	00	$36	48	_____	___
Ambrose, L.	240	08	43	69	_____	___
Baker, F.	200	15	35	68	_____	___
Buntel, M.	190	00	31	38	_____	___
Campbell, N.	220	05	36	26	_____	___
Chisholm, D.	208	00	38	45	_____	___
Fulton, F.	203	00	35	28	_____	___
Totals			−		=	

Grand Total

32.

Item	List Price		Discount		Net Price	
A	$238	43	$37	38	_____	___
B	173	15	25	30	_____	___
C	58	65	9	78	_____	___
D	216	75	23	48	_____	___
E	335	25	46	42	_____	___
F	86	89	12	75	_____	___
G	128	95	17	88	_____	___
Totals			−		=	

Grand Total

33.

Weekly Net Payroll Week of 10/15						
Employee	Gross Pay		Deductions		Net Pay	
A	$280	75	$73	52	_____	___
B	375	50	92	65	_____	___
C	347	38	87	35	_____	___
D	295	65	81	47	_____	___
E	356	90	86	38	_____	___
F	325	75	84	10	_____	___
G	328	63	84	20	_____	___
H	370	95	87	42	_____	___
Totals			−		=	

Grand Total

34.

Appliance Department						
Item	Selling Price		Cost Price		Gross Profit	
#1240	$237	75	$125	48	_____	____
#063	365	98	198	63	_____	____
#3057	179	58	93	75	_____	____
#1108	528	75	284	79	_____	____
#3124	472	85	265	47	_____	____
Totals		−		=		Grand Total

35.

Dep't	Gross Profit		Overhead		Net Profit	
Grocery	$3,462	58	$1,278	63	_____	____
Vegetables	2,678	94	963	47	_____	____
Dairy	1,875	58	694	78	_____	____
Delicatessen	1,684	54	573	38	_____	____
Nonfood	1,378	92	485	63	_____	____
Meat	2,872	65	984	72	_____	____
Totals		−		=		Grand Total

UNIT 3 Review of Chapter Two

TERMS:	• Minuend
	• Subtrahend
	• Difference
KEY PHRASES:	• "What is the difference?"
	• "How much greater is . . .?"
	• "How much less is . . .?"
	• "What is the net . . .?"
	• "By how much does something exceed . . .?"
HINTS:	• Line up the decimal points in vertical subtraction.
	• Check all subtraction.

Complete the following forms:

1.

Item	Original Price		Sales Price		Amount of Reduction	
A	$305	60	$248	75	_____	____
B	310	40	142	85	_____	____
C	508	00	329	95	_____	____
D	400	00	325	26	_____	____
E	705	05	584	88	_____	____
F	740	00	538	75	_____	____
G	825	90	634	95	_____	____
Totals		−		=		**Grand Total**

2.

Item	Original Price		Amount of Reduction		Sales Price	
A	$8,020	00	$3,530	75	_____	____
B	3,008	50	1,247	65	_____	____
C	2,400	60	785	55	_____	____
D	3,004	00	1,375	65	_____	____
E	6,070	40	2,386	55	_____	____
F	5,100	00	2,378	75	_____	____
G	4,030	70	1,647	65	_____	____
Totals		−		=		**Grand Total**

3.

Item	List Price		Discount		Net Price	
A	$248	95	$99	95	_____	___
B	163	00	19	99	_____	___
C	55	50	9	50	_____	___
D	235	75	29	75	_____	___
E	385	00	95	00	_____	___
F	82	48	19	50	_____	___
G	136	00	39	95	_____	___
Totals			−		=		Grand Total

4.

Invoice No.	Amount		Discount		Net Amount	
3714	$ 867	95	$ 35	65	_____	___
2117	285	65	28	57	_____	___
1332	1,650	85	165	08	_____	___
1325	758	75	75	80	_____	___
1862	425	35	68	55	_____	___
1525	967	69	128	65	_____	___
Totals			−		=		Grand Total

5.

List Price	$468	92
Trade Discount	194	68
Net Price		

6.

List Price	$943	65
Trade Discount	465	38
Net Price		

7.

List Price	$12,312	97
Trade Discount	5,460	98
Net Price		

8.

List Price	$15,942	86
Trade Discount	7,571	38
Net Price		

9.

Invoice No.	Amount		Cash Discount		Net Amount	
4137	$ 1,284	65	$ 28	74	_____	___
4332	3,524	32	75	28	_____	___
4253	12,863	75	253	68	_____	___
4315	13,615	92	273	95	_____	___
4528	15,225	63	342	75	_____	___
Totals			−		=	

Grand Total

10.

Employee	Gross Pay		Deductions		Net Pay	
A	$437	95	$ 83	78	_____	___
B	523	63	124	55	_____	___
C	532	38	98	43	_____	___
D	474	35	93	48	_____	___
E	465	83	92	65	_____	___
F	515	65	112	74	_____	___
Totals			−		=	

Grand Total

11.

Card No.	No. of Exemptions	Total Wages		Deductions								Total Deductions		Net Pay	
				Soc. Sec.		Fed. With. Tax		State Tax		City Tax					
101	2	$465	85	$32	61	$116	46	$28	53	$12	65	____	___	____	___
102	1	432	70	30	28	109	32	26	72	11	28	____	___	____	___
103	3	478	48	34	63	123	16	29	43	12	84	____	___	____	___
104	1	398	42	29	72	103	15	24	82	9	80	____	___	____	___
105	2	446	36	31	16	113	70	27	16	10	80	____	___	____	___
106	4	480	70	34	32	102	62	26	42	11	73	____	___	____	___

12.

Card No.	No. of Exemptions	Total Wages	Deductions Soc. Sec.	Fed. With. Tax	State Tax	City Tax	Total Deductions	Net Pay
)1	2	$493 70	$35 17	$124 62	$29 72	$14 34	____ __	____ __
)2	1	473 65	33 72	119 62	28 47	12 65	____ __	____ __
)3	3	485 54	35 28	122 16	29 86	13 15	____ __	____ __
)4	1	437 50	34 18	118 15	25 63	11 42	____ __	____ __
)5	2	458 85	31 61	114 24	27 86	11 21	____ __	____ __
)6	4	515 35	35 15	110 20	26 95	12 25	____ __	____ __

Solve the following problems:

13. Samantha earns $19,500 a year. Her federal, state, and city income taxes amount to $4,763.85. What is her net salary for the year?

14. A car sells for $9,050.25. Last year the same model car sold for $8,365.43. How much more does the car cost this year?

15. Sandy earns $1,060.05 a month. Her monthly expenses are as follows: rent, $345; food, $185.75; gas and electric, $85.95; car expenses, $79.60; other expenses, $135.45. How much of her salary is left after expenses?

CHAPTER **THREE**

Multiplication in Business

UNIT **1** Multiplication Skills

Anyone working in the business world must have a thorough knowledge of multiplication. When you are given the number of items purchased and the price of each, you find the total cost of the purchase by multiplication. Discounts are found by multiplication, as are sales taxes. Also, when larger units, such as feet, are changed to smaller ones, such as inches, it is necessary to multiply.

Review of Multiplication

Multiplication and addition are related operations in that multiplication is equivalent to repeated addition. For instance, when buying eight sparkplugs at $1.25 each, you can find the cost by adding $1.25 eight times, or you can multiply $1.25 by 8. Businesses, therefore, use multiplication every day—to find the total cost of a purchase, the total price of a sale, or the pay due to an employee at the end of the week.

In the above example, $1.25 is called the **multiplicand,** 8 is the **multiplier,** and the answer, $10.00, is the **product:**

$$
\begin{array}{r}
\$1.25 \leftarrow \text{Multiplicand} \\
\times \quad 8 \leftarrow \text{Multiplier} \\
\hline
\$10.00 \leftarrow \text{Product}
\end{array}
$$

There are three important *properties of multiplication:*

1. *Multiplying a number by 0, or 0 by a number, equals 0:*

$$9 \times 0 = 0 \times 9$$
$$0 = 0$$

2. *Multiplying a number by 1, or 1 by a number, equals the number:*

$$25 \times 1 = 1 \times 25$$
$$25 = 25$$

3. *Changing the order of the factors in a product does not change the answer:*

$$5 \times 6 = 6 \times 5$$
$$30 = 30$$

PROCEDURE: When the multiplier has *two or more* digits, the multiplication will result in *two or more* partial products that are *added to form the final product.*

1. Set up the numbers to be multiplied one under the other, aligning the ones digits in the multiplicand and multiplier.
2. Starting with the *rightmost digit* in the multiplier, and *moving right to left,* multiply *each digit* in the *multiplier* by *every digit* in the *multiplicand.* Place each partial product *directly under the digit with which you are multiplying.*
3. Continue this process with *each digit* in the multiplier.
4. *Add* the partial products to obtain the final product.
5. *Count* the *number of decimal places* to the *right of the decimal point* in both *multiplicand and multiplier.*
6. Moving *right to left,* place the decimal point in the *final product the same number of places to the left.*

Example 1   Multiply 1.25 by 0.75. (The 0 to the left of the decimal point in the multiplier indicates that the whole-number part of 0.75 is 0.)

STEP 1.

$$\begin{array}{r} 1.25 \\ \times\ 0.75 \end{array}$$

Align the ones digits in both multiplicand and multiplier.

STEP 2.

$$\begin{array}{r} \overset{1\ \ 2}{1.25} \\ \times\ 0.75 \\ \hline 6\ 2\overset{\downarrow}{5} \end{array}$$

Starting with the rightmost digit in the multiplier, 5, multiply every digit in the multiplicand. $5 \times 5 = 25$; write the 5 and carry the 2 to the column to the left.

STEP 3.

$$\begin{array}{r} \overset{1\ \ 3}{\underset{}{1.25}} \\ \times\ 0.75 \\ \hline 6\ 25 \\ 87\ 5 \end{array}$$

Multiply by 7.

$$\begin{array}{r} 1.25 \\ \times\ 0.75 \\ \hline 0.9375 \end{array}$$

4 places in the problem
4 places in the answer

Answer: $1.25 \times 0.75 = 0.9375$

Example 2   Multiply 423 by 105.

```
    423
 ×  105
  2 115
  0 00
 42 3
 44,415 Answer
```

Neither the multiplicand nor the multiplier has a digit to the right of the imaginary decimal point.

Therefore, no decimal point is placed in the product.

Checking Multiplication

To check the solution to a multiplication problem, use division to undo the multiplication.

Example 3   Multiply 423 by 234, and check the solution using a calculator.

Solution: Multiply as before, and check the solution on a calculator.

```
    423
 ×  234
  1692
  1269
  84
  486
 98,982
```

Check: Product ÷ Multiplicand = Multiplier

98982 ÷ 234 = 423 √

Answer: 423 × 234 = 98,982

Exercises

Exercise A   Solve the following problems, and check your answers:

1. 463 × 28	**2.** 763 × 54	**3.** 357 × 54
4. 468 × 75	**5.** 4,207 × 403	**6.** 3,604 × 607
7. 627.24 × 13	**8.** 823.32 × 27	**9.** 728 × 0.35
10. 832 × 0.42	**11.** 4,304 × 0.038	**12.** 5,624 × 0.020
13. 386 × 205	**14.** 695 × 107	**15.** 4,250.50 × 0.625

16. 2,532.75 × 0.045	**17.** 1,705.38 × 0.375	**18.** 2,345.50 × 0.125	**19.** 1,030.28 ×0.0975
20. 2,380.70 ×0.6025	**21.** 3,075.60 × 0.055	**22.** 1,235.80 × 0.6667	**23.** 4,206.35 ×0.0025
24. 6,432.08 × 0.085	**25.** 5,030.25 × 0.375	**26.** 3,300.85 × 7.251	

Exercise B Complete the following forms:

27.

Quantity	Description	Unit Price		Extension	
18 doz.	#1302 Stemware	$18	35/doz.	_____	____
32 sets	#1567 Translucent China	34	62/set	_____	____
27 sets	#158 Bavarian China	47	80/set	_____	____
18 sets	#758 Coffee Sets	12	73/set	_____	____
			Total		

28.

Quantity	Description	Unit Price		Extension	
28	12″ Chain Lamps #412	$12	75	_____	____
18	2-Bulb Pole Lamps #068	15	50	_____	____
24	3-Bulb Pole Lamps #4207	23	85	_____	____
36	Table Lamps #4238	9	50	_____	____
24	Floor Lamps #2705	24	75	_____	____
			Total		

29.

ORDERED BY: A. Rivera	SHIP: Before 9/15	SHIP VIA: Truck		TERMS: Usual	
Quantity	Description	Unit Price		Extension	
24 sets	Bone China, Service for 8, #1728	$19	75	_____	____
18 sets	Bone China, Service for 12, #2071	34	50	_____	____
36 sets	English Tea Sets, #509	12	45	_____	____
14 sets	Salad Sets, #1249	9	85	_____	____
24 sets	Tea and Dessert Sets, #1415	13	95	_____	____
			Total		

30.

ORDERED BY: S. Schmidt	SHIP: At Once	SHIP VIA: Truck		TERMS: Usual	
Quantity	Description	Unit Price		Extension	
348 yards	Corduroy, Maroon, #27	$ 8	45	_____	____
375 yards	Worsted, Striped, #107	12	65	_____	____
425 yards	Laner Felt, Beige	3	95	_____	____
635 yards	Lininy Satin, Black	4	25	_____	____
428 yards	Denim, Blue, #158	6	95	_____	____
		Total			

31.

SALESPERSON: G. Santini	DATE SHIPPED: 7/15	SHIPPED VIA: Freight	TERMS: 2/20, n 60	PURCHASE ORDER NO.: 4360	
Quantity	Description	Unit Price		Amount	
28 boxes	Floor Tiles #1106	$8	15	_____	____
150 boxes	Floor Tiles #1108	6	25	_____	____
248 boxes	Bathroom Tiles, Yellow	5	78	_____	____
175 boxes	Bathroom Tiles, Blue	5	49	_____	____
375 gal.	Tile Adhesive #708	2	86	_____	____
225 gal.	Tile Adhesive #710	3	25	_____	____
		Total			

32.

SALESPERSON: C. Benson	DATE SHIPPED: 9/22	SHIPPED VIA: Truck	TERMS: 2/10, n 30	PURCHASE ORDER NO: 1507	
Quantity	Description		Unit Price	Amount	
75	2-Slice Toasters #1513		$ 9 | 50	_____	_____
128	4-Slice Toasters #3025		15 | 78	_____	_____
48	3-Speed Blenders #702		17 | 49	_____	_____
75	Can Openers #2310		8 | 53	_____	_____
175	Electric Knives #1012		6 | 90	_____	_____
24	Grill Plates #2740		13 | 75	_____	_____
			Total		

33.

INVENTORY FORM					
Stock No.	Quantity	Description	Unit Price	Extension	
307	63	Sport Jackets	$ 27 | 85	_____	___
461	123	Overcoats	63 | 35	_____	___
107	235	Flared Slacks	12 | 95	_____	___
423	164	Sport Jackets	43 | 75	_____	___
613	417	Regular Slacks	15 | 65	_____	___
707	315	Raincoats	27 | 90	_____	___
321	128	Leather Belts	5 | 65	_____	___
			Total		

34.

MERCHANDISE RETURN				

Gentlemen:
We return merchandise this day and debit your account as follows:

Quantity	Description	Unit Price		Amount	
15	Blouses #2462	$ 8	75	_____	___
18	Skirts #628	12	45	_____	___
13	Blouses #1628	6	55	_____	___
14	Blouses #1827	7	95	_____	___
		Total		_____	___

Goods Shipped Via ___UPS_____

For Credit of Department ___Sportswear_____   By _S. Thompson._

35.

SOLD TO ___Handy Andy Hardware___   INVOICE NO. ___7342_____

___2316 Union Street_____   DATE ___May 14___   20 ___--___

___Cleveland, Ohio 44117___   OUR ORDER NO. ___3620_____

CUSTOMER'S ORDER NO. ___572___

TERMS ___3/15, net 45_____   SHIPPED VIA ___Truck_____

Quantity	Description	Unit Price		Total Amount	
245 gal.	Interior Latex, Flat, White	$ 7	85	_____	___
175 gal.	Interior Latex, Flat, Pink	9	85	_____	___
250 gal.	Interior Latex, Flat, Royal Blue	11	65	_____	___
175 gal.	Interior Latex, Flat, Moss Green	8	50	_____	___
235 gal.	Interior Latex, Flat, Lemon Sage	6	95	_____	___
265 gal.	Interior Latex, Flat, Burnt Orange	9	75	_____	___
		Total			

36.

TO	Tiffany Manufacturing Co.		No.	428
	113 Lake Shore Drive		Date	September 18, 20--
	Chicago, IL 60641		Your Invoice No.	6247

Gentlemen:
We return merchandise this day and debit your account as follows:

Quantity	Description	Unit Price		Amount	
3	Calculators #1018	$ 53	75	_____	____
6	Calculators #2515	128	60	_____	____
7	Calculators #621	38	95	_____	____
4	Calculators #2540	173	45	_____	____

Goods Shipped via ___Acme Trucking___

For Credit of Department ___Stationery___

Total _____ ____

By *W. Williams*

Word Problems

As with addition, the key phrases indicating multiplication are:

"What is the total?"
"Find the cost of. . . ."

Use multiplication if the problem gives you a unit price and you have to find the cost of a number of units, if you are asked to change a larger unit of measure to a smaller unit, or if you are given a salary rate and have to find a weekly, monthly, or yearly salary.

Many business problems have more than one part; you must add the total cost of one item to the total cost of another (see Exercise 43).

Exercise C   Solve the following problems:

37.   Ace Used Cars sells a car for $350 down and 36 monthly payments of $79. What is the total cost of the car?

Sample Solution: Solve the problem, and check the answer on a calculator.

First, outline the problem:

Given facts: 1. $350 is the down payment.
2. There are also 36 payments of $79 each.

Find: The total cost of the car.
The *total cost* will be the down payment, $350, *plus* 36 payments of $79 each.

Total cost = $350 + (36 × $79)
Evaluate the inside parentheses first.

Total cost = $350 + (36 × $79) Multiply first.
        = $350 + $2,844 Add.
        = $3,194

```
        36       2,844
      × 79      + 350
       324       3,194
       252
      2,844
```

Check: 350 ⊞ (36 ⊠ 79) ⊟ 3194 √
Answer: Total cost of the used car is $3,194.

38. Mary Taber earns $185 per week as a clerk-typist. What is her yearly salary?

39. Marking pens sell at $4.95 per dozen. How much will 124 dozen cost?

40. The J. & M. Paint Company bought 32 quarts of denatured alcohol at $2.95 per quart. How much did the 32 quarts cost?

41. The Mutual Insurance Company bought 18 four-drawer steel filing cabinets. The cost of each cabinet was $123.75. Find the total cost of the cabinets.

42. Electronic calculators are packed in cartons holding 18 units. If the price of each calculator is $73.65, what is the total value of 6 cartons of calculators?

43. What will be your gross pay for 51 hours of work in 1 week if you get paid $5 per hour and receive time and a half for work beyond 40 hours? (HINT: First find the cost of labor for 40 hours by multiplying 40 × $5. Then, find the cost of overtime by multiplying 11 hours by $7.50. Finally, find the total cost by adding the regular and the overtime pay.)

44. A traveling salesperson is reimbursed 57¢ per mile toward car expenses. How much will he be reimbursed for driving the following mileages in 1 week: 235, 267, 185, 227, 198, 225, and 186?

45. The cost analysis of producing a 19" color TV is as follows: parts, $67.35; labor, $43.75; overhead, $19.65; cost of selling, $22.85; advertising, $12.50; and shipping, $5.95. What is the total cost of producing 125 TV sets?

46. An office employs six clerks earning the following weekly salaries: $285, $315, $265, $247, $348, and $465. What is the total yearly payroll for all the clerks?

UNIT **2**   Rounding Numbers

You round numbers when you want to use an *approximate value* of a number, instead of its *exact value.*

- If, for a given year, the total sales of a company amounted to $2,845,698, the company may want to list the total sales as "close to 3 million dollars."

  The *exact amount,* $2,845,698, is *closer to* $3,000,000 than it is to $2,000,000. *Rounded to the nearest million:*

  $$\$2,845,698 \approx \$3,000,000$$

  The *symbol* ≈ means "is approximately equal to."

- If the solution to a problem involving *dollars and cents* is $19.3843, the number 3843 should be rounded to the nearest penny since fractions of a penny cannot be collected or paid.

  The *exact amount,* $19.3843, is *closer to* $19.38 than it is to $19.39. *Rounded to the nearest penny:*

  $$\$19.3843 = \$19.38$$

Review of Place-Value Columns and Names and Values of Numbers

Place-Value Columns

In a *mixed decimal number,* the *decimal point* separates the *whole-number* part from the *decimal part.*
For the number 628.247, the *place values* of the columns are as follows:

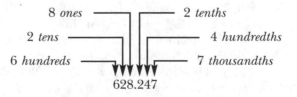

8 *ones* — 2 *tenths*
2 *tens* — 4 *hundredths*
6 *hundreds* — 7 *thousandths*
628.247

The number 628.247 is read as follows:

Six hundred twenty-eight and two hundred forty-seven thousandths

Note that the *decimal point* translates to the word *and.*

- With *whole numbers,* moving *left from the decimal point,* each column is *multiplied by 10,* and is *10 times as large* as the column to its *right.*

- With *decimal numbers,* moving *right from the decimal point,* each column is *divided by 10,* and is $\frac{1}{10}$ *the value* of the column to its *left.*

The accompanying table gives the names and values of whole numbers and decimal numbers.

Place-Value Columns of Whole Numbers and Decimal Numbers

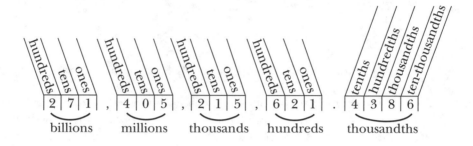

Names and Values of Numbers

- *Whole Numbers*
  A *three-digit* number names a value in *hundreds* (tens, ones).
  A *six-digit* number names a number in *thousands* (hundreds, tens, ones).
  A *nine-digit* number names a value in *millions* (thousands, hundreds, tens, ones).
  A *twelve-digit* number names a value in *billions* (millions, thousands, hundreds, tens, ones).

- *Decimal Numbers*
  A *one-place* decimal number names a value in *tenths.*
      0.5 = 5 tenths ($\frac{5}{10}$); 0.9 = 9 tenths ($\frac{9}{10}$)
          (1-place decimal: 1 zero in the number 10)
  A *two-place* decimal number names a value in *hundredths.*
      0.05 = 5 hundredths ($\frac{5}{100}$); 0.25 = 25 hundredths ($\frac{25}{100}$)
          (2-place decimal: 2 zeros in 100)
  A *three-place* decimal number names a value in *thousandths.*
      0.005 = 5 thousandths ($\frac{5}{1,000}$); 0.125 = 125 thousandths ($\frac{125}{1,000}$)
          (3-place decimal: 3 zeros in 1,000)
  A *four-place* decimal number names a value in *ten-thousandths.*
      0.0005 = 5 ten-thousandths ($\frac{5}{10,000}$); 0.0125 = 125 ten-thousandths
      ($\frac{125}{10,000}$) (4-place decimal: 4 zeros in 10,000)
As you continue moving *right from the decimal point,* each column is *divided by 10,* and is $\frac{1}{10}$ *the value* of the column to its *left.*

Review of Rounding Skills

Rounding Decimal Numbers

Underline the digit to be rounded. (In rounding to the *nearest penny,* underline the hundredths place.)

1. If the digit to the right is 5 or more, *add 1* to the *underlined digit.* If the digit to the right is less than 5, do *not* add 1.

2. Drop all digits to the right of the underlined digit.

Rounding Whole Numbers

Underline the digit to be rounded.

1. If the digit to the right is 5 or more, *add 1* to the *underlined digit.* If the digit is less than 5, do *not* add 1.

2. Replace all digits to the right of the underlined digit with zeros.

Example 1   Round $287.8967 to the nearest *penny.*

Solution: Underline the 9, the *hundredths* place, and check the digit to the right.

$287.8<u>9</u>67   Since the digit to the right of 9 is *more* than 5, *add* 1 to the 9, and drop all digits to the right of the rounded digit.

Answer: $287.8967 = $287.90 rounded to the nearest penny

Example 2   Round $257,489 to the nearest *thousand.*

Solution: Underline the 7, the *thousands* place, and check the digit to the right.

$25<u>7</u>,489   Since 4 is *less* than 5, do *not* add 1 to the 7. Replace all digits to the right of the underlined digit with zeros.

Answer: $257,489 = $257,000 rounded to the nearest thousand.

Example 3   What is the place value of each digit in $1,234,567.89?

- The 1 is in the *millions* place and means 1,000,000.
- The 2 is in the *hundred-thousands* place and means 200,000 (2 × 100,000).
- The 3 is in the *ten-thousands* place and means 30,000 (3 × 10,000).
- The 4 is in the *thousands* place and means 4,000 (4 × 1,000).
- The 5 is in the *hundreds* place and means 500 (5 × 100).
- The 6 is in the *tens* place and means 60 (6 × 10).
- The 7 is in the *units* place and means 7 (7 × 1).
- The 8 is in the *tenths* place and means 0.80 (8 × 0.10).
- The 9 is in the *hundredths* place and means 0.09 (9 × 0.01).

Exercises

Exercise A   Multiply, and round each answer to the indicated place.

1. $235.73
   × 0.36
        (cent)

2. $463.55
   × 0.30
        (cent)

3. $405.23
   × 0.025
        (dollar)

4. $524.53
   × 0.07
        (dollar)

5. $365.98
   × 0.06
        (cent)

6.   2,460.07
   × 0.345
        (cent)

7. $938.75
   × 0.025
        (dollar)

8. $1,238.75
   × 4.37
        (hundred)

9. $1,478.62
   × 0.075
        (cent)

10.   2,347.95
   × 1.0325
        (thousand)

11.   2,460.50
   × 1.405
        (thousand)

12.   3,548.16
   × 0.255
        (hundred)

13. $3,050.75
   × 0.005
        (cent)

14. $5,280.66
   × 0.45
        (cent)

15. $4,367.80
   × 0.0525
        (cent)

16. $3,450.38
   × 3.25
        (cent)

17. $5,362.78
   × 0.008
        (cent)

18. $8,428.62
   × 0.375
        (cent)

19. $4,378.92
   × 2.05
        (cent)

20. $7,630.08
   × 0.125
        (cent)

Exercise B Complete these forms, rounding each number to the nearest *cent*.

21.

Quantity	Description	Unit Price		Extension	
43.25 gal.	Alcohol, Wood	$ 6	75	_____	___
57.5 gal.	Paint Thinner	7	35	_____	___
85.35 gal.	Solvent #5	8	45	_____	___
73.65 gal.	Solvent #8	9	65	_____	___
65.65 gal.	Alcohol, Denatured	11	85	_____	___
128.80 gal.	Clear Lacquer	6	35	_____	___
			Total		

22.

Quantity	Description	Unit Price		Extension	
54.35 gal.	Alcohol, Wood	$ 6	75	_____	___
60.8 gal.	Paint Thinner	7	35	_____	___
83.53 gal.	Solvent #5	8	45	_____	___
56.73 gal.	Solvent #8	9	65	_____	___
57.56 gal.	Alcohol, Denatured	11	85	_____	___
128.18 gal.	Clear Lacquer	6	35	_____	___
			Total		

23.

Quantity	Description	Unit	Unit Price		Extension	
5.56 lb.	Potassium	Pound	$17	50	_____	___
7.38 kg	Magnesium	Kilogram	14	75	_____	___
7.53 lb.	Sulfur	Pound	22	47	_____	___
				Total		

24.

Quantity	Description	Unit	Unit Price		Extension	
3.78 lb.	Potassium	Pound	$17	50	————	——
5.63 kg	Magnesium	Kilogram	14	75	————	——
6.49 lb.	Sulfur	Pound	22	47	————	——
			Total			

25.

Quantity	Description	Unit Price		Extension	
23.8 tons	Wheat	$68	25	————	——
16.43 tons	Rice	83	37	————	——
18.63 tons	Soya Bean	72	46	————	——
20.31 tons	Corn	57	19	————	——
17.07 tons	Oat	63	85	————	——
		Total			

26.

Quantity	Description	Unit Price		Extension	
22.5 tons	Wheat	$68	25	————	——
15.32 tons	Rice	83	37	————	——
8.63 tons	Soya Bean	72	46	————	——
19.30 tons	Corn	57	19	————	——
17.15 tons	Oat	63	85	————	——
		Total			

Round each number to the place values indicated.

27.

Amount		$1	$100	$1,000	$10,000	$100,000
$ 356,247	93	___	___	___	___	___
474,563	42	___	___	___	___	___
1,263,437	59	___	___	___	___	___
835,726	40	___	___	___	___	___
452,374	75	___	___	___	___	___
168,935	15	___	___	___	___	___
244,568	53	___	___	___	___	___

Word Problems

Exercise C   Solve the following problems:

28.   A salesperson made the following sales: $879.50, $623.95, $735.85, and $928.45. If her commission is $12\frac{1}{2}\%$, how much did she earn in commissions? ($12\frac{1}{2}\% = 0.125$)

29.   Joise bought three blouses at $32.95 each, two skirts at $45.95 each, and a jacket for $65.95. If the sales tax is 6%, what is the total cost of her purchase? ($6\% = 0.06$)

30.   Andre is paid $6.75 per hour for a 40-hour week. If his overtime rate is $10.125 per hour, how much will he earn if he works 49 hours?

31.   An appliance manufacturer sells a refrigerator at a list price of $685.75 less a trade discount of 40%. What is the net price of the refrigerator? ($40\% = 0.40$)

32.   Lou deposits $2,750 in a certificate of deposit that pays 8.53% interest. How much will he have on deposit at the end of a year? ($8.53\% = 0.0853$)

UNIT **3** Developing Speed in Multiplication

In all businesses, speed as well as accuracy is needed in day-to-day calculations. A person with these two abilities will gain a positive reputation among supervisors and colleagues.

Multiplication by a Power of 10

A useful shortcut involves multiplying by a power of 10, such as 100 or 1,000. This type of multiplication can usually be done without written calculations.

PROCEDURE   To multiply by a power of 10:

1. When the multiplicand is a whole number, *multiply the numbers that are not zero and attach the same number of zeros to the product as there are zeros in the multiplicand and multiplier.* What you are really doing is moving the decimal point one place to the right for each zero in the multiplicand and multiplier.
2. When the multiplicand is a decimal or mixed decimal, *move the decimal point in the multiplicand to the right as many places as there are zeros in the multiplier.*

Whole numbers

$354 \times 1\underline{0}$	=	354×1	=	$3,54\underline{0}$	Attach $\underline{1}$ zero.
$354 \times 1\underline{00}$	=	354×1	=	$35,4\underline{00}$	Attach $\underline{2}$ zeros.
$354 \times 1\underline{,000}$	=	354×1	=	$354,\underline{000}$	Attach $\underline{3}$ zeros.
$25 \times 3\underline{0}$	=	25×3	=	$75\underline{0}$	Attach $\underline{1}$ zero.
$42\underline{0} \times 2\underline{0}$	=	42×2	=	$8,4\underline{00}$	Attach $\underline{2}$ zeros.
$13\underline{0} \times 3\underline{00}$	=	13×3	=	$39,\underline{000}$	Attach $\underline{3}$ zeros.

Decimals and mixed decimals

$0.354 \times 1\underline{0}$	=	0.354	=	3.54	Move the decimal point $\underline{1}$ place <u>to the right</u>.
$3.54 \times 1\underline{00}$	=	3.54	=	354	Move the decimal point $\underline{2}$ places <u>to the right</u>.
$3.54 \times 1\underline{000}$	=	3.540	=	$3,540$	Move the decimal point $\underline{3}$ places <u>to the right</u>.
$0.125 \times 3\underline{0}$	=	0.375	=	3.75	Move the decimal point $\underline{1}$ place <u>to the right</u>.
$1.25 \times 3\underline{00}$	=	3.75	=	375	Move the decimal point $\underline{2}$ places <u>to the right</u>.
$12.5 \times 3,\underline{000}$	=	37.500	=	$37,500$	Move the decimal point $\underline{3}$ places <u>to the right</u>.

Multiplication by a Decimal That Is a Power of 10

This method can also be used with decimals that are powers of 10, such as 0.1, 0.01, 0.001, and 0.0001.

PROCEDURE   To multiply a number by a decimal that is a power of 10, move the decimal point in the multiplicand as many places to the *left* as there are decimal digits in the multiplier, inserting zeros if necessary.

Note: When you multiply by a decimal of 10, or a power of 10, you are *decreasing the product* by 10 or powers of 10. Therefore, *move the decimal point to the left.*

123.45×0.1	$=$	12.345	Move the decimal point <u>1</u> place <u>to the left</u>.
123.45×0.01	$=$	1.2345	Move the decimal point <u>2</u> places <u>to the left</u>.
123.45×0.001	$=$	0.12345	Move the decimal point <u>3</u> places <u>to the left</u>.
123.45×0.0001	$-$	0.012345	Move the decimal point <u>4</u> places <u>to the left</u>.

Caution: When using this shortcut, disregard any zeros at the end of the multiplier. A decimal such as 0.10 or 0.100 will move the decimal point *one place* to the left in the multiplicand (0.100 = 0.10 = 0.1).

Exercises

Exercise A   Find the following products without using written calculations:

1. 427×0.01	**2.** 129×0.001	**3.** 0.534×100
4. $\$12.50 \times 10$	**5.** $\$5.15 \times 1{,}000$	**6.** 0.063×10
7. $\$28 \times 100$	**8.** $6.253 \times 1{,}000$	**9.** $\$0.09 \times 100$
10. $\$15 \times 0.30$	**11.** $\$12.50 \times 0.20$	**12.** $\$50 \times 4{,}000$
13. $\$30.15 \times 300$	**14.** $\$45.00 \times 20$	**15.** $300 \times \$10.50$
16. $2{,}000 \times 63$	**17.** $20\% \times 450$	**18.** $20\% \times \$7.50$
19. 43.50×200	**20.** 12.50×40	**21.** $1.50 \times 3{,}000$
22. $21.75 \times 1{,}000$	**23.** 13.50×200	**24.** $0.45 \times 4{,}000$

Exercise B   Complete the following forms, doing the multiplication without using written calculations:

25.

Quantity	Description	Unit Price		Amount	
200 boxes	#75 Screwdrivers	$ 3	75	_____	__
20 cases	#19 Nails	2	50	_____	__
1,000 boxes	#22 Nails		53	_____	__
3,000 boxes	#15 Nails	1	30	_____	__
200 boxes	6″ Bench Wire	12	41	_____	__
			Total		

26.

Quantity	Description	Unit Price		Amount	
100 boxes	#75 Screwdrivers	$ 3	75	_____	____
30 cases	#19 Nails	2	50	_____	____
2,000 boxes	#22 Nails		53	_____	____
2,000 boxes	#15 Nails	1	30	_____	____
100 boxes	6″ Bench Wire	12	41	_____	____
			Total		

27.

Quantity	Description	Unit Price		Amount	
20 boxes	#1207 Full-fashioned Sweaters	$47	75	_____	____
100 boxes	#157 Long-sleeve Blouses	24	75	_____	____
85	#307 Short Jackets	10	00	_____	____
32	#461 Full-length Jackets	30	00	_____	____
			Total		

28.

Quantity	Description	Unit Price		Amount	
10 boxes	#1207 Full-fashioned Sweaters	$47	75	_____	____
200 boxes	#157 Long-sleeve Blouses	24	75	_____	____
75	#307 Short Jackets	10	00	_____	____
32	#461 Full-length Jackets	30	00	_____	____
			Total		

29.

Quantity	Description	Unit Price		Amount	
200 doz.	#2 Pencils	$ 1	50	_____	____
60 gross	#7 Erasers	4	00	_____	____
180 doz.	#105 Ball-point Pens	20	00	_____	____
2,000	12″ Rulers		53	_____	____
5,000	8″ Rulers		30	_____	____
			Total		

30.

Quantity	Description	Unit Price		Amount	
300 doz.	#2 Pencils	$ 1	50	_____	___
50 gross	#7 Erasers	4	00	_____	___
240 doz.	#105 Ball-point Pens	20	00	_____	___
1,000	12″ Rulers		53	_____	___
6,000	8″ Rulers		30	_____	___
			Total		

UNIT 4   Review of Chapter Three

TERMS:	• Multiplicand
	• Multiplier
	• Product
KEY PHRASES:	• "What is the total?"
	• "Find the cost of . . . ."
HINTS:	• Set up your problem neatly on scratch paper.
	• Align all columns of digits carefully.
	• Check your work.
	• Use shortcuts when multiplying with powers of 10.
	• Round numbers when necessary.
	• Use multiplication as a shortcut for addition whenever the addends are the same.

Complete the following forms:

1.

Quantity	Description	Unit Price		Extension	
18.25 tons	Rice	$123	62	_____	___
24.262 tons	Corn	93	85	_____	___
15.032 tons	Lentil	131	75	_____	___
23.7 tons	Soya Bean	87	43	_____	___
13.623 tons	Sesame	78	65	_____	___
			Total		

2.

Quantity	Description	Unit Price		Extension	
36	Blouses #628	$ 5	75	_____	___
24	Jackets #506	15	25	_____	___
48	Skirts #812	11	60	_____	___
36	Dresses #930	15	65	_____	___
48	Dresses #960	9	95	_____	___
			Total		

3.

Quantity	Description	Unit Price		Extension	
500 boxes	#10 Paper Clips	$	20	_____	___
125 boxes	#063 Typ. Ribbons, Blue/Red	20	00	_____	___
2,000 bottles	Correction Fluid		70	_____	___
300 boxes	#6 Envelopes	1	20	_____	___
100 boxes	Desk Pads	14	60	_____	___
			Total		

4.

Quantity	Description	Unit Price		Extension	
52.45 gal.	Alcohol, Wood	$ 6	95	_____	___
59.18 gal.	Paint Thinner	7	55	_____	___
88.47 gal.	Solvent #5	8	95	_____	___
75.35 gal.	Solvent #8	9	75	_____	___
68.55 gal.	Alcohol, Denatured	11	95	_____	___
134.65 gal.	Clear Lacquer	6	85	_____	___
			Total		

Word Problems

Example   Samantha bought a new car and made a down payment of $1,800. If she pays the balance in 60 payments of $200 each, what is the total cost of the car?

Solution: Solve the problem using the shortcut method of multiplication by a power of 10.

Given facts: 1. Samantha made a down payment of $1,800.
                    2. She will make 60 payments of $200 each.

Find: The total cost of the car.
            Total cost is $1,800, plus 60 payments of $200 each.

Total cost = $1,800 + (60 × $200)
            = 1,800   + (6 × 2 increased by 3 zeros)
            = 1,800   + 12,000
            = 13,800
Total cost = $13,800

Check: 1800 ⊞ 〖 60 ⊠ 200 〗 ⊜ 13800√
Answer: Total cost of Samantha's car is $13,800.

Solve the following problems:

5. Find the cost of 2,000 springs priced at $0.055 each.

6. The terms of an invoice are "2% discount if paid within 10 days." Find the amount of discount on an invoice for $250.10 if paid within 10 days. (2% = 0.02)

7. How much will 100 filters cost at $12.50 each?

8. What will be the total cost of 230 thermostats selling at $20 each?

9. The Taylor Real Estate Company purchased eight electric typewriters at $972.50 each. What was the total cost of the typewriters?

10. The Gabriela family owns a home. The monthly mortgage payment is $345.90, and the monthly real estate tax payment is $115.35. Find the total in mortgage and tax payments for the year.

11. Aldo bought a new car, to be paid for in 36 monthly installments. Each monthly payment is $275.65. If his down payment was $500, what is the total cost of the car?

12. What will be your gross pay for 48 hours' work in 1 week if you are paid $8 per hour and receive time and a half for work beyond 35 hours?

13. Acme Motorcycles sells a motorcycle for $99 down and 36 monthly payments of $49.95. What is the total cost of the motorcycle?

14. What is the cost for 10 office sets (1 desk, 2 chairs) if the desks cost $450 and the chairs cost $150 per set?

15. Charles worked 54 hours last week. His hourly rate of pay is $4.75 for regular hours and $7.125 for all hours worked beyond 40 hours. What is his total pay for the week?

16. Erasers are priced at $0.125 each. If they are packed 12 in a box, how much will 25 boxes cost?

17. Alice is paid a 7% commission on sales. How much is her commission on a sale of $638.75?

CHAPTER **FOUR**

Division in Business

UNIT **1** Division Skills

Division is widely used by both businesses and consumers. In installment buying, the monthly payments are calculated by using division. When merchandise is purchased in quantity, the unit price is found by division. Averages, percent problems, and many other business computations also involve division.

Review of Division

Division and multiplication are inverse operations; that is, when you divide two numbers you are "undoing" a related multiplication. For example, when you multiply $0.25 by 6, you get a *product* of $1.50. When you *divide* $1.50 (the **dividend**) by $0.25 (the **divisor**), you get a **quotient** of 6; you have shown that there are 6 quarters in $1.50.

There are three ways of indicating division: the division symbol (÷), the fraction bar (–), and the division box ($\overline{)}$). If you want to divide the number 30 into 5 equal parts, you can indicate this division problem as

$$30 \div 5, \qquad \frac{30}{5}, \qquad \text{or} \qquad 5\overline{)30}$$

In each of the above notations, *30* is the *dividend*, and *5* is the *divisor.* The expression $30 \div 5$ means "30 divided by 5" and is written as $5\overline{)30}$. The 30 is *inside* the division box.

The expression $\frac{30}{5}$ also means "30 divided by 5" and is written as $5\overline{)30}$. A good way to remember this is to let the 30 "drop" into the division box $\left(\frac{30}{5} \searrow 5\overline{)30} \right)$.

In the problem 486 ÷ 3, you have to find how many 3's are contained in 486. To solve this problem, you need to perform a *series of separate problems using partial dividends. These partial dividends are used instead of the entire dividend.*

PROCEDURE: In the dividend, work from left to right. Move in as many digits as are necessary to make a *partial dividend* that is *as large as,* or *larger than,* the *divisor.*

STEP 1.   3)4|86

The 4 becomes the "new" dividend. Ask, "How many 3's are there in 4?"

STEP 2. $\overset{1}{3)4|86}$

Place 1 *directly* above the digit you are using, 4.

STEP 3. $\overset{1}{3)4|86}$
           3

Multiply the 1 by the divisor, 3. Place the product, 3, under the 4.

STEP 4. $\overset{1}{3)4|86}$
           3
           1

Subtract 3 from 4, and write the remainder, 1, under the 3.

STEP 5. $\overset{1}{3)4|86}$
           3↓
           1 8

To form a "new" dividend, bring down the next digit from the dividend, 8, in a straight line.

STEP 6. $\overset{1\ 6}{3)4|86}$
           3↓
           1 8
           1 8

You now have a "new" problem. How many 3's are there in 18? Place 6 *directly* above the 8, the digit you brought down. Multiply the 6 by the divisor, 3.

STEP 7. $\overset{1\ 6}{3)4|86}$
           3↓
           1 8
           1 8↓
             6

Subtracting 18 from 18 leaves no remainder, so bring down the last digit in the dividend, 6, to form the last partial dividend.

STEP 8. $\overset{1\ 62}{3)4|86}$
           3↓
           1 8
           1 8↓
             6
             6

3 goes into 6, then, 2 times. Place 2 directly above the 6 of the dividend and multiply it by 3. Since there are no more digits in the dividend and no remainder, you have completed the problem.

Check: To check a division problem, multiply the *quotient* by the *divisor.* The resulting *product* should be equal to the *dividend.*

Check: Quotient × Divisor = Dividend
           162 ⊠   3 ⊟ 486 √
Answer: 486 ÷ 3 = 162

Example 1   Divide 10,625 by 25.

STEP 1. $25\overline{)10,6|25}$

To form a partial dividend that is larger than the divisor, move 3 digits into the dividend.

STEP 2. $25\overline{)10,6|25}^{\,4}$

25 goes into 106, 4 times. Place 4 *directly* above the digit you are using, the 6.

STEP 3.
$$
\begin{array}{r}
4 \\
25\overline{)10,6|25} \\
10\ 0
\end{array}
$$

Multiply the 4 by the divisor, 25, and place the product, 100, under the 106.

STEP 4.
$$
\begin{array}{r}
4 \\
25\overline{)10,6|25} \\
10\ 0 \\
\hline
6
\end{array}
$$

Subtract 100 from 106.

STEP 5.
$$
\begin{array}{r}
4 \\
25\overline{)10,6|25} \\
10\ 0\downarrow \\
\hline
6\ 2
\end{array}
$$

Bring down the next digit, 2, from the dividend to form a "new" dividend.

STEP 6.
$$
\begin{array}{r}
4\ 2 \\
25\overline{)10,6|25} \\
10\ 0\downarrow \\
\hline
6\ 2 \\
5\ 0
\end{array}
$$

25 goes into 62, 2 times. Place 2 *directly* above the 2 in the dividend, and multiply it by 25.

STEP 7.
$$
\begin{array}{r}
4\ 2 \\
25\overline{)10,6|25} \\
10\ 0\downarrow \\
6\ 2 \\
5\ 0\downarrow \\
\hline
1\ 25
\end{array}
$$

Bring down the last digit, 5, from the dividend to form the last partial dividend.

STEP 8.
$$
\begin{array}{r}
4\ 25 \\
25\overline{)10,6|25} \\
10\ 0\downarrow \\
6\ 2 \\
5\ 0\downarrow \\
1\ 25 \\
1\ 25 \\
\hline
\end{array}
$$

25 goes into 125, 5 times. Place 5 *directly* above the 5 in the dividend, and multiply it by 25 to complete the problem.

Check: 425 ⊠ 25 ⊟ 10625
Answer: 10,625 ÷ 25 = 425

Division with a Remainder

When the divisor does not divide *evenly* into a dividend, you are left with a *remainder*. In such cases, the remainder is changed into a *fraction* with the divisor as its denominator, and the fraction is made part of the quotient.

Example 2   Divide 257 by 8.

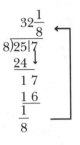

When you complete the division after bringing down the *last* digit in the dividend, you end up with a remainder of 1. To express the remainder as a fraction, place a fraction bar under the remainder, 1, and write the divisor, 8, under the fraction bar. The fraction $\frac{1}{8}$ becomes part of the quotient.

Check: Quotient × Divisor + Remainder = Dividend
$$32 \boxtimes 8 \quad \boxplus 1 \quad \boxminus 257 \checkmark$$

Answer: $257 \div 8 = 32\frac{1}{8}$

Division with Decimals

PROCEDURE: When the *dividend* is a decimal or *mixed decimal,* move the decimal point up to the *quotient directly above the decimal point in the dividend* before starting the division.

Example 3   Divide 475.82 by 37.

STEP 1. $37\overline{)475.82}$

Before starting the division, place a decimal point *directly above* the decimal point in the dividend.

Divide as with whole numbers.

Answer: $475.82 \div 37 = 12.86$

STEP 2.
$$
\begin{array}{r}
12.86 \\
37\overline{)475.82} \\
37 \\
\hline
105 \\
74 \\
\hline
31\,8 \\
29\,6 \\
\hline
22\,2 \\
22\,2 \\
\hline
\end{array}
$$

When the *divisor* is a decimal or *mixed decimal*, you must *first* change the divisor to a whole number and then do the division.

RULE: 1. To change a decimal divisor to a whole number, *move the decimal point in the divisor as many places to the right as are necessary to make the divisor a whole number.*
      2. Move the decimal point in the *dividend to the right. Move this decimal point the same number of places* you moved the decimal point in the divisor.

Example 4   Divide 132.24 by 3.8.

STEP 1.   3.8.$\overline{)132.2.4}$

Move the decimal point in both the divisor and the dividend 1 place to the right. (What you are really doing is multiplying both divisor and dividend by 10.)

STEP 2.
$$\begin{array}{r} 34.8 \\ 38\overline{)1,322.4} \\ \underline{1\ 14} \\ 182 \\ \underline{152} \\ 30\ 4 \\ \underline{30\ 4} \end{array}$$

Divide as with a whole-number divisor.

Check: 34 $\boxed{\cdot}$ 8 $\boxed{\times}$ 3 $\boxed{\cdot}$ 8 $\boxed{=}$ 132.24 √
Answer: 132.24 ÷ 3.8 = 34.8

Example 5   Divide 625.80 by 0.15.

STEP 1.   0.15.$\overline{)625.80.}$

In both divisor and dividend, move the decimal point 2 places to the right.

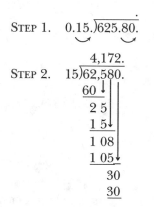

STEP 2.
$$\begin{array}{r} 4,172. \\ 15\overline{)62,580.} \\ \underline{60} \\ 2\ 5 \\ \underline{1\ 5} \\ 1\ 08 \\ \underline{1\ 05} \\ 30 \\ \underline{30} \end{array}$$

Divide as with a whole-number divisor. (In this problem you are multiplying both divisor and dividend by 100.)

Check: 4172 $\boxed{\times}$ 0 $\boxed{\cdot}$ 15 $\boxed{=}$ 625.80 √
Answer: 625.80 ÷ 0.15 = 4,172

Division with Zeros in the Quotient

A very common cause of mistakes in solving division problems is failure to place zeros in the quotient as placeholders when it is necessary to do so. The general rule to remember is that *every digit brought down from the dividend requires that an answer be placed above it in the quotient.*

RULE: When a partial dividend formed with a digit brought down from the dividend is smaller than the divisor, *you must place a zero in the quotient as a placeholder.*

Example 6   Divide 6,528 by 16.

STEP 1.
$$\begin{array}{r} 4 \\ 16\overline{)6,5|28} \\ 6\,4\downarrow \\ \hline 1\,2 \end{array}$$

Divide as before.

STEP 2.
$$\begin{array}{r} 4\,0 \\ 16\overline{)6,5|28} \\ 6\,4\downarrow \\ \hline 1\,2 \end{array}$$

After you have brought down the 2 from the dividend, the partial dividend, 12, is smaller than the divisor, 16. Place a zero in the quotient as a placeholder.

STEP 3.
$$\begin{array}{r} 4\,08 \\ 16\overline{)6,5|28} \\ 6\,4\downarrow\downarrow \\ \hline 1\,28 \\ \underline{1\,28} \end{array}$$

Bring down the next digit, 8, and complete the problem.

Check: 408 ⊠ 16 ⊟ 6528 √
Answer: 6,528 ÷ 16 = 408

Example 7   Divide 4,530 by 15.

Divide as before.

STEP 1.
$$\begin{array}{r} 3 \\ 15\overline{)4,5|30} \\ 45\downarrow \\ \hline 3 \end{array}$$

STEP 2.
$$\begin{array}{r} 3\,02 \\ 15\overline{)4,5|30} \\ 45\downarrow\downarrow \\ \hline 30 \\ \underline{30} \end{array}$$

As a placeholder, place a zero in the quotient above the 3. Then complete the problem.

Check: 302 ⊠ 15 ⊟ 4530 √
Answer: 4,530 ÷ 15 = 302

Example 8   Divide 2,485 by 8.

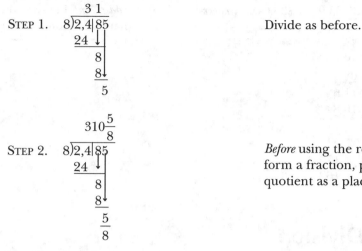

STEP 1.   Divide as before.

STEP 2.   *Before* using the remainder, 5, to form a fraction, place a zero in the quotient as a placeholder.

Check: 310 ☒ 8 ⊞ 5 ⊟ 2485 √

Answer: 2,485 ÷ 8 = 310$\frac{5}{8}$

Rounding in Division Problems

You will often have to round your answers in division, especially in problems dealing with money. The method used is to carry the division to one digit beyond the hundredths place (three decimal places).

PROCEDURE: To round an answer in division:

1. Carry out the division to three decimal places.
2. If the third digit is *5 or more,* add 1 to the hundredths digit and drop the last digit.
3. If the third digit is less than 5, do not add 1 to the hundredths digit. Drop the last digit.

Example 9   Divide $695.83 by 24 to the nearest *whole cent.*

$$
\begin{array}{r}
\$28.99②\;\;=\$28.99 \quad Answer\\
24\overline{)\$695.83\,\underline{0}}\\
\underline{48}\\
215\\
\underline{192}\\
23\ 8\\
\underline{21\ 6}\\
2\ 23\\
\underline{2\ 16}\\
70\\
\underline{48}\\
22
\end{array}
$$

Do not add a cent, because the third decimal place is *less than 5.*

You can attach as many *end zeros* to the right of the decimal point as are necessary without changing the value of the original number.

Example 10 Divide $659.51 by 18 to the nearest *whole cent*.

$$
\begin{array}{r}
\underline{\$36.63\,\textcircled{9}} = \$36.64 \quad \textit{Answer} \\
18\overline{)\$659.51}\ \underline{0} \\
\underline{54} \\
119 \\
\underline{108} \\
11\ 5 \\
\underline{10\ 8} \\
71 \\
\underline{54} \\
170 \\
\underline{162} \\
8
\end{array}
$$

Add a cent, because the third decimal place is more *than 5.*

Checking Division

It is important to check division problems because many errors occur in these calculations. Division is not hard, but you must be neat and accurate; always check your answers to be sure of accuracy.

HINT: Since division is the opposite of multiplication, it is best to check your answer by multiplying the divisor by the quotient and then adding the remainder. This figure should equal the dividend if you have divided correctly.

$$\text{Divisor} \times \text{Quotient} + \text{Remainder} = \text{Dividend}$$

Example 11 Divide 5,637 by 348.

$$
\begin{array}{r}
16\left(\dfrac{69}{348}\right) \\
348\overline{)5637} \\
\underline{348} \\
2157 \\
\underline{2088} \\
69
\end{array}
$$

Check: Quotient × Divisor + Remainder = Dividend

$$16\ \boxtimes\ 348 \quad \boxplus 69 \quad \boxminus 5637\ \checkmark$$

Answer: $5{,}637 \div 348 = 16\dfrac{69}{348}$

Exercises

Exercise A   Find the quotient in each of the following problems:

1. $0.012\overline{)14.232}$ 2. $23\overline{)47.162}$ 3. $15\overline{)12.405}$

4. $0.43\overline{)12.347}$ 5. $8.4\overline{)128.624}$ 6. $0.478\overline{)21.988}$

7. $640\overline{)4,480}$ 8. $4.16\overline{)142.597}$ 9. $0.358\overline{)223.392}$

10. $215\overline{)4,527}$ 11. $0.342\overline{)526.37}$ 12. $0.125\overline{)24,538}$

13. $41.7\overline{)9,678.57}$ 14. $0.285\overline{)427.685}$ 15. $305\overline{)65,885}$

16. $0.525\overline{)7,364.82}$ 17. $420\overline{)639.453}$ 18. $265\overline{)638,492}$

19. $280\overline{)481.880}$ 20. $3.35\overline{)80,735}$ 21. $415\overline{)88.435}$

22. $2.30\overline{)0.637521}$ 23. $0.149\overline{)538,620}$ 24. $301\overline{)10.0303}$

25. $0.238\overline{)74,763.5}$ 26. $318\overline{)72,535.8}$ 27. $24.67\overline{)0.0002467}$

Exercise B   Complete the following forms. Remember to round answers where necessary.

28.

Item	Bulk Unit	Bulk Price		Unit Price	
Knit Shirts	doz. in box	$27	60	____	____
Flannel Shirts	doz. in box	41	76	____	____
Knit Cardigans	½ doz. in box	53	40	____	____
Knit Socks	24 in box	35	52	____	____
Boxer Briefs	18 in box	24	48	____	____

29.

Item	Bulk Unit	Bulk Price		Unit Price	
#2 Pencils	doz. in box	$	72	____	____
Memo Pads	36 in box	47	16	____	____
Typ. Erasers	24 in box	1	92	____	____
Typ. Ribbons	18 in box	11	70	____	____
#10 Envelopes	8 boxes	73	36	____	____
#6 Envelopes	12 boxes	54	60	____	____

30.

Item	Total Amount		Price per Pound		Number of Pounds
Beef	$1,128	75	$2	15	————
Veal	837	38	2	98	————
Liver	466	25	3	73	————
Sirloin	518	40	4	05	————
Top Round	351	78	4	29	————

31.

Item	Total Amount		Price per Yard		Number of Yards
Carpeting, Blue	$ 850	50	$ 6	75	————
Carpeting, Plum	983	40	7	45	————
Carpeting, Gold	1,287	00	9	75	————
Carpeting, Brick Red	1,502	20	12	95	————
Carpeting, Royal Blue	1,718	75	13	75	————

32.

Item	Description	Price		Down Payment		Balance		Number of Payments	Amount of Each Payment	
#241	Television Set	$338	00	$ 50	00	———	———	18	———	———
#563	Color TV	556	00	100	00	———	———	12	———	———
#706	Refrigerator	676	00	100	00	———	———	24	———	———
#853	Refrigerator	724	00	100	00	———	———	24	———	———

33.

Quantity	Item	Description	Total Cost		Unit	Unit Price	
247 sq. yd.	Carpeting	#327 Shag	$1,482	00	Sq. yd.	———	———
315 boxes	Tiles	#10-5 Embossed	1,575	00	Box	———	———
80 yd.	Fabric	#48 Velvet	400	00	Yard	———	———
215 rolls	Wallpaper	#37-5 Textured	1,505	00	Roll	———	———
235 gal.	Paint	#511 Flat	1,175	00	Gallon	———	———

34.

Employee	Yearly Salary		Monthly Salary		Weekly Salary	
A	$18,675	00	————	——	————	——
B	16,525	00	————	——	————	——
C	19,780	00	————	——	————	——
D	17,685	00	————	——	————	——
E	20,950	00	————	——	————	——
F	21,475	00	————	——	————	——
G	18,950	00	————	——	————	——
H	19,675	00	————	——	————	——
I	22,750	00	————	——	————	——
J	20,750	00	————	——	————	——

35.

Amount of Loan		Number of Payments	Amount of Each Payment	
$2,475	65	24	————	——
6,570	90	36	————	——
1,258	75	12	————	——
8,562	80	36	————	——
9,675	65	48	————	——
4,860	45	36	————	——
7,637	85	48	————	——
3,578	80	24	————	——
5,685	75	36	————	——
1,325	80	12	————	——

36.

Amount of Loan		Number of Payments	Amount of Each Payment	
$3,472	65	36	————	——
4,865	79	48	————	——
2,575	35	18	————	——
5,627	75	48	————	——
897	62	12	————	——
1,516	34	24	————	——
3,872	95	24	————	——
2,347	55	18	————	——
4,213	83	36	————	——
2,874	64	24	————	——

37.

Item	Number of Pounds	Total Cost		Cost per Pound	
1	258	$ 315	08	——	——
2	337	1,120	00	——	——
3	139	495	63	——	——
4	453	1,305	72	——	——
5	532	1,620	05	——	——
6	263	1,432	35	——	——
7	385	1,724	50	——	——
8	657	2,128	72	——	——
9	315	1,015	62	——	——
10	225	1,420	68	——	——

38.

Installment Price		Down Payment	Number of Monthly Payments	Amount of Each Monthly Payment	
$ 628	68	$ 75	12	——	——
1,235	60	200	24	——	——
978	70	175	18	——	——
3,450	68	350	36	——	——
1,367	36	200	24	——	——
875	60	125	12	——	——
2,316	36	300	18	——	——
736	56	150	24	——	——
1,397	80	325	36	——	——

39.

Item	Number of Yards	Total Cost		Cost per Yard	
1	85	$ 347	60	——	——
2	105	529	55	——	——
3	215	767	90	——	——
4	325	943	35	——	——
5	467	1,415	70	——	——
6	235	3,267	90	——	——
7	435	4,585	38	——	——
8	355	5,628	15	——	——
9	525	7,293	80	——	——
10	437	6,585	95	——	——

40.

Item	Number of Items per Crate	Cost per Crate		Cost per Item	
1	48	$ 249	60	___	___
2	12	175	95	___	___
3	65	562	35	___	___
4	35	215	65	___	___
5	70	638	30	___	___
6	85	1,235	45	___	___
7	72	1,466	31	___	___
8	12	317	56	___	___
9	48	927	85	___	___
10	85	1,523	67	___	___

Word Problems

Key phrases indicating division include:

"What is the unit cost?"
"How much is each item?"
"What is the monthly cost?"
"How many months will be needed?"
"What is the ... per ...?"

Use division if you are given a large total and are asked to break it down into smaller parts (months, per piece, etc.).

Exercise C   Solve the following problems. Round answers where necessary.

41. The Adler Manufacturing Company ordered 450 yards of velvet at a total cost of $4,950. Find the cost per yard.

42. Albert Romano earns $18,200 a year. What is his weekly salary?

43. If 123 gallons of paint cost $615, what is the cost of 1 gallon?

44. Lucy Grant bought a car for $18,252. She made a down payment of $5,000 and has to pay the balance in 24 equal installments. How much will each payment be?

45. If four dozen sport shirts cost $348, how much does one shirt cost?

46. If bulbs are packed 24 to a box, how many boxes will be needed to pack 5,640 bulbs?

47. A skirt manufacturer shipped 75 skirts to a customer for a total cost of $1,725. What is the cost of each skirt?

UNIT **2** Developing Speed in Division

There are shortcuts in division that can speed the task and improve the accuracy. As noted previously, both speed and accuracy are qualities of major importance to persons in business.

The most useful shortcut in division involves dividing by 10 or a power of 10, that is, 100, 1,000, and so on. This shortcut is also useful when there are end zeros in both the dividend and the divisor.

Division by a Power of 10

PROCEDURE: When dividing by 10 or a power of 10, move the decimal point in the dividend *one place* to the *left* for each zero in the divisor. For example:

$$23. \div 10 \quad = 2.3$$
$$23. \div 100 \quad = 0.23$$
$$.0 \ 23. \div 1,000 = 0.023$$

Note: In the example $23 \div 1,000$, a zero is placed in front of the dividend because the decimal point was moved *three* places and the original dividend consisted of only *two* digits. The zero serves as a *placeholder* for the *tenths* column.

Here are three other examples:

$$\$13.50 \ \div 10 \quad = \$1.35$$
$$\$25.82 \ \div 100 \quad = \$0.2582 \text{ or } \$0.26$$
$$\$129.30 \div 1,000 = \$0.1293 \text{ or } \$0.13$$

Note: In business computations, you will find that many items are priced in lots of 100 or 1,000, or of a short ton, which equals 2,000 pounds. When calculating totals, remember that *cwt.* means *100 pounds, C* means *100 units,* and *M* means *1,000 units,* and use the power-of-10 shortcut to find the solution.

Example 1 Find the cost of 657 pounds of rice at $16.50 per cwt.

STEP 1. $657 \div 100 = 6.57$ Find the number of hundreds (cwt.) in 657 by moving the decimal point in 657 two places to the left.

STEP 2. $6.57 \times \$16.50 = \$108.4050$
              $= \$108.41$ *Answer*

Multiply 6.57, the number of hundreds in 657, by $16.50, the price per cwt.

Check: $108 \boxdot 41 \boxdot 16 \boxdot 5 \boxminus 6.57 \ \checkmark$

Example 2 Find the cost of 275 pens at $12.50 per 100 pens.

STEP 1. $275 \div 100 = 2.75$ Find the number of hundreds in 275 by moving the decimal point in 275 two places to the left.

STEP 2. $2.75 \times \$12.50 = \$34.3750$
= $34.38 *Answer* Multiply 2.75, the number of hundreds in 275, by $12.50, the price per 100.

Check: 34 · 375 ÷ 12 · 5 = 2.75 √

Division with End Zeros in Dividend and Divisor

When a division problem has end zeros in both dividend and divisor, you may cross out an *equal number* of end zeros in both *dividend* and *divisor*. What you are really doing is dividing both dividend and divisor by 10 or a power of 10.

Example 3 Divide 2,400 by 800.

$$2,4\cancel{00} \div 8\cancel{00} = 3 \text{ *Answer*} \qquad 8\cancel{00})\overline{24\cancel{00}} \atop 24 \;^{3}$$

Check: $800 \times 3 = 2,400$ √

Example 4 Divide 7,500 by 250.

$$7,50\cancel{0} \div 25\cancel{0} = 30 \text{ *Answer*} \qquad 25\cancel{0})\overline{750\cancel{0}} \atop 75\downarrow \;^{30} \atop 0$$

Check: $250 \times 30 = 7,500$

Example 5 Find the cost of 4,600 pounds of coal at $36.50 per ton.

STEP 1. $4,6\cancel{00} \div 2,0\cancel{00} = 46 \div 20 = 4.6 \div 2 = 2.3$ Find the number of tons in 4,600 pounds by dividing 4,600 by 2,000.

STEP 2. $2.3 \times \$36.50 = \$83.95$ *Answer* Multiply that number by $36.50, the price per ton.

Step 1 can sometimes be done without written calculation by using the following method:

PROCEDURE: When dividing by multiples of powers of 10:

1. Move the decimal point to the left as many places as there are zeros in the divisor.
2. Divide the new dividend by the left-hand digit in the original divisor.

In Example 5, the divisor 2,000 has three zeros. Therefore, the dividend 4,600 becomes 4.6, and the problem becomes $4.6 \div 2$.

Division by a Decimal That Is a Power of 10

PROCEDURE: Dividing by a decimal of 10 or power of 10 will *increase* the quotient by 10, 100, 1,000, and so forth. Therefore, move the decimal point in the *dividend* to the *right* as many places as there are decimal places in the *divisor.*

For example:

$$4.32 \div 1 = 4.32$$
$$4.32 \div 0.1 = 43.2$$

$$0.1\overline{)4.32} = 43.2$$

$$4.32 \div 0.01 = 432$$
$$4.32 \div 0.001 = 4{,}320$$

Note the insertion of the zero in 4,320, thus maintaining the position of the decimal point.

Example 6   Divide 1,350 by 0.02.

$$1{,}350 \div 0.02 = 135{,}000 \div 2$$
$$= 67{,}500 \; Answer$$

Exercises

Exercise A   Using the shortcuts shown in this unit, and without using written calculations, find the answer for each of the following problems:

1. $23.45 ÷ 10	**2.** 163 ÷ 100	**3.** $56.47 ÷ 1,000
4. 400 ÷ 20	**5.** 4,210 ÷ 1,000	**6.** 1,500 ÷ 300
7. $1.86 ÷ 100	**8.** 3,600 ÷ 300	**9.** 124,000 ÷ 1,500
10. 45,000 ÷ 120	**11.** 0.63 ÷ 10	**12.** 340 ÷ 10
13. 35 ÷ 100	**14.** 326,000 ÷ 200	**15.** $3,240 ÷ 1,000
16. $212 ÷ 10	**17.** $123.15 ÷ 1,000	**18.** $36,000 ÷ 300
19. $2,500 ÷ 500	**20.** $24,500 ÷ 2,000	**21.** $360 ÷ 0.2
22. $420.50 ÷ 0.02	**23.** $396.45 ÷ 0.03	**24.** $1,644.80 ÷ 0.4
25. $2,550 ÷ 0.05		

Exercise B   Using the shortcuts shown in this unit, in each of the following problems find the costs of the items listed:

26.

Total Number of Pounds	Description	Price per Cwt.		Amount	
375	Sugar	$7	35	_____	___
563	Salt	6	20	_____	___
1,243	Corn	3	15	_____	___
1,355	Coffee	8	75	_____	___
863	Pepper	5	45	_____	___

27.

Number of Items	Description	Price per C		Amount	
475	Pens	$ 9	50	_____	___
350	Notebooks	25	80	_____	___
1,250	Erasers	2	35	_____	___
1,465	Pencils	3	42	_____	___
970	Pens	6	25	_____	___

28.

Number of Items	Description	Price per M		Amount	
3,400	Memo Pads #248	$53	65	_____	___
5,625	Form #268	47	15	_____	___
12,410	Form #643	83	26	_____	___
15,675	Form #635	52	65	_____	___
13,127	Form #713	45	63	_____	___

29.

Total Number of Pounds	Description	Price per Ton		Amount	
8,400	Rice	$375	60	_____	___
12,648	Wheat	237	75	_____	___
7,820	Barley	347	50	_____	___
5,695	Peanuts	237	95	_____	___
10,150	Walnuts	425	50	_____	___

Word Problems

Exercise C   Solve the following problems, using the shortcut methods:

30. A hardware store pays $3.45 per C for #5 machine bolts. What is the cost of one bolt?

31. A retailer bought 10 watches for $475. How much did one watch cost?

32. Jeremy is paid a 10% commission on sales. He earned $563.55 in commissions. What was the total amount of the sales? (10% = 0.10)

33. Address labels are sold at $2.75 per M. How much will 6,750 labels cost?

34. If a 2% discount equals $24.40, what is the original amount? (2% = 0.02)

UNIT **3** Review of Chapter Four

TERMS:
- Dividend
- Divisor
- Quotient
- Remainder

KEY PHRASES:
- "What is the unit cost?"
- "How much is each item?"
- "What is the . . . per . . . ?"

HINTS:
- Read the problem carefully.
- Set up your work neatly, and leave enough space.
- Check your division by multiplication.
- Remember to use power-of-10 shortcuts.
- Round your answer if necessary.

Find the quotient in each of the following problems:

1. $48\overline{)74976}$

2. $213\overline{)7455}$

3. $478\overline{)21988}$

4. $706\overline{)37418}$

5. $38\overline{)81.70}$

6. $2.15\overline{)505.25}$

7. $0.015\overline{)63195}$

8. $4.5\overline{)1071}$

Find the quotient in each of the following problems, and round to the nearest *cent:*

9. $24\overline{)\$590.52}$

10. $130\overline{)\$3153.75}$

11. $215\overline{)\$4853.42}$

12. $425\overline{)\$92347.48}$

13. $321\overline{)\$43460.05}$

14. $572\overline{)\$76823.50}$

Find the quotient in each of the following problems. (Be alert for zeros in the quotient.)

15. $64\overline{)32320}$

16. $223\overline{)89869}$

17. $56\overline{)224168}$

18. $132\overline{)396660}$

19. $63\overline{)1260.252}$

20. $215\overline{)86001.075}$

21. $24\overline{)15128}$

22. $315\overline{)22062.607}$

Find the quotient in each of the following problems. (In problems involving dollars and cents, round to the nearest *cent*.)

23. $14.75 ÷ 100

24. $5.50 ÷ 10

25. 3,000 ÷ 500

26. $73 ÷ 1,000

27. 600 ÷ 30

28. 4,500 ÷ 1,500

29. 2,467 ÷ 1,000

30. 15.48 ÷ 100

31. 3,000 ÷ 1,500

32. 58.96 ÷ 100

Complete the following forms, rounding each number to the nearest *cent:*

33.

Installment Price		Down Payment		Number of Payments	Amount of Each Payment	
$ 865	95	$ 75	00	12	_____	___
1,535	45	150	00	18	_____	___
2,792	48	200	00	24	_____	___
5,478	90	550	00	36	_____	___
10,563	75	650	00	48	_____	___

34.

Employee	Yearly Salary	Monthly Salary		Weekly Salary	
A	$24,695	_____	___	_____	___
B	19,865	_____	___	_____	___
C	22,950	_____	___	_____	___
D	23,475	_____	___	_____	___
E	21,850	_____	___	_____	___

35.

Quantity	Description	Price	Amount	
675 lb.	Sugar	$4.15 per cwt.	_____	_____
1,275 lb.	Coffee	$6.45 per cwt.	_____	_____
8,460 lb.	Wheat	$267.25 per ton	_____	_____
12,250 lb.	Peanuts	$325.95 per ton	_____	_____

36.

Quantity	Description	Price	Amount	
515 units	Pens	$8.75 per C	_____	_____
485 units	Notebooks	$13.95 per C	_____	_____
4,225 units	Form #815	$23.15 per M	_____	_____
13,595 units	Memo Pads	$56.75 per M	_____	_____

Solve the following problems:

37. The First Federal Savings Bank bought 15 electronic calculators for $5,189.25. What was the cost of each calculator?

38. Mrs. Hernandez bought a refrigerator for $968.75. She made a down payment of $145 and will pay the balance in 36 monthly payments. How much will each payment be?

39. The Hartford Insurance Company ordered 1,685 calendars priced at $5.35 per 100, and 8,490 imprinted pens priced at $15.25 per 1,000. What was the total cost of the order?

40. Harry Gold bought a car for $9,875. Three years later he sold the car for $6,342. What was the depreciation percent of the car over the 3 years?

41. Mr. Gunfield bought 200 shares of stock at $63.75 each share. Two years later he sold the stock at a price of $86.25 each share. How much profit did he make?

CHAPTER **FIVE**

Fractions in Business

UNIT **1** Skill with Fractions

Many business transactions involve fractions, or parts of units. Fabrics are sold in yards or fractions of a yard. Many items are sold in pounds or fractions of a pound, in dozens or parts of a dozen. Hourly wages are computed with fractional parts of hours, and overtime pay is usually figured at $1\frac{1}{2}$ times the regular rate.

Review of Common Fractions

Parts of units are called **fractions.** The fraction $\frac{3}{4}$ *of a pound* means that a pound has been divided into *four equal parts,* and the fraction is representing *three of these parts.* The top number of a fraction tells *how many* parts are involved and is called the **numerator.** The bottom number tells the *total number* of equal parts in the fraction and is called the **denominator.** The denominator *names* the fraction: note the root *nomin* in the word *denominator.*

$$\frac{3}{4} \begin{array}{l} \leftarrow \text{Numerator} \\ \leftarrow \text{Denominator} \end{array}$$

A fraction is also another way of expressing division. The fraction $\frac{3}{4}$ is another way of writing $3 \div 4$. If \$3 is divided by 4, the answer is 75¢, or $\frac{3}{4}$ of a dollar.

A fraction can be used to *compare two numbers by division.* If 5 students are absent in a class of 35 students, the fraction $\frac{5}{35}$ compares the *number of students absent* to the *total number of students* in the class.

When a student correctly answers 8 questions out of a total of 10, the fraction $\frac{8}{10}$ compares the *number of questions answered correctly* to the *total number of questions.*

There are two important *properties of fractions:*

1. *Any fraction that has the same number for its numerator and denominator is equal to 1.*

$$\frac{4}{4} = 1, \qquad \frac{8}{8} = 1, \qquad \frac{27}{27} = 1$$

Writing a fraction with the same number for its numerator and denominator is a method of writing the number 1 as a fraction.

2. *Any fraction with a denominator of 1 is equal to its numerator.*

$$\frac{4}{1} = 4, \qquad \frac{8}{1} = 8, \qquad \frac{27}{1} = 27$$

Writing a fraction with a denominator of 1 is a method of writing a whole number as a fraction.

Equivalent Fractions

If you have two quarters $\left(\frac{2}{4}\right)$ or a half dollar $\left(\frac{1}{2}\right)$, you have $0.50, because both fractions have the same value. When two or more fractions written with different terms are equal in value, the fractions are called **equivalent fractions.** When you divide a unit into 8 equal parts and take 4 of these parts, you have taken $\frac{1}{2}$ of the unit, because

$$\frac{4}{8} = \frac{1}{2} \qquad \text{and} \qquad \frac{1}{2} = \frac{4}{8}$$

If the same unit is divided into 16 equal parts and you take 8 of these parts, you have also taken $\frac{1}{2}$ of the unit, because

$$\frac{8}{16} = \frac{1}{2} \qquad \text{and} \qquad \frac{1}{2} = \frac{8}{16}$$

Reducing Fractions

HINT: If the numerator and the denominator of a fraction are multiplied or divided by the same nonzero number, the value of the fraction is unchanged.

Example 1 Reduce $\dfrac{5}{20}$ to an equivalent fraction in lowest terms.

Solution: Since both numerator and denominator are divisible by 5, use 5 as the *common divisor* for both numerator and denominator.

$$\dfrac{5 \div \boxed{5}}{20 \div \boxed{5}} = \dfrac{1}{4}$$ Note that you divide by a fraction that is equal to 1 $\left(\dfrac{5}{5} = 1\right)$.

Dividing by a fraction that is equal to 1 will *reduce the fraction without changing its value.*

Answer: $\dfrac{5}{20} = \dfrac{1}{4}$ when reduced to lowest terms

Note: If both numerator and denominator *end in even numbers,* they are divisible by 2, or multiples of 2. If both numerator and denominator *end in 5 or 0,* they are divisible by 5, or multiples of 5.

You may use a more direct method for reducing fractions to lowest terms.

Example 2 Reduce $\dfrac{12}{16}$ to an equivalent fraction in lowest terms.

Solution: Since both numerator and denominator are even numbers, they are divisible by 2, or a multiple of 2.

$\Big|\dfrac{12}{16}$ Place a line to the left of the fraction to indicate division.

$2\,\Big|\,\dfrac{\cancel{12}}{\cancel{16}} = \dfrac{3}{4}$ Start with the number 2, and keep dividing by 2 until 2 no longer divides evenly into the numerator and the denominator.

$4\,\Big|\,\dfrac{\cancel{12}}{\cancel{16}} = \dfrac{3}{4}$ Since you see that 4 (a multiple of 2) divides evenly into 12 and 16, use 4 as the common divisor.

Answer: $\dfrac{12}{16} = \dfrac{3}{4}$ when reduced to lowest terms

Note: As in division, you can cross out an equal number of end zeros to simplify the fraction:

$$\dfrac{3\cancel{00}}{1,2\cancel{00}} = \dfrac{3}{12} = 3 \qquad \dfrac{3}{12} = \dfrac{1}{4}$$

Raising Fractions to Higher Equivalents

PROCEDURE: To raise a fraction to an equivalent fraction with higher terms, multiply the numerator and the denominator of the fraction by the *same* number.

For example:

$$\frac{1 \times \boxed{2}}{4 \times \boxed{2}} = \frac{2}{8}$$

$$\frac{1 \times \boxed{3}}{4 \times \boxed{3}} = \frac{3}{12}$$

Multiplying a fraction by 1 will not change its value, but will raise the fraction to higher equivalents.

$$\frac{1 \times \boxed{5}}{4 \times \boxed{5}} = \frac{5}{20}$$

In the following examples fractions are raised to higher equivalents that have *given* denominators.

Example 3   Raise $\dfrac{3}{4}$ to 16ths.

Solution: Rewrite the problem:

$$\frac{3}{4 \times \,?} = \frac{}{16} \qquad \textit{Think:} \quad 4 \times \text{ what number equals 16?}$$

$$\frac{3}{4 \times 4} = \frac{}{16} \qquad 4 \times 4 = 16$$

$$\frac{3 \times \boxed{4}}{4 \times \boxed{4}} = \frac{12}{16} \qquad \text{Multiply the numerator, 3, by 4, the same number.}$$

Multiplying by a fraction that is equal to 1 raises the given fraction to an equivalent fraction without changing its value.

Answer: $\dfrac{3}{4} = \dfrac{12}{16}$

Example 4   Raise $\dfrac{7}{15}$ to 30ths.

Solution: $\dfrac{7 \times 2}{15 \times 2} = \dfrac{14}{30}$

Answer: $\dfrac{7}{15} = \dfrac{14}{30}$

Example 5 Raise $\dfrac{4}{7}$ to 35ths.

Solution: $\dfrac{4 \times 5}{7 \times 5} = \dfrac{20}{35}$

Answer: $\dfrac{4}{7} = \dfrac{20}{35}$

Example 6 Raise $\dfrac{5}{8}$ to 40ths.

Solution: $\dfrac{5 \times 5}{8 \times 5} = \dfrac{25}{40}$

Answer: $\dfrac{5}{8} = \dfrac{25}{40}$

Improper Fractions

Any fraction that has a numerator that is the same as, or larger than, its denominator is called an **improper fraction**. The fractions $\dfrac{4}{4}$, $\dfrac{13}{8}$, and $\dfrac{25}{7}$ are examples of improper fractions.

An improper fraction represents a value equal to, or greater than, 1. For example:

$$\dfrac{4}{4} = 1 \qquad \text{and} \qquad \dfrac{8}{5} = 1\dfrac{3}{5}$$

Mixed Numbers

A mixed number represents *a whole number* plus *a fraction of a number.*

The mixed number $2\dfrac{5}{7}$ means $2 + \dfrac{5}{7}$. In problem solving with fractions, you sometimes need to change *mixed numbers* to *improper fractions.*

Example 7 Change $2\dfrac{5}{7}$ to an improper fraction.

Solution: Find how many sevenths are contained in $2\dfrac{5}{7}$. Then write $2\dfrac{5}{7}$ as an *improper fraction* with a *denominator of 7.*

You know that the number 1 = 7 sevenths, and 2 = 7 sevenths × 2. Therefore:

$$2\dfrac{5}{7} - (7 \text{ sevenths} \times 2) + 5 \text{ sevenths}$$

Write the expression as follows:

$$2\frac{5}{7} = \frac{(7 \times 2) + 5}{7}$$ Keep the same denominator.

$$= \frac{14 + 5}{7}$$ Multiply first.

$$= \frac{19}{7}$$ Add.

Answer: $2\frac{5}{7} = \frac{19}{7}$

Alternative Solution: You can use a more direct method to change a mixed number to an improper fraction:

$$2\frac{5}{7} = \frac{}{7}$$

$$\overset{+}{\underset{\times}{2}}\frac{5}{7} = \frac{19}{7}$$ *Think:* $7 \times 2 = 14$; $14 + 5 = 19$ as an improper fraction

$$2\frac{5}{7} = \frac{19}{7}$$

Example 8 Change $4\frac{5}{8}$ to an improper fraction.

Solution: $4\frac{5}{8} = 8 \times 4 = 32$; $32 + 5 = 37$

Answer: $4\frac{5}{8} = \frac{37}{8}$ as an improper fraction.

Example 9 Change $3\frac{2}{7}$ to an improper fraction.

Answer: $3\frac{2}{7} = \frac{23}{7}$

Example 10 Change $5\frac{2}{3}$ to an improper fraction.

Answer: $5\frac{2}{3} = \frac{17}{3}$

Example 11 Change $\frac{17}{5}$ to a mixed number.

Solution: Carry out the indicated division. Remember that $\frac{17}{5}$ means $17 \div 5$.

$$\begin{array}{r} 3\frac{2}{5} \\ 5)\overline{17} \\ \underline{15} \\ 2 \\ 5 \end{array}$$

Answer: $\frac{17}{5} = 3\frac{2}{5}$

Example 12 Change $\dfrac{28}{6}$ to a mixed number.

Solution: Divide the numerator by the denominator:

$$
\begin{array}{r}
4\frac{2}{3} \\
6\overline{)28} \\
\underline{24} \\
\frac{4}{6} = \frac{2}{3}
\end{array}
$$

Answer: $\dfrac{28}{6} = 4\dfrac{2}{3}$

Exercises

Exercise A Reduce each fraction to its lowest terms.

1. $\dfrac{5}{15}$ 2. $\dfrac{9}{27}$ 3. $\dfrac{6}{20}$ 4. $\dfrac{30}{45}$ 5. $\dfrac{24}{44}$

6. $\dfrac{32}{64}$ 7. $\dfrac{36}{48}$ 8. $\dfrac{42}{63}$ 9. $\dfrac{36}{84}$ 10. $\dfrac{500}{2,500}$

Raise each fraction to a higher equivalent of each given denominator.

11. $\dfrac{4}{5} = \dfrac{}{25}$ 12. $\dfrac{7}{8} = \dfrac{}{32}$ 13. $\dfrac{5}{6} = \dfrac{}{30}$ 14. $\dfrac{4}{7} = \dfrac{}{56}$

15. $\dfrac{11}{12} = \dfrac{}{48}$ 16. $\dfrac{5}{9} = \dfrac{}{36}$ 17. $\dfrac{7}{15} = \dfrac{}{60}$ 18. $\dfrac{5}{6} = \dfrac{}{54}$

19. $\dfrac{11}{24} = \dfrac{}{72}$ 20. $\dfrac{3}{4} = \dfrac{}{44}$

Change these improper fractions to mixed numbers.

21. $\dfrac{19}{5}$ 22. $\dfrac{28}{9}$ 23. $\dfrac{43}{12}$ 24. $\dfrac{18}{5}$ 25. $\dfrac{27}{8}$

26. $\dfrac{48}{15}$ 27. $\dfrac{32}{18}$ 28. $\dfrac{21}{6}$ 29. $\dfrac{17}{2}$ 30. $\dfrac{33}{6}$

31. $\dfrac{45}{8}$ 32. $\dfrac{20}{18}$ 33. $\dfrac{14}{13}$ 34. $\dfrac{28}{6}$ 35. $\dfrac{16}{12}$

36. $\dfrac{31}{21}$

Change these mixed numbers to improper fractions.

37. $4\frac{3}{7}$ **38.** $5\frac{4}{5}$ **39.** $12\frac{1}{3}$ **40.** $7\frac{6}{7}$ **41.** $15\frac{2}{3}$

42. $9\frac{7}{8}$ **43.** $6\frac{3}{4}$ **44.** $8\frac{5}{8}$ **45.** $2\frac{5}{7}$ **46.** $13\frac{1}{2}$

47. $7\frac{5}{6}$ **48.** $11\frac{4}{5}$ **49.** $12\frac{2}{3}$

Word Problems

Exercise B Solve the following problems:

50. (a) If you divide a yard of fabric into three equal parts, what will be the denominator of the fraction?
(b) If you took two of the parts in (a), how would you write that fraction?
(c) How would you write as a fraction the remaining part in (b)?

51. If the numerator and denominator of a fraction are the same, to what whole number is the fraction equal?

52. (a) Are the following fractions equal to the same number:

$$\frac{7}{7}, \frac{15}{15}, \frac{25}{25}, \text{ and } \frac{127}{127}?$$

(b) What is the number they are all equal to?

53. How would you write "15 divided by 20" as a fraction?

54. Write "35 ÷ 7" as a fraction.

55. If five boys have to share $3, how much money will each one get?

56. Last week John worked 3 days and was out 2 days.
(a) What fraction of the week did he work?
(b) What fraction of the week was he out?

57. A TV set selling for $75 was reduced by $\frac{1}{3}$. Write the amount of reduction as a fraction of the selling price.

58. Write $\frac{1}{4}$ of a year as a fraction of the days in a year.

59. Three partners had $30,000 to share equally.
(a) What fraction of the money did each one get?
(b) How many dollars did each one receive?

60. A retailer bought 200 suits and sold 50 suits.
(a) What fraction of the suits was sold?
(b) What fraction of the suits remained unsold?

61. A sport jacket that cost the retailer $25 is marked up $10. Write as a fraction the markup compared to the cost.

62. A lamp was reduced from $50 to $35.
(a) Write the portion of reduction as a fraction.
(b) What fraction of the original price remained?

63. In a shipment of glassware, 3 sets were damaged in shipping and 19 sets arrived undamaged.
    (a) What fraction of the shipment arrived damaged?
    (b) What fraction of the shipment arrived undamaged?

Reduce each answer to lowest terms.

64. A coat selling for $85 was reduced to $70. What is the fraction of reduction?

65. Mary bought nine oranges. What fraction of a dozen did she buy?

66. A loan was repaid in 90 days. In what fraction of a year was the loan repaid? (Note: A business year is considered to have 360 days.)

67. A retailer bought 144 sport shirts and sold 48. What fraction of the 144 shirts was sold?

68. If it takes 12 minutes to assemble a toaster, what fraction of an hour does this represent?

UNIT 2 Addition and Subtraction of Fractions and Mixed Numbers

Addition of Fractions and Mixed Numbers

Addition of Fractions

Fractions can be added only if they have the same (or a **common**) **denominator.**

PROCEDURE: To add fractions that have a common denominator:

      1. Add the numerators.
      2. Place the new numerator over the common denominator.
      3. Reduce the fraction.

Example 1   Add: $\dfrac{5}{32} + \dfrac{7}{32} + \dfrac{3}{32} + \dfrac{9}{32}$.

        Answer: $\dfrac{5}{32} + \dfrac{7}{32} + \dfrac{3}{32} + \dfrac{9}{32} = \dfrac{24}{32} = \dfrac{3}{4}$

Most of the time you will have to add fractions that do not have the same denominators. To solve such problems, you will have to raise all the fractions to equivalent fractions having the same denominators.

PROCEDURE: To add fractions that do not have a common denominator:

STEP 1. Circle the largest denominator and see whether the other denominators divide evenly into it. If the largest denominator is not a common denominator, *try multiples of the circled number* until you reach *a number that can be used as a common denominator.*

STEP 2. Raise all fractions to equivalent fractions that have the common denominator.

STEP 3. Add the numerators, and place the total (the new numerator) over the common denominator.

STEP 4. Simplify the answer. Change improper fractions to mixed numbers.

Example 2 Add: $\dfrac{2}{3} + \dfrac{3}{4} + \dfrac{9}{12}$.

Solution:

STEP 1. $\dfrac{2}{3} = \dfrac{}{12}$

$\dfrac{3}{4} = \dfrac{}{12}$

$+ \dfrac{9}{\boxed{12}} = \dfrac{}{12}$

$\dfrac{}{12}$

Arrange the fractions one under the other, and circle the largest denominator. Since the other denominators, 3 and 4, divide evenly into 12, 12 is the least common denominator (LCD) for the given fractions.

STEP 2. $\dfrac{2 \times 4}{3 \times 4} = \dfrac{8}{12}$

$\dfrac{3 \times 3}{4 \times 3} = \dfrac{9}{12}$

STEP 3. $\dfrac{9 \times 1}{12 \times 1} = \dfrac{9}{12}$

Raise the given fractions to equivalent fractions, and add their numerators.

STEP 4. $= \dfrac{26}{12}$

$= 2\dfrac{1}{6}$

Change the improper fraction to a mixed number:

$$\begin{array}{r} 2\frac{1}{6} \\ 12\overline{)26} \\ 24 \\ \hline \end{array}$$

$\dfrac{2}{12} = \dfrac{1}{6}$

Answer: $\dfrac{2}{3} + \dfrac{3}{4} + \dfrac{9}{12} = 2\dfrac{1}{6}$

Example 3 Add: $\dfrac{3}{4} + \dfrac{1}{2} + \dfrac{3}{5}$.

Solution:

STEP 1.
$$\dfrac{3}{4} = \dfrac{}{20}$$

$$\dfrac{1}{2} = \dfrac{}{20}$$

$$+ \ \dfrac{3}{\circled{5}} = \dfrac{}{20}$$

Arrange the fraction as before, and circle the largest denominator. Since 5 is not the LCD, try *multiples of 5* until you reach a number into which 4, 2, and 5 divide evenly.

$\cancel{5}, \cancel{10}, \cancel{15}, 20 \ \checkmark$

The LCD is 20.

$$\dfrac{}{20}$$

STEP 2. $\dfrac{3 \times 5}{4 \times 5} = \dfrac{15}{20}$

$+ \ \dfrac{1 \times 10}{2 \times 10} = \dfrac{10}{20}$

STEP 3. $\dfrac{3 \times 4}{5 \times 4} = \dfrac{12}{20}$

$$\begin{array}{r} 1\frac{17}{20} \\ 20\overline{)37} \\ \underline{20} \\ 17 \end{array}$$

STEP 4. $= \dfrac{37}{20} = 1\dfrac{17}{20}$

Answer: $\dfrac{3}{4} + \dfrac{1}{2} + \dfrac{3}{5} = 1\dfrac{17}{20}$

Addition of Mixed Numbers

PROCEDURE: Since mixed numbers are *whole numbers plus fractions,* you add mixed numbers in *three separate steps.*

1. Add the whole numbers first.
2. Add the fractions.
3. Combine the two answers into a final sum.

Example 4 Add: $15\dfrac{2}{3} + 11\dfrac{1}{2} + 18\dfrac{7}{12}$.

Solution: Write the numbers one under the other, and draw a vertical line to separate the fractions from the whole numbers.

STEP 1.
$$
\begin{array}{r|l}
15 & \dfrac{2}{3} \\[2mm]
11 & \dfrac{1}{2} \\[2mm]
+ \ 18 & \dfrac{7}{12} \\[2mm]
\hline
44 & 12
\end{array}
$$

Add the whole numbers.

Find the LCD (12).

STEP 2.
$$
\begin{array}{r|l}
15 & \dfrac{2}{3} \\[2mm]
11 & \dfrac{1}{2} \\[2mm]
+ \ 18 & \dfrac{7}{\circled{12}} \\[2mm]
\hline
44 &
\end{array}
$$

STEP 3.

$$15 \left|\ \frac{2 \times 4}{3 \times 4} = \frac{8}{12}\right.$$

$$11 \left|\ \frac{1 \times 6}{2 \times 6} = \frac{6}{12}\right.$$

$$+18 \left|\ \frac{7 \times 1}{12 \times 1} = \frac{7}{12}\right.$$

$$= \frac{21}{12} = \boxed{1\frac{3}{4}}$$

$$44$$
$$1\ \left|\ \frac{3}{4}\right.$$

$$45\ \left|\ \frac{3}{4}\right.$$

Raise the fractions to equivalent fractions, add the fractions, and change the improper fraction to a whole number.

$$1\frac{9}{12} = 1\frac{3}{4}$$
$$12\overline{)21}$$
$$\underline{12}$$
$$9$$

Combine the two sums.

Answer: $15\frac{2}{3} + 11\frac{1}{2} + 18\frac{7}{12} = 45\frac{3}{4}$

Example 5   Add: $1\frac{3}{5} + 3\frac{1}{2} + 4\frac{2}{3}$.

Solution: Set up the fractions, and solve as before.

$$1 \left|\ \frac{3}{⑤} = \frac{18}{30}\right.$$

$$3 \left|\ \frac{1}{2} = \frac{15}{30}\right.$$

$$4 \left|\ \frac{2}{3} = \frac{20}{30}\right.$$

$$8\ \ \ \ \frac{53}{30} = 1\frac{23}{30}$$

$$+\ 1\frac{23}{30}$$

$$9\frac{23}{30}$$

Find the LCD.

$\cancel{5}, \cancel{10}, \cancel{15}, \cancel{25}, 30\ \sqrt{}$ LCD

Think: $5 \times\ \ 6 = 30, 3 \times\ \ 6 = 18$
$\ \ \ \ \ \ \ \ \ \ \ 2 \times 15 = 30, 1 \times 15 = 15$
$\ \ \ \ \ \ \ \ \ \ \ 3 \times 10 = 30, 2 \times 10 = 20$

Answer: $1\frac{3}{5} + 3\frac{1}{2} + 4\frac{2}{3} = 9\frac{23}{30}$

Subtraction of Fractions and Mixed Numbers

In subtracting fractions and mixed numbers, you follow the same procedure as in addition except that, instead of *adding* the numerators, you *subtract* the numerators.

PROCEDURE: To subtract fractions and mixed numbers:

1. Arrange the fractions or mixed numbers one under the other.
2. If necessary, raise the fractions to equivalent fractions with a common denominator.
3. Subtract the numerators.

Example 6   Subtract: $\dfrac{2}{3} - \dfrac{3}{5}$.

$$\dfrac{2}{3} = \dfrac{10}{15}$$

$$-\dfrac{3}{5} = \dfrac{9}{15}$$

$$= \dfrac{1}{15}$$

The LCD is 15.

Think: $3 \times 5 = 15,\ 2 \times 5 = 10$

$5 \times 3 = 15,\ 3 \times 3 = 9$

To check, add the difference to the subtrahend. The answer should be the minuend.

Check: Difference + Subtrahend = Minuend

$$\dfrac{1}{15}$$

$$+\dfrac{9}{15}$$

$$\dfrac{10}{15} = \dfrac{2}{3}\ \checkmark$$

Answer: $\dfrac{2}{3} - \dfrac{3}{5} = \dfrac{1}{15}$

Example 7   Subtract: $20\dfrac{3}{4} - 15\dfrac{1}{3}$.

$$20\ \bigg|\ \dfrac{3}{4} = 20\dfrac{9}{12}$$
$$-\ 15\ \bigg|\ \dfrac{1}{3} = 15\dfrac{4}{12}$$
$$5\ \dfrac{5}{12}$$

Check: $5\ \bigg|\ \dfrac{5}{12} = \dfrac{5}{12}$
$+\ 15\ \bigg|\ \dfrac{1}{3} = \dfrac{4}{12}$
$20\ \dfrac{3}{4}\ \checkmark\ \dfrac{9}{12} = \dfrac{3}{4}$

Answer: $20\dfrac{3}{4} - 15\dfrac{1}{3} = 5\dfrac{5}{12}$

HINT: In subtracting mixed numbers, it may be necessary to *borrow* from the whole number when the numerator in the subtrahend is larger than the numerator in the minuend.

Example 8   Subtract: $23\dfrac{1}{5} - 17\dfrac{3}{4}$.

$$23\ \bigg|\ \dfrac{1}{5} = \dfrac{④}{20}$$
$$-\ 17\ \bigg|\ \dfrac{3}{4} = \dfrac{⑮}{20}$$

In this problem the numerator in the fraction in the subtrahend, 15, is larger than the numerator in the fraction in the minuend, 4. Since you cannot subtract a larger number from a smaller number, borrow 1 from the whole number and proceed as follows:

STEP 1.
$$\begin{array}{r|l}\overset{22}{\cancel{23}} & \frac{1}{5} = 1\frac{4}{20} \\[4pt] -\ 17 & \frac{3}{4} = \frac{15}{20}\end{array}$$

Borrow 1 from 23 and place it in front of the fraction $\frac{4}{20}$, resulting in the mixed number $1\frac{4}{20}$.

Change $1\frac{4}{20}$ to $\frac{24}{20}$, and complete the subtraction.

STEP 2.
$$\begin{array}{r|l}\overset{22}{\cancel{23}} & \frac{1}{5} = 1\frac{4}{20} = \frac{24}{20} \\[4pt] -\ 17 & \frac{3}{4} = \textcircled{$\frac{15}{20}$} \rightarrow \frac{15}{20} \\[4pt] \hline 5 & \frac{9}{20} \longleftarrow \textcircled{$\frac{9}{20}$}\end{array}$$

STEP 3.
$$\begin{array}{r|l}\overset{22}{\cancel{23}} & \frac{1}{5} = \frac{24}{20} \\[4pt] -\ 17 & \frac{3}{4} = \frac{15}{20} \\[4pt] \hline 5 & \frac{9}{20}\end{array}$$

Check:
$$\begin{array}{r|l} 5 & \frac{9}{20} \\[4pt] +\ 17 & \frac{15}{20} \\[4pt] \hline 22 & \frac{24}{20} = 1\frac{4}{20} = \textcircled{$1\frac{1}{5}$} \\[4pt] +\ 1 & \frac{1}{5} \longleftarrow \\[4pt] \hline 23 & \frac{1}{5} \checkmark\end{array}$$

Answer: $23\frac{1}{5} - 17\frac{3}{4} = 5\frac{9}{20}$

Example 9 Subtract: $21 - 5\frac{3}{4}$.

Solution: Arrange the problem as before:

$$\begin{array}{r|l} 21 & \\[4pt] -\ 5 & \frac{3}{4}\end{array}$$

Since 21 has no fraction, *borrow* 1 from the 21 and change the 1 you borrowed to $\frac{4}{4}$ $\left(\frac{4}{4} = 1\right)$. Write the $\frac{4}{4}$ above the $\frac{3}{4}$, and complete the problem.

$$
\begin{array}{r|l}
20 & \frac{4}{4} \\
\cancel{21} & \\
-\ 5 & \frac{3}{4} \\
\hline
15 & \frac{1}{4}
\end{array}
\qquad
\textit{Check:}\quad
\begin{array}{r|l}
15 & \frac{1}{4} \\
+\ 5 & \frac{3}{4} \\
\hline
20 & \frac{4}{4} = \boxed{1} \\
& \\
21 & \frac{1}{21}\ \checkmark
\end{array}
$$

Answer: $21 - 5\frac{3}{4} = 15\frac{1}{4}$

Exercises

Exercise A Solve the following problems:

1. $\frac{3}{5}$
$\frac{2}{3}$
$+\ \frac{9}{15}$

2. $\frac{3}{4}$
$\frac{7}{10}$
$+\ \frac{1}{5}$

3. $\frac{1}{4}$
$\frac{5}{8}$
$+\ \frac{13}{24}$

4. $\frac{5}{7}$
$\frac{1}{2}$
$+\ \frac{9}{14}$

5. $\frac{2}{8}$
$\frac{2}{3}$
$+\ \frac{5}{6}$

6. $13\frac{3}{4}$
$17\frac{4}{5}$
$+\ 23\frac{7}{8}$

7. $12\frac{3}{8}$
$5\frac{2}{3}$
$+\ 19\frac{6}{7}$

8. $24\frac{3}{4}$
$15\frac{11}{16}$
$+\ 18\frac{21}{32}$

9. $35\frac{2}{3}$
$15\frac{13}{15}$
$+\ 18\frac{3}{4}$

10. $13\frac{11}{14}$
$19\frac{2}{3}$
$+\ 22\frac{5}{7}$

11. $23\frac{1}{2}$
$19\frac{7}{8}$
$+\ 21\frac{4}{5}$

12. $25\frac{2}{3}$
$23\frac{4}{5}$
$+\ 18\frac{7}{10}$

13. $15\frac{2}{3}$
$18\frac{4}{5}$
$+\ 24\frac{5}{6}$

14. $35\frac{5}{8}$
$17\frac{3}{4}$
$+\ 1\frac{4}{5}$

15. $14\frac{2}{3}$
$20\frac{4}{5}$
$+\ 17\frac{1}{2}$

16. $\frac{5}{8}$
$-\ \frac{3}{16}$

17. $\frac{4}{5}$
$-\ \frac{3}{4}$

18. $\frac{2}{3}$
$-\ \frac{3}{7}$

19. $\frac{3}{5}$
$-\ \frac{5}{12}$

20. $\frac{5}{9}$
$-\ \frac{1}{4}$

21. $\frac{3}{4}$
$-\ \frac{2}{3}$

22. $23\frac{4}{5}$
$-\ 18\frac{2}{3}$

23. 19
$-\ 3\frac{7}{8}$

24. $45\frac{5}{16}$
$-\ 32\frac{3}{4}$

25. $37\frac{1}{5}$
$-\ 20\frac{5}{6}$

26. $18\frac{2}{7}$
$-\ 15\frac{1}{3}$

27. $23\frac{3}{8}$
$-\ 18\frac{2}{3}$

28. 21
$-\ 7\frac{9}{15}$

29. $15\frac{2}{3}$
$-\ 7\frac{5}{12}$

30. $43\frac{3}{12}$
$-\ 21\frac{14}{15}$

Exercise B   Complete the following forms:

31.

		Hours Worked						Total Hours Worked
Week Ending June 14, 20—								
Card No.	Name of Employee	M	T	W	T	F	S	
40	S. Alvarez	$8\frac{1}{2}$	$7\frac{3}{4}$	9	$8\frac{1}{4}$	$8\frac{3}{4}$	4	———
41	W. Baines	9	$8\frac{1}{4}$	$9\frac{1}{2}$	$7\frac{3}{4}$	$8\frac{1}{2}$	3	———
42	P. Belmore	$8\frac{3}{4}$	$9\frac{1}{2}$	$8\frac{1}{4}$	$8\frac{3}{4}$	$9\frac{3}{4}$	5	———
43	L. Caldwell	$9\frac{1}{2}$	$8\frac{3}{4}$	$8\frac{1}{4}$	$8\frac{3}{4}$	$9\frac{1}{2}$	4	———
44	N. Carter	$8\frac{1}{2}$	$9\frac{3}{4}$	$8\frac{1}{4}$	$8\frac{3}{4}$	$9\frac{1}{2}$	4	———
45	I. Cortez	$9\frac{1}{2}$	$8\frac{3}{4}$	$8\frac{1}{2}$	$9\frac{3}{4}$	$8\frac{1}{4}$	5	———
46	V. Elton	$8\frac{1}{2}$	$9\frac{3}{4}$	$8\frac{1}{4}$	$8\frac{3}{4}$	$9\frac{1}{2}$	4	———

32.

		Hours Worked						Total Hours Worked
Week Ending June 21, 20—								
Card No.	Name of Employee	M	T	W	T	F	S	
40	S. Alvarez	$8\frac{3}{4}$	$9\frac{1}{2}$	$8\frac{3}{4}$	$9\frac{1}{4}$	$8\frac{3}{4}$	4	———
41	W. Baines	$9\frac{1}{4}$	$8\frac{1}{2}$	$8\frac{3}{4}$	$9\frac{1}{2}$	$8\frac{1}{2}$	3	———
42	P. Belmore	$8\frac{1}{2}$	$9\frac{3}{4}$	$8\frac{3}{4}$	$9\frac{1}{4}$	$8\frac{1}{2}$	5	———
43	L. Caldwell	$9\frac{1}{2}$	$9\frac{3}{4}$	$8\frac{1}{4}$	$8\frac{3}{4}$	$9\frac{3}{4}$	4	———
44	N. Carter	$8\frac{3}{4}$	$8\frac{1}{2}$	$9\frac{1}{4}$	$9\frac{3}{4}$	$8\frac{1}{2}$	5	———
45	I. Cortez	$9\frac{1}{4}$	$8\frac{3}{4}$	$8\frac{3}{4}$	$9\frac{1}{2}$	$8\frac{3}{4}$	4	———
46	V. Elton	$8\frac{3}{4}$	$9\frac{1}{2}$	$8\frac{1}{4}$	$8\frac{3}{4}$	$9\frac{3}{4}$	5	———

33.

		Hours Worked						Total Hours Worked
Card No.	Name of Employee	M	T	W	T	F	S	
40	S. Alvarez	$8\frac{1}{2}$	$9\frac{3}{4}$	$9\frac{1}{2}$	$8\frac{1}{4}$	$8\frac{3}{4}$	4	———
41	W. Baines	$9\frac{3}{4}$	$8\frac{1}{2}$	$8\frac{1}{4}$	$9\frac{3}{4}$	$8\frac{1}{4}$	5	———
42	P. Belmore	$8\frac{3}{4}$	$9\frac{1}{2}$	$8\frac{1}{4}$	$9\frac{3}{4}$	$8\frac{1}{2}$	4	———
43	L. Caldwell	$9\frac{3}{4}$	$8\frac{3}{4}$	$8\frac{1}{2}$	$9\frac{1}{4}$	$8\frac{3}{4}$	4	———
44	N. Carter	$9\frac{1}{2}$	$9\frac{3}{4}$	$8\frac{1}{2}$	$9\frac{1}{4}$	$8\frac{3}{4}$	5	———
45	I. Cortez	$8\frac{3}{4}$	$9\frac{1}{2}$	$8\frac{1}{2}$	$9\frac{1}{4}$	$8\frac{3}{4}$	4	———
46	V. Elton	$8\frac{1}{2}$	$9\frac{3}{4}$	$8\frac{1}{4}$	$9\frac{1}{2}$	$9\frac{3}{4}$	4	———

Week Ending June 28, 20—

34.

		Hours Worked						Total Hours Worked
Card No.	Name of Employee	M	T	W	T	F	S	
40	S. Alvarez	$8\frac{3}{4}$	$9\frac{1}{2}$	$8\frac{1}{2}$	$8\frac{1}{4}$	$9\frac{3}{4}$	4	———
41	W. Baines	$9\frac{1}{2}$	$8\frac{3}{4}$	$9\frac{1}{2}$	$9\frac{1}{4}$	$8\frac{3}{4}$	5	———
42	P. Belmore	$9\frac{1}{4}$	$8\frac{1}{2}$	$9\frac{3}{4}$	$8\frac{1}{2}$	$9\frac{3}{4}$	4	———
43	L. Caldwell	$8\frac{3}{4}$	$8\frac{1}{2}$	$9\frac{1}{4}$	$9\frac{3}{4}$	$8\frac{1}{2}$	5	———
44	N. Carter	$9\frac{1}{2}$	$8\frac{3}{4}$	$9\frac{1}{4}$	$8\frac{3}{4}$	$8\frac{1}{2}$	3	———
45	I. Cortez	$8\frac{1}{2}$	$9\frac{3}{4}$	$8\frac{1}{2}$	$9\frac{1}{4}$	$8\frac{3}{4}$	4	———
46	V. Elton	$9\frac{3}{4}$	$8\frac{1}{2}$	$9\frac{1}{4}$	$8\frac{1}{2}$	$8\frac{3}{4}$	4	———

Week Ending July 5, 20—

Word Problems

Exercise C Solve the following problems:

35. A salesclerk sold the following pieces of material: $4\frac{1}{2}$ yards, $3\frac{1}{4}$ yards, $6\frac{2}{3}$ yards, and $5\frac{5}{6}$ yards. How many yards did the salesclerk sell?

36. Juan worked the following number of hours during the week: Monday, $8\frac{1}{2}$ hours; Tuesday, $9\frac{1}{4}$ hours; Wednesday, $7\frac{3}{4}$ hours; Thursday, $10\frac{1}{2}$ hours; and Friday, $9\frac{3}{4}$ hours. How many hours did he work?

37. A manufacturer needs the following pieces of material to make a suit: $1\frac{1}{2}$ yards for the jacket, $1\frac{2}{3}$ yards for the pants, and $\frac{4}{6}$ yard for the vest. Find the total number of yards needed to make the suit.

38. A carpenter needs four pieces of board to make a shelf unit: $13\frac{1}{2}$ feet, $15\frac{3}{4}$ feet, $12\frac{7}{8}$ feet, and $11\frac{1}{4}$ feet. How many feet of board does he need?

39. A mixture contains three ingredients, present in the following amounts: $5\frac{1}{2}$ pounds, $3\frac{1}{3}$ pounds, and $8\frac{7}{16}$ pounds. What is the total weight of the mixture?

40. Theresa bought $\frac{3}{4}$ of a yard of material and used $\frac{1}{3}$ yard. How much material was unused?

41. Mr. Brandt bought $\frac{5}{6}$ of a ton of coal and used $\frac{2}{3}$ ton. How much coal was left?

42. A bolt of rayon contained $35\frac{3}{4}$ yards. If a clerk sold $12\frac{1}{5}$ yards, how much rayon was left?

43. A carpenter had a piece of board measuring $24\frac{1}{2}$ feet. If he cut off a piece measuring $6\frac{2}{3}$ feet, how many feet of board were left?

44. Mrs. Schaeffer had $3\frac{1}{4}$ dozen eggs and used $2\frac{2}{3}$ dozen. How many eggs did she have left?

UNIT **3** Multiplication and Division of Fractions and Mixed Numbers

Multiplication of Fractions and Mixed Numbers

Multiplication of proper fractions and of mixed numbers is very important in business. Many items are purchased in whole units and parts of units, such as $6\frac{1}{2}$ yards, $5\frac{1}{3}$ pounds, or $4\frac{2}{3}$ tons, and these mixed numbers have to be multiplied by the price per unit.

When you need to find a fractional part of a number, a fraction, or a mixed number, the word *of* means multiplication. In the problems "How much is $\frac{2}{3}$ of $345.60?" "Find $\frac{1}{5}$ of $\frac{3}{4}$ ton," and "What is $\frac{3}{4}$ of $\frac{1}{2}$?" you can substitute the *multiplication sign* for the word *of.*

Multiplication of Fractions

PROCEDURE: To multiply fractions:

1. Multiply the numerators to produce a single numerator.
2. Multiply the denominators to produce a single denominator.
3. Reduce the resulting single fraction to the lowest terms possible.

Example 1 Multiply: $\frac{3}{4} \times \frac{2}{3} \times \frac{1}{5}$.

STEP 1. $\frac{3}{4} \times \frac{2}{3} \times \frac{1}{5} = \frac{6}{}$ Multiply the numerators.

STEP 2. $\frac{3}{4} \times \frac{2}{3} \times \frac{1}{5} = \frac{6}{60}$ Multiply the denominators.

STEP 3. $\frac{6}{60} = \frac{1}{10}$ Reduce your answer to the lowest terms, and check.

Answer: $\frac{3}{4} \times \frac{2}{3} \times \frac{1}{5} = \frac{1}{10}$

Shortcut: To simplify the multiplication of fractions, you may first reduce *any* numerator with *any* denominator. This will significantly shorten your time and help to eliminate mistakes.

Example 2 Multiply: $\frac{3}{4} \times \frac{8}{15} \times \frac{1}{2}$.

Solution: Set up the problem, and use *common divisors* to divide out *any numerator* and *any denominator before multiplying.*

$\frac{\overset{1}{\cancel{3}}}{4} \times \frac{8}{\underset{5}{\cancel{15}}} \times \frac{1}{2} = 3$ is a *common divisor* for *numerator 3* and *denominator 15.*

$\frac{\overset{1}{\cancel{3}}}{\underset{1}{\cancel{4}}} \times \frac{\overset{2}{\cancel{8}}}{\underset{5}{\cancel{15}}} \times \frac{1}{2} = 4$ is a *common divisor* for *denominator 4* and *numerator 8.*

$\frac{\overset{1}{\cancel{3}}}{\underset{1}{\cancel{4}}} \times \frac{\overset{\overset{1}{\cancel{2}}}{\cancel{8}}}{\underset{5}{\cancel{15}}} \times \frac{1}{\underset{1}{\cancel{2}}} = \frac{1}{5}$

Answer: $\frac{3}{4} \times \frac{8}{15} \times \frac{1}{2} = \frac{1}{5}$

Multiplication of Mixed Numbers

PROCEDURE: To multiply mixed numbers:

1. Change any mixed number to an improper fraction.
2. Reduce any numerator with any denominator.
3. Multiply the numerators and the denominators.
4. Change the resulting fraction to a mixed number.

Example 3   Multiply: $3\frac{3}{4} \times 4\frac{2}{3}$.

STEP 1. $3\frac{3}{4} \times 4\frac{2}{3} = \frac{15}{4} \times \frac{14}{3}$ Convert both numbers to improper fractions.

STEP 2. $\frac{\overset{5}{\cancel{15}}}{\underset{2}{\cancel{4}}} \times \frac{\overset{7}{\cancel{14}}}{\underset{1}{\cancel{3}}}$ Reduce where possible.

STEP 3. $\frac{\overset{5}{\cancel{15}}}{\underset{2}{\cancel{4}}} \times \frac{\overset{7}{\cancel{14}}}{\underset{1}{\cancel{3}}} = \frac{35}{2}$ Multiply the numerators and the denominators.

STEP 4. $\frac{35}{2} = 17\frac{1}{2}$

Answer: $3\frac{3}{4} \times 4\frac{2}{3} = 17\frac{1}{2}$

Note: Any number multiplied or divided by 1 equals the original number: $5 \times 1 = 5$ and $5 \div 1 = 5$. You may use this rule of arithmetic to change a whole number to an improper fraction by writing the number 1 as a denominator under the whole number.

Example 4   Multiply: $15 \times \frac{2}{3} \times \frac{5}{2}$.

Answer: $15 \times \frac{2}{3} \times \frac{5}{2} = \frac{\overset{5}{\cancel{15}}}{1} \times \frac{\overset{1}{\cancel{2}}}{\underset{1}{\cancel{3}}} \times \frac{5}{\underset{1}{\cancel{2}}} = \frac{25}{1} = 25$

Division of Fractions and Mixed Numbers

Division of Fractions

Examine the following two sets of problems:

(a) $15 \div 3 = 5$ (b) $18 \div 3 = 6$

    and   and

$$\frac{\overset{5}{\cancel{15}}}{1} \times \frac{1}{\underset{1}{\cancel{3}}} = 5 \qquad\qquad \frac{\overset{6}{\cancel{18}}}{1} \times \frac{1}{\underset{1}{\cancel{3}}} = 6$$

In each set of problems, when you *invert* the divisor (change 3 to $\frac{1}{3}$) and change the problem from division to multiplication, the answers to the division problems and multiplication problems are the same.

    Therefore, to divide two fractions, invert the divisor (the second fraction) and change the problem to a multiplication problem.

PROCEDURE: To divide any two fractions:

    1. Convert any mixed numbers to improper fractions.
    2. Invert the divisor, the second fraction.
    3. Change the operation to multiplication.
    4. Then reduce where possible and multiply to find the answer.

Example 5   Divide: $\frac{2}{3} \div \frac{4}{5}$.

STEP 1. $\frac{2}{3} \div \left(\frac{4}{5}\right) = \frac{2}{3} \times \frac{5}{4}$ and change the division sign to multiplication.

STEP 2. $\frac{\overset{1}{\cancel{2}}}{3} \times \frac{5}{\underset{2}{\cancel{4}}} = \frac{5}{6}$ Solve the multiplication problem, reducing where possible, and check your answer.

Check: $\frac{\overset{1}{\cancel{5}}}{6} \times \frac{4}{\underset{1}{\cancel{5}}} = \frac{4}{6} = \frac{2}{3}\,\checkmark$ Multiply the quotient by the divisor; the resulting fraction should equal the dividend.

Answer: $\frac{2}{3} \div \frac{4}{5} = \frac{5}{6}$

Division of Mixed Numbers

PROCEDURE: To divide any two mixed numbers, first change the mixed numbers to improper fractions. Then invert the divisor and multiply the two fractions.

Example 6 Divide: $\dfrac{5}{6} \div 3$.

$$\frac{5}{6} \div \frac{3}{1} = \frac{5}{6} \times \frac{1}{3} = \frac{5}{18}$$

Check: $\dfrac{5}{\overset{}{\underset{6}{18}}} \times \dfrac{\overset{1}{\cancel{3}}}{1} = \dfrac{5}{6}$ √

Answer: $\dfrac{5}{6} \div 3 = \dfrac{5}{18}$

Example 7 Divide: $5\dfrac{3}{5} \div 2\dfrac{4}{15}$.

STEP 1. $\dfrac{28}{5} \div \dfrac{34}{15}$ — Change the mixed numbers to improper fractions.

STEP 2. $\dfrac{28}{5} \div \dfrac{34}{15} = \dfrac{28}{5} \times \dfrac{15}{34}$ — Invert the divisor, and change the division symbol to the multiplication sign.

STEP 3. $\dfrac{\overset{14}{\cancel{28}}}{\underset{1}{\cancel{5}}} \times \dfrac{\overset{3}{\cancel{15}}}{\underset{17}{\cancel{34}}} = \dfrac{42}{17} = 2\dfrac{8}{17}$ — Solve the multiplication problem, reducing where possible. Change the improper fraction to a mixed number.

Check: $2\dfrac{8}{17} \times 2\dfrac{4}{15} = \dfrac{42}{\underset{1}{\cancel{17}}} \times \dfrac{\overset{2}{\cancel{34}}}{15} = \dfrac{84}{15} = 5\dfrac{3}{5}$ √

Answer: $5\dfrac{3}{5} \div 2\dfrac{4}{15} = 2\dfrac{8}{17}$

Exercises

Exercise A Solve the following problems:

1. $\dfrac{7}{8} \times \dfrac{14}{21}$

2. $\dfrac{3}{4} \times \dfrac{1}{2} \times \dfrac{3}{5}$

3. $\dfrac{7}{16} \times \dfrac{2}{3} \times \dfrac{4}{9}$

4. $\dfrac{3}{8} \times \dfrac{4}{8} \times 3\dfrac{2}{3}$

5. $\dfrac{4}{5} \times \dfrac{7}{8} \times \dfrac{2}{3}$

6. $3\dfrac{4}{5} \times 5\dfrac{5}{8}$

7. $6\dfrac{1}{2} \times 3\dfrac{1}{3}$

8. $4\dfrac{7}{8} \times 3\dfrac{1}{2} \times 4\dfrac{2}{3}$

9. $12 \times 2\dfrac{1}{5} \times \dfrac{1}{2}$

10. $4\dfrac{2}{3} \times 15 \times 3\dfrac{2}{5}$

11. $\dfrac{5}{8} \div \dfrac{3}{4}$

12. $\dfrac{5}{6} \div \dfrac{15}{18}$

13. $\dfrac{2}{3} \div \dfrac{9}{12}$

14. $\dfrac{5}{12} \div \dfrac{2}{3}$

15. $\dfrac{3}{5} \div \dfrac{5}{20}$

16. $3\dfrac{1}{2} \div 4\dfrac{3}{4}$

17. $15\dfrac{2}{3} \div 8\dfrac{5}{9}$

18. $16 \div 3\dfrac{4}{5}$

19. $8\dfrac{1}{2} \div 4$

20. $4\dfrac{2}{3} \div 7$

21. $4\dfrac{3}{4} \div 5\dfrac{1}{2}$

22. $3\frac{2}{3} \div 6\frac{3}{5}$ **23.** $8 \div \frac{3}{4}$ **24.** $2\frac{2}{3} \div 7\frac{1}{2}$

25. $14\frac{1}{2} \div 3\frac{5}{8}$ **26.** $3\frac{3}{4} \div 2\frac{2}{5}$

Word Problems

Exercise B Solve the following problems:

27. How many $\frac{1}{5}$'s of a yard are there in $\frac{3}{4}$ of a yard?

28. A lot measures $3\frac{4}{5}$ acres. Into how many $\frac{1}{3}$-acre parcels can you divide the lot?

29. A plane flies 980 miles in $1\frac{2}{3}$ hours. How many miles does the plane average in 1 hour?

30. It takes $3\frac{1}{2}$ hours to assemble a color TV set. How many TV sets can be assembled in 40 hours?

31. A bolt of material contains 45 yards of cotton. If it takes $2\frac{1}{5}$ yards to make a dress, how many dresses can be made from the bolt of cotton?

32. How much is $\frac{1}{3}$ of $\frac{3}{4}$ ton?

33. A TV selling for $636.45 was reduced by $\frac{1}{3}$. Find the amount of reduction.

34. Mr. Topic owned $\frac{2}{3}$ of a business and willed $\frac{2}{5}$ of his ownership to his nephew. What fraction of the business did Mr. Topic leave to his nephew?

35. John earns $250 a week. He spends $\frac{1}{3}$ on rent and utilities, spends $\frac{1}{5}$ on food, and saves the rest. How much money does John spend on each of these items: (a) rent and utilities, (b) food, (c) savings?

36. Ms. Morales owned $\frac{4}{5}$ of a business valued at $95,000. If she sold $\frac{1}{3}$ of her share in the business, what should have been the selling price of the $\frac{1}{3}$ share?

UNIT **4** Decimal Fractions

Review of Decimal Fractions

You have seen that parts of units can be expressed as common fractions. In a common fraction, the denominator tells into how many parts the unit has been divided while the numerator tells how many of these parts are being used.

A decimal fraction is different from a common fraction in two ways:

1. The denominator is 10 or a power of 10 such as 100, 1,000, or 10,000.

2. The denominator is not written but rather is determined by the number of digits to the right of the decimal point.

Thus, a decimal fraction with one digit to the right of the decimal point is understood to have a denominator of 10 and is read as "tenths." Two digits to the right of the decimal point represent "hundredths," three digits represent "thousandths," and so on.

For example:

$0.3 \quad = \dfrac{3}{10}$ "three tenths"
(a *1-place* decimal, *1 zero* in the number 10)

$0.73 \ = \dfrac{73}{100}$ "seventy-three hundredths"
(a *2-place* decimal, *2 zeros* in 100)

$0.491 = \dfrac{491}{1,000}$ "four hundred ninety-one thousandths"
(a *3-place* decimal, *3 zeros* in 1,000)

To help you read decimal fractions and determine their denominators, consider the number of places to the right of the decimal point as zeros in powers of 10.

Changing Decimal Fractions to Common Fractions

PROCEDURE: To change a decimal fraction to a common fraction:

1. Rewrite the decimal fraction as a common fraction with the equivalent power of 10 as its denominator.
2. Reduce the common fraction to its lowest terms.

For example:

$$0.5 = \frac{5}{10} = \frac{1}{2} \qquad\qquad 0.28 = \frac{28}{100} = \frac{7}{25}$$

$$0.125 = \frac{125}{1,000} = \frac{1}{8} \qquad\qquad 0.06 = \frac{6}{100} = \frac{3}{50}$$

The zero to the *left* of the decimal point indicates that the whole-number part of the decimal number is 0.

Changing Common Fractions to Decimal Fractions

A common fraction is another way of indicating division. For example, the fraction $\frac{3}{4}$ is equivalent to $3 \div 4$.

PROCEDURE: To change a common fraction to a decimal fraction:

1. Divide the numerator by the denominator, carrying the division one digit beyond the needed number of decimal places.
2. Round off the quotient to the required number of decimal places.

Example 1   Change $\frac{3}{8}$ to a decimal fraction to the nearest *hundredth*.

```
    0.37⑤= 0.38
8)3.00 0
  2 4
    60
    56
     4 0
     4 0
```

Answer: $\frac{3}{8} = 0.38$ to the nearest hundredth

Example 2   Change $\frac{2}{3}$ to a decimal fraction to the nearest *thousandth*.

```
   0.666 ⑥ = 0.667
3)2,000 0
  18
   20
   18
    20
    18
     2
```

Answer: $\frac{2}{3} = 0.667$ to the nearest thousandth

Exercises

Exercise A Change the following fractions to decimal fractions to the nearest *tenth:*

1. $\dfrac{5}{7}$ 2. $\dfrac{3}{4}$ 3. $\dfrac{8}{15}$ 4. $\dfrac{25}{32}$ 5. $\dfrac{12}{17}$ 6. $\dfrac{15}{40}$

Change the following common fractions to decimal fractions to the nearest *hundredth:*

7. $\dfrac{7}{8}$ 8. $\dfrac{11}{23}$ 9. $\dfrac{19}{45}$ 10. $\dfrac{16}{38}$ 11. $\dfrac{34}{47}$ 12. $\dfrac{21}{54}$

Change the following common fractions to decimal fractions to the nearest *thousandth:*

13. $\dfrac{18}{34}$ 14. $\dfrac{32}{70}$ 15. $\dfrac{15}{54}$ 16. $\dfrac{19}{20}$ 17. $\dfrac{31}{43}$ 18. $\dfrac{25}{82}$

Word Problems

Exercise B Solve the following problems:

19. A computer gear measures $\dfrac{21}{32}$ inch. How many thousandths of an inch does the gear measure?

20. How many hundredths of a mile is $\dfrac{7}{9}$ mile?

21. A part is produced with a tolerance of "plus or minus $\dfrac{3}{64}$ of an inch." How many thousandths of an inch is the tolerance?

22. How many tenths of a gallon is $\dfrac{5}{7}$ gallon?

23. How many tenths of an hour is $\dfrac{5}{6}$ hour?

24. Joseph bought 4 ounces of ham. What decimal fraction of a pound did he buy? (One pound equals 16 ounces.)

25. Pam bought 2 feet of fabric. How many *thousandths* of a yard did she buy? (One yard equals 3 feet.)

26. What decimal fraction of a dozen is 8 eggs?

27. Twelve seconds is what decimal fraction of a minute?

UNIT **5** Developing Speed with Fractions

In working with fractions, there are shortcuts that can help you compute more accurately and rapidly. With practice you can develop the skill of doing some of these computations without pencil and paper.

Complex Fractions

In business problems you may sometimes use a fraction that has another fraction for a numerator or a denominator, or for both. This type of fraction is called a **complex fraction.**

PROCEDURE: To simplify a complex fraction:

1. Since any fraction can be thought of as equivalent to a division problem, rewrite the complex fraction as the fraction in the numerator divided by the fraction in the denominator.
2. Complete the division by inverting the divisor and multiplying.

Example 1 Simplify: $\dfrac{\frac{3}{4}}{\frac{4}{5}}$

Solution: Rewrite the complex fraction as a division problem, and complete the indicated division.

$$\frac{\frac{3}{4}}{\frac{4}{5}} = \frac{3}{4} \div \frac{4}{5} = \frac{3}{4} \times \frac{5}{4} = \frac{15}{16} \; Answer$$

Example 2 Simplify: $\dfrac{5}{\frac{3}{4}}$

Solution: $\dfrac{5}{\frac{3}{4}} = 5 \div \frac{3}{4} = \frac{5}{1} \div \frac{3}{4} = \frac{5}{1} \times \frac{4}{3} = \frac{20}{3} = 6\frac{2}{3} = Answer$

Finding a Number When a Fractional Part Is Known

PROCEDURE: To find a number when you know a fractional part of it, divide the known fractional part (which is a given number) by the fraction.

Example 3   If $\frac{2}{5}$ of a number is 42, what is the number?

Solution: The above facts can be written as the problem

$$\frac{2}{5} \times ? = 42$$

Since division is the opposite of multiplication, you can change the multiplication problem $\frac{2}{5} \times ? = 42$ to the division problem

$$42 \div \frac{2}{5} = ?$$

$$\frac{42}{1} \div \frac{2}{5} = \frac{\overset{21}{\cancel{42}}}{1} \times \frac{5}{\underset{1}{\cancel{2}}} = 105 \; Answer$$

If the answer is correct, $\frac{2}{5}$ of 105 should equal 42.

Check: $\dfrac{2}{\underset{1}{\cancel{5}}} \times \dfrac{\overset{21}{\cancel{105}}}{1} = 42\surd$

Using the $\dfrac{\text{IS}}{\text{OF}}$ Fraction

There are many problems in business that are similar to percent problems but deal with *fractional* parts; for instance, "What happens if we sell only $\frac{2}{3}$ of that amount?"

HINT: People often divide incorrectly because they are not sure which number is the divisor and which is the dividend. A good way to keep them straight is to remember the word-fraction $\dfrac{\text{IS}}{\text{OF}}$. This memory device indicates that the number in the problem related to the word *IS* is written as the *numerator,* while the number related to *OF* is written as the *denominator.*

Example 4   56 is $\frac{2}{3}$ of what number?

STEP 1. $\boxed{56\ is}$ $\left(\frac{2}{3}\ of\right)$ what number?   Identify the numbers related to *IS* and *OF*.

STEP 2. $\dfrac{IS}{OF} = \dfrac{56}{\frac{2}{3}} = 56 \div \dfrac{2}{3}$ Set up the $\dfrac{IS}{OF}$ fraction, and divide.

$\dfrac{56}{1} \div \dfrac{2}{3} = \dfrac{\overset{28}{56}}{1} \times \dfrac{3}{\underset{1}{2}} = 84 \ Answer$

Check: $\dfrac{2}{\underset{1}{3}} \times \dfrac{\overset{28}{84}}{1} = 56 \ \checkmark$

Most problems, including word problems, can be restated to apply the $\dfrac{IS}{OF}$ fraction.

Example 5   Mary spends \$55 a week for food, which is $\frac{1}{5}$ of her income. Find her weekly income.

Problem restated: $\boxed{\$55\ is}$ $\left(\frac{1}{5}\ of\right)$ Mary's income.

$\dfrac{IS}{OF} = \dfrac{55}{\frac{1}{5}} = \dfrac{55}{1} \div \dfrac{1}{5} = \dfrac{55}{1} \times \dfrac{5}{1} = \$275 \ Answer$

Check: $\dfrac{1}{5} \times \dfrac{275}{1} = \$55 \ \checkmark$

Using the Basic Fraction Equation

Three basic types of word problems involve *fractions, numbers,* and *fractional parts* of numbers (the numerical equivalent of the fraction).

For most problems, you will be given two of the three factors in the equation, and you will have to *solve for the missing factor.*

You know that the word *of,* when used with fractions, means *multiplication,* and the word *is* translates into *equal.*

The *sentence* $\frac{3}{4}$ *of* 84 *is* 63 translates into the *equation* $\frac{3}{4} \times 84 = 63$.

To check the equation multiply the *left side.* The product should equal 63:

$$\frac{3}{\underset{1}{4}} \times \frac{\overset{21}{84}}{1} = \frac{63}{1}$$

$$63 = 63 \ \checkmark$$

From the above example the *basic fraction equation* is devised:

Fraction	×	*Total (number)*	=	*Fractional part*
$\frac{3}{4}$	×	84	=	63

PROCEDURE: To use the *basic fraction equation* to solve each of the three types of problems:

1. *Rewrite* the problem as a one-sentence statement.
2. *Translate* the sentence into an equation.
3. *Solve* for the missing factor in the equation.

Use the following translations to write the sentence as an equation:

1. The word *of* translates into *multiplication* ($\times$).
2. The word *is* means *equals* (=).
3. a) *What fraction* translates into U (unknown)
   b) *What number* translates into n or another variable.
   c) *A number* translates into n or another variable.

Let's solve Examples 3–5 again, this time using the basic fraction equation.

Example 3 If $\dfrac{2}{5}$ of a number is 42, what is the number?

Alternative Solution:
1. Rewrite the problem as a one-sentence statement.
2. Translate the sentence into an equation, and solve for the missing factor.

$$\frac{2}{5} \quad \textit{of what number is} \quad \textit{42?}$$
$$\downarrow \qquad\quad \downarrow \qquad\quad \downarrow \qquad \downarrow$$
$$\frac{2}{5} \;\times\; n \;=\; 42$$

$$\frac{\cancel{2}}{\cancel{5}}\; n \;=\; \frac{42}{\frac{2}{5}} \qquad \text{Divide both sides by } \frac{2}{5}.$$

$$n \;=\; 42 \div \frac{2}{5}$$

$$n \;=\; 42 \times \frac{5}{2} \qquad \text{Multiply by the reciprocal of } \frac{2}{5}.$$

$$= \frac{\overset{21}{\cancel{42}}}{1} \times \frac{5}{\underset{1}{\cancel{2}}}$$

$$= 105$$

To check the solution, substitute 105 for n, and solve the equation.

Check: *Fraction* $\times$ *Total* $=$ *Fractional part*

$$\frac{2}{\underset{1}{\cancel{5}}} \quad\times\quad \frac{\overset{21}{\cancel{105}}}{1} \quad=\quad \frac{42}{1} \checkmark$$

$$=\quad 42$$

Answer: 42 is $\dfrac{2}{5}$ of 105.

Example 4   56 is $\frac{2}{3}$ of what number?

Alternative Solution: Rewrite the problem as an equation, and solve for the missing factor.

$$\frac{2}{3} \times n = 56$$

$$\frac{\cancel{\frac{2}{3}}}{\cancel{\frac{2}{3}}} \quad n = \frac{56}{\cancel{\frac{2}{3}}} \qquad \text{To get } n \text{ by itself, divide both sides by } \frac{2}{3}.$$

$$n = 56 \div \frac{2}{3}$$

$$= \frac{\overset{28}{\cancel{56}}}{1} \times \frac{3}{\underset{1}{\cancel{2}}}$$

$$= 84$$

Check: $\frac{2}{\underset{1}{\cancel{3}}} \times \frac{\overset{28}{\cancel{84}}}{1} = 56 \checkmark$

Answer: 56 is $\frac{2}{3}$ of 84.

Example 5   Mary spends \$55 a week for food, which is $\frac{1}{5}$ of her income. Find her weekly income.

Alternative Solution: Rewrite the problem as an equation, and solve the equation.

$$\frac{1}{5} \times n = \$55$$

$$\frac{\cancel{\frac{1}{5}}}{\cancel{\frac{1}{5}}} \quad n = \frac{55}{\frac{1}{5}} \qquad \text{Divide both sides by } \frac{1}{5}.$$

$$n = \frac{55}{\cancel{\frac{1}{5}}}$$

$$= \frac{55}{1} \times \frac{5}{1} \quad \text{Multiply by the reciprocal of } \frac{1}{5}.$$

$$= 275$$

Check: $\frac{1}{5} \times \frac{275}{1} = 55 \checkmark$

Answer: Mary's weekly income is \$275.

Example 6   A coat regularly selling for $284 is reduced by $\frac{1}{4}$ of the regular price. What is the sale price of the coat?

Solution: Write the problem as an equation, and solve the equation.

$$\text{Sale price} = \$284 - (\frac{1}{4} \text{ of } \$284)$$

$$= 284 - (\frac{1}{4} \times 284)$$

$$= 284 - 71$$

$$= 213$$

$$\frac{1}{\underset{1}{4}} \times \frac{\overset{71}{\cancel{284}}}{1} = 71$$

$$\begin{array}{r} 284 \\ \underline{-71} \\ 213 \end{array}$$

Answer: Sale price of the coat is $213.

Alternative Solution: You can use a more direct method to solve this problem. If the *regular price* is *reduced* by $\frac{1}{4}$, then $\frac{3}{4}$, *the remaining fraction,* is the sale price.

$$\text{Sale price} = \frac{3}{4} \text{ of } \$284$$

$$= \frac{3}{\underset{1}{\cancel{4}}} \times \frac{\overset{71}{\cancel{284}}}{1} = \$213$$

It's easier to subtract the fractions than the dollar amounts.

Decimal Fraction and Common Fraction Equivalents

In problem solving that involves both fractions and decimal numbers, you may want to change fractions to decimals, or decimals to fractions, to make the problem easier to solve or to obtain a more accurate solution.

To change a *fraction to a decimal,* carry out the indicated division, that is, divide the numerator by the denominator.

For example, to change $\frac{3}{4}$ to a decimal, divide 3 by 4:

$$\begin{array}{r} 0.75 \\ 4\overline{)3.00} \\ \underline{2\,8} \\ 20 \\ \underline{20} \end{array}$$

The *numerator* is the *dividend.*

Since there is no remainder, the division is complete.

$\frac{3}{4} = 0.75$ The decimal value of $\frac{3}{4}$, that is, 0.75, is called a *terminating decimal.*

Sometimes the answer to a problem is a *repeating decimal.*

For example, to change $\frac{2}{3}$ to a decimal, divide 2 by 3:

$$
\begin{array}{r}
0.666 \\
3\overline{)2.000} \\
\underline{1\ 8} \\
20 \\
\underline{18} \\
20 \\
\underline{18} \\
2
\end{array}
$$

The pattern of the repeating digit will never end.

The *exact* decimal value of $\frac{2}{3}$ is $0.66\frac{2}{3}$ or $\frac{2}{3} = 0.667$ rounded to the nearest *thousandth.*

In problem solving, the *only way* to express the *exact value* of a nonterminating fraction ($\frac{1}{3}$, $\frac{1}{7}$, $\frac{1}{6}$, etc.) is to use the *fraction form* instead of the decimal equivalent.

You have seen that certain common fractions have easy-to-remember equivalents in decimal form. For instance, $\frac{1}{2} = 0.50$ and $\frac{1}{4} = 0.25$. By remembering the common decimal fraction/common fraction equivalents listed in the accompanying table, you can significantly cut the time required for certain computations.

Decimal Fraction/Common Fraction Equivalents

$0.25 = \frac{1}{4}$	$0.20 = \frac{1}{5}$	$0.33\frac{1}{3} = \frac{1}{3}$	$0.125 = \frac{1}{8}$
$0.50 = \frac{1}{2}$	$0.40 = \frac{2}{5}$	$0.66\frac{2}{3} = \frac{2}{3}$	$0.08\frac{1}{3} = \frac{1}{12}$
$0.75 = \frac{3}{4}$	$0.60 = \frac{3}{5}$	$0.16\frac{2}{3} = \frac{1}{6}$	$0.06\frac{1}{4} = \frac{1}{16}$
	$0.80 = \frac{4}{5}$	$0.83\frac{1}{3} = \frac{5}{6}$	

Note: These equivalents are especially useful for percent problems and money calculations.

HINT: When a problem includes multiplication by a fraction, you can sometimes save time and improve accuracy by converting a decimal fraction to a common fraction, or vice versa.

Example 7   Find the cost of 44 pounds of nails at 25¢ per pound.

STEP 1. $44 \times \$0.25$ Set up the problem.

STEP 2. $\dfrac{\overset{11}{\cancel{44}}}{1} \times \$\dfrac{1}{\underset{1}{\cancel{4}}} = \$11$ Recognizing that $0.25 is the same as $\dfrac{1}{4}$ of a dollar, multiply 44 by $\$\dfrac{1}{4}$.

$\$\dfrac{1}{4}$ of $44 = \$11$ Alternatively, *think:* "$\dfrac{1}{4}$ of 44 is 11."

Answer: Cost of 44 pounds of nails at 25¢ per pound is $11.

Example 8   Find 25% of $240. (25% = 0.25)

STEP 1. $\$240 \times 0.25$ Set up the problem.

STEP 2. $\$\dfrac{\overset{60}{\cancel{240}}}{1} \times \dfrac{1}{\underset{1}{\cancel{4}}} = \$60$ Recognizing that 0.25 is the same as $\dfrac{1}{4}$, multiply $240 by $\dfrac{1}{4}$.

$\dfrac{1}{4}$ of $\$240 = \$60$ Alternatively, *think:* "$\dfrac{1}{4}$ of $240 is $60."

Answer: 25% of $240 is $60.

Example 9   Find the cost: $36 @ 66\dfrac{2}{3}¢$.

STEP 1. $36 \times \$.66\dfrac{2}{3}$ Set up the problem.

STEP 2. $\dfrac{\overset{12}{\cancel{36}}}{1} \times \$\dfrac{2}{\underset{1}{\cancel{3}}} = \$24$ Recognizing that $\$0.66\dfrac{2}{3}$ is the same as $\dfrac{2}{3}$ of a dollar, multiply 36 by $\$\dfrac{2}{3}$.

$\$\dfrac{2}{3}$ of $36 = \$24$ Alternatively, *think:* "$\dfrac{1}{3}$ of 36 is 12, so $\dfrac{2}{3}$ of 36 is 24."

Answer: Cost is $24.

Example 10   Find the cost: 24 @ 75¢.

STEP 1. $24 \times \$0.75$ Set up the problem.

STEP 2. $\dfrac{\overset{6}{\cancel{24}}}{1} \times \$\dfrac{3}{\underset{1}{\cancel{4}}} = \$18$ Recognizing that $0.75 is the same as $\dfrac{3}{4}$ of a dollar, multiply 24 by $\$\dfrac{3}{4}$.

$\$\dfrac{3}{4}$ of $24 = \$18$ Alternatively, *think:* "$\dfrac{1}{4}$ of 24 is 6, so $\dfrac{3}{4}$ of 24 is 18."

Answer: Cost is $18.

Example 11   A TV regularly selling for $345 is reduced by $\frac{1}{3}$. What is the sale price of the TV?

Solution: If the regular price is reduced by $\frac{1}{3}$, then $\frac{2}{3}$ of the regular price remains as the selling price. Find $\frac{2}{3}$ of $345.

$$\text{Selling price} = \frac{2}{3} \text{ of } \$345$$

$$= \frac{2}{3} \times \frac{345}{1}$$

$$= \frac{2}{\cancel{3}} \times \frac{\overset{115}{\cancel{345}}}{1}$$

$$= 230$$

$$= \$230$$

Check: 230 ⊡ 345 ⊟ 0.666...

$$= \frac{2}{3} \checkmark$$

Answer: Selling price of the TV is $230.

Exercises

Exercise A   Use the $\frac{\text{IS}}{\text{OF}}$ fraction to solve the following problems:

1. $\frac{2}{3}$ of what number is 44?

2.   78 is $\frac{3}{4}$ of what number?

3. $\frac{4}{5}$ of a number is 60. Find the number.

4.   If $\frac{3}{7}$ of a number is 84, find the number.

5. $\frac{7}{8}$ of what number is 56?

6.   Find the number if $\frac{3}{5}$ of it is 93.

7. $\frac{5}{7}$ of a number is 95. Find the number.

8.   46 is $\frac{2}{3}$ of what number?

9. $\frac{2}{5}$ of a number is 104. Find the number.

10.   If 36 is $\frac{3}{4}$ of a number, find the number.

Solve the following problems, using the shortcuts of this unit:

11. 84 @ 25¢ _____

160 @ 25¢ _____

124 @ 25¢ _____

280 @ 25¢ _____

Total _____

12. 36 @ 50¢ _____

72 @ 50¢ _____

144 @ 50¢ _____

64 @ 50¢ _____

Total _____

13. 32 @ 75¢ _____

56 @ 75¢ _____

64 @ 75¢ _____

128 @ 75¢ _____

Total _____

14. 72 @ $12\frac{1}{2}$¢ _____

88 @ $12\frac{1}{2}$¢ _____

168 @ $12\frac{1}{2}$¢ _____

248 @ $12\frac{1}{2}$¢ _____

Total _____

15. 32 @ $37\frac{1}{2}$¢ _____

56 @ $37\frac{1}{2}$¢ _____

720 @ $37\frac{1}{2}$¢ _____

960 @ $37\frac{1}{2}$¢ _____

Total _____

16. 56 @ $62\frac{1}{2}$¢ _____

168 @ $62\frac{1}{2}$¢ _____

104 @ $87\frac{1}{2}$¢ _____

560 @ $87\frac{1}{2}$¢ _____

Total _____

17. 48 @ $33\frac{1}{3}$¢ _____

45 @ $33\frac{1}{3}$¢ _____

54 @ $33\frac{1}{3}$¢ _____

144 @ $33\frac{1}{3}$¢ _____

Total _____

18. 36 @ $66\frac{2}{3}$¢ _____

72 @ $66\frac{2}{3}$¢ _____

117 @ $66\frac{2}{3}$¢ _____

129 @ $66\frac{2}{3}$¢ _____

Total _____

19. 54 @ $16\frac{2}{3}$¢ _____

180 @ $16\frac{2}{3}$¢ _____

126 @ $16\frac{2}{3}$¢ _____

480 @ $16\frac{2}{3}$¢ _____

Total _____

20. 35 @ 20¢ _____

175 @ 20¢ _____

240 @ 25¢ _____

164 @ 25¢ _____

Total _____

21. 90 @ $33\frac{1}{3}$¢ _____

234 @ $66\frac{2}{3}$¢ _____

288 @ 75¢ _____

325 @ 20¢ _____

Total _____

22. 124 @ 50¢ _____

160 @ $12\frac{1}{2}$¢ _____

80 @ $6\frac{1}{4}$¢ _____

180 @ $6\frac{2}{3}$¢ _____

Total _____

Exercise B   Find the total amounts in the following invoices:

23.

Quantity	Unit Price	Amount	
472 lb.	25¢	———	——
630 lb.	50¢	———	——
355 lb.	20¢	———	——
480 lb.	75¢	———	——
	Total		

24.

Quantity	Unit Price	Amount	
369 pieces	$33\frac{1}{3}$¢	———	——
576 pieces	$66\frac{2}{3}$¢	———	——
184 pieces	$12\frac{1}{2}$¢	———	——
848 pieces	50¢	———	——
	Total		

25.

Quantity	Unit Price	Amount	
1,335 yd.	20¢	———	——
2,428 yd.	50¢	———	——
2,384 yd.	25¢	———	——
1,152 yd.	$33\frac{1}{3}$¢	———	——
	Total		

26.

Quantity	Unit Price	Amount	
132 qt.	$8\frac{1}{3}$¢	_____	___
600 qt.	$16\frac{2}{3}$¢	_____	___
656 qt.	$12\frac{1}{2}$¢	_____	___
984 qt.	10¢	_____	___
	Total		

Word Problems

You may use the $\dfrac{\text{IS}}{\text{OF}}$ fraction to solve word problems.

Example   A retailer makes \$35 profit on a stereo set. If the \$35 represents $\dfrac{2}{5}$ of the selling price, what is the total selling price of the stereo?

Solution: The facts of the problem are as follows: ($35 is) ($\frac{2}{5}$ of) the selling price.

$$\frac{\text{IS}}{\text{OF}} = \frac{35}{\frac{2}{5}} = \frac{35}{1} \div \frac{2}{5} = \frac{35}{1} \times \frac{5}{2} = \frac{175}{2} = \$87.50 \; Answer$$

Check: $\dfrac{2}{5} \times \dfrac{87.50}{1} = \$35 \; \checkmark$

Exercise C   Solve the following problems:

27.   The New York Insurance Company employs in its office 116 clerk-typists, who are $\dfrac{2}{3}$ of the total employees. Find the total number of employees of the company.

28.   The Hany Department Store spends $\dfrac{1}{5}$ of its yearly advertising budget on newspaper advertising. If it spends \$6,500 on newspaper advertising, what is the total advertising budget for the year?

29.   The Acme Appliance Store makes a profit of $\dfrac{1}{3}$ of the selling price on an 18-cubic-foot refrigerator. The cost of the refrigerator is \$250. Find the selling price.

30.   The average weekly charge sales of a department store amount to \$35,000. If this represents $\dfrac{4}{5}$ of the total sales, find the *weekly cash sales* of the department store.

31.   Henry bought a car and made a down payment of \$650, with the balance to be paid in 24 equal installments. If the down payment is $\dfrac{1}{6}$ of the cost of the car, how much will each installment be?

UNIT **6** Review of Chapter Five

TERMS:
- Common fraction
- Complex fraction
- Decimal fraction
- Denominator
- Equivalent fraction
- Improper fraction
- Mixed number
- Numerator

HINTS:
- Reduce all answers.
- Check your work.
- Add and subtract with common denominators *only*.
- Use decimal and common fraction equivalents.
- Use the $\dfrac{IS}{OF}$ fraction and the basic function equation to solve fraction problems.

Reduce each fraction to lowest terms.

1. $\dfrac{3}{24}$ 2. $\dfrac{15}{60}$ 3. $\dfrac{8}{18}$ 4. $\dfrac{32}{48}$ 5. $\dfrac{30}{300}$

Raise each fraction to the higher equivalent of each denominator.

6. $\dfrac{5}{7} = \dfrac{}{28}$ 7. $\dfrac{3}{4} = \dfrac{}{48}$ 8. $\dfrac{2}{3} = \dfrac{}{60}$

9. $\dfrac{12}{15} = \dfrac{}{45}$ 10. $\dfrac{3}{15} = \dfrac{}{90}$

Add the following fractions and mixed numbers:

11. $\dfrac{3}{4}$ $\dfrac{4}{5}$ $+\dfrac{7}{10}$

12. $\dfrac{3}{8}$ $\dfrac{2}{3}$ $+\dfrac{6}{7}$

13. $\dfrac{7}{15}$ $\dfrac{5}{6}$ $+\dfrac{4}{9}$

14. $15\dfrac{4}{5}$ $13\dfrac{2}{3}$ $+23\dfrac{3}{4}$

15. $19\dfrac{5}{8}$ $32\dfrac{3}{5}$ $+28\dfrac{13}{20}$

16. $17\dfrac{5}{7}$ $24\dfrac{5}{8}$ $+18\dfrac{11}{14}$

Subtract the following fractions and mixed numbers:

17. $\dfrac{2}{3}$

$-\dfrac{3}{5}$

18. $\dfrac{5}{7}$

$-\dfrac{1}{3}$

19. $\dfrac{5}{6}$

$-\dfrac{4}{16}$

20. $19\dfrac{1}{3}$

$-15\dfrac{5}{7}$

21. 20

$-14\dfrac{7}{8}$

22. $34\dfrac{1}{6}$

$-33\dfrac{3}{4}$

Multiply the following fractions and mixed numbers:

23. $\dfrac{4}{5} \times \dfrac{15}{16}$

24. $\dfrac{4}{7} \times \dfrac{5}{18} \times \dfrac{9}{20}$

25. $5\dfrac{1}{2} \times 6\dfrac{2}{3} \times 4\dfrac{4}{5}$

26. $5\dfrac{3}{4} \times 8 \times 3\dfrac{5}{7}$

27. 236

$\times\ 35\dfrac{1}{4}$

28. $1,240$

$\times\ 42\dfrac{5}{8}$

Divide the following fractions and mixed numbers:

29. $\dfrac{7}{8} \div \dfrac{15}{16}$

30. $\dfrac{2}{3} \div \dfrac{5}{12}$

31. $2\dfrac{1}{5} \div 4\dfrac{3}{10}$

32. $5 \div 2\dfrac{3}{4}$

33. $4\dfrac{3}{5} \div 5\dfrac{7}{15}$

34. $4\dfrac{1}{4} \div 8$

35. $\dfrac{2}{7}$ of what number is 70?

36. 105 is $\dfrac{3}{4}$ of what number?

37. $\dfrac{2}{3}$ of a number is 92. Find the number.

38. Find the number if $\dfrac{7}{8}$ of it is 56.

39. If 90 is $\dfrac{5}{6}$ of a number, find the number.

Solve the following problems without using pencil and paper:

40.   88 @ 25¢ _____

484 @ 25¢ _____

150 @ 50¢ _____

130 @ 50¢ _____

164 @ 75¢ _____

124 @ 75¢ _____

Total   _____

41.   96 @ $12\frac{1}{2}$¢ _____

24 @ $12\frac{1}{2}$¢ _____

64 @ $37\frac{1}{2}$¢ _____

160 @ $37\frac{1}{2}$¢ _____

104 @ $62\frac{1}{2}$¢ _____

480 @ $87\frac{1}{2}$¢ _____

Total   _____

Change the following common fractions to decimal fractions to the nearest *tenth:*

42. $\dfrac{5}{16}$ **43.** $\dfrac{4}{5}$ **44.** $\dfrac{7}{9}$ **45.** $\dfrac{14}{17}$

Change the following common fractions to decimal fractions to the nearest *hundredth:*

46. $\dfrac{5}{8}$ **47.** $\dfrac{1}{3}$ **48.** $\dfrac{2}{3}$ **49.** $\dfrac{18}{30}$

Change the following common fractions to decimal fractions to the nearest *thousandth:*

50. $\dfrac{7}{16}$ **51.** $\dfrac{14}{32}$ **52.** $\dfrac{5}{7}$ **53.** $\dfrac{23}{36}$

Solve the following problems:

54.   A clothing store sold $\dfrac{4}{5}$ of its stock of men's white shirts. If it sold 120 shirts, how many of the shirts are left in stock?

55.   Cynthia's take-home pay is $\dfrac{2}{3}$ of her gross income of $1,500 a month. If she saves $\dfrac{1}{8}$ of her take-home pay, how much does she save each month?

56.   A store marks up its merchandise $\dfrac{2}{5}$ of the cost price. If the store pays $495 for a stereo set, what should be the selling price of the set?

CHAPTER **SIX**

Solving Percent Problems

UNIT **1** Percents in Business

Percents are used throughout the business world. For instance, the sales tax is usually calculated as a percent of the total sale, as is a discount. Percents are used to measure sales increases and profits, and also to calculate salespersons' commissions.

Review of Percent

The word *percent* means "per hundred" or "out of every 100," and compares a *given number to 100*.

Percents are a type of *fractions* that have *denominators* of 100.

When you write 35%, you are *comparing* the *number 35* to *100*, and you can write 35% as the *fraction* $\frac{35}{100}$.

Understanding the Meanings of Percents

- A *7% sales tax rate* means that the *customer* pays an additional $0.07 on each $1 of taxable merchandise purchased.

- A *15% commission rate* means that a *salesperson* earns $15 on every $100 of merchandise sold.

- A *30% reduction sale* means that the *original price* of the merchandise on sale is reduced by $30 for every $100 of the original price. Also, the *sale price* is 70% (the remaining percent), or $70 for every $100 of the original price.

- A *100% attendance* means that *all the students* in a given class are present.

- If *25%* of the students in a class are *absent,* then 75% (the remaining percent) of the students are *present.*

  In problem solving with percents, you must *first* change the *given percent* to a *decimal.*

Changing Percents to Decimals

Since *percents* means "hundredths," write the *percent* as a *fraction* with a *denominator of 100,* and divide the numerator by 100. For example:

$$35\% = \frac{.35}{100} = 0.35$$ Dividing a number by 100 moves the decimal point two places to the left.

PROCEDURE: To change a percent to a decimal, *drop* the *percent sign,* and move the decimal point *two places* to the left.

Example 1   Change each percent to a decimal.

(a)   18% (b)   10.9% (c)   6%

(d)   8.7% (e)   0.8% (f)   0.05%

Solutions: In each case, drop the percent sign and move the decimal point two places to the left.

(a)   18% = 0.18 (b)   10.9% = 0.109 (c)   6% = 0.06

  = 0.18   = 0.109   Note the zero as a *placeholder.*

  (18 *hundredths*)   (109 *thousandths*)   (6 *hundredths*)

(d)   8.7% = 0.087 (e)   0.8% = 0.008 (f)   0.05% = 0.0005

  = 0.087   = 0.008   = 0.0005

  (87 *thousandths*)   (8 *thousandths*)   (5 *ten-thousandths*)

Changing Decimals to Percents

Multiplying a number *by 100* moves the decimal point *two places to the right.*

PROCEDURE: To change a *decimal* to a *percent, move the decimal point two places to the right* and write *the percent symbol to the right of the number.*

Example 2   Change each decimal number to a percent.

(a)   0.28   (b)   0.375   (c)   0.70

(d)   0.07   (e)   2.3   (f)   0.125

Solution: For each decimal number, move the decimal point two places to the right and add the percent symbol.

(a) $0.28 = 28.$
         $= 28\%$

(b) $0.375 = 37.5$
         $= 37.5\%$

(c) $0.70 = 70.$
         $= 70\%$

(d) $0.07 = 7.$
         $= 7\%$

(e) $2.3 = 230.$
         $= 230\%$

(f) $0.125 = 12.5$
         $= 12.5\%$

Using the Basic Percent Equation

Since percents are similar to fractions, a similar method is used to solve the three basic types of percent problems.

Suppose that you purchase $25 in taxable merchandise and that the sales tax rate is 6%. Multiply *$25* (the *base*) times *6%* (the *rate*) to obtain *$1.50* (the per-centage), which is the amount of sales tax that will be added to the cost of your merchandise.

The *basic percent equation* is as follows:

$$\text{Base} \times \text{Rate} = \text{Percentage}$$
$$25 \quad \times 6\% \ = \$1.50$$

$$\begin{array}{r} \$ \ \ 25 \\ \times \ 0.06 \\ \hline \$ \ 1.50 \end{array}$$

In *most* percent problems two of the factors are given, and you must solve for the missing factor.

Identifying the Three Factors in the Equation

1. The *base* is the *original* amount, or *total number.*

    A. In most problems, the *base* is the number to the *right* of the word *of.*

    B. In most problems, if the two given numbers are not percents, the *base* is the *larger* of the two numbers.

2. The *rate* is the number *with the percent sign.*

3. The *percentage* is the *part amount* or the number that is *derived from the base.* The percentage is the *numerical value* obtained by *multiplying* the *base* by the *rate.*

Example 3   Beth, who sells appliances, is paid a commission of 12% of total sales. If her sales for the week were $3,575, how much commission did she earn?

Solution: Identify the two given factors, and solve for the missing factor.

1. The *base* is *$3,575,* the *total sales.*

2. The *rate* is *12%,* the *number with the percent sign.*

The *percentage* is the missing factor, that is, the *commission amount* derived from the *base.*
Write the basic percent equation:

Base	×	Rate	=	Percentage		
$3.575	×	12%	–	commission		3,575
3,575	×	0.12	=	429		× 0.12
			=	$429		7150
						3575
						429.00

Check: Base × rate   = percentage

3575 ⊠ 0⎕12 ⊟   429 √

Answer: The commission Beth earned on $3,575 at 12% was $429.

Example 4   If Sarah buys a dress for $20 and the sales tax rate is 8%, how much sales tax will she pay?

Solution: The *base* is $20. The *rate* is 8%. The *percentage,* the amount derived from the base, is missing.

Base	×	Rate	=	Percentage		
$20	×	8%	=	sales tax amount		20
20	×	0.08	=	1.60		× 0.08
			=	$1.60		1.60

Check: Base × rate   = percentage

20 ⊠ 0⎕08 ⊟1.60 √

Answer: The sales tax amounts to $1.60.

Example 5   What is the total cost of a coat priced at $47.50 if the sales tax rate is 6%?

Solution: To determine the *total cost of the coat, first find* the *sales tax amount* and *then add* this amount to the cost of the coat.

1.	*Base*	×	*Rate*	=	*Percentage*	47.50
	$47.50	×	0.06	=	sales tax amount	× 0.06
	47.50	×	0.06	=	2.85	2.8500
				=	$2.85	

2.	*Total cost*	=	*Amount of sale*	+	*Sales tax amount*	47.50
		=	$47.50	+	$2.85	× 2.85
		=	$50.35			50.35

Alternative Solution: You can simplify the solution by using a more direct method.

  1. *Rewrite* the problem as a one-sentence statement.

  Total cost is the *amount of the sale,* $47.50, *plus* 6% *of* $47.50 (6% of $47.50 means 6% × $47.50).

  2. *Translate* into an equation.
  Total cost = $47.50 + (6% × $47.50) Evaluate inside the parentheses first.
          =   47.50 + 2.85
          =   50.35
          = $50.35

  Check: 47 ⬚.⬚ 50 ⊞ ⟦⟨0⬤ 06 ⊠ 47 ⬤ 50⟩⟧ = 50.35 ✓

  Answer: Total cost = $50.35

Exercises

Exercise A   Convert decimals to percents and percents to decimals:

1.	29%	**2.**	15%	**3.**	37.5%	**4.**	1.5%
5.	100%	**6.**	1%	**7.**	7.98%	**8.**	0.4%
9.	0.01%	**10.**	325%	**11.**	6.75%	**12.**	8.9%
13.	0.25	**14.**	2.50	**15.**	0.06	**16.**	0.005
17.	87.5	**18.**	1	**19.**	2	**20.**	0.07
21.	2.15	**22.**	0.2	**23.**	0.20	**24.**	0.0005
25.	$8\frac{1}{4}\%$	**26.**	$6\frac{1}{2}\%$	**27.**	$12\frac{1}{2}\%$		

Find the percentage in each of the following problems:

28.	10% of $128.70	**29.**	35% of $728
30.	5% of $163.80	**31.**	37.5% of $546
32.	64% of $58	**33.**	7.5% of $2,400
34.	8% of $3,257.50	**35.**	10% of $425.60
36.	12.5% of $572	**37.**	8% of $173.75
38.	125% of $315.36	**39.**	5% of $150.60

Exercise B   Complete the following forms:

40.

Earnings for Month Ending October 31, 20——				
Salesperson	Sales	Rate of Commission	Amount of Commission	
C. Allenby	$23,625	12%	_____	___
E. Altman	38,720	8	_____	___
W. Benson	46,628	5	_____	___
L. Bucknor	53,742	15	_____	___
P. Cuttler	43,127	7	_____	___
L. Elwood	41,285	9	_____	___
N. Evans	36,892	4	_____	___

41.

PENNY LANE SHOP

February 3   20--

SOLD TO _S. Tipsley_

ADDRESS _2110 Park Place_

CLERK S.T.	DEP'T 012	AM'T REC'D $1,265

QUAN.	DESCRIPTION	AMOUNT	
1	Recliner Chair	$258	00
1	Desk	576	00
1	Desk Chair	87	00
1	Bookcase	246	00
	Subtotal		
	8% Sales tax		
	Total		

POSITIVELY NO EXCHANGES MADE UNLESS
THIS SLIP IS PRESENTED WITHIN 3 DAYS.

42.

	EBERT'S DEPARTMENT STORE			
	October 15 20--			

SOLD TO *A. Bergen*

ADDRESS *128 Logan Lane*

CLERK *Joy*	DEP'T *Fabrics*	AM'T REC'D $93

QUAN.	DESCRIPTION	AMOUNT	
3 yd.	*Linen*	$18	00
5 yd.	*Velvet*	35	00
6 yd.	*Denim*	33	00
	Subtotal		
	8% Sales tax		
	Total		

POSITIVELY NO EXCHANGES MADE UNLESS
THIS SLIP IS PRESENTED WITHIN 3 DAYS.

Word Problems

Any problem asking for a percentage must supply you with a rate and a base. Most often, such problems will ask for the sales tax or the discount amount.

> "What is the tax on sales of $1,500 if the tax rate is 5%?"

> "Find the net price if the list price is $15.95 and the discount rate is 25%."

> "What is the cost overrun if the contract price was $1,100 and the overrun rate was 7.8%?"

Exercise C   Solve the following problems:

43.   The price of a stereo set was reduced by 40%. How many cents out of every dollar of the price represents the reduction?

44.   How many cents is 65% of $1.00?

45. If you save $33\frac{1}{3}$ cents on every dollar of the cost of a yard of carpeting, what is the percent of the savings?

46. A bar graph shows that 5 cents of every tax dollar is spent on education. What percent of the tax dollar is spent on education?

47. A bank pays $7.50 in interest for every $100 of savings. What is the percent of interest?

48. A retailer priced a TV set at $347. If the percent of profit is 35%, find the cost of the TV to the retailer.

49. Mr. Wells purchased a home for $48,990. If his down payment is 20%, find the amount of his mortgage.

50. A department store employs 2,475 people. If 68% of the employees are female, find the number of male employees.

51. Sally earns $1,175 a month. If she spends 20% on rent and 15% on food, how much of her monthly income remains?

52. A retailer has 265 shirts in stock. If he sells 57% of the stock, how many shirts are left?

53. A salesperson earns a commission of 15%. What is the commission on sales of $2,530?

54. An electric typewriter sells for $300, less a 40% discount. Find the net price of the typewriter.

UNIT 2　Percent: Finding the Rate

We learned that percent is a *rate,* just like *miles per hour* or *taxes per dollar.* As such, it relates the base to the percentage. The basic formula for solving percent problems is:

$$\text{Base} \times \text{Rate} = \text{Percentage}$$

$$\text{B} \times \text{R} = \text{P}$$

Example 1

Base	Subtotal of sale	$157.80
Rate	Tax rate	6.5%
Percentage	Amount of tax	$10.26

$$\$157.80 \times 0.065 = \$10.257$$
$$= \$10.26$$

Distinguishing Between Base and Percentage

One common problem with percent problems is distinguishing between the two nonpercent numbers: Which number is the base, and which is the percentage?

B (or base) is the number that occurs first in the time sequence of the problem:

- It is the cost before markup.
- It is the list price before a sale discount.
- It is the sales total before taxes.
- It is a number *before* any changes occur.

P (or percentage) is a number *derived from* (or added to or subtracted from) the base:

- It is the tax added onto a sale.
- It is the amount of money saved on a discounted item.
- It is the markup added to the cost to form the list price.
- It is the number that *alters* the base.

Example 2 A dress selling for $45 has been reduced to $9. Find the percent of reduction.

Solution: The *base* is $45.
The *percentage* is $9.
The *rate* is the missing factor.

Base $\times$ Rate = Percentage

$45 $\times$ Rate = $9

$\dfrac{\cancel{45}}{\cancel{45}} \times R = \dfrac{9}{45}$ Divide both sides by 45.

$\phantom{\dfrac{45}{45} \times}\ R = 0.20$

$\phantom{\dfrac{45}{45} \times}$ Rate = 20%

$$\begin{array}{r} 0.20 \\ 45\overline{)9.00} \\ \underline{9\,0} \end{array}$$

Check: Base $\times$ Rate = Percentage
 45 $\boxtimes$ 0$\boxdot$20 $\boxed{=}$ 9 $\checkmark$

Answer: The reduction percent is 20%

In solving problems such as Example 2, it may be difficult to remember which number should be divided into which. A good way to remember which number becomes the dividend and which the divisor is to think of the word fraction $\dfrac{\text{IS}}{\text{OF}}$.

The number in the problem related to *IS* is written as the *dividend* or *numerator*. The number related to *OF* is written as the *divisor* or *denominator*.

Example 3 During a special sale, a retailer sold 51 men's suits out of his stock of 204 suits. What percent of the suits did he sell?

Solution: STEP 1.   The base is 204 suits.

Step 2. The change is 51 suits.

Step 3. Rephrased, the problem is: (51 is) what percent (of 204) suits?

Step 4. $\dfrac{IS}{OF} = \dfrac{51}{204} = .25$

Step 5. 25% *Answer*

Alternative Solution: The *base* is 204. The *percentage* is 51.

Base × Rate = Percentage

$\dfrac{\cancel{204}}{\cancel{204}} \times R = \dfrac{51}{204}$ Divide both sides by 204.

$R = 0.25$

Rate = 25%

Check: Base × Rate = Percentage

204 ⊠ 0⊡25 ⊟ 51 ✓

Answer: The retailer sold 25% of the suits in stock.

Example 4 The Hunts bought a house for $60,000 and were able to finance $45,000. Find the percent of the down payment.

Solution: The problem gives the *total price of the house,* $60,000, and the *amount of the mortgage,* $45,000. You have to find the *percent* that the *down payment is of the total price.*

1. Find the down payment.
    Down payment = $60,000 − $45,000 = $15,000

2. Use the basic percent equation to find the rate.

Base × Rate = Percentage

$60,000 × R = $15,000

$\dfrac{\cancel{60,000}}{\cancel{60,000}} \times R = \dfrac{15,000}{60,000}$ Divide both sides by 60,000.

$R = \dfrac{15,\cancel{000}}{60,\cancel{000}} = \dfrac{1}{4} = 0.25$

$= 25\%$

Check: $60,000 × 25% = $15,000

60000 ⊠0⊡25 ⊟ 15000 ✓

Answer: Down payment percent = 25%

Alternative Solution: *Rewrite* the problem as a one-sentence *statement,* and *translate* the sentence into an equation.

Down payment percent *is* $60,000 *minus* $45,000 *divided* by $60,000.

$$
\begin{aligned}
\text{Down payment} \; &= (\$60{,}000 - \$45{,}000) \div \$60{,}000 \\
&= (60{,}000 - 45{,}000) \div 60{,}000 \\
&= 15{,}000 \div 60{,}000 \qquad \textit{Subtract first.} \\
&= \frac{15{,}000}{60{,}000} = \frac{15}{60} = \frac{1}{4} \\
&= 0.25
\end{aligned}
$$

Answer: Down payment percent = 25%

Example 5   Last year Fred earned $12,500, and this year his salary is $14,500. Find the percent of increase in Fred's salary.

Solution: First find the *amount* of increase, and then find the *percent* of increase.

$$
\begin{aligned}
\text{Amount of increase} &= \$14{,}500 - \$12{,}500 \\
&= \$2{,}000
\end{aligned}
$$

$$
\text{Base} \quad \times \quad \text{Rate} \quad = \quad \text{Percentage}
$$

$$
\$12{,}500 \quad \times \quad R \quad = \quad \$2{,}000
$$

$$
\frac{\cancel{12{,}500}}{\cancel{12{,}500}} \times R = \frac{\overset{4}{\cancel{2{,}000}}}{\underset{25}{\cancel{12{,}500}}} = \frac{4}{25} = 0.16 = 16\%
$$

Check: $12500 \;\boxtimes\; 0 \boxdot 16 \;\boxminus\; 2000 \;\checkmark$

Answer: Fred's salary increase was 16%.

Example 6   Because of more efficient machinery, the Sonic Radio Corporation was able to reduce the cost of manufacturing a radio from $36 to $31.50. Find the percent of decrease in the cost of producing the radio.

Solution:
$$
\begin{aligned}
\text{The amount of decrease} &= \$36 - \$31.50 \\
&= \$4.50
\end{aligned}
$$

$$
\begin{aligned}
\text{Base} \;\times\; \text{Rate} \;&=\; \text{Percentage} \\
\$36 \;\times\; R \;&=\; \$4.50 \\
\frac{\cancel{36}}{\cancel{36}} \;\times\; R \;&=\; \frac{4.50}{36} \\
R \;&=\; 0.125 \\
&=\; 12.5\%
\end{aligned}
$$

Check: Base $\times$ Rate = Percentage
$$
36 \;\boxtimes\; 0\boxdot125 \;\boxminus\; 4.50 \;\checkmark
$$

Answer: The percent of decrease is 12.5%.

Alternative Solution:

STEP 1.   The base is $36.00.

STEP 2.   The percentage decrease is $36.00 − $31.50 = $4.50, amount of decrease

STEP 3.   ($4.50 is) what percent (of $36.00) ?

STEP 4. $\dfrac{IS}{OF} = \dfrac{\$4.50}{\$36.00} = 0.125$

STEP 5.   12.5% Decrease *Answer*

Example 7   Jason earns 6% annual interest on his savings account. Last year he earned $93 in interest. How much money did he have in the bank before the interest was added?

Solution:

$$
\begin{array}{lcccl}
\text{Base} & \times & \text{Rate} & = & \text{Percentage} \\
B & \times & 6\% & = & \$93 \\
\dfrac{B}{} & \times & \dfrac{\cancel{0.06}}{\cancel{0.06}} & = & \dfrac{93}{0.06} \\
B & & & = & 1550
\end{array}
$$

Original amount in bank = $1,550 *Answer*

Check: Base × Rate = Percentage
1550 ⊠ 0⨯06 ⊟ 93 √

Alternative Solution:

STEP 1.   The amount of change in the account was $93, so this is the percentage.

STEP 2.   The rate of change is 6%.

STEP 3.   Rephrased, the problem is: ($93 is) (6% of) what number?

STEP 4. $\dfrac{IS}{OF} = \dfrac{\$93}{0.06} = \$1,550$ *Answer*

Example 8   Carmela earns 8% on a time deposit and cannot withdraw the $80 interest she has earned. How much is in the time deposit account now?

Caution: This problem is similar to Example 7 but asks a different question. Here, you have to find the original base and then *add* the interest to find the current balance.

Solution:

$$
\begin{array}{lcccl}
\text{Base} & \times & \text{Rate} & = & \text{Percentage} \\
\text{Base} & \times & 8\% & = & \$80 \\
\dfrac{B}{} & \times & \dfrac{\cancel{0.08}}{\cancel{0.08}} & = & \dfrac{80}{0.08} \\
& & B & = & 1,000
\end{array}
$$

Original deposit = $1,000
Current balance = $1,000 + $80
                 = $1,080   *Answer*

Check: Base ×   Rate   = Percentage
1,000 ⊠ 0⨯08 ⊟ 80 √

Alternative Solution:

STEP 1.   The percentage is $80.

STEP 2.   The rate is 8%.

STEP 3. $80 is 8% of what number?

STEP 4. $\dfrac{\text{IS}}{\text{OF}} = \dfrac{\$80}{0.08} = \$1{,}000$ (Original amount)

STEP 5.   Current balance = $1,000 + $80 = $1,080 *Answer*

Example 9   Sara bought a coat for $78.30, including a sales tax of 8%. Find the price of the coat and the amount of tax.

Solution: The *price* of the coat *plus* the *sales tax* can be expressed as *108%* (100% for the *price* of the coat plus *8%* sales tax).

1. The *rate* is *108%*.

2. The *percentage* is *$78.30*.

3. The *base* is *missing*.

Base × Rate = Percentage
 B × 108% = $78.30
 $\dfrac{B \times 1.08}{1.08} = \dfrac{78.30}{1.08}$ Divide both sides by 1.08.
 B   =   72.50
Price of coat = $72.50

    $78.30   Total amount
    −72.50   Price of the coat
    $ 5.80   Sales tax

Check: Base   × Rate = Percentage
    72 . 50 × 1 . 08 = 78.30 √

Answer: The price of the coat is $72.50. The amount of sales tax is $5.80.

Alternative Solution:

PROCEDURE: The total cost of $78.30 represents the cost of the coat plus 8% sales tax. The price of the coat without the sales tax can be represented by 100% (the price of the coat is 100% of itself). The price of the coat plus the sales tax can be expressed as 100% + 8% = 108%. Therefore, $78.30 is the equivalent of 108%.

STEP 1.   The percentage is $78.30.

STEP 2.   The rate is 108%.

STEP 3.　($78.30 is) (108% of) what number?

STEP 4.　$\dfrac{IS}{OF} = \dfrac{\$78.30}{1.08} = \$72.50$ Price of coat

STEP 5.
$$\begin{array}{l} \$78.30 \quad \text{Total amount} \\ \underline{-72.50} \quad \text{Price of coat} \\ \$\ 5.80 \quad \text{Sales tax} \end{array} \Big\} \textit{Answers}$$

Example 10　The price of a car is $8,350. If this is 15% more than last year's price, what was the cost of the car last year?

Solution:　The price of the car, $8,350, can be expressed as 115% (100% for last year's price plus the 15% increase).

1.　The *rate* is *115%*.

2.　The *percentage* is $8,350.

3.　The *base* is *missing*.

Base $\times$ Rate $=$ Percentage
$B \times \cancel{115\%} = \$8,350$
$B \times \dfrac{\cancel{1.15}}{\cancel{1.15}} = \dfrac{8,350}{1.15}$
$B \qquad\qquad = 7,260.869$

Check: Base　　　$\times$　Rate　$=$　Percentage
7260$\boxed{.}$87 $\boxed{\times}$ 1$\boxed{.}$15 $\boxed{=}$ 8350 $\checkmark$

Answer:　The price last year was $7,260.87 rounded to the nearest penny.

Alternative Solution:

STEP 1.　The percentage is $8,350.

STEP 2.　$8,350 is 100% plus 15% of last year's price. The rate is therefore 115%.

STEP 3.　($8,350 is) (115% of) what number?

STEP 4.　$\dfrac{IS}{OF} = \dfrac{\$8,350}{1.15} = \$7,260.869$

STEP 5.　$7,260.87　*Answer* (rounded off)

Exercises

Exercise A　Solve the following problems, and check your answers:

1.　56 is what percent of 64?　　　**2.**　43 is what percent of 78?

3.　24 is what percent of 125?　　**4.**　28 is what percent of 135?

5. What percent of 36 is 9?

6. What percent of 225 is 180?

7. What percent of 270 is 150?

8. What percent of 3,400 is 5,400?

9. 24 is what percent of 120?

10. 16 is what percent of 150?

11. 93 is what percent of 248?

12. What percent of 30 is 20?

13. What percent of 114 is 19?

14. What percent of 86 is 15?

15. What percent of 85 is 125?

16. 80 is what percent of 240?

17. $35 is what percent of $70?

18. $12.50 is what percent of $75?

19. $146 is what percent of $250?

20. $247 is what percent of $160?

21. What percent of $216 is $85?

22. What percent of $415 is $78?

23. $8 is what percent of $150?

24. $3.75 is what percent of $9.60?

25. $54.50 is what percent of $95?

26. $96.75 is what percent of $50?

27. What percent of $325 is $75?

28. What percent of $324 is $24.50?

In each of the following problems, find the percent of increase or decrease:

29. $315 decreased to $250

30. $475 increased to $550

31. $128 increased to $325

32. 375 increased to 550

33. $478 increased to $579

34. $428 decreased to $348

35. 18,240 decreased to 14,380

36. $1,237 increased to $1,450

37. $515 increased to $735

38. 450 decreased to 375

39. $235 increased to $650

40. $748 decreased to $670

41. 6,434 increased to 8,420

42. 2,360 decreased to 1,930

43. $3,500 decreased to $2,300

44. $24,000 decreased to $18,000

Solve the following problems, rounding where necessary, and check your answers:

45. 35% of what amount is $72?

46. $375.50 is 108% of what amount?

47. 45% of what amount is $395?

48. $78.75 is 115% of what amount?

49. $369 is $33\frac{1}{3}$% of what amount?

50. 125% of what amount is $230.25?

51. 235 is 40% of what number?

52. 210% of what amount is $85.50?

53. 25% of what number is 2,460?

54. $48.95 is 105% of what amount?

55. $248 is 110% of what amount?

56. $112\frac{1}{2}$% of what amount is $215.75?

57. 560 is 125% of what number?

58. 135% of what amount is $65.38?

59. 150% of what amount is $4,250.60?

60. $243.62 is 108% of what amount?

61. 105% of what amount is $76.50?

62. 103% of what amount is $97.65?

63. 3,275 is 135% of what number?

64. 165% of what amount is $28.65?

Exercise B   Find the missing items in the following forms, rounding where necessary:

65.

Sale Reduction Rates						
Original Price		Sale Price		Reduction Amount		Reduction Percent
$235	65	_____	___	$ 82	48	___
330	33	$198	20	_____	___	___
175	85	_____	___	_____	___	35%
575	95	316	77	_____	___	___
425	75	_____	___	140	50	___
380	25	197	73	_____	___	___
298	95	194	32	_____	___	___
605	85	_____	___	_____	___	28

66.

New Yearly Balances							
Interest Earned		Interest Rate	Amount on Deposit		New Balance		
$123	85	8.65 %	_____	___	_____	___	
228	69	9.703	_____	___	_____	___	
185	35	_____	$1,844	27	_____	___	
87	63	8.5	_____	___	_____	___	
113	25	8.35	_____	___	_____	___	
142	75	_____	_____	___	$1,645	38	
173	34	8.73	_____	___	_____	___	
195	45	7.75	_____	___	_____	___	
163	92	_____	2,041	34	_____	___	
147	35	9.6	_____	___	_____	___	

67.

Totals Paid Including Sales Tax							
Amount Paid		Sales Tax Rate		Amount of Sale		Sales Tax Amount	
$ 85	78	6 %		——	——	——	——
128	65	——		$119	12	——	——
246	19	5.5		——	——	——	——
193	35	8.25		——	——	——	——
216	48	——		——	——	$10	31
342	31	4		——	——	——	——
259	17	——		248	01	——	——
342	20	6.5		——	——	——	——

68.

Price Changes for Year Ending Dec. 20——							
Price This Year		Rate of Increase		Price Last Year		Amount of Increase	
$578	65	13%		——	——	——	——
423	75	——		——	——	$55	27
682	90	12		——	——	——	——
329	25	——		$302	06	——	——
526	45	14		——	——	——	——
685	95	15		——	——	——	——
419	20	——		——	——	48	23
398	50	——		355	80	——	——
248	65	11		——	——	——	——

Word Problems

The key phrases indicating a rate problem will not give you a numerical rate, but will ask for the rate or percent:

"What is the percent of …?"
"What is the rate of …?"

The major difficulty lies in correctly identifying the base and the percentage. Read the problem carefully, analyze it logically, and then assign the correct values to both the base and the percentage.

Exercise B   Solve the following problems, and check your answers:

69.   Angel earns $975 a month. His rent is $175 a month. What percent of his monthly earnings does he spend on rent?

70.   There are 16 girls and 26 boys in a class. What percent of the class consists of boys?

71.   A piano regularly selling for $825 was reduced to $650. What is the percent of the reduction?

72.   A retailer sells a 20-cubic-foot freezer for $615. If his profit is $210, find the percent of profit based on the cost of the freezer.

73.   Ms. Donato earns $248 on a sale of $1,250. What is her rate of commission?

74.   Mr. Wright bought a house for $128,640. Five years later he sold the house for $136,900. Find the percent of increase in the value of the house.

75.   The Lang Department Store's sales for December were $68,750. Sales for January were $53,230. Find the percent of decrease for the month of January.

76.   A clothes washer was reduced from $336.90 to $215.90. Find the percent of reduction.

77.   The average weekly food cost for a family of four is $78.50. Two years ago, the average weekly food cost for a family of four was $52.75. What is the percent of increase for the 2 years?

78.   The price of a ton of coal dropped from $38.60 to $26.35. Find the percent of decrease.

Percent problems in which you must find the base will always give you a rate and a percentage. It is essential to *correctly identify* each of the given numbers as the rate or the percentage. Read the problem carefully to make sure you understand what the question is asking for.

Exercise C   Solve the following problems, rounding where necessary, and check your answers:

79.   A retailer pays $125.50 for a dishwasher. If this will represent 65% of the selling price, find the selling price.

80.   A municipal bond pays 10.5% interest. If it paid $110 in interest, what is the value of the bond?

81.   A retailer made $53,500 in net profits last year. If this represents 15% of his total sales, what were his total sales last year?

82.   A manufacturing concern employs 824 people, 15% more than it employed last year. Find the number of employees it had last year.

83.   Rachel earns 25% more this year than last year. If she earns $16,575 this year, find the salary she earned last year.

UNIT **3** Review of Percent Problems

The basic formula for solving percent problems is

$$\text{Base} \times \text{Rate} = \text{Percentage}$$

Example 1   If you buy a dress for $20 and the sales tax is 8%, how much sales tax will you pay?

Solution: In this problem you are given two facts—the amount of the sale and the percent of tax—and you have to find the unknown fact—the amount of tax. Substitute in the basic formula, and your problem looks like this:

$$
\begin{array}{rclcl}
\text{Base} & \times & \text{Rate} & = & \text{Percentage} \\
\$20 & \times & 0.08 & = & u \\
20 & \boxtimes & 0\boxed{.}08 & = & 1.6 \\
& & & = & 1.60 \\
& & 1.60 & - & u \\
\text{Sales tax} & & & = & \$1.60 \quad \textit{Answer}
\end{array}
$$

Check: Base × Rate = Percentage
20 ⊠ 0⌊.⌋08 ⊟ 1.60 √

You may use the basic formula to solve a percent problem algebraically if any *two* of the *three* facts in the basic formula are given.

Example 2   Suppose that in Example 1 you are given the cost of the dress, $20, and the amount of tax, $1.60. What is the rate of percent?

Solution: Using the basic formula, substitute the known facts, and your problem will look like this:

$$
\begin{array}{rclcl}
\text{Base} & \times & \text{Rate} & = & \text{Percentage} \\
\$20 & \times & u & = & 1.60 \\
& & 20u & = & 1.60 \\
& & \dfrac{\cancel{20}u}{\cancel{20}} & = & \dfrac{1.60}{20} \\
& & u & = & 0.08 = 8\% \\
\text{Rate} & = & \$1.60 & & \textit{Answer}
\end{array}
$$

Check: Base × Rate = Percentage
20 ⊠ 0⌊.⌋08 ⊟ 1.60 √

Example 3   A salesclerk earned a commission of $84.41 on a sale of $562.75. What is his rate of commission?

Solution: Using the basic formula, substitute the known facts:

$$\begin{aligned}
\text{Base} \quad \times \quad &\text{Rate} \;=\; \text{Percentage}\\
\$562.75 \;\times\; &\quad u \;=\; \$84.41\\
562.75u \;&=\; 84.41
\end{aligned}$$

$$\frac{562.75u}{562.75} \;=\; \frac{84.41}{562.75}$$

Divide both sides of the equation by 562.75.

$$84\;\boxed{.}\;41 \;\boxed{\div}\; 562\;\boxed{.}\;75 \;\boxed{=}\; 0.14\underline{9}\dots$$
$$= 0.15$$

$$u \;=\; \frac{84.41}{562.75}$$

$$\text{Rate of commission} \;=\; 0.15 = 15\% \quad \textit{Answer}$$

Check: Base   × Rate   = Percentage
$$562\;\boxed{.}\;75 \;\boxed{\times}\; 0\;\boxed{.}\;15 \;\boxed{=}\; 84.41 \;\checkmark$$

Example 4   During a sale, $32.81 was taken off the price of a dress selling for $93.75. What was the percent of reduction?

Solution:

$$\begin{aligned}
\text{Base} \quad \times \quad &\text{Rate} \;=\; \text{Percentage}\\
\$93.75 \;\times\; &\quad u \;=\; \$32.81\\
93.75u \;&=\; 32.81
\end{aligned}$$

$$\frac{93.75u}{93.75} \;=\; \frac{32.81}{93.75}$$

$$u \;=\; \frac{32.81}{93.75}$$

$$32\;\boxed{.}\;81 \;\boxed{\div}\; 93\;\boxed{.}\;75 \;\boxed{=}\; 0.34.99$$
$$= 0.35$$

$$\text{Percent of reduction} \;=\; 0.35 = 35\% \quad \textit{Answer}$$

Check: Base   × Rate   = Percentage
$$93\;\boxed{.}\;75 \;\boxed{\times}\; 0\;\boxed{.}\;35 \;\boxed{=}\; 32.81 \;\checkmark$$

Answer: The percent of reduction is 35%

Example 5   A retailer reduces the price of a lamp by 45%. If the amount of reduction is $57.83, what was the original price of the lamp?

Solution:

$$\begin{aligned}
\text{Base} \;\times\; \text{Rate} \;&=\; \text{Percentage}\\
u \;\times\; 45\% \;&=\; \$57.83
\end{aligned}$$

Note: Expressions of this type are usually written with the numerical factor first.

$$\begin{aligned}
u45\% \;&=\; \$57.83\\
0.45u \;&=\; 57.83
\end{aligned}$$

$$\frac{0.45u}{0.45} \;=\; \frac{57.83}{0.45}$$

$$u \;=\; \frac{57.83}{0.45}$$

$$57\;\boxed{.}\;83 \;\boxed{\div}\; 0\;\boxed{.}\;45 \;\boxed{=}\; 128.51\underline{1}\dots$$
$$= 128.51$$

$$\text{Original price} \;=\; \$128.51 \quad \textit{Answer}$$

Check: Base $\times$ Rate = Percentage
128 $\boxed{\cdot}$ 51 $\boxed{\times}$ 0 $\boxed{\cdot}$ 45 $\boxed{=}$ 57.82|9 . . .
= 57.83
= $57.83 $\checkmark$

Example 6 Jane has a savings account that earns 5.75% interest. How much did she have on deposit if at the end of the year she earned $90.56 in interest?

Solution:

Base	$\times$	Rate	=	Percentage
u	$\times$	5.75%	=	$90.56
u	$\times$	0.0575x	=	90.56

$$u \qquad \frac{\cancel{0.0575}u}{\cancel{0.0575}} = \frac{90.56}{0.0575}$$

$$u = \frac{90.56}{0.0575}$$

$$= 90$$

90 $\boxed{\cdot}$ 56 $\boxed{\div}$ 0 $\boxed{\cdot}$ 0575 $\boxed{=}$ 1574.96

Amount on deposit = $1,574.96 *Answer*

Check: Base $\times$ Rate = Percentage
$1,574.96 $\times$ 5.75% = $90.56
1574 $\boxed{\cdot}$ 96 $\boxed{\times}$ 0 $\boxed{\cdot}$ 0575 $\boxed{=}$ 90.56 $\checkmark$

Exercises

Word Problems

Solve the following problems, using equations:

1. The price of a refrigerator was reduced by 23%. If the amount of reduction was $174.56, what was the original price of the refrigerator?

2. Janice bought a car for $8,625 and later sold it for $6,790. What was the depreciation percent of the car? (HINT: First find the amount of depreciation.)

3. Mr. Hernandez spends 20% of his weekly income on food. If he spends $85 on food, how much is his weekly income?

4. Soong Lee deposited $2,855 in a savings account. At the end of the year he earned $246.95 in interest. What interest rate does his bank pay?

5. A store marks up its merchandise 45% of the selling price. If the markup amount on a camera is $265.75, what is the selling price of the camera?

6. Ms. DeMato received a 15% increase in salary. If the amount of increase is $2,978.25, what was her salary before the increase?

7. An insurance company employs 244 clerks, of whom 183 are women. What percent of the total clerks are women?

8. A house is assessed at $85,000 for real estate tax purposes. If the real estate tax for the year is $3,854.25, what is the percent of the real estate tax?

9. An appliance store makes a 5% net profit on each appliance sold. If the profit on a refrigerator is $39.50, what is the selling price of the refrigerator?

10. The shoe department of a store increased its sales this month over last month by $2,636.12. If the sales last month were $18,829.45, what is the percent of increase?

11. A trade discount on a stereo is 45% off list price, and the discount amount is $375.82. What is the list price of the stereo?

12. Sandra took out a loan of $4,550. If her interest for the year was $540, what is the interest rate charged by the bank?

13. The cost of manufacturing a desk rose from $73.42 to $95.67. What was the percent of increase in the cost? (HINT: First find the amount of increase.)

14. The terms of an invoice are as follows: 3% discount if paid within 15 days. What is the amount of the invoice if the discount is $28.76?

15. The purchase of a house requires a down payment of 25%. If the down payment is $16,497.50, what is the price of the house?

UNIT 4 Using Ratios

Ratios

A *ratio* compares two numbers by division, and shows the *relationship* between the two numbers. If you know that of the 36 passengers on a bus there are 12 females and 24 males, you can compare the number of *females* on the bus to the number of *males* as the ratio "12 to 24." You can write the ratio of *females* to *males* as:

$$12 \text{ to } 24 \quad \text{or} \quad 12{:}24 \quad \text{or} \quad \text{the fraction } \frac{12}{24}$$

In each case, the ratio is read as "12 to 24."
When writing a ratio as a fraction, you can reduce the ratio to lowest terms *without changing the relationship of the ratio.* Thus:

$$\frac{12}{24} = \frac{1}{2} \text{ reduced to lowest terms}$$

The ratio $\frac{12}{24}$ shows the same relationship as the ratio $\frac{1}{2}$.

In the bus-passenger example, the relationship of *males* to *females* is the ratio "24 to 12" and can be written as:

$$\frac{24}{12} \text{ reduced to } \frac{2}{1}$$

Unlike fractions, a ratio must have a denominator to *show the relationship between the two terms of the ratio.*

The *improper fraction* $\frac{24}{12}$ is reduced to $\frac{2}{1} = 2$.

The *ratio* $\frac{24}{12}$ is reduced to $\frac{2}{1}$ and is read as "2 to 1."

From the given facts, the following ratios can be written:

females to *total* passengers, $\frac{12}{36}$ reduced to $\frac{1}{3}$, "1 to 3,"

males to *total* passengers, $\frac{24}{36}$ reduced to $\frac{2}{3}$, "2 to 3."

Example 1 During a given day, a retail store had 520 sales. If 5 out of every 8 sales were cash sales, how many sales were credit sales?

PROCEDURE: From the facts in the problem, write the following ratios:

cash sales: $\frac{5}{8}$ credit sales: $\frac{3}{8}$

To find the number of credit sales, find "$\frac{3}{8}$ of 520":

$$\frac{3}{\overset{}{\underset{1}{8}}} \times \frac{\overset{65}{\cancel{520}}}{1} = 195 \text{ credit sales } Answer$$

Check: If 195 credit sales is correct, then the number of cash sales should be 325 (520 − 195 = 325):

$$\frac{5}{\overset{}{\underset{1}{8}}} \times \frac{\overset{65}{\cancel{520}}}{1} = 325 \text{ cash sales } \checkmark$$

Example 2 For every $5 of sales, a retailer spends $2 on salaries. If the average weekly sales are $36,500, what is the average weekly expenditure on salaries?

PROCEDURE: The ratio of *salary* to *sales* is "2 out of 5" or the ratio $\frac{2}{5}$. To find

the expenditure on salaries, find "$\frac{2}{5}$ of 36,500":

$$\frac{2}{\overset{}{\underset{1}{5}}} \times \frac{\overset{7,300}{\cancel{36,500}}}{1} = 14,600 \text{ spent on salaries } Answer$$

Check: If $14,600 is correct, then $21,900 of the average weekly sales is the remainder:

$$\frac{3}{\overset{}{\underset{1}{5}}} \times \frac{\overset{7,300}{\cancel{36,500}}}{1} = \$21,900 \checkmark$$

Ratios as Rates

Ratios can also be used to compare quantities that are not alike such as *miles* per *hour*, *price* per *unit of measure*, *pay* per *hour*, and *gallons of gas* per *miles*.

A ratio that compares unlike quantities becomes a *rate* when it is *reduced to an equivalent ratio with a denominator of 1*.

If a truck driver travels 120 miles in 3 hours, his rate of speed per hour is 40 miles per hour.

To find the rate of speed, reduce the ratio to an equivalent ratio with a denominator of 1.

$$\frac{120}{3} = \frac{}{1} \qquad \frac{120 \div 3}{3 \div 3} = \frac{40}{1} = 40 \text{ miles/hour}$$

Example 3   Sally earned $294 last week. If she worked 42 hours last week, what is the hourly rate of pay?

PROCEDURE: To find Sally's hourly rate of pay, *reduce* the ratio $\dfrac{\$294}{42 \text{ hours}}$ to an equivalent ratio with a denominator of 1.

$$\frac{\$294}{42} = \frac{}{1} \quad \bigg| \quad \frac{294 \div 42}{42 \div 42} = \frac{7}{1} = \$7/\text{hour} \quad \textit{Answer}$$

Example 4   Turkey sells for $0.79 per pound. How much will an 18-pound turkey cost?

PROCEDURE: Since you are given the rate per pound, raise the given ratio, $0.79 per pound, to an equivalent ratio with a denominator of 18.

$$\frac{\$0.79}{1} = \frac{}{18} \quad \bigg| \quad \frac{0.79 \times 18}{1 \times 18} = \frac{14.22}{18} = \$14.22 \quad \textit{Answer}$$

Example 5   A retailer pays $45 for 1 dozen T-shirts. How much will he pay for 96 T-shirts?

PROCEDURE: Since the given rate is $45 per dozen, change the 96 T-shirts to 8 dozen (96 ÷ 12 = 8).

$$\frac{\$45}{1} = \frac{}{8} \quad \bigg| \quad \frac{45 \times 8}{1 \times 8} = \frac{360}{8} = \$360 \quad \textit{Answer}$$

You can also write the given ratio as:

$$\frac{\$45}{12} = \frac{}{96} \quad \bigg| \quad \frac{45 \times 8}{12 \times 8} = \frac{360}{96} = \$360$$

Exercises

Write each expression as a ratio in fraction form reduced to lowest terms.

1. 9 to 12   **2.** 6 to 8   **3.** 15 to 5   **4.** 25:40   **5.** 24:3   **6.** 4 ounces to 1 pound   **7.** 12 out of 50   **8.** 2 pints to 1 gallon   **9.** 3 shirts for $27 **10.** 90 miles in 2 hours   **11.** $3.60 for 3 pounds   **12.** 110 miles on 5 gallons of gas   **13.** $.10 per $1   **14.** $15.90 for 3 yards of fabric **15.** $3.48 for 6 pounds

Word Problems

16. A department store ordered the following sizes in men's sport shirts: 25 dozen, large; 35 dozen, medium; and 15 dozen, small. What is the ratio of:
a. Large to medium? _____
b. Large to small? _____
c. Large to total? _____
d. Medium to total? _____

17. A coat regularly selling for $160 is on sale at $\frac{1}{4}$ off. What is the amount of the reduction?

18. A store purchased blouses at $30 per dozen. How much will 5 dozen blouses cost the store?

19. A clothing store had 288 pairs of slacks in stock. If $\frac{3}{8}$ of the slacks were sold, how many pairs of slacks were sold?

20. Two partners in a business share profits in the ratio of 5:3. How much money will each partner get if the profits are $56,000?
Partner A _____
Partner B _____

UNIT **5** Using Proportions

Proportions

You know that raising or reducing a ratio to an equivalent ratio does not change the value or relationship of the ratio.

The ratios $\dfrac{6}{36} = \dfrac{1}{6}$ state that the relationship of 6 to 36 is the same as the relationship of 1 to 6. *When two ratios are equivalent, they form a proportion.* The equivalent ratios

$$\frac{5}{8} = \frac{15}{24}$$

form the proportion

$$\frac{5}{8} = \frac{15}{24}$$

The proportion is read as "*5 is to 8 as 15 is to 24.*"

$$\frac{5}{8} \quad = \quad \frac{15}{24}$$

In the proportion

The 8 and the 15 are called the *means*

The 5 and the 24 are called the *extremes*

extremes

$5{:}8 = 15{:}24$

means

The Property of Proportions

In any proportion, the *product of the means is equal to the product of the extremes.*

$8 \times 15 = 120$
$5 \times 24 = 120$
$120 = 120$

$6 \times 10 = 60$
$5 \times 12 = 60$
$60 = 60$

You can use the *property of proportions* to find any one of the missing terms in the above proportion

(a) $\quad \dfrac{x}{8} = \dfrac{15}{24}$

Cross multiply
(the x term first).

$24x = 120$

$\dfrac{24x}{24} = \dfrac{120}{24}$

Divide both sides
of the equation.
by 24.

$x = 5$

To *check* the solution, substitute *5* for x and cross multiply.

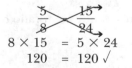

$8 \times 15 = 5 \times 24$

$120 = 120 \ \checkmark$

(b) $\dfrac{5}{x} = \dfrac{15}{24}$

$\dfrac{5}{x} \diagdown\!\!\!\diagup \dfrac{15}{24}$ Cross multiply.

$15x = 120$

$\dfrac{\cancel{15}x}{\cancel{15}} = \dfrac{\cancelto{8}{120}}{\cancel{15}}$ Divide both sides of the equation by 15.

$x = 8$

Check: Substitute 8 for *x*.

$$\frac{5}{8} = \frac{15}{24}$$

$$120 = 120 \checkmark$$

(c) $\dfrac{5}{8} = \dfrac{x}{24}$

$\dfrac{8x}{8} = \dfrac{120}{8}$

$x = 15$

Check: $\dfrac{5}{8} = \dfrac{15}{24}$

$8 \times 15 = 5 \times 24$

$120 = 120 \checkmark$

(d) $\dfrac{5}{8} = \dfrac{15}{x}$

$\dfrac{5x}{5} = \dfrac{120}{5}$

$x = 24$

Check: $\dfrac{5}{8} = \dfrac{15}{24}$

$120 = 120 \checkmark$

You can apply the property of proportions to solve any one of the three basic types of percent problems.

Finding the Percentage

In the preceding units several methods of solving business problems were explained and illustrated. Some students like to use the *basic percent formula*, while others prefer the *proportion method* or $\dfrac{\text{IS}}{\text{OF}}$ method (fraction).

It may be helpful to use *one method* to solve problems, and use the *other method* to check solutions.

Example 1 A CD player regularly selling for $475 is on sale at 40% off. Find the amount of reduction.

PROCEDURE: In Unit 1 percent was defined as a rate that compares a given number to 100. Therefore, you can write the 40% as the ratio $\frac{40}{100}$, and write the following proportion:

$$40\% \text{ is to } 100\% \text{ as } x \text{ is to } \$475$$

$$\frac{40}{100} = \frac{x}{\$475}$$

Important: *When setting up the proportion, corresponding terms in each ratio must compare corresponding relationships.*

$$\frac{40 \text{ (reduction \%)}}{100 \text{ (total \%)}} \quad \frac{x(\text{reduction amount})}{\$475 \text{ (total amount)}}$$

$$\frac{40}{100} = \frac{x}{\$475}$$

$$\frac{0.40}{1.00} \; \frac{x}{\$475} \quad \text{Reduce the first ratio by dividing both terms by 100.}$$

$$x = 190$$

$$475 \boxed{\times} 0 \boxed{.} 40 = 190$$

Amount of reduction $= \$190$ *Answer*

Check: Proportion

$$\frac{0.40\%}{1.00\%} = \frac{\$190}{\$475}$$

$$\frac{0.40}{1} \quad \frac{190}{475}$$

$$190 = 475 \boxed{\times} 0 \boxed{.} 40 \boxed{=} 190$$

$$190 = 190 \checkmark$$

Check: Base $\times$ Rate = Percentage

$$\$475 \times 0.40 = \text{Percentage}$$

$$190 \qquad\quad = \$190 \checkmark$$

Finding the Rate

Example 2 A TV selling for $528 was reduced by $132. Find the percent of reduction.

PROCEDURE: From the facts of the problem, write the following proportion:

$$x\% \text{ is to } 100\% \text{ as } \$132 \text{ is to } \$528$$

$$\frac{x \text{ (reduction \%)}}{100 \text{ (total \%)}} = \frac{\$132 \text{ (reduction amount)}}{\$528 \text{ (total amount)}}$$

$$\frac{x}{100} = \frac{\$132}{\$528} \quad \text{Set up the proportion.}$$

$$\frac{x}{1} = \frac{132}{528} \quad \text{Reduce the first ratio.}$$

$$528x = 132 \quad \text{Cross multiply.}$$

$$\frac{528x}{528} = \frac{132}{528} \quad \text{Divide both sides by 528.}$$

$$= 32 \boxed{\div} 528 \boxed{=} 0.25$$
$$x = 0.25$$
$$\text{Percent of reduction} = 25\% \quad \textit{Answer}$$

Check: Base $\times$ Rate = Percentage
$\quad$ \$528 $\times$ 25% = \$132 $\checkmark$
$\quad$ 528 $\boxed{\times}$ 0 $\boxed{.}$ 25 $\boxed{=}$ 132

Finding the Base

Example 3 A refrigerator is on sale at 45% off the regular price. If the amount of reduction is \$279, what was the original price of the refrigerator?

PROCEDURE: From the facts in the problem, write the following proportion:

45% is to *100%* as *\$279* is to *x*

$$\frac{45 \text{ (reduction \%)}}{100 \text{ (total \%)}} = \frac{\$279 \text{ (reduction amount)}}{x \text{ (total amount)}}$$

$$\frac{45}{100} = \frac{\$279}{x}$$

$$\frac{0.45}{1.00} = \frac{279}{x}$$

$$\frac{0.45x}{0.45} = \frac{279}{0.45}$$

$$x = 620$$

Original price = \$620 *Answer*

Check: Base $\times$ Rate = Percentage
$\quad$ \$620 $\times$ 0.45 = \$279
$\quad$ 620 $\boxed{\times}$ 0 $\boxed{.}$ 45 $\boxed{=}$ 279 $\checkmark$

Exercises

Find the missing quantities. Check each answer.

1. $\dfrac{35}{14} = \dfrac{x}{2}$ 2. $\dfrac{4}{5} = \dfrac{36}{x}$ 3. $\dfrac{x}{48} = \dfrac{5}{8}$ 4. $\dfrac{35}{42} = \dfrac{5}{x}$ 5. $x{:}6 = 40{:}48$

6. $5{:}8 = 45{:}x$ 7. $5{:}x = 45{:}63$ 8. 24 is to x as 3 is to 4

9. 2 is to 13 as x is to 1.105   10. $242{:}x = 11$ is to 12   11. $5{:}11 = x{:}693$

12. $2{:}3 = 1{,}268{:}x$ 13. 6 oz.:1 lb. $= x{:}592$ lb.   14. $3{:}5 = x{:}\$575$

15. 15% of $235   16. $54 is what percent of $180?

17. 25% of what number is 130?

Word Problems

18. What is the price per pound of a 4-oz. jar of instant coffee selling for $2.55?

19. Jane is paid a commission of 12% of total sales. If she earned $393 in commissions, what were her total sales?

20. Tim deposits $2,575 into a savings account that pays 8.5% interest. What will be his balance at the end of the year?

21. An appliance store sells a refrigerator for $625. If the gross profit is 40%, what is the amount of the gross profit?

22. The Rivera family made a down payment of 15% on the purchase of a new home. If the down payment was $8,250, what was the purchase price of the house?

UNIT **6** Review of Chapter Six

1.

			Wholesaler's Trade Discounts				
			Effective January 1–July 1				
Item Code	List Price	Trade Discount	Amount of Discount			Net Price	
A	$127	40%	____	____		____	____
B	163	45	____	____		____	____
C	272	55	____	____		____	____
D	245	35	____	____		____	____
E	286	43	____	____		____	____
F	342	52	____	____		____	____
G	678	47	____	____		____	____

2.

		Stock Price Changes for November				
Stock	Price	Percent of Increase or Decrease*	Amount of Increase or Decrease		New Price	
A	$28	+6%	____	____	____	____
B	63	+3	____	____	____	____
C	85	−4	____	____	____	____
D	42	−5	____	____	____	____
E	53	+12	____	____	____	____
F	16	+8	____	____	____	____
G	73	+14	____	____	____	____

*Plus (+) means an increase in the price; minus (−) means a decrease in the price.

Find the amount of interest and the new balance for each of the following amounts. Round off each number to the nearest cent.

3.

Amount on Deposit		Interest Rate	Amount of Interest		New Balance	
$1,238	65	8.752%	___	___	___	___
1,578	42	9.75	___	___	___	___
2,415	70	8.025	___	___	___	___
2,571	81	9.65	___	___	___	___
3,682	55	10.0325	___	___	___	___
3,520	60	11.652	___	___	___	___

Find the amount to the nearest penny or whole unit.

4. 42% of what number is 625?

5. $322 is 115% of what amount?

6. 125% of what amount is $2,422.75?

7. $462.75 is 112% of what amount?

8. Find the percent of increase or decrease to the nearest whole percent.

   (a) $242 increased to $353   (b) $410 increased to $650

   (c) $565 decreased to $427   (d) $4,200 decreased to $2,300

9. Janet Gomez earns a 10% commission on all her sales. In January, her sales were $53,694.75, and in February her sales were $42,785.50.

   (a) How much less commission did she earn in February?

   (b) What was the percent of decrease in her earnings for February as compared to January?

10. Harry Gold bought a car for $9,875. Three years later he sold the car for $6,342. What was the depreciation percent of the car over the 3 years?

11. Sam Grotin earned $728.50 in interest on his saving account last year. If the rate of interest is $6\frac{1}{2}$%, how much did Sam have on deposit at the beginning of last year?

12. A retailer sold 375 coats this year. If she sold 35% more coats this year than last year, how many coats did she sell last year?

13. At the end of a full year Mary Garber had $6,248.95 in her savings account. If the rate of interest was 12.253%, how much money did Mary have in the bank at the beginning of the year?

CHAPTER **SEVEN**

Statistics and Business Graphics

UNIT **1** Measures of Central Tendency

Most people are familiar with averages. An **average** serves as a **measure of central tendency.** It is a representative number around which the related measures tend to center.

There are other statistical methods of calculating central tendencies, and the purpose of the information will determine which method you will use.

The Mean (Average)

The **mean,** also called the **average,** is the most commonly used measure.

PROCEDURE: To find the mean:

1. Add all the numbers in a given set.
2. Divide the sum by the number of items in the set.

Example 1 Find the *mean* (average) of the following set of numbers:

80, 70, 75, 90, 68, 80, 74

STEP 1. Add the numbers: $80 + 70 + 75 + 90 + 68 + 80 + 74 = 537$

STEP 2. Divide the sum by the number of items in the set:

537 ⊡ 7 ⊟ 76.7 |14 . . .
       = 76.7

Answer: The mean (average) of the set of numbers is 76.7

The Median

The **median** is the number located in the *middle* of a set of numbers that have been arranged in sequence according to their numerical values.

PROCEDURE: To find the median in sets with an *odd* number of elements:

1. Arrange the numbers in ascending order.
2. Locate the number in the middle of the set, and circle it. The circled number is the median.

Example 2 Find the median in the following set of numbers:

12, 10, 6, 8, 9, 10, 15, 11, 11, 12, 18, 11, 16, 13, 19

STEP 1. Arrange the numbers in ascending order:

6, 8, 9, 10, 10, 11, 11, 11, 12, 12, 13, 15, 16, 18, 19

STEP 2. Since there are *15* numbers in the set, the 8th number is in the middle. Circle the 8th number:

6, 8, 9, 10, 10, 11, 11, ⑪ 12, 12, 13, 15, 16, 18, 19
                          ↓
                       Median

Answer: The circled number, 11, is the median.

PROCEDURE: To find the median in sets with an *even* number of elements:

1. Arrange the numbers in ascending order.
2. Count how many entries you have, and then add 1.
3. Divide this sum by 2.
4. Take the average of the middle two numbers.

Example 3 Find the median in the following set of numbers:

30, 80, 60, 40, 50, 70, 80, 70

STEP 1. Arrange the numbers in ascending order.

$$30, 40, 50, 60, 70, 70, 80, 80$$

STEP 2. Since there are *eight* numbers in the set, the *median* is the *average* of the *two middle numbers*.

STEP 3. Circle the two middle numbers, and find the average:

$$30, 40, 50, \widehat{60, 70,} 70, 80, 80$$

$$60 \boxplus 70 \boxed{=} 130 \boxdiv 2 \boxed{=} 65$$

Answer: The median is the average of 60 and 70.

Note: The median minimizes the impact of extremely high or low numbers, whereas the mean reflects them.

The Mode

The **mode** is the *number that appears most frequently* in the set of numbers being considered.

PROCEDURE: To find the mode, tally the number of times each number appears. The number that appears most frequently is the mode.

Example 4   Find the mode for the following set of numbers:

$$80, 70, 75, 90, 68, 80, 74$$

STEP 1.   90 | On a scratch pad, tally the number of times each
          80 || number occurs.
          75 |
          74 |
          70 |
          68 |

STEP 2. Note which number appears most frequently.

Answer: The mode is 80, because this number occurs most often.

Note: The mode is unaffected by variations in the distribution of scores; it only identifies the most frequent score.

Comparison of Measures of Central Tendency

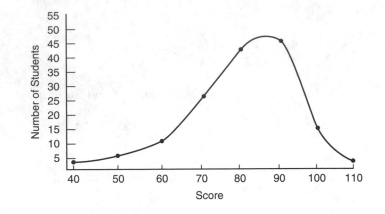

On a recent test of 10 questions plus a bonus question, 171 members of the freshman class received these marks:

Score	Number of Students
40%	2
50	5
60	12
70	30
80	48
90	52
100	18
110	4

HINTS: To find the *average,* take 2 × 0.40 plus 5 × 0.50, etc., and then divide by 171. This gives an average of

$$\frac{139.10}{171} = 0.81345 = 81.35\%$$

To find the *median,* count in 86 people from the top and from the bottom. The score of the person right in the middle is the median score. In this case, the median score is 80%.

To find the *mode,* the score that occurs most frequently, count the number of times each number occurs. In this case, the mode is 90%.

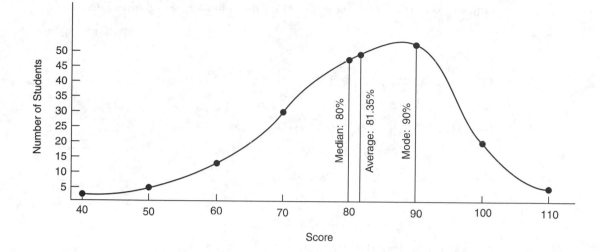

Notice that of the above three measures only the *median* (in a set with an odd number of items) and the *mode* are items that are actually contained in the given sets of numbers. When deciding which of the three measures you should use with a given set of statistics, you must determine the purpose of the information:

- If you need a number that is typical of the set, the *mean* can be used, unless a large number of high or low scores cause the mean to be nonrepresentative.
- If you need a number about which the others are evenly spaced, the *median* can be used.
- If you need a number that is more prominent because of its frequency, the *mode* can be used.

Exercises

Exercise A   Find the *mean* for each set of numbers.

1. 20, 28, 45, 25, 34, 40

2. 115, 98, 105, 125, 110, 95, 103

3. 325, 340, 315, 330, 310, 305

4. 70, 65, 75, 85, 80, 90, 73, 81

5. 260, 242, 251, 263, 250

6. 53, 72, 65, 80, 57, 75, 82, 67

7. 460, 443, 455, 470, 462

8. 84, 92, 70, 87, 95, 85, 75, 78

9. 18, 22, 16, 19, 20, 17, 21, 19, 24, 25

10. 40, 50, 70, 60, 80, 50, 70

Find the *median* and the *mode* in each of the following sets of numbers:

		Median	Mode
11.	70, 85, 80, 65, 70	____	____
12.	215, 245, 231, 220, 235, 231	____	____
13.	24, 32, 24, 20, 32, 25, 32	____	____
14.	150, 135, 140, 155, 120, 135, 150, 135	____	____
15.	191, 152, 183, 191, 140, 170, 164	____	____
16.	80, 75, 105, 90, 75, 80, 95, 80	____	____
17.	42, 53, 40, 61, 40, 64, 58, 40	____	____
18.	345, 430, 410, 350, 430, 450, 425, 435	____	____
19.	195, 170, 180, 190, 165, 170, 185	____	____
20.	121, 143, 132, 145, 132, 140	____	____

Word Problems

Exercise B Solve the following problems:

21. A salesperson made the following sales last week: Monday, $248.50; Tuesday, $310.78; Wednesday, $278.65; Thursday, $320.43; Friday, $315.15; and Saturday, $343.85. What is the daily average of the sales made?

22. A retailer bought equal numbers of the following lines of blouses: group A at $9.50, group B at $11.75, group C at $12.65, group D at $8.75, and group E at $9.50.

    (a) What is the average price paid for the blouses?
    (b) What is the median price of the blouses?
    (c) What is the mode price of the blouses?

23. An office employs six clerks at the following salaries: $9,850; $8,975; $11,475; $10,500; $12,250; and $9,750.

    (a) What is their mean annual salary?
    (b) What is their median salary?

24. A furniture store sells dining room sets in the following price ranges: $1,850.75; $1,675.50; $1,495.85; $1,965.90; and $1,575.75.

    (a) What is the median price of the dining room sets?
    (b) What is the mean price of the dining room sets?

25. The average weekly salary of six salesclerks is $195. Five of the salesclerks earn the following salaries: $185, $190, $205, $195, and $200. What is the salary of the sixth salesclerk? (HINT: Since the average salary is $195, the total weekly salaries amount to $195 × 6, or $1,170.)

UNIT **2** Line Graphs

Just as a picture can show things that are difficult to describe in words, a graph can show relationships among numbers which are difficult to discern from tables of numbers or columns of figures.

The **line graph** is often used to show how a quantity *changes* over a period of *time*.

Interpreting Line Graphs

A line graph will show at a glance whether a quantity is **increasing** (the line is rising), **decreasing** (the line is falling), or **remaining the same** (the line is horizontal).

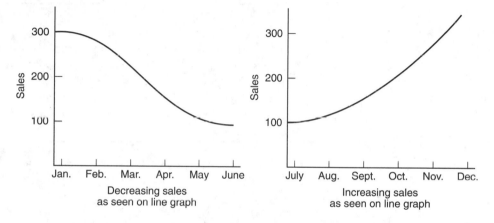

A line graph has a **horizontal** scale and a **vertical** scale, which are drawn at right angles to each other. The vertical scale usually indicates the quantity that is changing, while the horizontal scale shows the change in time (or sometimes in distance).

Preparing Line Graphs

PROCEDURE: To construct a line graph:

1. Collect the data, which may have to be rounded. For example, the following figures were used for the line graph in Exercise A on page 165:

Appliance Department Sales for 2000

Month	Sales	Sales to the Nearest $1,000
January	$15,468.95	$15,000
February	18,763.50	19,000
March	20,394.75	20,000
April	16,643.25	17,000
May	25,415.30	25,000
June	23,146.90	23,000
July	34,861.40	35,000
August	37,419.70	37,000
September	24,718.20	25,000
October	21,953.75	22,000
November	32,385.70	32,000
December	27,410.90	27,000

2. Label the scales in uniform units, choosing the intervals so that both scales are of appropriate length. (You may use as a guide the line graph in Exercise A.) If using graph paper, allow five squares between each of the major divisions.

3. Plot the graph on the two scales by placing a dot for each set of the rounded-off figures. For instance, using the graph in Exercise A as an example, for the month of January you would move up the vertical scale until you reach the line labeled "15" and place a dot where the "January" line and the "15" line meet. For February, you would move up the vertical scale until you reach the line that represents "19" (thousands). NOTE: In the line graph in Exercise A, each major division on the vertical scale represents $5,000 in sales and each subdivision represents $1,000 in sales. Therefore, you would place a dot four subdivision lines up from the line labeled "15," and then continue this process for the remaining months.

4. Using a ruler, connect all the dots in order.

5. Label the graph.

Exercises

Exercise A Examine the line graph below, and answer the questions that follow.

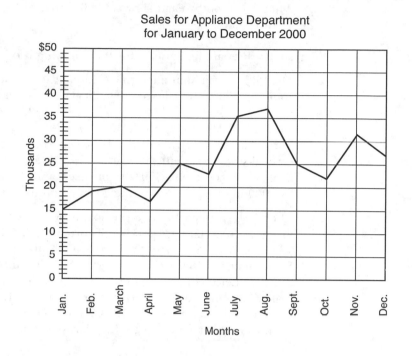

Sales for Appliance Department
for January to December 2000

1. What information does the graph represent?

2. What do the lines on the horizontal scale represent?

3. How many $1,000 in sales is represented by each major division on the vertical scale?

4. How many $1,000 in sales is represented by each subdivision on the vertical scale?

5. (a) In what month were the sales the highest?
    (b) How much was sold in that month?

6. (a) What month had the lowest sales?
    (b) How much was sold that month?

7. In what two months was the amount of sales the same?

8. What was the percent of increase in sales in July over sales in May?

9. Which months showed increases in sales over the previous month?

10. Which months showed decreases in sales over the previous month?

11. (a) Which month had the greatest increase in sales over the previous month?
    (b) What were the sales of that month?

12. (a) Which month had the greatest decrease in sales over the previous month?
    (b) How much was the drop in sales for that month?

13. In what month were the sales $22,000?

14. What month shows a drop in sales of $12,000?

15. What month shows an increase in sales of $12,000?

16. What two months each show $3,000 decreases in sales over the previous month's sales?

Exercise B Prepare line graphs for the following two groups of data:

17. The Photo-Tech Manufacturing Company introduced a dry-method photo-copier in 1990. The sales for 1991-2000 were as follows: 1991, $52,365; 1992, $87,872; 1993, $138,410; 1994, $211,865; 1995, $263,635; 1996, $315,880; 1997, $290,235; 1998, $364,415; 1999, $415,605; 2000, $475,675. Let the horizontal scale represent the 10-year period from 1991 to 2000 and the vertical scale represent the yearly sales. Let each major division on the vertical scale represent $50,000 in sales and each subdivision represent $10,000 in sales. Round off the given amounts to the nearest $10,000.

18. The Western Department Store spent the following amounts on TV advertising last year: January, $33,620; February, $24,465; March, $29,780; April, $36,345; May, $41,870; June, $38,460; July, $29,775; August, $28,475; September, $35,643; October, $38,240; November, $46,300; December, $53,975. Let the horizontal scale represent the 12 months and the vertical scale represent the TV advertising expenditures. Let each major division on the vertical scale represent $10,000 and each subdivision represent $2,000. Round the given amounts to the nearest $1,000.

UNIT **3** Bar Graphs and Pictographs

Bar graphs and **pictographs** are used to compare changes in given quantities or values and to show the relationships of these quantities to one another. The basic difference between bar graphs and pictographs is that a pictograph uses a sketch of the item represented.

Interpreting Bar Graphs and Pictographs

Since these graphs are used to show *comparisons* between given quantities or values, the differences in the length of the bars or in the number of pictorial units indicate the relationships of the quantities being represented.

Bar graphs and pictographs can be vertical or horizontal, depending upon the way the scales are laid out and the nature of the pictures to be used. For instance, the vertical bar graph shown on the next page can be drawn horizontally by merely interchanging the vertical and horizontal scales. (See the graph in Exercise A, page 165.)

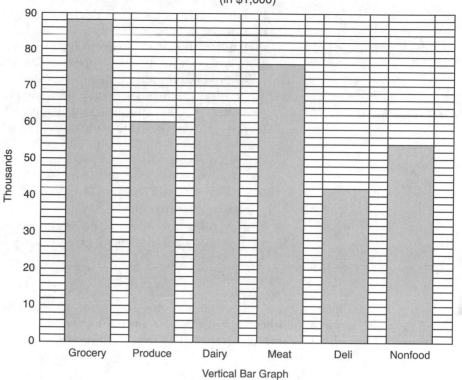

Thrifty Supermarket Sales by Department for 2000
(in $1,000)

Vertical Bar Graph

Preparing Bar Graphs and Pictographs

PROCEDURE: To construct a vertical bar graph:

1. Collect the data, rounding the figures if necessary. For example, these figures were used for the vertical bar graph shown above:

Thrifty Supermarket Sales by Department for 2000

Department	Sales	Sales to the Nearest $1,000
Grocery	$88,465.90	$88,000
Produce	59,864.75	60,000
Dairy	63,593.50	64,000
Meat	76,253.48	76,000
Deli	42,480.70	42,000
Nonfood	53,505.80	54,000

2. Decide on appropriate lengths for both the vertical scale and the horizontal scale, and label the scales in uniform units.
3. Plot the graph on the two scales by placing a dot for each set of rounded figures. In the preceding bar graph, for instance, each major division on the vertical scale represents $10,000 in sales, and each subdivision represents $2,000 in sales.

    Therefore, to indicate the grocery department sales, you would move up the vertical scale until you reach the line that represents $88,000 (the line that is four subdivisions above the line marked "80" [thousand]) and place a dot where the "Grocery" line and the "88" line meet. For the produce department sales, you would move up the vertical scale until you reach the line that represents "60" (thousand) and place a dot at that point. This process would be continued for the remaining departments.
4. Using a ruler, draw bars of equal widths from the zero of the horizontal scale to the dots. Leave the same amount of space between bars.
5. Label the graph.

A pictograph is very much like a bar graph, but the quantities are represented by pictorial units that illustrate the given information. For instance, the pictograph illustrated on page 170 represents the yearly car sales for Ace Car Company for 1995 to 2000.

PROCEDURE: To construct a pictograph:

1. Collect the data, rounding the figures if necessary. For the pictograph illustrated, the basic data were as follows:

**Yearly Car Sales for the Ace Car Company
for 1995 to 2000**

Year	Number of Cars Sold
1995	355
1996	490
1997	445
1998	653
1999	624
2000	853

2. Select a suitable picture to represent the data and decide how many units each picture will represent.
3. Find out how many pictures are needed to represent each rounded-off number of the given information. To do this, divide each rounded-off number by the number of units each picture represents. (In the pictograph illustrated on page 170, for 1995 the rounded-off number of cars is 360. $360 \div 100 = 3\frac{3}{5}$, or slightly more than $3\frac{1}{2}$.)

4. Insert the required number of pictures, including proportionate parts of the picture for each rounded-off number of the given information.

5. Label the graph and include an illustration of the picture and the number of units it represents.

Exercises

Exercise A Examine the horizontal bar graph below and answer the questions that follow.

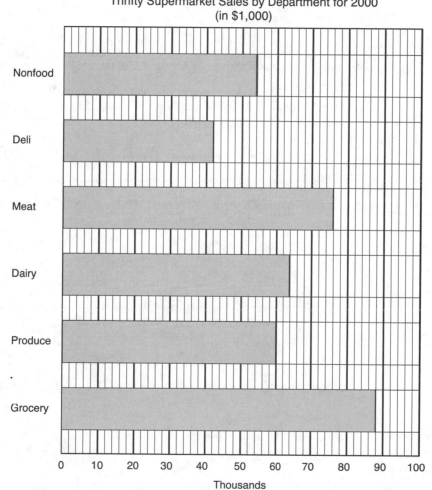

Thrifty Supermarket Sales by Department for 2000
(in $1,000)

1. What information does the graph represent?

2. What do the bars represent?

3. How many $1,000 in sales is represented by each major division on the horizontal scale?

4. How many $1,000 in sales is represented by each subdivision on the horizontal scale?

5. (a) What department had the highest sales?
   (b) What were the sales of that department?

6. (a) What department had the lowest sales?
   (b) What were the sales of that department?

7. What were the sales of the deli department?

8. What department sold between $60,000 and $70,000?

9. What departments had sales of under $60,000 each?

10. What departments had sales of over $60,000 each?

11. Which two departments show the greatest difference in sales?

12. What were the total sales of all departments?

13. What percentage of the total sales is the sales of the grocery department?

14. What is the difference in sales between the deli and nonfood departments?

15. List the departments in descending order according to sales.
    (a) Which department sold $42,000?
    (b) Which two departments show a difference of $24,000?

Exercise B Examine the horizontal pictograph below and answer the questions that follow.

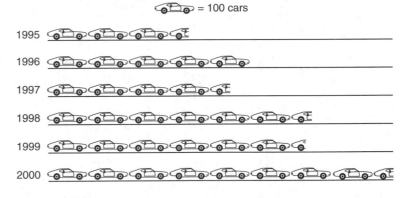

Yearly Car Sales for the Ace Car Company for 1995 to 2000

= 100 cars

16. What information does the graph represent?

17. Which year had the lowest sales?

18. Which year had the highest sales?

19. How many cars were sold in 1997?

20. In what year were 625 cars sold?

21. How many cars were sold in 1995?

22. How many cars were sold in 1999?

23. What is the percent of increase in sales in 2000 over the sales in 1999?

24. Which two years show decreases in sales compared to their preceding years?

Word Problems

Exercise C   Prepare the following graphs:

25.   Prepare a vertical bar graph for the following data:

The Acorn Manufacturing Company sold the following amounts in its five territories last month: territory A, $47,625.80; B, $32,249.75; C, $51,817.45; D, $26,485.75; E, $29,525.35.

Let the horizontal scale represent the five territories and the vertical scale represent the amounts of monthly sales. Let each major division on the vertical scale represent $10,000 in sales and each subdivision represent $2,000 in sales. Round the given amounts to the nearest $1,000.

26.   Prepare a horizontal bar graph for the following data:

A salesman earned the following commissions for the first 6 months of this year: January, $1,875.50; February, $2,148.65; March, $2,465.95; April, $1,953.72; May, $1,748.50; June, $2,615.68. Let the horizontal scale represent the monthly commission earned and the vertical scale represent the 6 months.

27.   Prepare a pictograph for the following data:

The average tuition costs for 1 year at a state college during 1997 to 2001 were as follows:

1997, $5,175; 1998, $5,768; 1999, $6,448; 2000, $6,848; 2001, $7,281. Round off each tuition cost to the nearest $100. Use the picture of a $1,000 bill,

 , to represent $1,000.

UNIT **4**   Circle Graphs

The **circle graph** is used to show the relative size of each part of a quantity to the whole.

   With a glance, you can get an idea of the relative values of each item as a part of the whole.

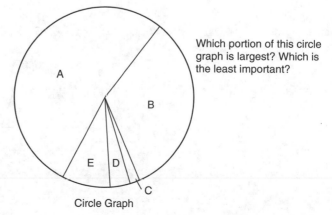

Which portion of this circle graph is largest? Which is the least important?

Circle Graph

Interpreting Circle Graphs

The circle graph is used to show the *relationship* of the parts of a quantity to the whole. The 360 degrees (360°) of the circle represent 100% of the quantity being considered. The sectors of the circle are constructed so that an item with a value of 20% will be represented by a sector that is 20% of the circle.

Preparing Circle Graphs

PROCEDURE: To construct a circle graph:

1. Change the data to percents of the whole quantity being considered. For example, the circle graph of Exercise A on page 173 represents the Fernandez family budget based on a yearly income of $28,500. The expenditures for the year were as follows:

Food	$ 5,700	20%
Rent	6,270	22
Savings	4,275	15
Clothing	2,280	8
Recreation	4,845	17
Health	1,425	5
Charity	1,140	4
Miscellaneous	2,565	9
	$28,500	100%

HINT: The $\dfrac{\text{IS}}{\text{OF}}$ method is helpful here. Since you want to know, for example, what percent is $5,700 of $28,500, write $\dfrac{\$5,700}{\$28,500}$ and divide:

$$\begin{array}{r} 0.20 \\ 285\overline{)57.00} \\ 57\ 0 \end{array} = 20\%$$

2. Change each percent to degrees of a circle.

Food = 360° × 20% = 72°

3. Using a compass, draw a circle large enough to show the divisions of the circle graph. Then, use a protractor and ruler to mark off the sectors in degrees for each item. For example:

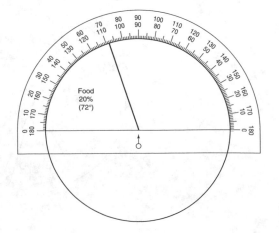

Exercises

Exercise A   Examine the circle graph below and answer the questions that follow.

Distribution of the Fernandez Annual Income of $28,500

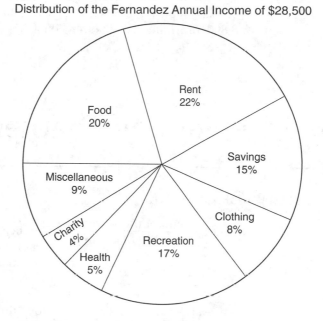

1.   What information does the graph represent?

2.   What do the sectors of the circle represent?

3.   What should be the total percent of all the sectors added together?

4.   What expenditure is represented by the largest sector of the circle?

5.   What expenditure is represented by the smallest sector of the circle?

6.   What two expenditures combined are equal to the miscellaneous expenditure?

7.   What is the total percent of the three largest expenditures?

8.   How many degrees are there in the sector representing the food expenditure? (HINT: There are 360 degrees in a circle; therefore find 20% of 360°.)

9.   How much money does the Fernandez family spend on rent?

10.   How much money does the Fernandez family spend on charity?

11.   How much more money does the Fernandez family spend on rent than on food?

12.   What is the total amount of money spent on food, rent, and recreation?

Exercise B   Draw circle graphs for the following two groups of data:

13.   The breakdown in sales of the Bee Gee Appliance Company for last year was as follows: refrigerators, $178,464; washers, $118,976; dryers, $75,712; dishwashers, $54,080; television sets, $81,120; stereos, $32,448.

14.   Last year, there were 110,000 accidental deaths in the United States. Their causes were as follows: motor vehicle, 38,500; falls, 22,000; firearms, 18,700; burns, 8,800; drowning, 7,700; other, 14,300.

UNIT 5 Review of Chapter Seven

SUMMARY OF KEY POINTS

- Mean (average) $= \dfrac{\text{Sum of the scores}}{\text{Number of scores}}$ The mean is the best all-around measure of central tendency, but gives an answer that does not relate to any one real score.

- Median is the *middle* score of a set.   Most times, the median gives an actual score. It also tends to minimize the effect of a few abnormally high or low scores.

- Mode is the *single most popular* score.   The mode is an actual score, being the single most popular score. The mode is immune to extremes.

- Line graphs should be used to demonstrate changes and trends over time.

- Bar graphs or pictographs should be used to show comparisons between groups in *real numbers* (dollars, units, etc.).

- Circle graphs should be used to show comparisons between groups in *relative* terms (percent).

Find the mean in each of the following sets of numbers:

1.   35, 45, 30, 43, 32, 48, 33

2.   68, 93, 74, 70, 95, 81, 78

3.   320, 348, 372, 328, 350, 365

Find the *median* and the *mode* in each of the following sets of numbers:

	Median	Mode

4. 28, 44, 36, 32, 34, 46, 36 _____ _____

5. 85, 70, 95, 80, 75, 70, 75, 70 _____ _____

6. 285, 295, 284, 278, 295, 288 _____ _____

Examine the line graph below, and answer the questions that follow.

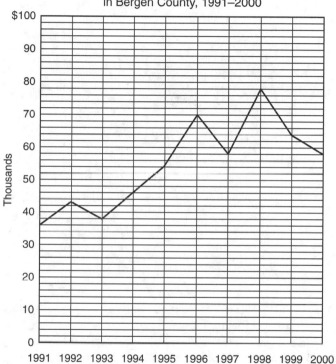

Average Cost of One-Family Homes (in $1,000)
in Bergen County, 1991–2000

7. (a) In what year was the cost the highest?
     (b) How much was the cost that year?

8. What year showed the largest drop in cost from the preceding year?

9. What year showed the largest increase from the preceding year?

10. (a) If someone bought a home in 1993 and sold it in 2000, how much profit was made?
     (b) What would be the percent of increase?

11. Arrange all the yearly prices as a set. Find the mean, median, and mode of the prices represented by the graph.

Examine the bar graph below, and answer the questions that follow.

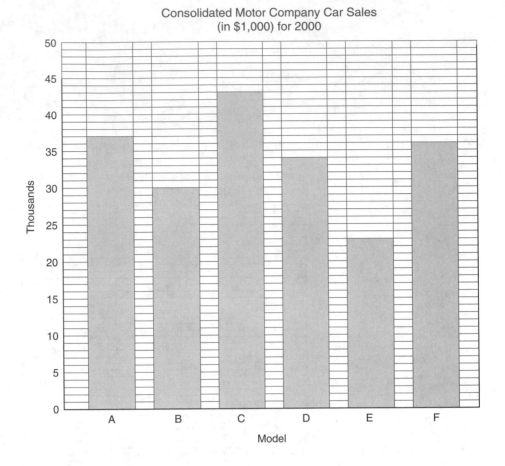

12. (a) What two models had the smallest difference in sales?
    (b) How much was the difference?

13. What is the difference in the number of cars sold between the model that had the lowest sales and the model that had the highest sales?

14. What two models had a difference in sales of 15,000 cars?

15. What is the model C sales percent of the total cars sold?

16. Arrange all the sales of models as a set. Find the mean and median averages of the total number of cars sold.

Examine the circle graph below, and answer the questions that follow.

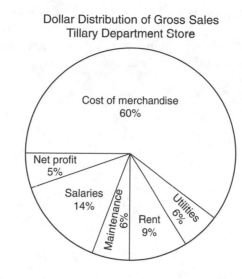

Dollar Distribution of Gross Sales
Tillary Department Store

17. What two expenditures are equal to the salary expenditure?

18. How many degrees does each sector of the graph represent?

19. If the gross sales are $1,328,467, find the expenditure for each item in the graph.

20. Last year, the store purchased $741,270 worth of merchandise. What should the gross sales have been?

21. If the net profit for a year is $71,157.85, what would be the cost of merchandise for the year?

Examine the pictograph below, and answer the questions that follow.

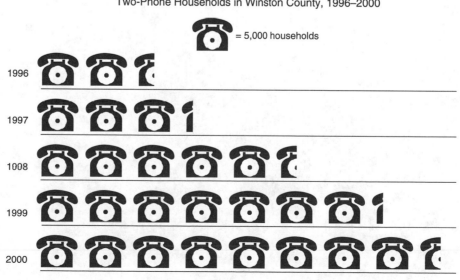

Two-Phone Households in Winston County, 1996–2000

22. How many two-phone households were there in 1998?

23. How many more two-phone households were there in 2000 than in 1996?

24. What is the number of two-phone households for each of the years covered by the graph?

CHAPTER **EIGHT**

Measurements/English and Metric Systems

UNIT **1** Addition and Subtraction of Mixed Units of Measure

In business, you will often be dealing with measurements made up of mixed units. For example, you may have to add 3 yards to 6 feet or subtract 5 pounds 13 ounces from 8 pounds 6 ounces. Measurements such as these are called **denominate numbers** and are often composed of two or more mixed units.

TABLE 1   Units of Measure

Length
1 foot (ft.) = 12 inches
1 yard (yd.) = 3 feet or 36 inches
1 mile (mi.) = 5,280 feet or 1,760 yards

Capacity
1 pint (pt.) = 16 liquid ounces
1 quart (qt.) = 2 pints or 32 liquid ounces
1 gallon (gal.) = 4 quarts or 128 liquid ounces = 8 pints

Weight
1 pound (lb.) = 16 ounces
1 short ton (s.t. or T) = 2,000 pounds
1 long ton (l.t.) = 2,240 pounds

Quantity
1 dozen (doz.) = 12 units
1 gross (gr.) = 12 dozen or 144 units
1 score = 20 units

Changing Units of Measure to Equivalent Units

To solve problems that involve units of measure, it may at times be necessary to change a quantity expressed in one particular unit of measure into a different unit of measure.

Example 1   Change 78 inches to feet.

        PROCEDURE: Set up a proportion that compares the number of inches in 1 foot to the number of inches in the problem.

                1 foot is to 12 inches as *x feet is to 78 inches.*

Solution:

$$\frac{1 \text{ (ft.)}}{12 \text{ (in.)}} = \frac{x \text{ (ft.)}}{78 \text{ (in.)}}$$

$$\frac{1}{12} = \frac{x}{78}$$

$$\frac{\cancel{12}x}{\cancel{12}} = \frac{78}{12}$$

$$x = 6.5$$

$$= 6\frac{1}{2} \text{ ft.}$$

Check: 78 ⊡ 12⊟ 6.5

$$= 6\frac{1}{2} \text{ ft. } \checkmark$$

Answer: 78 in. $= 6\frac{1}{2}$ ft.

Example 2   Change $5\frac{1}{4}$ feet to inches.

Solution: $$\frac{1 \text{ (ft.)}}{12 \text{ (in.)}} = \frac{5\frac{1}{4} \text{ (ft.)}}{x \text{ (in.)}}$$

$$\frac{1}{12} = \frac{5\frac{1}{4}}{x}$$

$$x = 5\frac{1}{4} \times \frac{12}{1} = \frac{21}{\cancel{4}_{1}} \times \frac{\cancel{12}^{3}}{1} = \frac{63}{1}$$

$$x = 63$$

$$= 63 \text{ in.}$$

Alternative Solution:

$$\frac{1}{12} = \frac{5.25}{x}$$

$$x = 12 \times 5.25$$

$$= 12 \boxtimes 5 \boxed{.} 25 \boxed{=} 63$$

Answer: $5\frac{1}{4}$ ft. = 63 in.

Example 3 Change $4\frac{3}{4}$ gallons to liquid ounces.

Solution: $\dfrac{1 \text{ (gal.)}}{128 \text{ (oz.)}} = \dfrac{4\frac{3}{4} \text{ (gal.)}}{x \text{ (oz.)}}$

$$x = 128 \times 4\frac{3}{4} = \frac{19}{\underset{1}{\cancel{4}}} \times \frac{\overset{32}{\cancel{128}}}{1} = 608$$

$$= 608 \text{ oz.}$$

Answer: $4\frac{3}{4}$ gal. = 608 liquid ounces

Example 4 Change 47 pints to gallons.

Solution: $\dfrac{1 \text{ (gal.)}}{8 \text{ (pt.)}} = \dfrac{x \text{ (gal.)}}{47 \text{ (pt.)}}$

$$\frac{1}{8} = \frac{x}{47}$$

$$\frac{\cancel{8}x}{\cancel{8}} = \frac{47}{8}$$

$$= 47 \boxed{\div} 8 \boxed{=} 5.875$$

$$x = 5.875$$

$$= 5\frac{7}{8} \text{ gal.}$$

Answer: 47 pt. = $5\frac{7}{8}$ gal.

Addition of Mixed Units of Measure

PROCEDURE: To add mixed units of measure:

1. Lay out the problem with like units under each other.
2. Add the smallest units first.
3. Convert this sum to a proper mixed unit, and carry the larger unit to the next column.
4. Add the column with the next smallest units.
5. Continue with Steps 3 and 4 until all units are added. Label your answer and check your addition.

Example 1   Add: 6 ft. 8 in. + 3 ft. 5 in. + 4 ft. 10 in.

Solution: STEP 1.

6 ft.	8 in.
3 ft.	5 in.
+4 ft.	10 in.

Lay out the problem in columns, with like units under each other.

STEP 2.

6 ft.	8 in.
3 ft.	5 in.
+4 ft.	10 in.
13 ft.	23 in.

Add the smallest units—in this case, inches, and then add the feet column.

STEP 3.   23 in. ÷ 12 in. = 1 ft. 11 in.

$$\begin{array}{r} 1 \text{ ft. } 11 \text{ in.} \\ 12\overline{)23} \\ \underline{12} \\ 11 \text{ in.} \end{array}$$

Convert your answer to a mixed unit by division. To *convert inches to feet, divide the number of inches by 12* (the number of inches in a foot). Note that the whole number of the quotient is the number of feet in 23 inches, while the remainder is the number of inches.

STEP 4.

6 ft.	8 in.
3 ft.	5 in.
+ 4 ft.	10 in.
13 ft.	
+1 ft.	11 in.
14 ft.	11 in.

Combine both answers.

Answer: 6 ft. 8 in. + 3 ft. 5 in. + 4 ft. 10 in. = 14 ft. 11 in.

Example 2   Add: 12 gal. 2 qt. 1 pt. + 8 gal. 4 qt. 3 pt. + 3 gal. 10 qt. 9 pt.

Solution:

1.   Arrange the mixed units one under the other, and add each column.

12 gal.	2 qt.	1 pt.
8 gal.	4 qt.	3 pt.
+ 3 gal.	10 qt.	9 pt.
23 gal.	16 qt.	13 pt.

Starting with the pints, add each column and write the sum under the column.

2.   Moving from right to left, convert the units in each column to the units in the column to its left.

12 gal.	2 qt.	1 pt.
8 gal.	4 qt.	3 pt.
3 gal.	10 qt.	9 pt.
23 gal.	16 qt.	13 pt.
5 gal.	6 qt.	1 pt.
28 gal.	22 qt.	1 pt.
	2 qt.	

Divide 13 pt. by 2, the number of pints in 1 qt.

$$\begin{array}{r} 6 \text{ qt.} \\ 2\overline{)13} \text{ pt.} \\ \underline{12} \\ 1 \text{ pt.} \end{array}$$

Divide 22 qt. by 4, the number of quarts in 1 gal.

$$\begin{array}{r} 5 \text{ gal.} \\ 4\overline{)22} \text{ qt.} \\ \underline{20} \\ 2 \text{ qt.} \end{array}$$

Answer: 12 gal. 2 qt. 1 pt. + 8 gal. 4 qt. 3 pt. + 3 gal. 10 qt. 9 pt. = 28 gal. 2 qt. 1 pt.

Subtraction of Mixed Units of Measure

PROCEDURE: To subtract mixed units of measure:

1. Write the problem with like units of measure under each other.
2. Subtract the smallest units first, borrowing where necessary.
3. Continue subtracting each unit of measure.
4. Label your answer and check your subtraction.

Example 3   Subtract 4 pounds 13 ounces from 9 pounds 7 ounces.

Solution:

STEP 1.
$$\begin{array}{r} 9 \text{ lb.} \quad 7 \text{ oz.} \\ -\,4 \text{ lb.} \; 13 \text{ oz.} \\ \hline \end{array}$$
Write the problem with like units of measure under each other.

STEP 2.
$$\begin{array}{r} \overset{8}{\cancel{9}} \text{ lb.} \; \overset{23}{\cancel{7}} \text{ oz.} \\ -\,4 \text{ lb.} \; 13 \text{ oz.} \\ \hline 10 \end{array}$$
Borrow 1 lb. from 9 lb., convert the 1 lb. to 16 oz., and add it to the 7 oz. Subtract 13 oz. from 23 oz.

STEP 3.
$$\begin{array}{r} \overset{8}{\cancel{9}} \text{ lb.} \; \overset{23}{\cancel{7}} \text{ oz.} \\ -\,4 \text{ lb.} \; 13 \text{ oz.} \\ \hline 4 \quad\;\; 10 \end{array}$$
Continue the subtraction for larger units of measure.

STEP 4.   4 lb. 10 oz. *Answer*
Label the answer and check the subtraction

Example 4   Subtract 18 eggs from 8 gross.

Solution:

$$\begin{array}{r} \overset{7}{\cancel{8}} \text{ gross} \; \overset{\overset{10}{\cancel{12}}}{\cancel{0}} \text{ doz.} \; \overset{24}{\cancel{0}} \text{ units} \\ -\qquad\qquad\qquad\qquad 18 \text{ units} \\ \hline 7 \text{ gross} \; 10 \text{ doz.} \quad 6 \text{ eggs} \quad \textit{Answer} \end{array}$$

Exercises

Exercise A   Find the sums, and simplify your answers.

1.
$$\begin{array}{r} 5 \text{ ft.} \quad 7 \text{ in.} \\ 11 \text{ ft.} \; 11 \text{ in.} \\ +\,7 \text{ ft.} \quad 8 \text{ in.} \\ \hline \end{array}$$

2.
$$\begin{array}{r} 8 \text{ yd.} \; 2 \text{ ft.} \\ 12 \text{ yd.} \; 1 \text{ ft.} \\ +15 \text{ yd.} \; 2 \text{ ft.} \\ \hline \end{array}$$

3.
$$\begin{array}{r} 5 \text{ gross} \; 8 \text{ doz.} \\ 7 \text{ gross} \; 9 \text{ doz.} \\ +12 \text{ gross} \; 10 \text{ doz.} \\ \hline \end{array}$$

4.
$$\begin{array}{r} 12 \text{ lb.} \; 11 \text{ oz.} \\ 8 \text{ lb.} \quad 9 \text{ oz.} \\ +15 \text{ lb.} \; 14 \text{ oz.} \\ \hline \end{array}$$

5.
$$\begin{array}{r} 8 \text{ gal.} \; 3 \text{ qt.} \\ 6 \text{ gal.} \; 2 \text{ qt.} \\ +12 \text{ gal.} \; 3 \text{ qt.} \\ \hline \end{array}$$

6.
$$\begin{array}{r} 5 \text{ yd.} \; 2 \text{ ft.} \quad 8 \text{ in.} \\ 13 \text{ yd.} \; 2 \text{ ft.} \; 10 \text{ in.} \\ +10 \text{ yd.} \; 1 \text{ ft.} \quad 9 \text{ in.} \\ \hline \end{array}$$

7. 12 gal. 2 qt. 1 pt.
    8 gal. 2 qt. 1 pt.
  + 9 gal. 19 qt. 1 pt.

8.   9 gross 11 doz. 10 units
  11 gross 7 doz. 11 units
  + 6 gross 10 doz. 8 units

9. 18 gal. 3 qt.
   7 gal. 3 qt.
  +15 gal. 2 qt.

10. 4 yd. 2 ft. 11 in.
  7 yd.   9 in.
  + 5 yd. 1 ft.

Subtract, then check your answers.

11.   9 ft. 11 in.
  − 5 ft. 6 in.

12. 13 yd. 1 ft.
  − 5 yd. 2 ft.

13. 15 gross 9 doz.
  − 8 gross 11 doz.

14. 12 gal. 3 qt. 1 pt.
  − 8 gal. 3 qt. 1 pt.

15. 15 yd. 2 ft. 10 in.
  − 6 yd. 2 ft. 11 in.

16. 14 lb.
  − 7 lb. 14 oz.

17. 8 gross 5 doz. 9 units
  − 5 gross 8 doz. 11 units

18. 9 yd. 2 ft. 6 in.
  − 5 yd. 2 ft. 9 in.

19. 8 gross   9 units
  − 3 gross 5 doz. 10 units

20. 15 yd.   8 in.
  − 8 yd. 2 ft. 9 in.

Word Problems

Exercise B Solve the following problems:

21. From a 50-pound bag of rice, a grocer sold the following weights: 6 pounds 10 ounces, 4 pounds 11 ounces, and 8 pounds 14 ounces. How many pounds of rice are left in the sack?

22. A bolt of fabric had 38 yards 23 inches. If a salesperson sold three lengths of fabric measuring 5 yards 19 inches, 8 yards 15 inches, and 4 yards 31 inches, how much material was left on the bolt?

23. Ribbon sells for $2.75 per foot. What is the total cost of the following lengths of ribbon: 2 yards 1 foot, 3 yards 18 inches, 4 yards 30 inches?

24. A stationery store sold the following orders of ball-point pens: 4 gross 8 dozen, 6 gross 4 dozen, and 8 gross 6 dozen. If the pens sell for $7.50 per gross, what was the total amount for the three sales?

25. Pedro bought the following weights of cold cuts: 1 pound 10 ounces of ham, 1 pound 6 ounces of salami, and 1 pound 9 ounces of roast beef. What was the total weight of all the cold cuts?

UNIT **2** Multiplication and Division of Mixed Units of Measure

At times, you will have to multiply or divide mixed units. For example, if a manufacturer needs 2 yards 6 inches of material to make one dress, how many yards and inches will he need to make a dozen dresses? In this case, you would be dealing with a mixed unit number (2 yd. 6 in.) and a whole number (12 dresses).

Multiplying a Mixed Unit Number by a Whole Number

PROCEDURE: To multiply a mixed unit number by a whole number:

1. Multiply each unit by the whole number multiplier (as if there were two separate problems).
2. Simplify.
3. Label and check your final answer.

Example 1 The manufacturer of the dresses in the problem discussed above would have to multiply 2 yd. 6 in. by 12. He would do this as follows:

STEP 1.
$$\begin{array}{r} 2 \text{ yd.} \quad 6 \text{ in.} \\ \times \qquad 12 \\ \hline 24 \text{ yd. } 72 \text{ in.} \end{array}$$

Multiply each unit by the whole number multiplier.

STEP 2.
$$\begin{array}{r} 2 \leftarrow \text{yards} \\ 36\overline{)72} \\ \underline{72} \end{array}$$

Change the 72 inches to yards by dividing 72 by 36 (the number of inches in a yard).

STEP 3.
$$\begin{array}{r} 24 \text{ yd.} \\ + \ 2 \text{ yd.} \\ \hline 26 \text{ yd.} \end{array}$$

Alternative Solution:

Set up a proportion:

$$\frac{1 \text{ (yd.)}}{36 \text{ (in.)}} = \frac{x \text{ (yd.)}}{72 \text{ (in.)}} \quad \left| \quad \frac{1}{36} = \frac{x}{72} \right.$$

$$\frac{36x}{36} = \frac{72}{36}$$

$$x = 2 \text{ yd.}$$

Then complete the problem, labeling and checking your answer.

Answer: To make 12 dresses, the manufacturer will need 26 yd. of fabric.

Example 2   Multiply 4 lb. 9 oz. × 4.

STEP 1.   4 lb.   9 oz.
            ×   4
          16 lb. 36 oz.

Multiply each unit by the whole number multiplier.

STEP 2.   2 ← pounds
            16)36
               32
                4 ← ounces

Change the 36 ounces to pounds and ounces by dividing 36 by 16 (the number of ounces in 1 pound). NOTE: The whole number part of the quotient is the number of pounds, while the remainder is the number of ounces.

STEP 3.   16 lb.
         + 2 lb. 4 oz.
          18 lb. 4 oz.

Then complete the problem, labeling and checking your answer.

Answer: 4 lb. 9 oz. × 4 = 18 lb. 4 oz.

Dividing a Mixed Unit Number by a Whole Number

PROCEDURE: To divide a mixed unit number by a whole number:

1. Divide the whole number into the largest unit of measure, and place your answer in the quotient above the corresponding units of the dividend.
2. Convert the remainder and add it to the like unit of measure in the dividend.
3. Continue this process for each unit of measure in the dividend.
4. Check your division and label your answer.

Example 3   Divide 12 ft. 5 in. by 5.

STEP 1.   2
            5)12 ft. 5. in.
               10
                2 ft. ← Remainder

Divide the 5 into 12 feet, placing the whole number of the quotient (2) in the appropriate answer space.

STEP 2.

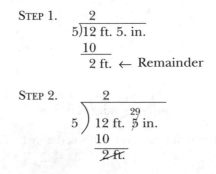

Convert the remainder (2 feet) to inches by multiplying by 12, and add the product (24) to the 5 inches of the dividend (24 + 5 = 29).

STEP 3.

$$2 \quad\quad 5\frac{4}{5}$$

$$5\overline{)\begin{array}{cc} 12\text{ ft.} & \overset{29}{\cancel{5}}\text{ in.} \\ \underline{10} & \underline{25} \\ \cancel{2\text{ ft.}} & 4 \end{array}}$$

Divide 5 into 29 inches, getting a quotient of $5\frac{4}{5}$ inches.

STEP 4. 2 ft. $5\frac{4}{5}$ in.   *Answer*

Label the answer and check the solution.

Changing Mixed Units to Mixed Fractions

In solving certain problems with mixed units, it may be easier to *change the mixed units to mixed fractions of the larger units.*

PROCEDURE: To solve problems with mixed units:

1. Change the mixed units to mixed fractions of the larger units.
2. Then, as the problem requires, either add, subtract, multiply, or divide the mixed fractions, and label your answer.

Example 4   Add: 8 ft. 6 in. + 5 ft. 3 in.

STEP 1. 8 ft. 6 in. $= 8\frac{1}{2}$ ft. $\left(6\text{ in.} = \frac{6}{12} = \frac{1}{2}\right)$

5 ft. 3 in. $= 5\frac{1}{4}$ ft. $\left(3\text{ in.} = \frac{3}{12} = \frac{1}{4}\right)$

Change the mixed units to mixed fractions of the larger unit.

STEP 2.   (a) $8\frac{1}{2}$ ft. $= 8\frac{2}{4}$ ft.

$$\underline{+5\frac{1}{4}\text{ ft.} = 5\frac{1}{4}\text{ ft.}}$$

$$13\frac{3}{4}\text{ ft.}$$

Add the mixed fractions and label your answer.

OR

(b) $\begin{array}{r} 8.50 \\ + 5.25 \\ \hline 13.75 \end{array} = 13\frac{3}{4}$ ft.

$13\frac{3}{4}$ ft., or 13 ft. 9 in.   *Answer*

Example 5   Subtract: 15 yd. 2 ft. − 4 yd. 1 ft.

STEP 1.   15 yd. 2 ft. = $15\frac{2}{3}$ yd.   Change the mixed units to mixed fractions of the larger unit.

4 yd. 1 ft. = $4\frac{1}{3}$ yd.

STEP 2. $15\frac{2}{3}$ Subtract the mixed fractions and label your answer

$-\ 4\frac{1}{3}$

$\overline{11\frac{1}{3}}$ yd.

$11\frac{1}{3}$ yd., or 11 yd. 1 ft. *Answer*

Example 6   Multiply: 6 lb. 4 oz. × 8.

STEP 1.   6 lb. 4 oz. = $6\frac{1}{4}$ lb.   Change the mixed unit to a mixed fraction of the larger unit.

STEP 2.   (a) $6\frac{1}{4} \times 8 = \dfrac{25}{\underset{1}{\cancel{4}}} \times \dfrac{\overset{2}{\cancel{8}}}{1} = 50$ lb.   Carry out the multiplication and label your answer.

OR

(b) $\begin{array}{r} 6.25 \\ \times\ \ \ \ 8 \\ \hline 50.00 \text{ lb.} \end{array}$

50 lb.   *Answer*

Example 7   Divide 15 doz. 9 units by 3.

STEP 1.   15 doz. 9 units = $15\frac{3}{4}$ doz.   Change the mixed unit to a mixed fraction of the larger unit.

STEP 2.   (a) $15\frac{3}{4} \div 3 = \dfrac{\overset{21}{\cancel{63}}}{4} \times \dfrac{1}{\underset{1}{\cancel{3}}} = \dfrac{21}{4}$ $\begin{array}{r} 5\frac{1}{4} \\ 4\overline{)21} \\ \underline{20} \\ 1 \end{array}$ Carry out the division and label your answer.

OR

(b) $\begin{array}{r} 5.25 \\ 3\overline{)15.75} \\ \underline{15}\ \ \ \ \\ 7\ \ \\ \underline{6}\ \ \\ 15 \\ \underline{15} \end{array}$

$5\frac{1}{4}$ doz., or 5 doz. 3 units   *Answer*

Multiplying Two Mixed Unit Numbers

Area is a measure of surface within given linear measurements. For instance, a room that is 10 ft. wide by 15 ft. long has a floor surface of 150 sq. ft. Area measures are always in *square units*. You multiply *10 ft. × 15 ft.*, but your answer is *150 sq. ft.*

Note how *linear* measures change to *square* measures:

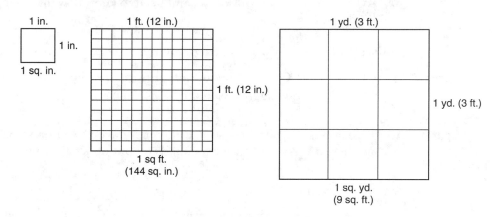

1 in. / 1 in. / 1 sq. in.

1 ft. (12 in.) / 1 ft. (12 in.) / 1 sq ft. (144 sq. in.)

1 yd. (3 ft.) / 1 yd. (3 ft.) / 1 sq. yd. (9 sq. ft.)

To find the area of a square or rectangle, use this formula:

$$A = L \times W$$
Area = Length × Width

The answer will always be in *square units* (square inch, square foot, square yard, etc.).

PROCEDURE: To multiply two mixed unit numbers:

1. Convert both measures to the same units.
2. Multiply the mixed unit numbers.
3. Label in square measure, and check your answer.

Example 8 Find the area of a warehouse measuring 60 ft. by 80 yd.

STEP 1.   80 yd. – 240 ft.   Convert the measures to the same units.

STEP 2.   60 × 240 = 14,400   Multiply the two measures.

STEP 3.   14,400 sq. ft.   *Answer*   Label your answer and check your arithmetic.

HINT: You could also have changed 60 ft. to 20 yd. Doing the problem a second time with different units is a good way to check your work.

Check: 20 yd. × 80 yd. = 1,600 sq. yd.

1,600 × 9 = 14,400 sq. ft. √   There are 9 square feet in a square yard.

Dividing Two Mixed Unit Numbers

You will commonly have to divide one mixed unit number by another in two types of problems:

1. When you are given an area and the length of one side, and must find the other side.
2. When you are given a distance, and need to know how many lengths will go into it.

PROCEDURE: To divide two mixed unit numbers:

    1. Convert the units of measure to a like unit.
    2. Then divide, and label your answer.

Example 9   You have access to a 30,000-sq.-ft. warehouse, but you need only 16,000 sq. ft. If the building is 250 ft. wide, where should you put up a partition?

STEP 1.   Sketch the problem.

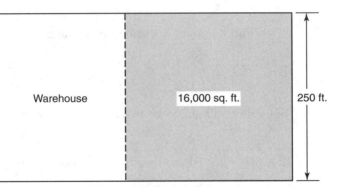

STEP 2.   Length × Width = Area   Carry out the division and label your answer.

$$\text{Length} = \frac{\text{Area}}{\text{Width}}$$

$$= \frac{\overset{64}{\cancel{16,000}} \text{ sq. ft.}}{\cancel{250} \text{ ft.}}$$

$$= 64 \text{ ft.}$$

To create a space that measures 16,000 sq. ft., you would put up a partition 64 ft. from one end.   *Answer*

Exercises

Exercise A   Multiply and simplify.

1. 3 ft. 9 in.
    × 5

2. 6 lb. 11 oz.
    × 7

3. 4 yd. 2 ft. 7 in.
    × 8

4. 5 gross 6 doz. 8 units
    × 4

5. 6 gal. 3 qt. 1 pt.
    × 8

6. 7 yd. 1 ft. 10 in.
    × 6

7. 8 lb. 15 oz.
    × 6

8. 9 gross 7 doz. 8 units
    × 5

9. 2 yd. 8 in.
    × 12

10. 5 gross 11 doz.
    × 15

Divide and simplify. Round off each answer to the nearest whole smaller unit.

11. 5)9 ft. 10 in.

12. 4)7 yd. 2 ft.

13. 4)12 lb. 8 oz.

14. 8)23 gross 10 doz.

15. 12)30 gal. 3 qt.

16. 15)22 yd. 2 ft.

17. 7)14 lb. 15 oz.

18. 8)30 ft. 11 in.

19. 6)15 gross 11 doz. 8 units

20. 8)19 yd. 2 ft. 6 in.

Word Problems

Exercise B   Solve the following problems:

21. A box holds 3 gross 7 dozen 8 units of memo pads.

    (a) How many memo pads will six boxes hold?
    (b) If the memo pads cost 60¢ per dozen, what is the cost of six boxes of memo pads?

22. A manufacturer uses 3 yards 2 feet 6 inches of material to make a dress. How much material is needed to manufacture a dozen dresses?

23. A typewriter packed for shipping weighs 13 pounds 14 ounces.

    (a) What is the total weight of six typewriters?
    (b) If the cost of shipping each typewriter is $9.95, what is the total cost of the shipment?

24. A candy mix weighing 8 pounds 12 ounces is packaged into six boxes. To the nearest ounce, what will be the weight of each box?

25. A drum of liquid adhesive containing 20 gallons 3 quarts is to be poured into eight containers. How much would each container hold? (Round to the nearest quart.)

UNIT **3** The Metric System

The units of measure commonly used in the United States—miles, yards, feet, inches, acres, gallons, pints, pounds, ounces—are part of the **English system** of measures. The English system is generally used in countries with historical ties to Great Britain. All other countries use the **metric system,** which is named after the basic unit of length, the meter.

How the Metric System Works

The metric system is based on the decimal system; that is, all its standard units increase or decrease by powers of 10. Therefore, converting from one unit to another is much simpler in the metric system.

The metric system consists of three basic units:

1. The basic unit of *length* is the **meter** (a little longer than a yard).
2. The basic unit of *liquid measure* is the **liter** (slightly larger than a quart).
3. The basic unit of *weight* is the **gram** (500 grams is about 1 pound).

These basic units combine with six Greek or Latin prefixes to form all the units in the metric system. The following three prefixes show how the standard units *increase* in powers of 10 to form *larger* units:

• **Deca**—means *ten* (10), and **decameter** means 10 meters.

• **Hecto**—means *hundred* (100), and **hectoliter** means 100 liters.

• **Kilo**—means *thousand* (1,000), and **kilogram** means 1,000 grams.

Similarly, the following prefixes show how the standard units *decrease* in powers of 10 to form *smaller* units:

• **Deci**—means *tenth* $\left(\dfrac{1}{10}\right)$, and **decimeter** means 0.1 $\left(\dfrac{1}{10}\right)$ meter.

• **Centi**—means *hundredth* $\left(\dfrac{1}{100}\right)$, and **centiliter** means 0.01 $\left(\dfrac{1}{100}\right)$ liter.

• **Milli**—means *thousandth* $\left(\dfrac{1}{1,000}\right)$, and **milligram** means 0.001 $\left(\dfrac{1}{1,000}\right)$ gram.

TABLE 2 Metric Units of Measure

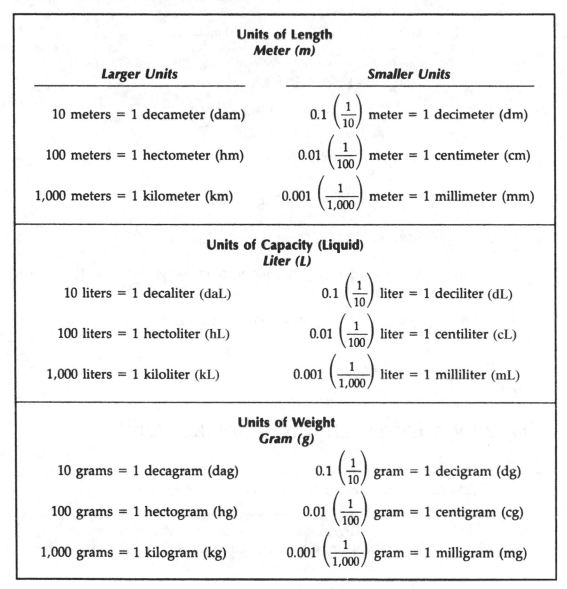

Changing a Smaller Unit to a Larger Unit

PROCEDURE: To change a smaller unit of measure to a larger unit:

1. Determine how many smaller units are contained in each larger unit.
2. *Divide* the given number of smaller units by this number.
3. Label your answer.

Example 1   Change 15,500 meters to kilometers.

STEP 1.   From Table 2, 1 kilometer = 1,000 meters.

STEP 2.   Divide the given number of meters by 1,000 by moving the decimal point three places *to the left*.

$$15,500 \div 1,000 = 15.500 = 15.5$$

STEP 3.   15,500 m = 15.5 km   *Answer*

Example 2   How many grams are there in 425 centigrams?

STEP 1.   From Table 2, 1 gram = 100 centigrams.

STEP 2.   Divide the given number of centigrams by 100 by moving the decimal point two places to the left.

$$425 \div 100 = 4.25 = 4.25$$

STEP 3.   425 cg = 4.25 g   *Answer*

Changing a Larger Unit to a Smaller Unit

PROCEDURE: To change a larger unit to a smaller unit:

1. Determine how many smaller units are contained in each larger unit.
2. *Multiply* the given number of larger units by this number.
3. Label your answer.

Example 3   Change 5 meters to centimeters.

STEP 1.   From Table 2, 1 centimeter = 0.01 meter. Multiplying by 100 gives 1 meter = 100 centimeters.

STEP 2.   Multiply the given number of meters by 100 by moving the decimal point two places *to the right*.

$$5 \times 100 = 500$$

STEP 3.   5 m = 500 cm   *Answer*

Example 4 Change 0.015 kilogram to milligrams.

STEP 1. From Table 2, 1 kilogram = 1,000 grams. Since 1 milligram = 0.001 gram, multiplying by 1,000,000 gives 1 kilogram = 1,000,000 milligrams.

STEP 2. Multiply the given number of kilograms by 1,000,000 by moving the decimal point six places to the right.

$$0.015 \times 1,000,000 = 0.015000 = 15,000$$

STEP 3. 0.015 kg = 15,000 mg   *Answer*

The metric system uses many specialized units of measure, and prefixes for nearly all powers of 10. However, you will get along very well with the metric system if you know *the three basic measures (liter, meter, and gram) and the three most common prefixes (milli-, centi-, and kilo-).*

Remember: When changing from a *smaller unit* to a *larger unit,* you will end up with *fewer units.* Therefore, use division.

When changing from a *larger unit* to a *smaller unit,* you will end up with *more* units. Therefore, use multiplication.

Exercises

Exercise A By moving the decimal point, you should be able to perform most of the multiplications and divisions without written calculations. Change:

1. 240 cm to meters
2. 2,750 m to kilometers
3. 0.53 m to millimeters
4. 15.7 km to meters
5. 573 mL to liters
6. 4,637 m to kilometers
7. 4.15 cL to liters
8. 0.45 L to milliliters
9. 53 cg to milligrams
10. 675 g to kilograms
11. 4,375 mm to meters
12. 3,325 kg to grams
13. 0.6 g to milligrams
14. 6.8 mL to centiliters
15. 0.08 km to meters
16. 23 cL to liters
17. $23 \frac{1}{2}$ g to centigrams
18. 235 mg to centigrams
19. $5 \frac{1}{4}$ L to centiliters
20. 250 mm to meters
21. 235 L to centiliters
22. 0.25 cm to millimeters
23. 432 cg to kilograms
24. $\frac{1}{8}$ kg to centigrams
25. 0.05 kL to mililiters
26. 243 cm to meters
27. 0.4 km to meters
28. 535 mg to kilograms
29. 635 cm to millimeters
30. 45 mm to centimeters

Word Problems

Exercise B   Solve the following problems:

31. A vial holds 55 milliliters. How many liters will 48 vials contain?

32. A certain cut of meat costs $5.75 per kg. How much will 13,500 cg cost?

33. How many 50-mL vials can be filled with $2 \frac{1}{2}$ liters of liquid?

34. A coaxial cable sells at 25 cm for 35¢. How much will 15 meters cost?

35. A piece of tubing measures 1.5 m. How many pieces of 50-cm length can be cut?

UNIT **4** Metric-English Conversions

The United States has taken steps to change to the metric system. You may have noticed that almost all food products are now using the metric system as well as the English system in stating the weight, measure, or capacity on the packages. This is also true of machinery, equipment, tools, and the sizes of nuts and bolts. Scientists uniformly use the metric system.

Since the metric system is being used more and more frequently in business and industry, it is becoming increasingly necessary to change from the metric system to the English system and vice versa.

PROCEDURE: To convert measurements from one system to another, multiply the original measurement by the equivalent measure of the new system:

1. To convert from the English system, multiply the English measurement by the metric equivalent from Table 3.
2. To convert from the metric system, multiply the metric measurement by the English equivalent from Table 4.

TABLE 3   English to Metric

Metric Equivalents of English Measures
1 in. = 25.4 mm = 2.54 cm
1 ft. = 0.30 m
1 yd. = 0.91 m
1 mi. = 1.61 km
1 qt. (liquid) = 0.95 L
1 qt. (dry) = 1.1 L
1 oz. = 28.35 g
1 lb. = 0.45 kg
1 s.t. = 0.91 metric ton

TABLE 4   Metric to English

English Equivalents of Metric Measures
1 m = 39.37 in. = 3.28 ft. = 1.09 yd.
1 cm = 0.39 in.
1 mm = 0.039 in.
1 km = 0.62 mi.
1 L = 1.06 qt. (liquid)
1 L = 0.91 qt. (dry)
1 g = 0.04 oz.
1 kg = 2.2 lb.
1 l.t. = 2,240 lb.

Example 1 How many yards are there in 130 meters (to the nearest yard)?

STEP 1. From Table 4, 1 meter = 1.09 yards.

STEP 2.
$$
\begin{array}{r}
130 \\
\times\ 1.09 \\
\hline
11\ 70 \\
130\ 0 \\
\hline
141.70 = 142 \text{ yd.} \quad \textit{Answer}
\end{array}
$$

Proportion Method

$$\frac{1 \text{ (in.)}}{1.09 \text{ (yd.)}} = 1\frac{30 \text{ (in.)}}{x \text{ (yd.)}}$$

$$\frac{1}{1.09} = \frac{130}{x}$$

$$x = 141.70 = 142 \text{ yd.}$$

Example 2 How many meters are there in 14 yards (to the nearest meter)?

STEP 1. From Table 3, 1 yard = 0.91 meter.

STEP 2.
$$
\begin{array}{r}
0.91 \\
\times\ 14 \\
\hline
3\ 64 \\
9\ 1 \\
\hline
12.74 = 13 \text{ m} \quad \textit{Answer}
\end{array}
$$

Proportion Method

$$\frac{1 \text{ (yd.)}}{0.9 \text{ (in.)}} = \frac{14 \text{ (yd.)}}{x}$$

$$x = 12.74 = 13 \text{ m.}$$

Example 3 Change 30 gallons to liters.

STEP 1. Since there are 4 quarts in 1 gallon, 30 gallons = 30 × 4 = 120 quarts.

STEP 2. From Table 3, 1 quart = 0.95 liter.

STEP 3.
$$
\begin{array}{r}
120 \\
\times\ 0.95 \\
\hline
6\ 00 \\
108\ 0 \\
\hline
114.00 = 114 \text{ L} \quad \textit{Answer}
\end{array}
$$

Proportion Method

$$\frac{1 \text{ (qt.)}}{0.95 \text{ (L)}} = \frac{120 \text{ qt.}}{x \text{ (L)}}$$

$$\frac{1}{0.95} = \frac{120}{x}$$

$$x = 114 \text{ L}$$

Example 4 Change 2.3 kilograms to ounces.

STEP 1. As there are 1,000 g in 1 kg, 2.3 kg = 2,300 g.

STEP 2. 2,300 g = 2,300 × 0.04 oz. = 92 oz. *Answer*

Proportion Method

$$\frac{1 \text{ (g.)}}{0.04 \text{(oz.)}} = \frac{2,300}{x}$$

$$x = 92 \text{ oz.}$$

Exercises

Exercise A Convert as indicated, rounding each answer to the nearest whole number.

1. 20 m to feet
2. 10 m to yards
3. 130 km to miles
4. 125 L to quarts
5. 42 oz. to grams
6. 25 in. to meters
7. 115 km to miles
8. 43 lb. to kilograms
9. 15 dry qt. to liters
10. 86 in. to meters
11. $3\frac{1}{2}$ kg to pounds
12. $\frac{3}{4}$ m to inches
13. 2,300 lb. to metric tons
14. 18.3 km to miles
15. $3\frac{1}{4}$ in. to millimeters
16. 2,500 g to pounds
17. 2.3 ft. to decimeters
18. 435 cm to inches
19. 86 oz. to kilograms
20. $\frac{3}{4}$ mile to meters

21. 32.8 cm to inches (nearest *tenth*)
22. 18.3 in. to centimeters (nearest *tenth*)
23. $\frac{3}{4}$ kg to pounds (nearest *hundredth*)
24. 0.21 metric ton to pounds (nearest *tenth*)

Word Problems

Exercise B Solve the following problems:

25. What is the width in inches of 35-mm film? (nearest *hundredth*)
26. A can of coffee weighs 850 grams. How many ounces does it weigh? (nearest *tenth*)
27. How many liters are there in 5 quarts of milk? (nearest *tenth*)
28. A box is $3\frac{1}{4}$ meters high. How high is the box in feet? (nearest *tenth*)
29. A room measures 3.6 m by 6.5 m. What are the room measurements in feet? (nearest *tenth*)

UNIT **5** Review of Chapter Eight

TERMS:
- Mixed units
- Distance—linear measures
- Area—square measures
- Meter, liter, gram
- Deka- (10), hecto- (100), kilo- (1,000)
- Deci $\left(\dfrac{1}{10}\right)$, centi- $\left(\dfrac{1}{100}\right)$, milli- $\left(\dfrac{1}{1,000}\right)$

HINTS:
- When changing *smaller* units to *larger* units, *divide.*
- When changing *larger* units to *smaller* units, *multiply.*
- When possible, change mixed units to mixed fractions of the larger unit.

Add or subtract as indicated and simplify your answer.

1.　4 yd. 2 ft. 11 in.
　12 yd. 1 ft. 　9 in.
　+13 yd. 2 ft. 10 in.

2.　8 gross 　9 doz. 　8 units
　9 gross 10 doz. 10 units
　+11 gross 　8 doz. 　9 units

3.　14 gross 6 doz. 　8 units
　− 4 gross 9 doz. 10 units

4.　12 yd. 　　　7 in.
　− 5 yd. 2 ft. 10 in.

Multiply or divide as indicated. Simplify and round to the nearest whole smaller unit.

5.　8 gal. 2 qt. 1 pt.
　×　　　13

6.　12 lb. 14 oz.
　×　　16

7.　14)‾34‾gross 9 doz. 6 units

8.　12)‾15‾yd. 2 ft. 8 in.

Change the following metric units without using written calculations:

9.　0.8 g to mg

10.　235 mg to cg

11.　$8\frac{1}{4}$ L to cL

12.　3,422 m to km

13.　0.73 km to m

14.　53 m to cm

15.　115 cL to mL

16.　$\frac{3}{4}$ kg to cg

Change the following units and round each answer to the nearest whole unit:

17. 53 oz. to g

18. $15 \frac{1}{2}$ in. to cm

19. 42.7 km to mil.

20. $12 \frac{3}{4}$ mil. to m

21. $1 \frac{1}{8}$ in. to mm

22. 43.5 cm to in.

Solve these area problems:

23. An office measures 12 ft. 6 in. by 16 ft. 9 in. How many square yards of carpeting are needed to cover the floor?

24. A large office is to be subdivided into four equal work stations. If the office measures $9 \frac{1}{2}$ meters by $14 \frac{1}{4}$ meters, what will be the area of each work station?

PART II

MATHEMATICS OF PERSONAL FINANCE

CHAPTER NINE

Banking and Investments

UNIT 1   Savings Accounts

The safest and most convenient way of saving money is to open a savings account at a bank or through a credit union. Money deposited will then earn interest for its owner, and the account is protected by a United States government agency.

Banks pay interest for the use of this money, which they invest in government bonds, mortgages, and business and personal loans. These investments then make money for the bank.

There are two major types of savings accounts: withdrawal accounts and time deposits. The traditional savings account is a **withdrawal account,** that is, you can withdraw your money on demand. Banks prefer time deposits, however, and will pay a higher rate of interest for such savings. With a **time deposit account** you cannot withdraw the money for a stated period of time unless a penalty is paid for early withdrawal.

Types of Savings Accounts

The most common type of savings account is the *day-of-deposit-to-day-of-withdrawal account,* with a current interest rate of more than 5%. Money may be deposited and withdrawn from this account without any restrictions, and the account will be active so long as there is a balance.

With a *6-month certificate of deposit* (CD), the depositor agrees to leave his or her deposit with the bank for 6 months. Many banks also require a large minimum deposit. Under federal law, if a depositor breaks the agreement and withdraws the money before the 6-month period expires, a substantial financial penalty will be imposed. Earned interest may be withdrawn at any time or left in the account until the 6-month period is over. At this point the certificate is said to **mature,** and the principal and interest can be withdrawn without penalty.

Other certificates have the same general features, varying in the length of time and the rate of interest. Typically, the higher interest rates come with CDs of longer duration.

Calculating Interest

Note to users of this text: In the preceding chapters we have used several methods of solving business problems. It has been our experience that individual students show preferences for different methods that can be used for solving such problems. Some students like the basic percent formula; others, the $\frac{IS}{OF}$ formula; and still others, the proportion method. With this in mind, we will continue to use the three methods, where applicable, so that you can make your own choice as to which method is best for you.

Two types of interest are commonly used in banking: simple interest and compound interest.

Simple interest is calculated on the **principal** (the money deposited) at a given rate, over a period of time (typically, by the year). To compute simple interest, multiply the *principal* by the *interest rate* by the *time*. This can be written as the formula:

$$I = P \times R \times T$$
$$\text{Interest} = \text{Principal} \times \text{Rate} \times \text{Time}$$

Note: Because the interest percent is an *annual rate,* the period of time must be years or fractional parts of a year, such as months or days.

With compound interest, your money starts earning interest on the day of deposit, and when the interest earned is added to your account, the subsequent interest calculation includes the interest on your original deposit *plus* the interest credited previously. With compound interest, your principal grows more rapidly than with simple interest at the same rate. With simple interest, the principal is the same until the end of the period.

For example, $1,000 savings account will grow as shown, based upon a 5.5% interest rate:

COMPOUND INTEREST				SIMPLE INTEREST		
Principal	Today's (Day 1) Interest			Principal	Cumulative Interest	Today's (Day 1) Interest
$1,000	$0.15	Day	1	$1,000		$0.15
1,004.53	0.15	Day	30	1,000	$ 4.37	0.15
1,013.65	0.15	Day	90	1,000	13.41	0.15
1,056.54	0.16	Day	365	1,000	54.85	0.15
$1,056.54				Total principal and interest		$1,055
5.654%				Effective annual yield		5.5%

Note: **Effective annual yield** means that the annual interest rate compounded daily is equal to a higher simple interest rate. In this example, a 5.5% rate of interest compounded daily is equal to (has an effective annual yield of) 5.654%. Note also that, if you were to withdraw your interest from a compound interest account, your effective annual yield would be the same as under simple interest.

The calculating of exact compound interest is a long process and somewhat complicated. For our purposes, therefore, we will be dealing with *simple interest only*, which does not include the daily increases of principal.

PROCEDURE: To compute simple interest:

1. Multiply the *principal* (the money on deposit) by the *rate* (the interest paid by the bank) by the *time* (the length of time the deposit remains in the bank).
2. To find the new balance: add the interest earned to the principal.

Example 1   Pedro opens a day-of-deposit savings account with $750. If the interest rate is 5.5%, how much will he have in the bank at the end of a year?

STEP 1. $I = P \times R \times T$ Write the formula.

STEP 2. $I = \$750 \times 5.5\% \times 1$ year   Substitute known values.

STEP 3. $I = \dfrac{\overset{7.50}{\cancel{750}}}{1} \times \dfrac{5.5}{\underset{1}{\cancel{100}}} \times \dfrac{1}{1}$ Solve for I.

$= 7.50 \times 5.5$

$- 7 \boxed{.} 50 \boxed{\times} 5 \boxed{.} 5 \boxed{=} 41.25$

$= 41.25$

$= \$41.25$

STEP 4.   New balance $= P + I$ Calculate the new balance.

$= \$750 + \$41.25$

$= \$791.25$ *Answer*

Check: $\dfrac{\cancel{05.5\%}}{\cancel{100\%}} = \dfrac{x}{\$750}$

$x = .055 \times 750$
$= 41.25$
$= \$41.25$

Note: When calculating interest for 1 year, you may alter the formula to $I = P \times R$, because multiplying a number by 1 does not change the value of the number.

Example 2   Beth deposited $900 into a savings account. After 90 days she withdrew the money to pay some bills. If the interest rate was 4.5%, how much money did she have after the 90 days?

STEP 1. $I = P \times R \times T$ Write the formula.

STEP 2. $I = \$900 \times 4.5\% \times 90$ days   Substitute the values.

STEP 3. $\quad I = \dfrac{\overset{9}{\cancel{900}}}{1} \times \dfrac{4.5}{\underset{1}{\cancel{100}}} \times \dfrac{\overset{1}{\cancel{90}}}{\underset{4}{\cancel{360}}}$ $\qquad$ Solve for I.

$\qquad = \dfrac{\cancel{40.5}}{4} \qquad = 10.125 = 10.13$ $\qquad$ Calculate the new balance.

$\qquad = 40\,\boxed{.}\,5\ \boxed{\div}\ 4\ \boxed{=}\ 10.12\,\underline{|5}$
$\qquad\qquad = \$10.13$

STEP 4. $\quad$ New balance $= \quad P \ \ + I$
$\qquad\qquad\qquad\quad = \ \$900 \ + \$10.13$
$\qquad\qquad\qquad\quad = \$910.13 \quad Answer$

$\qquad$ *Check:* $\quad \dfrac{4.5\%}{100\%} = \dfrac{x}{\$900}$

$\qquad\qquad\qquad \dfrac{\cancel{.}04.5}{\cancel{100}} = \dfrac{x}{900}$

$\qquad\qquad\quad x \quad = \ 0.045 \times 900$

$\qquad\qquad\quad x \quad = \ \dfrac{40.50}{4}$

$\qquad\qquad\qquad\quad = \ 10.12\,\underline{|5}$
$\qquad\qquad\qquad\quad = \ \$10.13 \text{ for } 90 \text{ days}$

Note: A business year is considered to consist of 360 days, or 12 months of 30 days each month.

Example 3 $\quad$ Carmen has \$1,100 in a savings account. If she earned \$74.25 interest in a year, what interest rate was paid by the bank?

Method 1: Equation Method

$\qquad$ The basic formula is:

Principal	$\times$	Rate	$=$	Interest
P	$\times$	R (unknown)	$=$	I

$\qquad \$1{,}100u = \$74.25$
$\qquad 1{,}100u = \quad 74.25$

$\qquad \dfrac{\cancel{1{,}100}u}{\cancel{1{,}100}} = \dfrac{74.25}{1{,}100}$

$\qquad\qquad u = \dfrac{74.25}{1{,}100}$

$\qquad\qquad = 74\,\boxed{.}\,25\ \boxed{\div}\ 1100\ \boxed{=}\ 0.0675$
$\qquad\qquad\qquad = \ 6.75\% \quad Answer$

Check:

$\dfrac{x(\%)}{100(\%)} = \dfrac{74.25}{1{,}100}$

$\dfrac{x}{100} = \dfrac{74.25}{1{,}100}$

$\dfrac{\cancel{1{,}100}x}{\cancel{1{,}100}} = \dfrac{7425}{1{,}100}$

$x = 6.75 = 6.75\%$

Method 2: $\dfrac{\text{IS}}{\text{OF}}$ Method

The problem can be rephrased as " $74.25 is what percent of $1,100 ?"

$$\frac{\text{IS}}{\text{OF}} = \frac{\$74.25}{\$1,100} = 0.0675 = 6.75\% \qquad \textit{Answer}$$

Example 4   Mr. Logan deposits $20,000 in a 6-month certificate of deposit that pays an annual interest rate of 13.871% with an effective annual yield of 14.561%.

(a) How much interest will he earn for the 6 months if he withdraws his interest every month?

Since Mr. Logan is withdrawing the interest every month, you will use the base interest rate of 13.871%.

STEP 1. $I = \quad P \quad \times \quad R \quad \times \quad T$ Write the formula.

STEP 2. $I = \$20,000 \times 13.871\% \times 6 \text{ months}$ Substitute the values.

STEP 3. $I = \dfrac{\overset{100}{\cancel{20,000}}}{1} \times \dfrac{13.871}{\cancel{100}} \times \dfrac{\overset{1}{\cancel{6}}}{\underset{\underset{1}{\cancel{2}}}{\cancel{12}}} = 1,387.10$ Solve for I.

$= 100 \boxed{\times} 13 \boxed{.} 871 \boxed{=} 1387.1$
$= \$1,387.10$

Answer: Mr. Logan earns $1,387.10 in interest.

(b) How much interest will he earn for the 6 months if he leaves the interest in the bank for the 6-month period?

In this case, Mr. Logan leaves the interest in the bank for the 6-month period. Therefore, you will use the effective annual yield rate of 14.561%.

STEP 1. $I = \quad P \quad \times \quad R \quad \times \quad T$ Write the formula.

STEP 2. $I = \$20,000 \times 14.561\% \times 6 \text{ months}$ Substitute the values.

STEP 3. $I = \dfrac{\overset{100}{\cancel{20,000}}}{1} \times \dfrac{14.561}{\cancel{100}} \times \dfrac{\overset{1}{\cancel{6}}}{\underset{\underset{1}{\cancel{2}}}{\cancel{12}}} = 1,456.10$ Solve for I.

$= 100 \boxed{\times} 14 \boxed{.} 561 \boxed{=} 1456.1$
$= \$1,456.10$

Answer: Mr. Logan earns $1,456.10 in interest.

Exercises

Exercise A   Each of the following accounts had no withdrawals or deposits for the period shown. Find the amount of interest and the new balance for each account.

	Amount	Interest Rate	Period of Time	Amount of Interest		New Balance	
1.	$ 8,400	5.5%	2 years	_____	____	_____	____
2.	6,500	6	3 years	_____	____	_____	____
3.	11,000	$5\frac{1}{2}$	1 year	_____	____	_____	____
4.	7,600	5.75	2 years	_____	____	_____	____
5.	5,800	$5\frac{1}{4}$	2 years	_____	____	_____	____
6.	9,500	5.25	3 years	_____	____	_____	____
7.	10,000	$8\frac{1}{2}$	4 years	_____	____	_____	____
8.	5,575	7.5	3 years	_____	____	_____	____
9.	11,765	$9\frac{1}{4}$	2 years	_____	____	_____	____
10.	14,895	10.25	3 years	_____	____	_____	____

	Amount	Interest Rate	Period of Time	Amount of Interest		New Balance	
11.	$15,000	6%	3 months	_____	____	_____	____
12.	10,500	5.75	90 days	_____	____	_____	____
13.	8,440	$8\frac{1}{4}$	6 months	_____	____	_____	____
14.	13,500	$9\frac{1}{2}$	30 days	_____	____	_____	____
15.	18,750	8.5	8 months	_____	____	_____	____
16.	9,675	$10\frac{3}{4}$	60 days	_____	____	_____	____
17.	14,725	11.75	2 months	_____	____	_____	____
18.	17,435	9.25	45 days	_____	____	_____	____
19.	24,000	$10\frac{1}{4}$	15 days	_____	____	_____	____
20.	19,200	8.25	30 days	_____	____	_____	____

Fill in the blanks in the following table:

	Amount	Interest Rate	Period of Time	Amount of Interest	New Balance	
21.	$5,850	_____	1 year	$ 394.88	_____	___
22.	_____	8.75%	1 year	630.00	_____	___
23.	4,675	_____	1 year	245.44	_____	___
24.	8,350	_____	1 year	780.73	_____	___
25.	_____	11.63	1 year	1,133.93	_____	___
26.	_____	10.55%	1 year	1,107.75	_____	___

Find the interest earned for each of the following accounts, using the appropriate interest rate—the annual rate *or* the effective yield.

	Amount	Certificate of Deposit	Annual Rate	Effective Yield	Interest Withdrawn	Interest Earned	
27.	$12,000	30 months	12%	12.94%	Yes	_____	___
28.	9,500	6 months	9.871	10.561	No	_____	___
29.	4,000	30 months	12.5	13.475	No	_____	___
30.	11,750	6 months	11.523	12.251	Yes	_____	___
31.	14,250	6 months	13.95	14.63	Yes	_____	___
32.	7,500	30 months	12.75	13.721	No	_____	___
33.	8,500	30 months	12.5	13.475	Yes	_____	___
34.	15,500	6 months	13.95	14.63	Yes	_____	___
35.	12,800	6 months	12.125	13.89	No	_____	___
36.	3,700	30 months	12	12.94	Yes	_____	___

Fill in the following table, showing the amount of interest and new balances on a 6-month CD.

	Amount on Deposit		Interest Rate	Amount of Interest		New Balance at End of 6 Months	
37.	$1,465	75	8.752%	_____	___	_____	___
38.	1,786	45	9.75	_____	___	_____	___
39.	2,528	80	8.025	_____	___	_____	___
40.	2,895	75	9.65	_____	___	_____	___
41.	4,521	48	10.035	_____	___	_____	___
42.	4,865	80	11.652	_____	___	_____	___

Word Problems

Exercise B Solve the following problems:

43. Meghan opened a savings account, paying 6% interest, with $5,300. Six months later she deposited another $1,000. If she does not withdraw interest for the entire year, how much money will she have in her account at the end of a year?

44. To help pay for his college education, Frank has a trust fund of $38,000 that pays an annual interest rate of 18.75%. He wants to withdraw his interest only on a monthly basis. How much money can he withdraw each month?

45. Rachel has a savings account of $18,000. If she earned $2,610 in 1 year, what rate of interest did the bank pay her?

46. Yaffa deposited $9,000 into a 30-month certificate of deposit that paid an interest rate of 13.871% with an effective annual yield of 14.561%.

   (a) How much interest will she earn if she withdraws her interest when earned during the 30-month period?
   (b) How much more interest will she earn if she does not withdraw her interest for the 30-month period?

47. Sara put $15,000 into a 6-month certificate of deposit, paying an annual rate of 12.65%, with an effective annual yield of 13.7%. After 6 months, she renewed her certificate of deposit, and the new interest rate was 13.25% annual rate, with an effective annual yield of 14.85%. How much money will Sara have at the end of a year if she does not withdraw any interest?

UNIT **2** Checking Accounts

A **checking account** is a convenient way of paying bills, as you can write a check for an exact amount and then make payments by mail. The canceled check, which usually is eventually returned to you, represents proof of payment.

When you open a checking account, the bank supplies you with deposit slips and checks printed with your name and address.

You can then deposit paychecks and other income into your checking account, and write checks to pay bills. You must make sure that you have sufficient funds to cover all the checks written: if there is not enough money in your account to cover a check, the bank will not transfer money to the payee, but will instead return the check, stamped "Insufficient Funds." The bank will also charge you a penalty for having overdrawn your account.

There is a *service charge* for most checking account services. One basic plan has a monthly service charge of a few dollars per month, plus a charge for each check written. Another plan has a larger monthly service charge, but with no charge for the checks written. Other plans have no charge at all if you maintain a specified minimum balance in either the checking or a savings account.

Because of this diversity, you should shop around for the plan that suits you best, depending on how many checks you write and how much cash you have available.

Making a Deposit

To put money into your checking account, you must make out a deposit slip, listing the money to be deposited.

Let us suppose you are depositing the following items. You would make out a deposit slip, noting that all cash must be added together and put on the deposit slip as a single entry.

> Three $20 bills
> Five $10 bills
> Two $5 bills
> Three $1 bills
> Five quarters
> A paycheck for $92.65
> Checks for $35.85, $63.70, and $25.80

Here is how your deposit slip would look:

Next, you would endorse each check by signing the reverse side.

Finally, you would give the teller the deposit slip, the cash, and the checks. The teller would then credit your account for $342.25 and give you a receipt.

Caution: Depending upon the bank and your credit history, the $218 in checks may not be immediately available to you in cash. Many banks require checks to clear before they will release money against the checks. This usually takes 2 to 3 days for checks drawn on a local bank and up to 2 weeks for checks drawn on an out-of-state bank.

Writing a Check

When paying bills, you will write checks from the checkbook supplied by the bank. For example, to pay the rent for August in the amount of $175, you would write the following check:

```
                                              No. 109

                      August 5    20 ____

Pay to the
order of  Ace Realty Co.                      $ 175.00

One hundred seventy-five and 00/00       Dollars


For  Aug. Rent                    John Klug
```

PROCEDURE: To write and record a check:

Check number: If the check number is not preprinted by the bank, write in the number of the check.

Date: Enter the date in the register and on the check.

Pay to the order of: The check is an authorization by you for your bank to pay another party (in this example, the Ace Realty Co.) the amount written on the check. Fill in the name of the other party on the check and in the register.

For: Record the purpose of the check. Note that in this example "Aug. Rent" was written on the check.

Amount: Write the amount on the check in two places: *as a number,* after the $ sign, and *in written form,* with the cents as a number, on the line below "Pay to the order of." The value of the cents in the amount is always written as a fraction of a dollar: $\frac{00}{100}$ for "no cents," or $\frac{25}{100}$ for $0.25.

Signature: The bank has a record of your signature, so sign the check in exactly the same way.

In the checkbook, the checks are separate from the register.

The register is your record of the transaction in your checking account of checks written and deposits made. To avoid the costly penalty for writing checks not covered by funds in your account, an accurate record must be kept.

The "balance carried forward" from the previous check becomes the "balance brought forward." In this example the balance from the previous check was $109.75.

PROCEDURE: To calculate the balance in your checking account:

Amount deposited: Enter the amount of your last deposit (in this example, $342.25).

Total: Add together the previous balance and the deposit to obtain the total amount available in the account (in this example, $452).

Amount of this check: Enter the amount of the check (in this example, $175).

Balance carried forward: Subtract the amount of the check from the total; the sum left ($277) is the amount remaining in the account. The "balance carried forward" becomes the "balance brought forward."

Balancing a Checkbook

A **bank statement** is sent out once a month. It lists the beginning and ending balances and all deposits for the preceding month. It also lists all checks clearing the bank during that period. Usually enclosed with the bank statement are your canceled checks.

Almost always, the balance you keep in the checkbook will not agree with the balance shown in the bank statement. This is so because:

1. Check charges and service charges will be included in the bank statement.
2. Deposits made after the statement closing date will not appear.
3. Checks will not appear if they have not cleared by the closing date.
4. There may be errors in either the bank statement or the checkbook. Errors might include:
   a. Omitted deposits in checkbook registers or a deposit entered twice.
   b. Arithmetic errors in keeping the checkbook balance.
   c. A difference in the amount of a check and the amount entered in the register.

Every month you will have to *reconcile* the bank statement balance with the checkbook balance.

PROCEDURE: To reconcile your bank statement and checkbook balances:

1. Deduct the bank's check charges and service charges from the checkbook balance. This amount is the checkbook's *trial balance.*
2. Put the returned checks in numerical order, and match each check amount against the register amount. It is best to put a red check by the amount in the register so you know which checks have cleared.
3. Make a list of all checks (number and amount) *that have not cleared,* and subtract this total from the bank's closing balance.
4. Compare your record of deposits with the bank's, and *add* deposits not shown on the bank statement to the total from Step 3. This will give you the *bank's trial balance.*
5. Check that the checkbook's trial balance equals the bank's trial balance. If it does not, there is an error in the checkbook or the bank statement.

If the trial balances do not agree, subtract the two balances. The difference is the amount of the error(s).

PROCEDURE: To find the error when the trial balances do not agree:

1. Review the statement, looking specifically for the amount of difference. The error may be a service charge that you missed or a check that was processed but not returned to you.
2. Review your register, looking for this amount. The error could be in listing a check as cleared when it had not.
3. Check your addition and subtraction.

Your bank statement shows a balance of $483.55; your checkbook shows a balance of $241.70. After checking your canceled checks against the checkbook register, you find that three checks are outstanding, in the amounts of $48.75, $35.50, and $65.10, and that a deposit of $95.50 was omitted on the stub. The bank statement also shows a $3 service charge.

This is how your *reconciliation statement* would look:

Checkbook Balance		Bank Statement Balance	
	$241.70		$483.55
Add:		*Add:*	
Deposit omitted in register	95.50		
	$337.20		
Deduct:		*Deduct:*	
Service charge	3.00	Checks outstanding	149.35
Adjusted balance	$334.20	Adjusted balance	$334.20

Exercises

Exercise A Using the forms provided, fill out a deposit slip for each of the following:

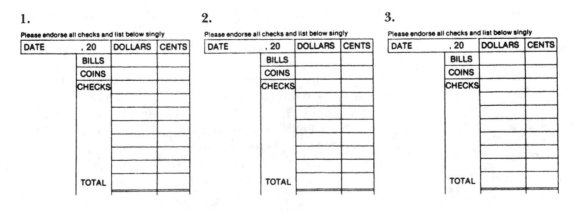

1.

Please endorse all checks and list below singly			
DATE , 20		DOLLARS	CENTS
	BILLS		
	COINS		
	CHECKS		
	TOTAL		

2.

Please endorse all checks and list below singly			
DATE , 20		DOLLARS	CENTS
	BILLS		
	COINS		
	CHECKS		
	TOTAL		

3.

Please endorse all checks and list below singly			
DATE , 20		DOLLARS	CENTS
	BILLS		
	COINS		
	CHECKS		
	TOTAL		

4.

Please endorse all checks and list below singly

DATE	, 20	DOLLARS	CENTS
	BILLS		
	COINS		
	CHECKS		
	TOTAL		

5.

Please endorse all checks and list below singly

DATE	, 20	DOLLARS	CENTS
	BILLS		
	COINS		
	CHECKS		
	TOTAL		

6.

Please endorse all checks and list below singly

DATE	, 20	DOLLARS	CENTS
	BILLS		
	COINS		
	CHECKS		
	TOTAL		

1. Bills: 3 $20's, 2 $10's, 4 $5's, 7 $1's
    Coins: 6 quarters, 7 dimes, 8 nickels, 17 pennies
    Checks: $85.70, $24.50, $17.05

2. Bills: 6 $20's, 4 $10's, 3 $5's, 11 $1's
    Checks: $123, $75.75, $38.50

3. Bills: 5 $20's, 5 $10's, 6 $5's, 11 $1's
    Checks: $98.75, $63.15, $35.38, $18

4. Bills: 2 $50's, 3 $20's, 6 $10's, 3 $5's
    Checks: $63.50, $52.75, $47

5. Bills: 3 $20's, 4 $10's, 5 $5's, 12 $1's
    Checks: $73.30, $84.75

6. Bills: 5 $20's, 4 $10's, 5 $5's, 9 $1's
    Checks: $38.25, $115.75, $68.48

Using the blank forms provided, prepare checks according to the information in Problems 7 through 12. The initial balance brought forward is $219.85; find each succeeding balance carried forward.

7.

No._____

_____ 20._____

Pay to the
order of _____ $ _____

_____ Dollars

For _____   _____

8.

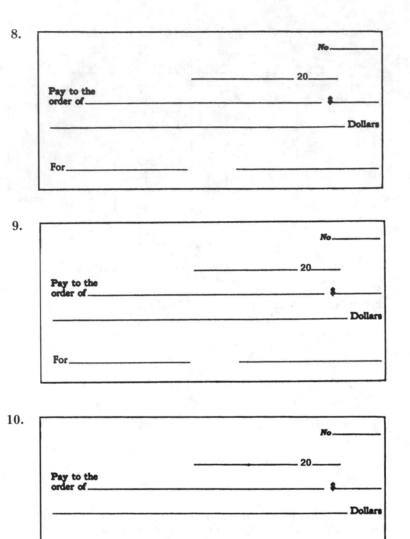

9.

10.

11.

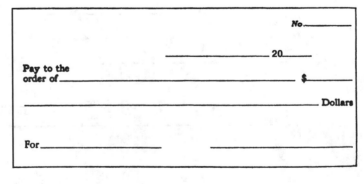

12.

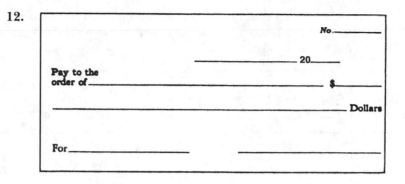

7.   Check #110:   To Consolidated Utility Co. for July electric bill; amount of check, $48.75; date of check, August 5.

8.   Check #111:   Deposit, $185.50; amount of check, $98.75; to City Trust Bank for car payment; date, August 7.

9.   Check #112:   Deposit, $315; amount of check, $215; to Ace Realty for August rent; date, August 8.

10.   Check #113:   Amount of check, $68.78; to Kings Supermarket for groceries; date, August 11.

11.   Check #114:   Amount of check, $55; to Lang's Department Store for charge account payment; date, August 11.

12.   Check #115:   Deposit, $335.50; amount of check, $78.60; to Mutual Insurance Co. for car insurance; date, August 15.

Exercise B Prepare a reconciliation statement for each of the following accounts, using the reconciliation statement on page 214 as a guide. What is the corrected balance for each?

	Checkbook Balance	Bank Statement Balance	Outstanding Checks	Service Charge	Other Adjustments	Corrected Balance
13.	$313.64	$365.39	$23.50 20.75 75.65	$3.15	$65 deposit recorded twice	_____
14.	$245.75	$255.20	$70.50 13.95	None	$75 deposit not on bank statement	_____
15.	$146.18	$324.26	$27.13 23.25 30.70	$3.00	$100 deposit omitted from check stub	_____
16.	$250.25	$442.00	$24.25 65.40 30.60	$3.50	$75 deposit omitted from check stub	_____
17.	$281.90	$289.90	$ 63.25 101.50 25.25	$2.00	$180 deposit not on bank statement	_____
18.	$260.35	$167.00	$23.55 23.10	None	$140 deposit not on bank statement	_____
19.	$259.25	$369.10	$128.85 64.30 20.70	$4.00	$100 deposit recorded twice on check stubs	_____
20.	$347.85	$258.00	$35.65 24.50	None	$150 deposit recorded twice on check stubs	_____
21.	$662.40	$557.20	$ 75.60 109.62 71.83	$3.50	$258.75 deposit not on bank statement. $100 check omitted on checkbook stub	_____
22.	$161.10	$273.70	$42.25 50.85 19.50	None	None	_____

Word Problems

Exercise C Solve the following problems:

23. Henry's checking account showed a balance brought forward of $243.65. He wrote the following checks: $175.50; $68.78; $47.65; and $109.15. If he deposited $87.50 in cash plus his paycheck of $265.80, what is his new balance brought forward?

24. The balance brought forward in Sally's checkbook was $138.75. In checking her register, she noticed that she had forgotten to enter a deposit of $195. She then wrote the following checks: $165.85, $48.72, $18.29, and $63.15. She also deposited her paycheck of $289.70. Find the new balance brought forward.

25. Tony's checkbook balance was $321.75 but he had neglected to record a check for $225. If he then writes checks for $132.50, $78.95, and $63.75, and deposits $235.65, what is his current checkbook balance?

26. Sandy wrote the following checks: $185.50, $53.75, $28.65, and $49.65. If she deposited $265.75 and her balance carried forward was $168.50, find her balance brought forward.

27. Raphael had $215.72 in his checking account and wrote checks for $63.75, $49.75, and $57.50. Find his new balance if he deposited $186.90 in his account.

Prepare a reconciliation statement for each of the following accounts:

28. Sam's checkbook balance was $327.50. He received his monthly bank statement showing a balance of $200.15. After reviewing his checks and register, he found that three checks were still outstanding, in the amounts of $87.50, $28.90, and $34.65. He also found that a deposit of $275 sent in late in the month had not been credited on the bank statement. The bank also added a service charge of $3.50. What is his corrected balance?

29. Marcia received her bank statement for July, showing a balance of $429.71. Her check stubs showed a balance of $45.30. In reviewing her checkbook and the canceled checks, she found three checks outstanding for $125.63, $65.10, and $23.18. She had also omitted from her checkbook register a deposit of $175. The bank service charge was $4.50. What is her corrected balance?

30. Mark's bank balance was $264.58; his checkbook balance was $542.50. He reviewed his canceled checks and register and found checks outstanding in the amounts of $19.63, $87.70, and $48.75. He also found a deposit of $225 entered twice on his stubs and a deposit of $215 not credited on his bank statement. The bank service charge was $4. Find his corrected balance.

UNIT **3** Investments: Stocks

Most people will open a savings account to build a cushion for future needs. Sometimes, however, those seeking to increase the rate of growth of these savings may decide to take money out of savings accounts and invest in *stocks* or *bonds*.

The Stock Market

It is estimated that there are more than 2 million corporations in the United States. Many of these are **closed corporations,** owned by a small number of shareholders (the organizers of the corporation or members of a family). The Ford Motor Company, for example, was a closed corporation until 1956, when some of its stock was offered for sale to the general public.

Most corporations are **publicly owned** through *stock* that can be bought by anyone. More than 30 million Americans own shares in publicly held corporations. Some of these people own as little as one share, while others own large numbers of shares.

TERMS

Stock certificate   A document that proves ownership of a part of a corporation. There are two basic types of stock, *common* and *preferred.*

Common stock   A type of stock that usually carries the right to vote for the directors of the company, but earns dividends only *after* dividends have been paid to the owners of preferred stock.

Preferred stock   The type of stock that has a claim on the company's earnings *before dividends may be paid on common stock* and that has a prior claim on the corporation's assets in the event of liquidation. However, preferred stock usually has no voting rights.

Dividend   Money designated by the board of directors to be distributed among the stockholders. It is usually stated as a dollar amount per share (e.g., $3.25/share). Many corporations do not declare dividends on a regular basis either because of financial inability or in order to reinvest the money to create future growth. Investors who must live off the dividends of their investments should select stocks with a history of regular dividend payments.

Offer   The price at which an owner of shares of stock is ready to sell a stock.

Bid   The highest price anyone has declared he or she is willing to pay for a stock.

Market order   An order by a customer to a broker to buy or sell at the best price available.

Round lot   A unit of trading or a multiple thereof. On most stock exchanges, the unit of trading is 100 shares, and in some stocks, it is 10 shares.

Odd lot   An amount of stock less than the established round lot.

Stock exchange   A marketplace where stocks of approved companies are listed, bought, and sold. There are stock exchanges in New York, Chicago, Los Angeles, and other major cities.

Because of the public interest in buying and selling stocks, the financial pages of most newspapers publish a record of the daily transactions at some of these exchanges. Page 222 shows a section of one of these reports of stocks listed on the New York Stock Exchange. You can also check stock reports on the Internet.

Note the large number of fractions that appears with the price of the stocks. Each fraction represents a fractional part of a dollar. All stocks are sold in whole dollars and fractional parts of a dollar. Notice that these fractions are eighths of a dollar or multiples of eighths. The following table will help you to translate the fractions of a dollar to their decimal value:

$$\$\frac{1}{8} \quad = 12\,\frac{1}{2}\text{¢} = \$0.125$$

$$\$\frac{1}{4} \quad = 25\text{¢} \quad = \$0.25$$

$$\$\frac{3}{8} \quad = 37\,\frac{1}{2}\text{¢} = \$0.375$$

$$\$\frac{1}{2} \quad = 50\text{¢} \quad = \$0.50$$

$$\$\frac{5}{8} \quad = 62\,\frac{1}{2}\text{¢} = \$0.625$$

$$\$\frac{3}{4} \quad = 75\text{¢} \quad = \$0.75$$

$$\$\frac{7}{8} \quad = 87\,\frac{1}{2}\text{¢} = \$0.875$$

If you sell a share for $19\,\frac{1}{2}$, the purchaser will pay $\$19\,\frac{1}{2}$ or $\$19.50$. If you buy a share for $27\,\frac{7}{8}$, you will pay $\$27\,\frac{7}{8}$, or $\$27.875$.

Understanding Stock Market Reports

The stock market reports published in newspapers usually contain the following information:

Under the heading *52-Week High/Low*, the columns show the highest and lowest prices of the stock in trading for the preceding 52 weeks.

Under the heading *Stock* is the abbreviation of the company name.

From: *THE NEW YORK TIMES,* Wednesday May 24, 2000

NEW YORK STOCK EXCHANGE

Continued From Preceding Page

52-Week High	52-Week Low	Stock	Div	Yld %	P/E	Sales 100s	High	Low	Last	Chg
14	5 1/2	JilinCh	.12 e	1.8	3	51	6 3/4	6 1/2	6 1/2	− 1/2
17 1/4	8	JoAnnSt A	...	...	6	311	9	9	9	+ 1/16
13 1/8	6	JoAnnSt B	...	...	6	94	8	7 15/16	7 15/16	...
22 5/16	**13 7/16**	**JHFnSrv n**	...	...	...	**10073**	**21 3/4**	**20 1/2**	**21 3/4**	**+1**
43 11/16	33 1/2	JNuveen	1.04	2.5	14	429	41 7/8	41 1/8	41 3/8	+ 3/16
15	7 7/16	JohnsMnv	.24	2.0	7	549	12	11 3/4	11 13/16	− 5/16
106 7/8	66 1/8	JohnJn	1.28 f	1.5	33	28055	88 3/16	86 1/8	87	+ 1/8
73 7/8	46 7/8	JohnsnCtrl	1.12	1.8	13	3119	61 1/8	60	60 3/4	+ 3/8
35 7/16	20 1/8	JonesApp	...	...	17	3133	28	27 3/4	27 15/16	+ 7/16
32	9 3/16	JonesLL	...	...	dd	388	15 1/16	15	15	− 1/16
23	11 7/16	JrnlReg	...	...	13	197	14 3/16	13 13/16	13 13/16	− 7/16

K

52-Week High	52-Week Low	Stock	Div	Yld %	P/E	Sales 100s	High	Low	Last	Chg
10 9/16	6 3/16	K2 Inc	...	...	12	480	7 19/32	7 5/16	7 9/16	+ 3/16
2 3/8	3/16	vjKCS	...	...	6	1096	1 1/4	15/16	1 1/16	+ 1/8
29 1/16	16 3/4	KLM n	...	...	...	485	21 1/16	20 1/2	20 1/2	...
17 1/2	7 5/16	K mart	...	...	11	18466	8	7 3/4	7 15/16	+ 1/8
47 1/2	23 3/8	KN En01	3.55	7.9	...	508	44 15/16	44	44 15/16	+ 9/16
143 7/16	39 11/16	KPN	1.04 e	1.4	...	409	77 15/16	76 1/16	76 1/8	−2 5/8
32 13/16	14 3/4	KV Ph B	...	...	18	45	22 3/8	22	22	− 1/4
32 5/8	14 3/8	KV Ph A	...	...	18	133	22	21 1/2	21 3/4	+ 1/8
9 11/16	2 15/16	KaisAl	...	...	dd	748	4 9/16	4 3/8	4 3/8	+ 1/8
32 5/8	22	KanPipLP	2.80	11.3	11	117	24 15/16	24 3/4	24 7/8	− 1/16
6 15/16	4	Kaneb	...	...	3	171	5 3/16	5 1/16	5 1/8	− 1/16
29	20 13/16	KCtyPL	1.66	6.9	22	1354	24 3/8	23 5/8	24 3/16	+ 1/8
93 7/8	37 1/2	KC Sou	.04 j	...	21	3272	70	68 1/8	68 7/16	−1 13/16
17 1/4	**7 5/8**	**KatyInd**	**.30**	**2.7**	**10**	**110**	**11 1/2**	**11**	**11**	**− 3/4**
25 9/16	16 3/4	KaufBH	.30	1.7	6	2186	17 7/8	17 7/16	17 7/16	− 1/16
34 3/4	21 9/16	Kaydon	.44	1.9	13	352	23 5/8	22 3/4	22 7/8	− 3/16
36 1/8	21 3/4	Keebler	.11 p	...	29	1722	35 3/16	34 1/2	34 7/8	− 1/16
74	**8 3/16**	**Keithly**	**.22 f**	**0.4**	**27**	**1791**	**62 1/8**	**56 3/16**	**56 1/4**	**−3 9/16**
40 15/16	20 3/4	Kellogg	.98	3.2	32	13479	30 3/4	29	30 7/16	+1 1/8
27 13/16	13 3/4	Kellwood	.64	3.9	49	555	16 11/16	16 1/4	16 1/4	− 3/16
88 7/16	**16 3/4**	**Kemet**	...	...	**38**	**9752**	**76 3/4**	**63 1/2**	**64 3/8**	**−12 1/2**
9 5/16	7 7/16	KmpHi	.97	12.3	q	445	7 7/8	7 13/16	7 7/8	+ 1/16
7 3/16	6 1/8	KmplGv	.54	8.5	q	1044	6 3/8	6 1/4	6 3/8	+ 1/8
9 3/8	7 11/16	KmpMl	.93 a	11.3	q	466	8 1/4	8 1/16	8 1/4	+ 1/8
12 15/16	9 7/16	KmpMu	.82	7.7	q	802	10 13/16	10 5/8	10 11/16	− 1/16
17 3/8	12 1/8	KmpSlnc	1.80	13.2	q	46	13 7/8	13 5/8	13 5/8	− 5/16
12 1/16	9 3/8	KmpStr	.75	7.3	q	308	10 5/16	10 1/8	10 5/16	+ 3/16
33 7/8	22 5/8	Kennmtl	.68	2.5	17	1746	27 3/8	26 11/16	26 15/16	...
46 1/8	17 5/8	KCole s	...	...	29	479	37 3/4	36 1/2	37 1/2	+ 1/2
42	**12**	**KentEl**	...	...	**43**	**1577**	**28 1/8**	**26 7/8**	**26 7/8**	**−1 3/8**
67 15/16	39 7/8	KerrMc	1.80	3.1	12	3511	59 13/16	58 1/2	58 1/2	− 3/8
53 1/4	30 13/16	KerrM04 n	1.83	3.5	...	2215	52 1/2	51 1/2	52 1/8	− 1/16
12 1/4	3	KeyEng	...	...	dd	2574	11 7/16	11	11 3/16	+ 1/16
15 3/8	6 3/4	KeyPrd	...	...	16	735	14 5/16	13 1/4	13 5/8	− 3/8
36	15 9/16	Keycorp	1.12	5.6	8	18418	20 9/16	19 1/4	19 7/8	+ 11/16
31 1/16	20 3/16	Keyspan	1.78	6.2	15	2202	29 3/16	28 13/16	28 7/8	...
7 11/16	3 3/4	KeyCon	...	...	dd	35	4	3 13/16	4	...
26 1/2	18	KilroyR	1.80 f	7.8	16	808	23 3/4	23 1/16	23 1/8	− 3/8
69 9/16	42	KimbClk	1.08	1.8	18	10356	60 1/16	57 3/4	59 3/4	− 1/4
42 1/4	30 7/8	Kimco	2.64	6.4	16	466	41 1/2	40 3/4	41 1/8	+ 5/16
45 5/8	35 1/4	KindME	3.10 f	8.2	14	1330	38 1/4	37 1/4	37 5/8	− 5/16
34 1/2	12 3/16	KindMorg	.80	2.6	15	2578	31 1/4	30 3/8	30 15/16	+ 1/8
68 3/4	13 7/8	KingPh s	...	...	78	1525	51 3/4	51	51 1/2	...
3 3/4	1 1/8	▼Kinross g	...	...	...	7512	1 3/16	1 1/16	1 1/16	− 1/8
24 5/8	16 1/2	Kirby	...	...	21	147	23	22 3/8	22 1/2	− 1/2
65	44 3/16	KnightR	.92	1.8	11	3819	51 15/16	50 5/16	51	+ 3/8
19 3/16	14 1/4	KogerEq	1.40	7.9	14	100	17 3/4	17 3/8	17 11/16	+ 5/16
54 3/4	30 3/4	Kohls s	...	...	65	18277	53 1/2	52 3/16	52 5/8	+1 3/8
22 7/8	8 7/8	Kolmor	.08	0.4	20	195	22 3/4	22 11/16	22 11/16	...
9 3/16	4 3/4	Konover	.50	10.3	dd	51	5 1/16	4 7/8	4 7/8	− 3/16
24 3/4	16	Koor	.69 e	3.9	dd	61	18 1/4	17 3/4	17 3/4	− 5/8
21 3/4	11 3/4	KoreaElc	.27 e	1.7	...	2190	15 9/16	14 13/16	15 1/2	+ 11/16
5 15/16	3 1/16	KoreaEqt	...	...	q	303	3 3/16	3 1/8	3 3/16	− 1/16
17 13/16	11 1/8	Korea	...	...	q	1811	11 7/16	11 3/16	11 3/16	− 5/16
79 7/8	30 1/16	KoreaTel	.20 e	0.6	...	6094	34	33 1/4	33 3/4	+ 1/4
9 1/8	5 1/2	KoreaInv	...	...	q	1393	6	5 5/8	5 15/16	− 1/16
44 1/8	12 1/2	KornFer	...	...	...	212	22 3/4	22 5/16	22 1/2	...
14 1/8	7 1/2	Kranzc	1.30	14.3	22	197	9 1/4	8 15/16	9 1/16	− 1/16
31 3/8	14 1/16	Kroger s	...	...	27	33536	20 1/4	19 9/16	19 9/16	− 7/16
86 1/2	54	Kubota	1.13 e	1.5	31	5	74	73	74	+2
280 15/16	51 1/16	Kyocera	.57 e	0.4	...	277	144 1/4	140 3/4	141 3/4	+1 1/4

L

52-Week High	52-Week Low	Stock	Div	Yld %	P/E	Sales 100s	High	Low	Last	Chg
58 3/4	**34 1/4**	**L-3 Com**	...	...	**30**	**2086**	**55 3/4**	**51 15/16**	**55 1/4**	**+3 1/16**
23 13/16	15 1/4	LG&E	1.27	5.4	15	2522	23 3/4	23 5/8	23 11/16	+ 1/8
3 3/4	3/4	LLE Ry	.24 e	6.9	7	353	3 5/8	3 7/16	3 1/2	− 1/16
24	16 1/2	LNR Pr	.05	0.3	7	51	19 3/16	18 7/8	18 7/8	− 1/16
90 3/8	**16 3/4**	**LSI Log s**	...	...	**55**	**31544**	**46 3/8**	**42**	**42 5/8**	**−2 3/8**
13 7/8	4	LTC Prp	1.16 m	20.0	11	615	6	5 13/16	5 13/16	...
7 7/16	2 5/8	LTV	.12	3.9	dd	2759	3 1/8	3	3 1/16	− 1/16
24 9/16	13 1/2	LaZBoy	.32	2.1	10	549	15 1/4	15 1/16	15 1/16	+ 1/16
28 3/8	7 5/8	LabrRdy s	...	...	24	617	9 11/16	9 7/16	9 11/16	...
25 1/2	15 7/8	LabChile	1.03 e	5.3	...	22	19 3/4	19 9/16	19 9/16	− 3/16
74 5/8	22 1/2	LabCp s	...	...	39	1347	67 7/16	65 3/8	66 1/2	+ 3/8
15 3/4	9 1/16	LaBrnch n	...	...	7	563	11 3/4	11 1/2	11 3/4	...
23 3/4	17 1/2	LaclGas	1.34	6.8	15	132	19 5/8	19 3/8	19 9/16	+ 3/16
36 7/8	18 13/16	Lafarge	.60	2.4	7	1310	26 5/8	25 1/16	25 3/16	− 11/16
8	7/16	Laidlaw	.07 j	...	dd	11914	9/16	15/32	1/2	− 1/16
45 15/16	32	LakehdP	3.50	9.3	16	419	38 1/8	37 9/16	37 3/4	− 1/4
8 3/4	4 5/16	LamSes	...	...	5	19	8	8	8	+ 1/8
30 1/2	15 9/16	LandAmer	.20	1.1	10	143	18 1/2	18 1/16	18 1/16	− 7/16
10 3/16	6 1/16	Landrys	.03 p	...	dd	769	8 1/2	8 3/8	8 7/16	...
83 1/2	27 1/4	LandsE	...	...	14	1319	33 11/16	32 9/16	32 13/16	− 3/8
6 1/2	1 5/16	LanierW n	...	...	...	2154	1 9/16	1 7/16	1 7/16	− 1/16
16 1/8	10 13/16	LaSalleH	1.52	11.0	16	243	13 15/16	13 5/8	13 13/16	+ 1/8
18 5/8	10 7/8	LaSalleRe	...	...	dd	59	13	12 7/8	13	...
4 1/16	3 1/8	LaserMtg	...	...	dd	17	3 13/16	3 3/4	3 13/16	...
8 3/16	4 1/8	Lasmo	.63 e	11.2	80	88	5 11/16	5 3/8	5 5/8	− 1/16
14 5/16	8 1/4	LatAEqt	...	...	q	118	10 5/8	10 1/2	10 9/16	− 1/16
13 7/16	7 1/8	LatADisc	.03 e	0.3	q	436	8 15/16	8 1/2	8 7/8	+ 1/8
14 5/16	9 9/16	LatAInv	.50 e	...	q	34	12 11/16	12 5/8	12 5/8	− 1/8
53	19 1/4	LearCorp	...	...	6	2078	26 15/16	25 1/4	25 1/4	− 3/4
32 1/4	19 11/16	LeeEnt	.64	3.0	12	401	21 1/8	20 11/16	21 1/16	+ 3/8
51 1/4	30 5/8	LeggMas	.26	0.6	18	1004	43 1/16	41 1/16	41 15/16	+ 9/16
28 5/16	15 1/4	LeggPlat	.40 f	2.0	13	2841	19 7/8	19 1/2	19 11/16	+ 1/16
107 1/2	47 9/16	LehmBr	.44 f	0.6	10	7902	82 3/4	78 7/16	78 7/8	−2 13/16
25 7/8	21 5/8	LehBr35	2.08	9.2	...	102	22 5/8	22 1/2	22 5/8	...
24 15/16	13 1/16	Lennar	.05	0.3	7	957	17 7/8	17 7/16	17 3/4	− 1/4
19 7/8	7 7/8	Lennox n	.38	3.3	7	1199	11 1/2	10 7/8	11 7/16	+ 1/2
25 3/8	20 1/8	LeucNtl s	1.58 e	7.0	15	283	23 1/4	22 5/8	22 11/16	+ 1/16
12 7/8	8 13/16	LexCrpP	1.20	11.2	10	97	10 3/4	10 9/16	10 11/16	+ 1/16
135 7/8	**59 5/8**	**Lexmark**	...	...	**30**	**28861**	**80 1/2**	**71 15/16**	**72 3/4**	**−8 1/4**

DIVIDENDS DECLARED

Company	Period	rate	Stk of record	Payable
IRREGULAR				
Coflexip Spons ADR	x	.5307	6-6	6-27
x- approx amount.				
Delta-Galil IndADS	x	.0931	5-25	6-12
Gabelli EquityTr	...	.27	6-16	6-26
Liberty All-Star	...	.36	6-2	6-19
Liberty All-StarGwth	...	.33	6-2	6-19
LUMH Moet ADR	x	.4392	6-5	6-26
x- approx amount.				
Mesa Offshore	...	.0018	5-31	7-31
Mesa Royalty Tr	...	.2669	5-31	7-31
Supermercado Unimarc	...	.1581	5-30	6-9
Swiss Helvetia Fd	...	.045	5-31	6-7
Torch EnergyRoy	...	.342	5-31	6-12
CORRECTION				
Intel Corp	x	.02	8-7	9-1
x- increased amount payable on post split shares.				
Penn-American Grp	x	.0525	6-3	6-19
x- correcting pay date.				
Std Register	x	.23	5-26	6-9
x- correcting record date.				
INCREASED				
Gibraltar Steel	Q	.03		
x- dates unannounced.				
Home-Stake Oil	Q	.05	5-31	6-15
PAB Bkshrs	Q	.1075	6-30	7-14
Roslyn Bncp	Q	.15	6-2	6-13

Company	Period	rate	Stk of record	Payable
FINAL				
Dominguez Svcs	...	.25	5-22	5-26
REDUCED				
JDN Realty	x	.30		
x- dates unannounced.				
Municipal Advantage	x	.06		
x- dates unannounced.				
REGULAR				
Advanta Cp A,	Q	.063	5-30	6-16
Advanta Cp B,	Q	.0756	5-30	6-16
Amer Bal Fd	M	.14	5-19	5-22
Becton Dickinson	Q	.0925	6-9	6-30
Blockbuster Inc	Q	.02	6-5	6-19
CenturyTel Inc	Q	.0475	6-2	6-16
Columbus McKinnon	Q	.07	6-22	7-6
Community Bk Syst	Q	.25	6-15	7-10
Corporate Office	Q	.19	6-30	7-17
Craftmade Intl	Q	.02	6-30	7-14
Doral Fncl A,	M	.2917	5-26	5-31
Edison Intl	Q	.28	7-5	7-31
Fst BanCorp PR,	Q	.11	6-15	6-30
Fst Fedl BcshrsArk	Q	.10	6-9	6-23
1st Midwest Fncl	Q	.13	6-15	7-3
Florida Progress	Q	.555	6-5	6-20
Gabelli Conv Secs	Q	.20	6-16	6-26
Gables Resident	Q	.53	6-16	6-30
Gulf CdaResadjpf1 g	Q	.024	5-31	6-12
HCB Bnshrs Inc AR,	Q	.06	6-15	6-29
HSBC Bk ADR A,	Q	.5546	5-26	6-15

Company	Period	rate	Stk of record	Payable
REGULAR				
HSBC Bk ADR B,	Q	.6406	5-26	6-15
HSBC Bk ADR C,	Q	.5703	5-26	6-15
HSBC Bk ADR D,	Q	.5968	5-26	6-15
Hartford Life Inc	Q	.10	6-1	7-3
Home City Fncl	Q	.105	6-5	6-15
Home Fedl Bncp	Q	.1375	6-20	7-3
Magna Intl A,	Q	.30	5-31	6-15
Martin Marietta	Q	.13	6-1	7-3
Merchants NY Bncp	Q	.125	6-15	6-29
NUI Corp	Q	.245	6-1	6-15
Natl City Bkshrs	Q	.21	6-21	7-7
Precision Castpart	Q	.06	6-2	7-3
Presidentl Rlty A,	Q	.16	6-9	6-30
Prosperity Bcshrs	Q	.09	6-16	7-3
Salisbury Bncp	Q	.13	6-30	7-28
Scientific-Atlanta	Q	.01	6-1	6-16
Sentinel Bd A,	M	.035	5-24	5-31
Sentinel Bd B,	M	.031	5-24	5-31
Sentinel Gvt Secs	M	.052	5-24	5-31
Sentinel PA TxFr	M	.052	5-24	5-31
Sentinel Sht/Mat	M	.053	5-24	5-31
Suffolk Bncp	Q	.23	6-15	7-3
UB Bancorp	Q	.215	6-1	6-15
US Indus	Q	.05	6-30	7-21
Unocal Corp	Q	.20	7-10	8-10
Westvaco Corp	Q	.22	6-2	7-3

g- payable in Canadian funds.

52-Week High	52-Week Low	Stock	Div	Yld %	P/E	Sales 100s	High	Low	Last	Chg
33 3/4	24 5/8	Libbey	.30	1.0	10	114	29 5/16	29	29 1/16	− 1/4
3 13/16	3	Liberte	.06 e	2.0	50	7	3 1/8	3	3	...
14 1/8	9 3/4	LbtyASE	1.38 e	12.4	q	1329	11 1/4	11 1/16	11 1/8	...
11 9/16	9 5/16	LbtyASG	1.24 e	12.3	q	604	10 1/4	10 1/16	10 1/16	− 1/8
54 9/16	30 3/4	LibtyCp	.88	2.6	12	153	34 1/8	33 1/2	33 5/8	− 1/8
29 11/16	17 7/8	LibFin	.40	1.8	10	377	22 1/4	21 11/16	21 7/8	− 5/16
61 7/16	30 7/8	LibtyMA s	...	...	...	37900	40 1/4	38 3/4	39 11/16	− 1/8
73 1/8	32	LibtyMB s	...	...	cc	8	45 1/4	45	45 1/4	− 3/4
25 7/8	20 7/8	LibtProp	2.08	8.2	13	835	25 1/2	25 5/16	25 5/16	...
80 1/2	54	LillyEli	1.04	1.4	28	17110	76 3/16	73 7/8	75 9/16	+ 3/8
19 3/4	10 1/2	LillyInd	.32	2.3	10	552	14 7/16	13 7/8	13 7/8	− 1/4
51 3/4	28 7/8	Limitd	.60 b	1.2	23	6309	49 11/16	48 5/16	48 3/4	− 1/2
21	12 3/4	LncNtC	.80	4.9	q	71	16 1/4	16 1/8	16 1/4	+ 1/4
57 1/2	22 5/8	LincNat s	1.16	3.2	17	5704	36 7/8	34 7/8	36 3/8	+1 1/8
12 7/8	9 9/16	LincNIF	.96 a	9.2	q	43	10 7/16	10 7/16	10 7/16	− 1/16
21 1/4	13 5/8	Lindsay	.14	0.7	18	37	18 3/4	18 7/16	18 11/16	+ 5/16
49 1/2	17 15/16	Linens	...	...	23	2006	30 9/16	30	30 5/16	− 1/8
23 3/4	11 5/8	LithiaMot	...	...	7	253	12 15/16	12 3/8	12 1/2	− 1/8
74 5/8	26 13/16	Litton	...	...	16	3568	42 3/8	40 5/8	40 7/8	− 1/8
48 5/16	30 15/16	LizClab	.45	1.1	13	2387	42 5/16	41 13/16	42 1/16	+ 3/8
42 1/4	**16 3/8**	**LockhdM**	**.44 m**	**1.8**	**18**	**11093**	**25 5/16**	**23 5/8**	**25 1/8**	**+1 9/16**
7 1/8	2 3/16	▼Lodgian	...	...	dd	1221	2 7/16	2	2 5/16	...
11 1/8	2 1/4	LoewsCin	...	...	dd	86	2 13/16	2 5/8	2 5/8	...
82 1/2	38 1/4	Loews	1.00	1.6	13	3801	65 1/16	63 1/4	64	+ 3/4
32 3/4	4 3/8	LondnPc s	.23 e	2.3	...	839	10 9/16	10	10 1/8	− 3/8
53 5/16	14 7/16	LoneStTch	...	...	cc	279	49 9/16	48 3/4	48 7/8	− 13/16
36 7/8	15 15/16	LongDrg	.56	2.8	12	417	20 11/16	20 1/4	20 1/4	− 3/16
17 3/4	11 1/16	LongvF	.32 a	2.7	18	645	12 1/2	11 13/16	11 7/8	− 9/16
25 3/4	7 9/16	LoralSp	...	...	dd	18904	8 7/16	7 15/16	7 15/16	...
34	15 3/4	LDryNG	...	...	38	1613	33 1/4	32 5/8	33 1/16	+ 3/8
24 7/8	10 13/16	LaPac	.56	4.3	6	4873	13 5/16	12 13/16	12 7/8	− 5/8
67 1/4	40 3/4	Lowes	.14	0.3	25	13821	49 5/8	48	48 5/16	− 9/16
33 7/8	23	Lubrizol	1.04	4.2	12	1285	25	24 3/8	24 1/2	− 3/8
17 1/4	8 3/4	Lubys	.80	7.8	8	522	10 7/16	10 1/8	10 5/16	+ 1/16
84 3/16	49 13/16	Lucent	.08	0.1	49	98199	56 3/8	54 9/16	54 9/16	+ 1/16
27	13 7/8	Luxottc	.16 e	0.7	34	207	24 1/2	24 1/8	24 7/16	+ 3/16
12 7/8	5 1/8	Lydall	...	...	12	419	10 5/16	10 3/16	10 1/4	...
22 1/2	8 7/16	Lyondell	.90	4.9	12	x4896	18 7/8	18 1/4	18 5/16	− 3/16

M

52-Week High	52-Week Low	Stock	Div	Yld %	P/E	Sales 100s	High	Low	Last	Chg
575	357	M&T Bank	5.00	1.2	13	z15180	424	410	422	+11 5/16
68 7/8	36 5/16	MBIA	.82 f	1.4	13	4249	57 1/8	55 1/4	56 5/8	+ 3/4
24 15/16	19 3/8	MBIA38	1.74	8.5	...	13	20 13/16	20 9/16	20 9/16	...
33 1/4	19 1/2	MBNA	.32	1.2	22	21186	27 15/16	26 15/16	27 7/16	+ 11/16
26 15/16	**17**	**MCN Engy**	**1.02**	**4.8**	**dd**	**6174**	**22 15/16**	**21 7/16**	**21 7/16**	**−1**
14 1/4	4 7/8	MSC Sft	...	...	15	315	8 3/4	8 5/16	8 3/4	+ 1/8
22	13 3/8	MDC	.24	1.3	4	228	19 3/16	18 7/8	19	+ 1/16
32	25 1/2	MDS gn	.07 e	...	...	8	31 1/4	30 7/8	30 7/8	− 1/8
24 3/4	17 5/8	MDU	.84	4.0	14	347	22	21 1/4	21 1/4	− 5/8
24 1/4	**7 3/4**	**MEMC**	...	...	**dd**	**2275**	**14 7/8**	**13 3/16**	**14**	**+ 7/8**
9 3/16	7 3/4	MCR	.79	10.0	q	1025	7 15/16	7 13/16	7 15/16	+ 1/16
6 5/16	5 5/8	MGF	.52	8.9	q	643	5 7/8	5 13/16	5 7/8	+ 1/16
6 1/2	5 15/16	MIN	.55	9.1	q	1289	6 1/8	6	6 1/16	− 1/16
6 3/4	5 1/2	MMT	.59	10.4	q	915	5 13/16	5 11/16	5 11/16	− 1/8
8 1/2	6 3/8	MFM	.53	7.5	q	365	7 1/16	7	7 1/16	+ 1/16
17 11/16	13	MFV	1.65	12.6	q	54	13 1/2	13 1/8	13 1/8	− 3/8
9 15/16	2 1/4	MGI Prp s	26.50 c	...	2	425	2 3/8	2 1/4	2 1/4	− 1/16
62 3/4	31 15/16	MGIC	.10	0.2	11	3932	49 7/8	47 9/16	49	+ 5/8
35 1/4	18 7/16	MGM Gr s	...	...	31	4140	33 7/16	32 7/8	33	− 1/8
20 3/16	12 3/4	MISchott	.20	1.2	4	26	16 3/4	16 11/16	16 11/16	− 3/16
18 5/16	9 7/8	MIIX n	.20	1.8	7	37	11 3/8	11 3/8	11 3/8	− 1/16
5 1/4	3 1/2	ML Macad	.50	10.3	9	56	4 7/8	4 13/16	4 7/8	+ 1/16
22 3/16	7 1/2	MSC Ind	...	...	31	851	21 1/4	21 1/16	21 1/16	+ 1/16
24 15/16	19 3/16	MSDW38	1.78	8.8	...	306	20 3/8	20 1/8	20 5/16	+ 1/16
46 3/4	19 3/4	McDrmd	.08	0.4	16	724	20 3/4	20 3/8	20 9/16	− 3/16
27 1/4	17 5/16	Macerich	2.04	9.2	19	555	22 15/16	22 3/16	22 1/4	+ 1/4
10	2 3/4	MacGry	...	...	dd	1218	3	2 13/16	2 13/16	− 3/16
33 3/16	22 3/4	MackCali	2.32	8.5	13	1661	27 1/2	27 1/16	27 3/8	+ 3/8
15 15/16	7 5/8	Madeco	...	...	6	109	8 1/4	8 1/8	8 1/8	− 1/4
10 1/2	1 3/4	Magellan	...	...	dd	802	2 5/16	2 3/16	2 1/4	...
62 3/4	38 3/16	Magnal g	1.20	2.3	...	1735	52 7/8	49 7/8	51 1/4	+1 7/16
11 5/8	6 1/8	Magntk	...	...	7	277	8 1/8	8 1/16	8 1/16	+ 1/16
17 13/16	6 3/4	MailWell	...	...	7	511	9 3/8	9	9 3/16	− 1/8
15 7/8	11 7/8	MalanR	1.70	12.4	15	68	13 3/4	13 5/8	13 11/16	+ 3/16
7 13/16	5 1/8	Malaysa	...	...	q	94	5 1/4	5 3/16	5 3/16	− 1/16
37 9/16	22 3/16	Malinckr	.66	2.2	11	1781	30 13/16	30 1/4	30 5/16	− 1/16
10 9/16	8	MgdHi	1.01	12.4	q	993	8 3/16	8 1/8	8 1/8	...
11 7/16	9	MgHiYld	1.26	13.5	q	227	9 3/8	9 1/4	9 5/16	...
12 5/8	9 9/16	▼MgHiYP	1.50	16.0	q	2056	9 11/16	9 3/8	9 3/8	− 5/16
10 13/16	9	MgdMun	.60	6.5	q	1085	9 3/16	9 1/8	9 3/16	...
10 7/8	8 15/16	MgdMun2	.60	6.6	q	397	9 1/8	9 1/16	9 1/8	...
24 1/2	12 7/8	Mandalay	...	...	16	6564	22 3/8	21 3/4	22 1/16	+ 1/8
43 3/4	24 9/16	Manitow	.30	0.9	13	263	33 13/16	33 1/16	33 1/4	− 1/8
28 1/16	6 7/16	ManorCare	...	...	dd	1299	7	6 13/16	6 7/8	− 1/16
39 15/16	21	Manpwl	.20	0.6	34	2632	36 3/4	35 5/16	35 7/8	+ 3/8
26 15/16	22 1/4	ManufHm	1.66 f	6.6	23	779	24 3/8	24 1/16	24 5/16	+ 3/16
16 11/16	10 1/4	▲Manulif gn	...	...	...	4590	17 1/2	16 3/16	17	+ 11/16
14 5/8	8 3/16	Marcus	.21	2.0	14	28	10 7/8	10 1/2	10 1/2	...
31 5/16	**11 5/16**	**MarineDrl**	...	...	**cc**	**5745**	**27 1/2**	**25 5/8**	**27 1/2**	**+1 13/16**
12 1/8	8 7/16	MarineMx	...	...	7	29	9 1/4	9 3/16	9 1/4	...
6 15/16	4 3/4	Maritrn	.40	7.0	7	29	5 3/4	5 5/8	5 3/4	+ 1/8
23 7/8	16 1/2	MarkIV	.25 f	1.1	13	614	22 1/16	21 13/16	21 13/16	...
192	111 1/2	Markel	...	...	20	175	141	140 1/8	140 7/8	+ 3/16
40 13/16	26 1/8	MarIntA	.24 f	0.7	22	2479	36 3/16	35 7/16	35 5/8	− 9/16
110 11/16	61 3/4	MarshMcL	2.00 f	1.9	38	4979	106 1/4	104	104 15/16	−1 5/16
70	42 3/4	Marshlls	1.06 f	2.2	15	2087	49 7/8	48 11/16	49	− 1/16
47 1/2	13 1/16	MStewrt n	...	...	54	232	17 15/16	17 7/16	17 7/16	− 5/16
64 1/2	35 1/4	MartMM	.52	1.0	19	1260	52	50 15/16	51 1/2	− 3/4
9 1/8	4 1/16	MarvelEnt	...	...	dd	1124	4 5/16	4 3/16	4 1/4	+ 1/16
33 11/16	17 1/16	Masco	.48	2.4	15	17517	20 5/16	19 9/16	20 3/16	+ 3/8
17 11/16	10 5/8	MascoTch	.32	2.6	7	1001	12 11/16	12 5/16	12 7/16	+ 1/8
23 3/4	17 5/8	MassCp	1.72 a	8.0	q	53	21 7/16	20 15/16	21 3/8	+ 3/8
11 3/4	8 1/2	MasPrt	.96 a	9.8	q	51	9 3/4	9 5/8	9 3/4	+ 1/16
90 1/4	**21 1/2**	**Mastec**	...	...	**35**	**2534**	**76**	**69 3/4**	**70 1/4**	**−3**
49 15/16	25 13/16	Matav	.15 e	0.5	...	x748	29 1/2	28 15/16	28 15/16	+1 1/16
16	9 1/2	MatSci	...	...	9	142	10 3/8	10 1/4	10 1/4	− 1/4
5 15/16	1 7/16	Matlack	...	...	dd	108	1 3/4	1 5/8	1 3/4	+ 1/4
303	173 1/2	Matsu	1.17 e	0.5	76	37	235 5/16	231	231	+1
26 3/4	8 15/16	Mattel	.36	2.8	dd	71300	13 1/4	12 5/16	13	+ 5/8
3 7/8	2 5/16	Mavesa	.08 e	3.0	7	1353	2 3/4	2 5/8	2 5/8	...
38 15/16	20 3/4	Maximus	...	...	15	306	22 1/4	21 7/8	22 1/16	− 1/16
44 3/4	23 3/4	MayDS	.93	3.1	11	10934	29 15/16	29 5/16	29 5/8	+ 1/16
74 13/16	25 15/16	Maytag	.72	2.0	10	3336	36 9/16	34 11/16	35 13/16	+1 1/4
45 1/8	28 3/4	McClatchy	.40	1.3	16	198	29 7/8	29 1/2	29 13/16	+ 1/8
36 9/16	23 3/4	McCorm	.76	2.3	22	1112	33 5/8	33 5/16	33 7/16	...
30 3/16	7 1/4	McDerl	.20	2.1	67	1921	9 7/16	9	9 3/8	+ 1/8
49 9/16	29 13/16	McDnlds	.20	0.5	27	24521	39 1/4	37 3/4	39 1/8	+ 1/4
26 3/16	21 5/8	McDn36	1.88	8.2	...	76	23 1/16	22 7/8	23 1/16	...
26	21 3/4	McDn37	1.87	8.2	...	55	22 15/16	22 3/4	22 15/16	+ 1/8
63 1/8	41 7/8	McGrH	.94	1.9	22	3965	50 1/4	49 1/16	49 13/16	+ 5/16
39	16 1/8	McKHBOC	.24	1.5	6	8214	17	16 3/8	16 1/2	+ 1/8
25	11 5/8	McMoRn	...	...	dd	1202	13 3/8	12 3/4	13 3/8	+ 1/2
19 3/4	10 7/8	McWhrtr	...	...	21	437	19 5/8	19 7/16	19 1/2	+ 1/16
46 5/16	**28 1/8**	**Mead**	**.68**	**2.1**	**21**	**10919**	**33 3/4**	**31 3/4**	**32 1/16**	**−1 11/16**
14 1/16	4 3/4	Mdbklns	.12	2.4	dd	73	5 1/8	5 1/16	5 1/16	− 3/16
10 1/2	5 1/2	MedPtTAP	1.44	17.7	...	159	8 1/4	7 15/16	8 1/8	+ 1/16
9 1/4	3 1/16	MediaArt	...	...	4	125	4 5/8	4 5/8	4 5/8	...
84	64	MediaOne	...	...	9	21657	67 1/16	65 5/16	65 83/128	− 125/128
135	78 1/2	MediaO 01	1.56	1.8	...	22	84 1/2	81 1/2	84 1/2	+2 1/2
59 1/2	36 3/4	Media02 n	3.04	7.8	...	1005	39 7/8	38 1/16	39	+ 5/8
29	10	MedAsr	...	...	6	459	11 1/2	10 7/8	11 1/4	+ 3/8
51 15/16	20 1/4	Medicis	...	...	29	1562	46 1/2	44 1/8	45 7/8	+1 1/2
14 1/4	1 13/16	Meditrust	...	...	4	1777	2	1 15/16	1 15/16	− 1/16
57 7/8	**29 15/16**	**Medtrnic s**	**.16**	**0.3**	**61**	**67987**	**49 1/2**	**46 1/16**	**47 7/8**	**−2 7/16**
40 3/16	26 13/16	MellonFnc	.88 f	2.4	19	18458	37	35 7/16	36 1/8	+ 15/15
8 3/8	6 15/16	MentInc	.72	10.0	q	490	7 1/4	7 1/8	7 3/16	+ 1/16
81 1/8	52	Merck	1.16 f	1.6	29	47473	73 13/16	72 5/8	73 13/16	+1 1/2
37 1/8	20 15/16	MercGn	.96	3.6	12	432	26 5/8	25 3/4	26 9/16	+ 11/16
42	**22 3/8**	**Meredith**	**.32**	**1.1**	**17**	**954**	**29 3/16**	**27 9/16**	**29 1/8**	**+1 7/16**
9 3/16	3 13/16	MeridGld	.05	0.8	dd	393	6 1/4	5 15/16	6 1/8	+ 1/8
6 1/8	2 9/16	MeridRes	...	...	9	767	4 15/16	4 3/4	4 3/4	− 1/16
24 1/16	14 7/16	MeriStHsp	2.02	10.7	8	1185	19 1/8	18 7/8	18 15/16	− 1/8
4 1/2	2 1/8	MeriStHR	...	...	11	350	2 7/8	2 3/4	2 13/16	...
13 1/2	8 3/4	MeritagCp	...	...	3	39	11 11/16	11 1/2	11 11/16	+ 1/8
26 1/2	12 3/4	Meritor	.42	3.2	3	1760	13 1/4	12 15/16	13	+ 1/16
115 3/16	62	MerrLyn	1.20 f	1.2	14	25480	103 3/8	99 3/8	99 3/8	−2 7/16
54 1/2	34	MLCBR01	4.26	12.4	...	87	35	34	34 3/8	+ 3/16
13 3/16	11 7/16	ML DJ03	...	...	...	6	12 1/8	12 1/8	12 1/8	...
25	14 1/2	MLIGL01	2.39	13.2	...	129	18 1/4	18	18 1/8	+ 1/8
10 5/8	9	ML Nik02	...	...	...	20	9 1/8	9 1/8	9 1/8	− 1/16
24 15/16	19 7/8	MLSP01	...	...	...	88	22 9/16	22 1/2	22 1/2	− 3/16
18 5/8	15	MLSP02	...	...	...	34	16 3/4	16 11/16	16 11/16	− 1/16
12 1/8	10 1/4	MLSP905	...	...	...	28	11 3/8	11 1/8	11 1/8	− 3/16
11	9	MLSP07	...	...	...	8	10 1/2	10 1/2	10 1/2	− 1/8
18 1/16	15 3/4	ML Tech01	...	...	...	11	17 3/4	17 3/4	17 3/4	+ 1/16
3 3/8	2 3/16	Mesab	.38 e	13.2	...	70	3 1/16	2 7/8	2 7/8	− 1/16
23	14 3/16	Mestek	1.31 t	...	8	72	16 3/4	16 1/2	16 1/2	...
13 5/8	8 11/16	MetPro	.32	3.6	8	1144	8 15/16	8 11/16	8 13/16	+ 1/16
13 1/2	6 3/16	Metals	.03 p	...	6	287	6 1/2	6 5/16	6 5/16	− 3/16
19 11/16	14 5/16	MetLife n	...	...	...	20939	19	18 1/4	18 7/8	+ 5/8
64 1/4	50	MetLife un	...	...	...	2116	62 1/4	60 9/16	62	+1 1/16

The abbreviation *Div* stands for *dividend,* and the figures under this heading represent the current annual dividend per share, which is based on the latest quarterly or semiannual declarations, unless otherwise noted.

The next column, *YLD %*, stands for **yield,** or the percentage return represented by the annual dividend at the current stock price.

The *PE Ratio* refers to the **price/earnings ratio,** that is, the number of times by which the company's latest 12-month earnings must be multiplied to obtain the current stock price.

Sales 100s refers to the volume of shares in consolidated trading. Thus, 150 in the sales column would mean 15,000 shares traded.

The *High/Low/Last* columns refer to the day's trading price. The *High* column states the highest price paid for the stock during the day's trading session. The *Low* column tells the lowest price during the day's trading. The *Last* column shows the closing price, or the last sale of the day for each stock.

The abbreviation *Chg.* stands for *change* and represents the difference—plus, minus, or no change—between the day's last reported price and the preceding day's closing price.

These terms are summarized in the following diagram:

52-Week High	52-Week Low	Stock	Div	Yld %	P/E	Sales 100s	High	Low	Last	Chg
14	5 1/2	JilinCh	.12 e	1.8	3	51	6 3/4	6 1/2	6 1/2	− 1/2
17 1/4	8	JoAnnSt A	...	...	6	311	9	9	9	+ 1/16
13 1/8	6	JoAnnSt B	...	...	6	94	8	7 15/16	7 15/16	...
22 5/16	**13 7/16**	**JHFnSrv n**	...	...	...	**10073**	**21 3/4**	**20 1/2**	**21 3/4**	**+1**
43 11/16	33 1/2	JNuveen	1.04	2.5	14	429	41 7/8	41 1/8	41 3/8	+ 3/16
15	7 7/16	JohnsMnv	.24	2.0	7	549	12	11 3/4	11 13/16	− 5/16
106 7/8	66 1/8	JohnJn	1.28 f	1.5	33	28055	88 3/16	86 1/8	87	+ 1/8
73 7/8	46 7/8	JohnsnCtrl	1.12	1.8	13	3119	61 1/8	60	60 3/4	+ 3/8
35 7/16	20 1/8	JonesApp	...	...	17	3133	28	27 3/4	27 15/16	+ 7/16
32	9 3/16	JonesLL	...	...	dd	388	15 1/16	15	15	− 1/16
23	11 7/16	JrnlReg	...	...	13	197	14 3/16	13 13/16	13 13/16	− 7/16
		K								
10 9/16	6 3/16	K2 Inc	...	...	12	480	7 19/32	7 5/16	7 9/16	+ 3/16
2 3/8	3/16	vjKCS	...	...	6	1096	1 1/4	15/16	1 1/16	+ 1/8
29 1/16	16 3/4	KLM n	...	...	...	485	21 1/16	20 1/2	20 1/2	...
17 1/2	7 5/16	K mart	...	...	11	18466	8	7 3/4	7 15/16	+ 1/8
47 1/2	23 3/8	KN En01	3.55	7.9	...	508	44 15/16	44	44 15/16	+ 9/16
143 7/16	39 11/16	KPN	1.04 e	1.4	...	409	77 15/16	76 1/16	76 1/8	−2 5/8
32 13/16	14 3/4	KV Ph B	...	...	18	45	22 3/8	22	22	− 1/4
32 5/8	14 3/8	KV Ph A	...	...	18	133	22	21 1/2	21 3/4	+ 1/8
9 11/16	2 15/16	KaisAl	...	...	dd	748	4 9/16	4 3/8	4 3/8	+ 1/8
32 5/8	22	KanPipLP	2.80	11.3	11	117	24 15/16	24 3/4	24 7/8	− 1/16
6 15/16	4	Kaneb	...	...	3	171	5 3/16	5 1/16	5 1/8	− 1/16
29	20 13/16	KCtyPL	1.66	6.9	22	1354	24 3/8	23 5/8	24 3/16	+ 1/8
93 7/8	37 1/2	KC Sou	.04 j	...	21	3272	70	68 1/8	68 7/16	−1 13/16
17 1/4	**7 5/8**	**KatyInd**	**.30**	**2.7**	**10**	**110**	**11 1/2**	**11**	**11**	**− 3/4**
25 9/16	16 3/4	KaufBH	.30	1.7	6	2186	17 7/8	17 7/16	17 7/16	− 1/16
34 3/4	21 9/16	Kaydon	.44	1.9	13	352	23 5/8	22 3/4	22 7/8	− 3/16
36 1/8	21 3/4	Keebler	.11 p	...	29	1722	35 3/16	34 1/2	34 7/8	− 1/16
74	**8 3/16**	**Keithly**	**.22 f**	**0.4**	**27**	**1791**	**62 1/8**	**56 3/16**	**56 1/4**	**−3 9/16**
40 15/16	20 3/4	Kellogg	.98	3.2	32	13479	30 3/4	29	30 7/16	+1 1/8
27 13/16	13 3/4	Kellwood	.64	3.9	49	555	16 11/16	16 1/4	16 1/4	− 3/16
88 7/16	**16 3/4**	**Kemet**	...	...	**38**	**9752**	**76 3/4**	**63 1/2**	**64 3/8**	**−12 1/2**
9 5/16	7 7/16	KmpHi	.97	12.3	q	445	7 7/8	7 13/16	7 7/8	+ 1/16
7 3/16	6 1/8	KmplGv	.54	8.5	q	1044	6 3/8	6 1/4	6 3/8	+ 1/8
9 3/8	7 11/16	KmpMI	.93 a	11.3	q	466	8 1/4	8 1/16	8 1/4	+ 1/8
12 15/16	9 7/16	KmpMu	.82	7.7	q	802	10 13/16	10 5/8	10 11/16	− 1/16
17 3/8	12 1/8	KmpSInc	1.80	13.2	q	46	13 7/8	13 5/8	13 5/8	− 5/16
12 1/16	9 3/8	KmpStr	.75	7.3	q	308	10 5/16	10 1/8	10 5/16	+ 3/16
33 7/8	22 5/8	Kennmtl	.68	2.5	17	1746	27 3/8	26 11/16	26 15/16	...
46 1/8	17 5/8	KCole s	...	...	29	479	37 3/4	36 1/2	37 1/2	+ 1/2
42	**12**	**KentEl**	...	...	**43**	**1577**	**28 1/8**	**26 7/8**	**26 7/8**	**−1 3/8**
67 15/16	39 7/8	KerrMc	1.80	3.1	12	3511	59 13/16	58 1/2	58 1/2	− 3/8
53 1/4	30 13/16	KerrM04 n	1.83	3.5	...	2215	52 1/2	51 1/2	52 1/8	− 1/16
12 1/4	3	KeyEng	...	...	dd	2574	11 7/16	11	11 3/16	+ 1/16
15 3/8	6 3/4	KeyPrd	...	...	16	735	14 5/16	13 1/4	13 5/8	− 3/8
36	15 9/16	Keycorp	1.12	5.6	8	18418	20 9/16	19 1/4	19 7/8	+ 11/16
31 1/16	20 3/16	Keyspan	1.78	6.2	15	2202	29 3/16	28 13/16	28 7/8	...
7 11/16	3 3/4	KeyCon	...	...	dd	35	4	3 13/16	4	...
26 1/2	18	KilroyR	1.80 f	7.8	16	808	23 3/4	23 1/16	23 1/8	− 3/8
69 9/16	42	KimbClk	1.08	1.8	18	10356	60 1/16	57 3/4	59 3/4	− 1/4
42 1/4	30 7/8	Kimco	2.64	6.4	16	466	41 1/2	40 3/4	41 1/8	+ 5/16
45 5/8	35 1/4	KindME	3.10 f	8.2	14	1330	38 1/4	37 1/4	37 5/8	− 5/16

- The difference between the preceding day's last price and the current day's last price.
- The sales prices of the particular day: the highest price, the lowest price, and the price of the day's last sale.
- The volume of sales in round lots of 100.
- The price/earnings ratio (the current stock price divided by the company's last 12-month earnings).
- The percentage return of the annual dividends divided by the current price of the stock.
- The current annual dividend per share, based on the latest quarterly or semiannual declaration.
- The abbreviation of the company name.
- The highest and the lowest prices of the stock in the last 52 weeks.

Example 1   What was the performance of McDonald's common stock as it appears on the stock market report on page 222?

STEP 1.   Go down the list until you find McDnlds. This is the abbreviation for McDonald's common stock.

STEP 2.   In the last four columns, you will find:

a.   Its high price was $39\frac{1}{4}$ ($39.25)

b.   Its low price was $37\frac{3}{4}$ ($37.75).

c.   Its closing (last price) was $39\frac{1}{8}$ ($39.125).

d.   It is up $\frac{1}{4}$ ($0.25) since yesterday.

Note also that the stock is selling midway between its low and high values for the past year ($49\frac{9}{16}$ and $29\frac{13}{16}$).

Brokerage Fees on Stocks

Stock exchanges provide meeting places where exchange members can buy and sell securities. Individuals can buy or sell securities through brokers or commission houses who are members of the exchange and who act for the buyers and sellers.

A stockbroker charges a fee for his or her services in buying or selling stocks. This fee is in the form of a **commission** or **brokerage fee.** Some states also have a **transfer tax,** which the seller of stocks is charged. Since this is only a small part of the cost of selling securities, we will not consider the transfer tax in this unit.

Commission rates for buying or selling stocks are based on the money value of the transactions and the number of shares involved. A new system of competitive rates is in effect now, and brokerage firms are permitted to charge commissions at varying rates. The rates of some firms vary somewhat depending on the extent of the services offered, frequency of transactions, and size of the order.

Prevailing rates generally do not differ greatly from the minimum commission rates in the following brokerage fee table.

Minimum Commission Rates for Brokers
(Per 100-Share Orders and Odd-Lot Orders of Less than 100 Shares)

Money Involved in the Order	Minimum Commission
$100 but under $800	2.0% plus $ 6.40
$800 but under $2,500	1.3% plus $12.00
$2,500 and above	0.9% plus $22.00
Odd Lot = $2 less	

Example 2   John Gates purchased through his broker 400 shares of Gulf Oil at $46 $\frac{1}{4}$.

(a) Find the broker's fee.
(b) What is the total cost of the shares including the broker's fee?

HINT: Since the brokerage fee table shown is based on the dollar value per 100 shares, you must first find the cost plus brokerage fee on 100 shares of the purchase, then multiply this amount by the number of 100 shares in the purchase.

STEP 1.   Cost of 100 shares

$$= 100 \times \$46\frac{1}{4}$$
$$= 100 \times \$46.25.$$
$$= \$4,625$$

STEP 2.   Broker's fee on 100 shares

$$= 0.9\% \times \$4,625 + \$22$$
$$= 0.009 \times \$4,625 + \$22$$
$$= \$41.625 = \$41.63 + \$22$$
$$= \$63.63$$

STEP 3.   Broker's fee on 400 shares

$$= \$63.63 \times 4$$
$$= \$254.52$$

STEP 4.   Cost plus broker's fee of 100 shares

$$= \$4,625 + \$63.63$$
$$= \$4,688.63$$

STEP 5.   Cost plus broker's fee of 400 shares

$$= \$4,688.63 \times 4$$
$$= \$18,754.52 \quad Answer$$

Example 3   Mary Tanaka asked her broker to sell 300 shares of Greyhound. The stock was sold at $14 $\frac{7}{8}$ a share. After brokerage fees were deducted, what were the net proceeds of the sale?

As in Example 2, using the table on page 224, first find the selling price and broker's fee on 100 shares. Next, multiply the broker's fee on 100 shares by 3, the number of 100s in 300 shares sold.

HINT: To find the net proceeds, subtract the total broker's fee from the total amount of the selling price.

STEP 1.   Selling price of 100 shares

$$= 100 \times \$14.87.5$$
$$= \$1,487.50$$

STEP 2.   Broker's fee on 100 shares

$$= 1.3\% \times \$1,487.50 + \$12$$
$$= 0.013 \times \$1,487.50 + \$12$$
$$= \$19.34 \qquad\qquad + \$12$$
$$= \$31.34$$

STEP 3.   Broker's fee on 300 shares

$$= \$31.34 \times 3$$
$$= \$94.02$$

STEP 4. Selling price of 300 shares   = $1,487.50 × 3

                                               = $4,462.50

STEP 5. Net proceeds of sale   = $4,462.50 − $94.02

                                = $4,368.48   *Answer*

Example 4   James Williams purchased through his broker 70 shares of Norris at $41\frac{1}{4}$. What is the total cost of the shares including the broker's fee?

HINT: First find the cost of the 70 shares. Then, since this is an odd-lot order, refer to the brokerage fee table and use the appropriate minimum commission fee *less $2* (in this example, 0.9% plus $22 less $2).

STEP 1. Cost of 70 shares   = $70 × \$41\frac{1}{4}$

                           = 70 × $41.25

                           = $2,887.50

STEP 2. Broker's fee on 70 shares   = 0.9% × $2,887.50 + $20

                                     = 0.009 × $2,287.50 + $20

                                     = $25.99   + $20

                                     = $45.99

STEP 3. Cost plus broker's fee on 70 shares   = $2,887.50 + $45.99

                                                     = $2,933.40   *Answer*

Exercises

Exercise A   Rewrite each of the following stock prices in equivalent decimal form:

1. $21\frac{1}{4}$
2. $16\frac{1}{8}$
3. $48\frac{3}{8}$
4. $19\frac{1}{2}$
5. $63\frac{5}{8}$
6. $14\frac{1}{2}$
7. $36\frac{7}{8}$
8. $42\frac{3}{8}$
9. $19\frac{3}{4}$
10. $65\frac{5}{8}$

Find the net cost of the following lots of stocks at the indicated prices. (Change each price to a mixed decimal form.)

11. 40 at $67\frac{1}{4}$

12. 200 at $42\frac{1}{8}$

13. 75 at $63\frac{1}{2}$

14. 235 at $24\frac{3}{8}$

15. 400 at $36\frac{1}{8}$

16. 625 at $18\frac{5}{8}$

17. 450 at $23\frac{1}{4}$

18. 375 at $37\frac{3}{8}$

19. 175 at $53\frac{7}{8}$

20. 425 at $17\frac{1}{4}$

Find the preceding day's closing prices in each of the following stock prices. (Change all fractions to decimal equivalents.)

21. $18 $-\dfrac{1}{2}$

22. $15 $\dfrac{1}{4}+\dfrac{1}{8}$

23. $62 $\dfrac{3}{4}-\dfrac{7}{8}$

24. $27 $\dfrac{1}{8}-\dfrac{3}{8}$

25. $41 $-\dfrac{7}{8}$

26. $15 $\dfrac{1}{2}+\dfrac{3}{4}$

27. $22 $\dfrac{3}{4}-1\dfrac{7}{8}$

28. $34 $\dfrac{1}{8}+2\dfrac{1}{4}$

29. $62 $\dfrac{1}{4}-\dfrac{7}{8}$

30. $25 $\dfrac{7}{8}-\dfrac{1}{8}$

Refer to the stock market quotations on page 222. Find the net price of 350 shares of each of the following stocks that were bought at the prices indicated. (NOTE: The net totals do not include brokers' fees and other expenses.)

	Company	When Bought	Price per Share		Net Total Price	
31.	Lucent	Low	_____	_____	_____	_____
32.	KLM n	Last	_____	_____	_____	_____
33.	Kroger s	High	_____	_____	_____	_____
34.	Mead	High	_____	_____	_____	_____
35.	K mart	Last	_____	_____	_____	_____
36.	LizClab	Low	_____	_____	_____	_____
37.	MBNA	Last	_____	_____	_____	_____
38.	Mattel	Low	_____	_____	_____	_____
39.	LaZBoy	High	_____	_____	_____	_____
40.	Keyspan	Low	_____	_____	_____	_____

Exercise B Find the brokerage fee on each of the following sales of stock:

	Number of Shares	Price per Share	Brokerage Fee	
41.	200	$13\frac{1}{4}$	_____	____
42.	20	$87\frac{3}{4}$	_____	____
43.	50	$15\frac{1}{2}$	_____	____
44.	15	$74\frac{7}{8}$	_____	____
45.	600	$9\frac{5}{8}$	_____	____
46.	38	$64\frac{1}{2}$	_____	____
47.	75	$93\frac{1}{4}$	_____	____
48.	400	20	_____	____
49.	63	$12\frac{3}{4}$	_____	____
50.	32	76	_____	____

Find the total cost, including brokerage fees, for the following sales of stock:

	Number of Shares Bought	Price per Share	Selling Price		Brokerage Fee		Total Cost	
51.	300	$23	_____	____	_____	____	_____	____
52.	100	$17\frac{1}{2}$	_____	____	_____	____	_____	____
53.	500	$8\frac{3}{4}$	_____	____	_____	____	_____	____
54.	100	$25\frac{3}{4}$	_____	____	_____	____	_____	____
55.	60	$88\frac{7}{8}$	_____	____	_____	____	_____	____

Find the net proceeds for each of the following sales:

	Number of Shares Sold	Price per Share	Selling Price		Brokerage Fee		Net Proceeds	
56.	200	18\frac{1}{2}$						
57.	300	31$\frac{3}{4}$						
58.	100	63$\frac{5}{8}$						
59.	400	28$\frac{1}{2}$						
60.	500	14$\frac{7}{8}$						

Word Problems

Exercise C Refer to the stock market quotations on page 222 in solving the following problems:

61. Frank Greene bought 250 shares of JNuveen at the low price in the quotations.

(a) How much did he pay for the stock?
(b) How much did he save by not buying the shares at the high for the day?

62. James Vargas bought 400 shares of Korea at the previous 52-week low listed in the quotations.

(a) How much did he pay for the stock?
(b) If he sold the 400 shares at the 52-week high, how much profit did he make?

63. Janice Frank bought 275 shares of Libbey at the last price as listed in the quotations.

(a) How much did she pay for the stock?
(b) How much money did she save by not buying the stock at the preceding day's closing price?

64. If Mr. Rodriguez had purchased 500 shares of Maytag at the low for the day rather than at the high, how much would he have saved?

65. Mrs. Washington owned 350 shares of LabCp s, which she had bought at the previous 52-week low. If she sold the shares at the preceding day's closing price, how much profit did she make?

66. John Battaglio purchased 300 shares of Loews at the high for the day.

(a) What was the cost of the shares only?
(b) How much were the brokerage fees?
(c) What was the total amount he had to pay his broker?

67. Mrs. Sanchez bought 400 shares of MStewrt n at the 52-week low and sold the shares at the 52-week high.

(a) How much did the shares cost?
(b) How much profit did she make?

68. What were the net proceeds on 400 shares of MStewart n that sold at $17 $\frac{3}{4}$?

UNIT **4** Investments: Bonds

The Bond Market

Corporations raise large sums of money by issuing stock or borrowing money. When a corporation needs a sum of money that is too large to borrow from a lending institution, it will issue and sell *bonds* to the public through institutions that underwrite bond issues. These bonds are traded publicly on exchanges in the same manner that stocks are traded.

The basic difference between a stock and a bond is that stock represents ownership in a corporation, while a bond is like an IOU, representing money lent to a corporation or a government.

TERMS

Bond   Basically, a promissory note. The person who invests in a bond is lending a company or government a sum of money for a specified time with the understanding that the borrower will pay it back and pay a fixed interest for using it. Bonds are generally issued in denominations of $1,000.

Corporate bond   A bond issued by a corporation.

Government bond   A bond issued by the United States government.

Municipal bond   A bond issued by a state or a political subdivision, such as a county, city, town, or village.

Market value   The price at which a bond can be purchased between the time of issue and the date of maturity. Depending on market conditions, this can be higher or lower than par value.

Par value   The price of the bond at the time of issue.

Understanding Bond Market Reports

Bond market sales appear daily in newspapers in much the same way as stock market sales. Page 231 shows a section of one of these reports of corporate bond issues on the New York Stock Exchange.

STOCK EXCHANGE BOND TRADING

TUESDAY, MAY 23, 2000

NYSE BONDS

Company	Cur. Yld	Vol	Price	Chg
AMR 9s16	8.9	3	101 1/2	− 1 5/8
ATT 7 1/8 02	7.2	65	99 1/2	+ 1/8
ATT 6 3/4 04	6.9	45	97 3/4	+ 1 7/8
ATT 5 5/8 04	6.0	124	93 1/8	...
ATT 7 1/2 06	7.6	25	99 1/8	− 1/4
ATT 6s09	6.9	32	86 1/2	+ 1/2
ATT 8 1/8 22	8.3	97	97 1/2	+ 3/8
ATT 8 1/8 24	8.5	462	95 7/8	− 1 1/8
ATT 8 5/8 31	8.8	324	98 1/2	− 3/8
Aames 10 1/2 02	13.4	6	78 1/4	− 1 3/4
Alza 5s06	cv	15	131	+ 3

Company	Cur. Yld	Vol	Price	Chg
Alza zr14	...	35	66	+ 1 1/2
Amresco 10s03	19.6	16	51	− 2 1/8
Amresco 10s04	20.8	22	48	− 5
BkrHgh zr08	...	250	79 1/4	+ 1 1/4
BellPa 7 1/8 12	7.7	31	92 1/8	+ 1/8
BellsoT 6 1/4 03	6.5	31	96	− 2 1/8
BellsoT 7s05	7.1	150	98 5/8	+ 1/4
BellsoT 6 1/2 05	6.9	10	94 5/8	+ 1/4
BellsoT 5 7/8 09	6.8	22	86 1/8	+ 1/4
BellsoT 8 1/4 32	8.3	13	99 5/8	− 3/8
BellsoT 7 1/2 33	8.3	128	90 1/8	+ 1/2
BellsoT 6 3/4 33	8.3	138	81 1/8	− 1/4
BellsoT 7 5/8 35	8.3	2	91 1/2	− 1/8
BethSt 8 3/8 01	8.5	63	98	− 1

Company	Cur. Yld	Vol	Price	Chg
BethSt 8.45s05	9.1	53	93	− 1
CIT Gp 5 7/8 08	6.9	10	85	+ 1/4
CalEgy 9 7/8 03	9.9	25	100 1/8	− 2 7/8
CamdPr 7.33s01	cv	15	116	+ 1
CaterpInc 9 3/8 00	9.4	5	99 27/32	− 11/32
CentrTrst 7 1/2 01	cv	73	96 1/4	+ 1/4
ChaseM 6 1/2 05	7.0	10	92 1/4	− 1 3/4
ChaseM 6 1/8 08	7.0	2	88	...
CPoM 7 1/4 12	7.8	15	92 5/8	− 1/8
ChespkE 9 5/8 05	10.0	89	96	− 3/8
ChespkE 9 1/8 06	10.0	4	91 3/4	...
ChiqBr 10s09	12.6	350	79 1/4	− 3 7/8
ClrkOil 9 1/2 04	11.2	18	85	...
Coastl 8 1/8 02	8.1	20	100	...
Coeur 6 3/8 04	cv	145	41	− 6 7/8
Consec 8 1/8 03	11.8	26	69	− 7/8
Conseco 10 1/2 04	14.3	1	73 1/2	− 1 7/8
Conseco 10 1/4 02	15.8	70	65	− 1
ConPort 10 1/2 04	15.9	30	66	+ 3
DR Hrtn 10s06	10.0	37	99 5/8	+ 2 3/4
Deere 8 1/2 22	8.3	50	101 7/8	− 1/8
Dole 7s03	7.5	18	93 1/2	− 1
DukeEn 6 3/8 08	7.1	50	90	+ 3/8
DukeEn 7 7/8 24	8.3	7	95 3/8	...
DukeEn 6 3/4 25	8.2	50	82	− 1/2
DukeEn 7 1/2 25	8.4	10	89 3/4	− 1 1/8
FedDS 8 1/2 03	8.4	55	100 3/4	+ 3/4
FordCr 6 3/8 08	7.1	20	89 3/8	...
GBCB 8 3/8 07	9.5	40	88	...
GEICap 7 7/8 06	7.5	120	105	+ 1 3/8
GMA 6 7/8 01	7.2	37	96 1/8	− 1 7/8
GMA 7s02	7.1	15	98 1/2	− 3/8
GMA 8 1/2 03	8.3	15	102	...
GMA 5 7/8 03	6.2	1	95 1/8	+ 1/8
GMA dc6s11	7.3	34	82 1/4	+ 5/8
GMA zr12	...	8	349	− 2
GMA zr15	...	6	295	+ 5
GenesisH 9 3/4 05f	...	1476	13 1/2	...
HlthcrR 6.55s02	cv	24	88 1/4	− 1
Hilton 5s06	cv	215	75 7/8	− 1
Hollngr 8 5/8 05	9.0	50	95 3/4	+ 1
Honywll zr01	...	5	91	− 1
Honywll zr07	...	95	55 1/2	− 3/8
InldStl 7.9s07	10.5	5	75 1/2	− 4 1/2
IBM 6 3/8 00	6.4	25	99 27/32	− 1/32
IBM 7 1/4 02	7.3	10	99 7/8	+ 3/8

Company	Cur. Yld	Vol	Price	Chg
IBM 6.45s07	7.0	30	92 1/4	− 3/4
IBM 7 1/2 13	7.6	20	98 3/4	+ 3/4
IntShip 9s03	9.1	25	99	− 1 1/8
JCPL 6 3/8 03	6.7	5	95 1/4	− 5/8
JCP 6 3/4 25	8.3	15	81	+ 5
vjKCS En 8 7/8 08f	...	556	53 3/4	+ 3/4
KentE 4 1/2 04	cv	10	84 3/4	− 1/2
KerrM 5 1/4 10	cv	3	110	+ 1
KerrM 7 1/2 14	cv	84	92 3/4	− 1
LehmnBr 8 3/4 02	8.6	15	102	+ 1/2
Leucadia 7 3/4 13	8.5	76	90 3/4	+ 1/2
Lilly 8 1/8 01	8.1	15	100	− 1/8
LglsLt 7.05s03	7.3	10	96 5/8	...
Lucent 6.9s01	6.9	25	99 3/8	− 1/8
Lucent 7 1/4 06	7.4	10	98	+ 1/2
MSC Sf 7 7/8 04	cv	97	89	− 1
Malan 9 1/2 04	cv	31	89 7/8	+ 1/8
Mascotch 03	cv	23	75 1/2	+ 1/4
McDnl 6 5/8 05	7.0	10	94 1/2	− 5/8
Medtrst 9s02	cv	10	78	− 4 1/4
NatData 5s03	cv	73	81 1/2	− 2 1/2
NRurU 6 1/8 05	6.6	5	92 1/2	+ 1 3/8
NETelTel 4 1/2 02	4.8	65	93 1/4	− 1 1/8
NETelTel 7 7/8 22	8.2	2	96	− 1 7/8
NETelTel 6 7/8 23	8.1	5	84 1/2	+ 1/2
NYTel 4 5/8 02	4.8	50	96	+ 7/8
NYTel 7s25	8.3	25	84 3/4	+ 1 1/4
Noram 6s12	cv	25	84	− 1/2
OcciP 10 1/8 01	9.9	5	102 5/8	− 3/8
OcciP 10 1/8 09	9.2	110	110 1/4	− 1 1/4
OreStl 11s03	16.1	162	68 1/8	− 3 7/8
OutbM 7s02	cv	93	75 1/8	− 8 7/8
ParkerD 5 1/2 04	cv	71	71	− 5
PepBoys zr11	...	10	54 1/4	+ 1/4
PhilEl 6 1/2 03	6.8	2	96	...
PhilPt 7.2s23	8.6	10	83 3/8	− 1 7/8
PotEl 5s02	cv	130	94	+ 1/4
PrmHsp 9 1/4 06	9.5	10	97 1/2	...
PSvEG 6 1/8 02	6.4	10	96 1/2	− 1/8
Quanx 6.88s07	cv	29	83 5/8	− 3/8
Rallys 9 7/8 00	10.4	272	95	...
RalsP 9 1/4 09	8.7	70	105 7/8	− 3/8
RalsP 7 7/8 25	8.3	10	94 7/8	+ 2 1/8
RelGrp 9s00	10.0	4	90 1/4	+ 7/8
ReiGrp 9 3/4 03	15.2	10	64	+ 1/2
ReynTob 7 5/8 03	9.9	27	76 7/8	−, 3/8

Company	Cur. Yld	Vol	Price	Chg
ReynTob 8 3/4 04	11.1	35	79	+ 1
ReynTob 8 3/4 05	12.0	45	73	+ 1
Ryder 8 3/4 17	9.0	1	97	− 3
SearsAc 6 3/4 05	7.2	19	94	− 1 1/8
SilicnGr 5 1/4 04	cv	54	70	+ 1/2
SouBell 6s04	6.5	12	92 3/4	...
StdCmcl 07	cv	30	48 1/4	+ 1/4
StoneC 10 3/4 02A	10.7	115	100 1/4	+ 1/8
StoneC 10 3/4 02O	10.5	100	102 1/8	+ 3/8
StoneC 11 1/2 04	11.0	5	104 1/4	+ 1/8
StoneCn 6 3/4 07	cv	46	76	− 4
SunCo 7.95s01	8.0	15	98 7/8	− 1/2
SwiftE 6 1/4 06	cv	78	91 1/8	− 1 7/8
TVA 8 1/4 34	8.4	50	98 5/8	− 3/8
TVA 7 1/4 43	7.9	69	91 7/8	− 1/8
TVA 7.85s44	8.3	45	95	− 1
Tenet 6s05	cv	15	81 5/8	+ 1 7/8
Tenet 8s05	8.5	10	94 1/4	+ 1/8
Tenet 8 5/8 07	9.2	40	93 1/2	− 1
TmeWar 7.98s04	8.0	57	99 1/2	+ 1
TmeWar 7 3/4 05	7.8	10	99	+ 3/4
TmeWar 8.11s06	8.2	318	99 1/4	+ 3/8
TmeWar 8.18s07	8.3	11	99 1/8	...
TmeWar 8.05s16	8.0	10	100	...
US Timb 9 5/8 07	11.1	10	87	...
VaRy 6s2008	7.0	25	86	− 1/4
WsteM 4s02	cv	46	91 1/8	+ 5/8
Webb 9 3/4 03	9.8	60	100	+ 1/4
Webb 9 3/4 08	11.3	3	86 1/2	+ 1 1/2
Webb 10 1/4 10	12.3	152	83 1/2	− 2
Weirton 10 3/4 05	10.8	10	99 7/8	− 1/2
WhlPit 9 3/8 03	9.1	15	103 1/4	+ 1/8

AMEX BONDS

Company	Cur. Yld	Vol	Price	Chg
AltLiv 5 1/4 02	cv	10	49	+ 1 1/2
ArchCm 10 7/8 08f	...	37	50	− 7 1/2
ExcelLeg 9s04	cv	3	81	...
ExcelLeg 10s04	13.8	1	72 1/2	− 4 1/2
Paxson 11 5/8 02	11.3	3	103	+ 1/2
TWA 11 3/8 06	38.9	25	29 1/4	− 3/8
Trump 11 3/4 03f	...	7	77 1/4	− 1 1/4

BOND TABLES EXPLAINED

Bonds are interest-bearing debt certificates. Their value is usually quoted as a percentage, with 100 equaling par, or face value. This table shows the issuing company, then the original coupon rate (interest rate) and the last two digits of the maturity year.

Current yield represents the annual percentage return to the purchaser at the current price. The **Price** column refers to the bond's closing price, and **Chg** is the difference between the day's closing price and the previous daily closing price. A majority of bonds, and all municipal or tax-exempt bonds, are not listed on exchanges; rather they are traded over the counter

Other footnotes:

cv Bond is convertible into stock under specified conditions
cld Called
dc Selling at a discounted price
f Dealt in flat — traded without accrued interest
k Treasury bond, non resident aliens exempt from witholding tax
m Matured bonds
na No accrual of interest
p Treasury note, non-resident aliens exempt from witholding tax
r Registered
rp Reduced principal
st Stamped
t Floating rate
x Ex interest
vj In bankruptcy or receivership or being reorganized under the Bankruptcy Act, or securities assumed by such companies
wd When distributed
wl When issued
zr Zero coupon issue

Much of the material in the bond market report is the same as that for the stock report. There are, however, a few differences. The *par value* of every bond sold on the New York Stock Exchange is \$1,000. Every price quotation is given as a percent of the par value. Thus a quotation of $85\frac{5}{8}$ means that the price of the bond is $85\frac{5}{8}\%$ of its par value of \$1,000.

Example 1 Find the market value of a bond listed at $85\frac{5}{8}$.

$$\text{Market value} = 85\frac{5}{8} \text{ of } \$1{,}000$$

$$= 85.625\% \times \$1{,}000$$

$$= 0.856.25 \times \$1{,}000$$

$$= \$856.25 \quad \textit{Answer}$$

Shortcut: To determine the market value of a bond:

1. Change the quotation to a mixed decimal.
2. Move the decimal point two places to the right.

Example 2 Find the market value of a bond listed at $95\frac{3}{4}$.

STEP 1. $95\frac{3}{4} = 95.750$

STEP 2. $= 95.7{,}50$

$= \$957.50$ market value *Answer*

Another difference in the bond market report is in the *Net Change (Net Chg.)* quotations.

Shortcut: As with price quotations:

1. Convert the net change figure to a mixed decimal.
2. Move the decimal point one place to the right to convert to a dollar amount.

Example 3   If the net change of a bond is $-\frac{3}{8}$, how much will the bond have decreased in value from the preceding day's closing price?

STEP 1. $-\dfrac{3}{8}$ = -0.375

STEP 2.   = $-0.3\underset{\smile}{7}5$
             = $-\$3.75$

Net change = $3.75 less than preceding day's closing price.   *Answer*

Similarly, a net change of $+1\frac{1}{4}$ is changed to the mixed decimal 1.250 and is equal to an increase of $12.50 over the preceding day's closing price. A net change of –2 is written as 2.000 and is equal to a $20.00 decrease over the preceding day's closing price.

The name of the issuing company is followed by the original interest rate and the last two digits of the year of maturity. In the listing "ABrnd $9\frac{3}{4}$07," the "$9\frac{3}{4}$" indicates that the company is paying an interest rate of $9\frac{3}{4}$% per year to the holders of these bonds. The numeral "07" after the interest rate tells you that the bond matures in 2007. This means that the company will pay off the debt to the holders of this bond in 2007.

The column heading *Cur. Yld.* stands for *current yield* and represents the annual rate of return to the purchaser *based on the current price.* To help you understand this, let us assume that you purchased one ABrnd bond at the quoted price of "$95\frac{1}{4}$," or the market price of $952.50. The annual interest rate of the bond is $9\frac{3}{4}$% on $1,000 (the par value of the bond). The amount of interest paid by the company is $97.50 ($1,000 $\times$ $9\frac{3}{4}$%). If you hold the bond for a full year, you will earn $97.50 on *your investment of $952.50.* To find the *current yield,* or the actual yield, on your investment, you will have to find what percent $97.50 is of $952.50 . Recalling the $\frac{\text{IS}}{\text{OF}}$ formula, carry out the division indicated by the fraction:

$$\frac{\text{IS}}{\text{OF}} = \frac{\$97.50}{\$952.50} = 0.1024 = 10.24\%$$

$$\text{Proportion Method} \qquad \frac{x}{100} = \frac{97.50}{952.50}$$

$$\frac{\overset{1}{\cancel{952.50}}x}{\underset{1}{\cancel{952.50}}} = \frac{97.50}{952.50}$$

$$x = 97 \boxed{.}5 \boxed{\div} 952 \boxed{.}5 \boxed{=} 0.1023 \underline{|6\ldots}$$
$$= 10.24\%$$

Example 4 Find the current yield of a bond purchased at $87 \frac{1}{8}$ and paying an annual interest rate of $11\frac{1}{4}\%$. The cost of the bond is $871.25.

To find the current yield:

STEP 1. Interest paid $= 11\frac{1}{4}\% \times \$1,000$ Find the interest paid on the par value.

$= 0.1125 \times \$1,000$

$= \$112.50$

STEP 2. Current yield $= \$112.50 \div \$871.25$ Find what percent the interest paid is of the market value.

$\left(\dfrac{\text{IS}}{\text{OF}} = \dfrac{\$112.50}{\$871.25} \right)$

$= 0.1291$

$= 12.9\%$ *Answer*

$$\text{Proportion Method} \qquad \frac{x}{100} = \frac{112.50}{871.25}$$

$$\frac{\cancel{871.25}x}{\cancel{871.25}} = \frac{11{,}250}{871.25}$$

$$x = 11250 \boxed{\div} 871 \boxed{.}25 \boxed{=} 12.9 \underline{|12}$$
$$= 12.9\%$$

Brokerage Fees on Bonds

Stockbrokers charge a fee for the selling and buying of bonds for their clients. The fees of some firms may vary, but the following table is fairly representative of the prevailing rates.

Brokerage Rates on Bonds
(Quotations per Bond)

Bond Quotation	Minimum Fee
30 but under 50	$2.75
50 but under 70	$4.25
70 but under 90	$6.75
Over 90	$8.50

Example 5 Find the brokerage fee on three bonds sold at $87\frac{3}{4}$.

STEP 1. The quotation of $87\frac{3}{4}$ is between the rate "70 but under 90."
Therefore: Brokerage fee per bond = $6.75

STEP 2. Brokerage fee for three bonds = $6.75 × 3
= $20.25 *Answer*

Exercises

Exercise A Change each of the following bond price quotations to the actual price:

	Price Quotation	Price			Price Quotation	Price	
1.	$93\frac{1}{2}$	_____	__	2.	$78\frac{3}{4}$	_____	__
3.	$85\frac{3}{8}$	_____	__	4.	87	_____	__
5.	$102\frac{1}{4}$	_____	__	6.	$63\frac{1}{8}$	_____	__
7.	$47\frac{3}{4}$	_____	__	8.	81	_____	__
9.	$115\frac{1}{8}$	_____	__	10.	$52\frac{7}{8}$	_____	__
11.	$94\frac{5}{8}$	_____	__	12.	$78\frac{1}{2}$	_____	__
13.	$89\frac{1}{4}$	_____	__	14.	$104\frac{3}{8}$	_____	__
15.	$95\frac{1}{8}$	_____	__	16.	$77\frac{7}{8}$	_____	__

Convert each of the following net change quotations for bonds to the actual dollar equivalent:

	Net Change Quotation	Net Change	
17.	$+\dfrac{3}{4}$	___	___
19.	$-\dfrac{5}{8}$	___	___
21.	$-2\dfrac{1}{8}$	___	___
23.	$+1\dfrac{5}{8}$	___	___
25.	$-1\dfrac{3}{4}$	___	___

	Net Change Quotation	Net Change	
18.	$+1\dfrac{1}{2}$	___	___
20.	-3	___	___
22.	$+\dfrac{7}{8}$	___	___
24.	$-2\dfrac{1}{4}$	___	___
26.	$-3\dfrac{7}{8}$	___	___

Refer to the bond market quotations on page 231 to find the interest rate and the maturity date for each of the following bonds:

	Company	Interest Rate	Maturity Year
27.	AMR	___	___
28.	Coastl	___	___
29.	TVA	___	___
30.	Hilton	___	___
31.	Deere	___	___
32.	US Timb	___	___
33.	Trump	___	___

Find the cost for the number of bonds purchased in each of the following transactions:

	Number of Bonds	Quotation per Bond	Price per Bond		Total Price	
34.	3	$87\frac{1}{2}$	——	—	——	—
35.	5	$68\frac{3}{4}$	——	—	——	—
36.	4	$105\frac{1}{8}$	——	—	——	—
37.	5	$75\frac{3}{4}$	——	—	——	—
38.	8	$57\frac{5}{8}$	——	—	——	—
39.	12	$67\frac{1}{2}$	——	—	——	—
40.	13	$48\frac{1}{4}$	——	—	——	—
41.	15	$58\frac{7}{8}$	——	—	——	—

Using the bond market quotation report on page 231, find the total cost for the number of bonds bought at the indicated quotations.

	Company	Number of Bonds	Price per Bond		Total Price	
42.	ATT $\left(8\frac{1}{8}24\right)$	5	——	—	——	—
43.	Amresco $\left(10s04\right)$	3	——	—	——	—
44.	GMA $\left(8\frac{1}{2}03\right)$	8	——	—	——	—
45.	Dole	12	——	—	——	—
46.	IBM $\left(7\frac{1}{2}13\right)$	8	——	—	——	—
47.	PepBoys	15	——	—	——	—
48.	TVA $\left(7\frac{1}{4}43\right)$	14	——	—	——	—
49.	SearsAc	13	——	—	——	—

Find the current yield on each of the following bonds:

	Quotation	Price Paid		Interest Rate	Annual Interest		Current Yield
50.	$87\frac{1}{2}$	————	——	$9\frac{3}{4}\%$	————	——	——
51.	$102\frac{1}{4}$	————	——	$14\frac{1}{8}$	————	——	——
52.	$64\frac{3}{8}$	————	——	$11\frac{3}{4}$	————	——	——
53.	$85\frac{3}{4}$	————	——	13	————	——	——
54.	$56\frac{1}{8}$	————	——	$11\frac{3}{8}$	————	——	——

Exercise B Find the total brokerage fee on each of the following bond sales:

	Number of Bonds	Market Value	Fee per Bond		Total Fee	
55.	5	$53\frac{1}{2}$	——	——	——	——
56.	3	$47\frac{3}{8}$	——	——	——	——
57.	8	$69\frac{1}{4}$	——	——	——	——
58.	12	84	——	——	——	——
59.	15	$35\frac{7}{8}$	——	——	——	——
60.	9	$105\frac{1}{4}$	——	——	——	——
61.	6	$90\frac{1}{8}$	——	——	——	——
62.	11	$78\frac{3}{4}$	——	——	——	——
63.	14	$86\frac{1}{4}$	——	——	——	——
64.	13	$98\frac{3}{8}$	——	——	——	——

Find the total cost of each of the following bond purchases:

	Number of Bonds	Market Value	Fee per Bond		Total Fee		Total Cost	
65.	5	$95\frac{1}{2}$	——	—	——	—	——	—
66.	4	$115\frac{1}{4}$	——	—	——	—	——	—
67.	8	$69\frac{7}{8}$	——	—	——	—	——	—
68.	12	$46\frac{3}{8}$	——	—	——	—	——	—
69.	9	$86\frac{3}{4}$	——	—	——	—	——	—
70.	6	$78\frac{1}{2}$	——	—	——	—	——	—
71.	15	$48\frac{1}{8}$	——	—	——	—	——	—
72.	13	$35\frac{1}{4}$	——	—	——	—	——	—
73.	16	$65\frac{5}{8}$	——	—	——	—	——	—
74.	15	$89\frac{7}{8}$	——	—	——	—	——	—

Word Problems

Exercise C   Refer to the bond market report on page 231, and solve the following problems:

75.   Mrs. Wilson bought 12 bonds of ATT, paying 6% annual interest and maturing in the year 2009.

(a) How much did she pay for the bonds?
(b) If she keeps the bonds for a full year, how much interest will she earn?
(c) What is the current yield for each bond?

76.   Juana Vargas bought 8 bonds of BellPa.

(a) What was the total cost of the bonds?
(b) If she had bought the bonds at the preceding day's closing quotation, how much would she have paid for the bonds?
(c) After keeping the bonds for a full year, she sold them at the quotation price of $105 $\frac{1}{2}$.

(1) How much interest did she earn for the year?
(2) What was her profit in the sale of the bonds?

77. Mr. Romano bought 14 JCP bonds.

(a) What was the cost of the 14 bonds?
(b) How much was the brokerage fee for the sale?
(c) What was the total cost of the bonds?

78. Joel Berman sold 18 GMA ($8\frac{1}{2}$ 03) bonds.

(a) What was the total amount of the sale of the bonds?
(b) How much was the brokerage fee?
(c) What were the net proceeds the stockbroker sent to Mr. Berman?

UNIT 5 Review of Chapter Nine

Each of the following accounts had no withdrawals or deposits for the periods shown. Find the amount of interest and new balance for each account.

	Amount	Interest Rate	Period of Time	Amount of Interest		New Balance	
1.	$ 6,570	$6\frac{1}{4}\%$	3 years	_____	____	_____	____
2.	12,450	5.75	180 days	_____	____	_____	____
3.	8,340	13.263	30 months	_____	____	_____	____
4.	7,462	7.15	45 days	_____	____	_____	____
5.	15,600	12.725	6 months	_____	____	_____	____
6.	13,600	11.315	90 days	_____	____	_____	____
7.	4,400	14.72	3 months	_____	____	_____	____
8.	18,500	12.63	$2\frac{1}{2}$ years	_____	____	_____	____

Using the blank forms provided, prepare deposit slips for the following deposits:

9.

10.

11.

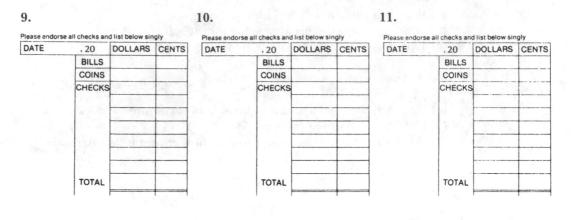

Please endorse all checks and list below singly			
DATE	, 20	DOLLARS	CENTS
	BILLS		
	COINS		
	CHECKS		
	TOTAL		

Please endorse all checks and list below singly			
DATE	, 20	DOLLARS	CENTS
	BILLS		
	COINS		
	CHECKS		
	TOTAL		

Please endorse all checks and list below singly			
DATE	, 20	DOLLARS	CENTS
	BILLS		
	COINS		
	CHECKS		
	TOTAL		

9. Bills: 7 $20's, 13 $10's, 16 $5's, 27 $1's
Checks: $142.75, $193.68, $186.48, $137.64

10. Bills: 12 $20's, 17 $10's, 27 $5's, 35 $1's
Checks: $235.80, $342.92, $167.87, $296.58

11. Bills: 15 $20's, 23 $10's, 28 $5's, 29 $1's
Checks: $143.79, $258.53, $178.38, $375.84

Using the blank forms provided, prepare the following checks. The balance brought forward is $816.92.

12.

No._____

_____20_____

Pay to the
order of_____ $_____

_____ Dollars

For_____   _____

13.

No._____

_____20_____

Pay to the
order of_____ $_____

_____ Dollars

For_____   _____

14.

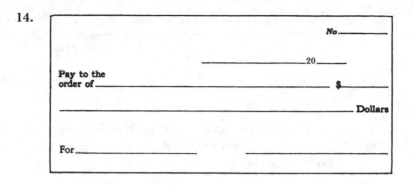

12. Check #142: To Federal Savings Bank for February mortgage payment; amount of check, $635.45; date of check, February 3.

13. Check #143: To American Express for February statement; amount of check, $235.63; date of check, February 6; deposit, $423.75.

14. Check #144: To New York Telephone Company for February bill; amount of check, $78.67; date of check, February 10.

Prepare a reconciliation statement for each of the following accounts:

	Checkbook Balance	Bank Statement Balance	Outstanding Checks	Service Charge	Other Adjustment	Corrected Balance
15.	$ 880.93	$845.75	$ 89.45 115.67 142.25	$3.75	$378.80 deposit not on bank statement	_____
16.	$1,072.06	$683.47	$132.91 261.30	None	$482.80 deposit not on bank statement; $300 arithmetic error in bank's favor	_____

Rewrite each of the following stock prices in equivalent decimal forms:

17. $63 $\frac{1}{8}$

18. $28 $\frac{1}{2}$

19. $18 $\frac{7}{8}$

20. $14 $\frac{3}{8}$

21. $31 $\frac{5}{8}$

Find the net cost of the following lots of stocks at the indicated prices:

22. 150 at $53 $\frac{1}{2}$

23. 225 at $62 $\frac{5}{8}$

24. 475 at $19 $\frac{1}{8}$

25. 650 at $8 $\frac{3}{8}$

Find the preceding day's closing price for each of the following stock prices:

26. 21\frac{3}{4}$ − $\frac{1}{2}$

27. 40\frac{1}{4}$ + 1$\frac{1}{8}$

28. 46\frac{1}{2}$ − $\frac{7}{8}$

29. 47\frac{7}{8}$ + $\frac{5}{8}$

For Problems 30 to 32, refer to the stock market quotations on page 222. Find the price per share and the net price of 475 shares of each of the following stocks that were bought at the prices indicated:

	Company	When Bought	Price per Share	Net Total Price	
30.	Kaneb	High	————	————	———
31.	JohnJn	Last	————	————	———
32.	MMT	High	————	————	———

Find the brokerage fee on each of the following sales of stock:

	Number of Shares	Price per Share	Brokerage Fee	
33.	300	23\frac{1}{8}$	————	———
34.	500	14$\frac{1}{4}$	————	———
35.	75	53$\frac{3}{8}$	————	———

Find the total cost including brokerage fees for each of the following sales of stock:

	Number of Shares Bought	Price per Share	Selling Price		Brokerage Fee		Total Cost	
36.	400	32\frac{3}{4}$	————	———	————	———	————	———
37.	600	9$\frac{7}{8}$	————	———	————	———	————	———
38.	200	45$\frac{1}{8}$	————	———	————	———	————	———

Find the net proceeds for each of the following sales:

	Number of Shares Sold	Price per Share	Selling Price		Brokerage Fee		Net Proceeds	
39.	300	16\frac{1}{4}$	———	—	———	—	———	—
40.	400	47$\frac{3}{8}$	———	—	———	—	———	—
41.	100	87$\frac{7}{8}$	———	—	———	—	———	—

Change each of the following bond quotations to the actual price:

42. $87\frac{1}{2}$ **43.** $105\frac{1}{8}$

44. $68\frac{7}{8}$ **45.** $95\frac{3}{4}$

Change each of the following net changes in bond quotations to the actual dollar equivalent:

46. $+\frac{7}{8}$ **47.** $-1\frac{1}{4}$

48. $-2\frac{1}{8}$ **49.** $+\frac{5}{8}$

Use the bond market quotations on page 231 to do the following problems:

	Company	Interest Rate	Maturity Year
50.	Aames	———	———
51.	CentrTrst	———	———
52.	Ryder	———	———

Find the cost for the number of bonds purchased in each of the following transactions:

	Number of Bonds	Quotation per Bond	Price per Bond		Total Price	
53.	8	78$\frac{1}{4}$	———	—	———	—
54.	12	93$\frac{5}{8}$	———	—	———	—
55.	15	61$\frac{3}{8}$	———	—	———	—

Find the annual interest and current yield on each of the following bonds:

	Quotation	Price Paid		Interest Rate	Annual Interest		Current Yield
56.	$93\frac{1}{2}$	——	——	$8\frac{1}{4}\%$	——	——	——
57.	$87\frac{1}{8}$	——	——	$13\frac{1}{8}$	——	——	——
58.	$72\frac{1}{4}$	——	——	$12\frac{3}{8}$	——	——	——

Find the brokerage fee on each of the following bond sales:

	Number of Bonds	Market Value	Fee per Bond		Total Fee	
59.	8	$79\frac{1}{4}$	——	——	——	——
60.	11	$96\frac{3}{8}$	——	——	——	——
61.	15	$88\frac{3}{4}$	——	——	——	——

Find the brokerage fee and total cost for each of the following purchases:

	Number of Bonds	Market Value	Fee per Bond		Total Fee		Total Cost	
62.	9	$105\frac{1}{8}$	——	——	——	——	——	——
63.	13	$99\frac{7}{8}$	——	——	——	——	——	——
64.	15	$83\frac{3}{8}$	——	——	——	——	——	——

Word Problems

Solve the following problems:

65. Maria has a savings account that earns an interest rate of 13.28%. If she earns a monthly interest of $134.50, how much money does she have in her savings account?

66. Carlos earned $5,375 in interest over a 3-year period. He opened his account 3 years ago with $36,480. What is the interest rate on Carlos's account?

67. Joel needs $375 a month to supplement his education expenses. If a bank pays an interest rate of 13.7%, how much money will Joel have to deposit to earn the monthly amount that he needs?

68. Samantha's checkbook shows a balance carried forward of $369.47. Her three previous checks were in the amounts of $243.60, $93.72, and $123.75. She also deposited $278.25. How much did she have in her checking account before she wrote the three checks?

69. Mark's checkbook shows a balance brought forward of $471.32. He wrote checks for $375.81, $167.25, and $87.77. In reviewing his check stubs, he noticed that he had made an error in entering a deposit of $386.95 as $586.95; he corrected this and also deposited a paycheck of $375.80. What should be his corrected balance carried forward on his last check stub?

CHAPTER **TEN**

Loans and Credit

UNIT **1** Promissory Notes

Banks earn a large part of their income from making personal and business loans. However, loans are also made by individual investors, businesses, and credit unions.

Generally, loans are guaranteed by a note, which identifies the terms of the transaction.

With an interest-bearing note (also called a **promissory note**), the person borrowing the money agrees to pay back the loan plus interest after a specified period of time.

For example, on August 23, Frank Cruz borrowed $450 from Hal Parker at 12% interest, to be paid back in 60 days. He gave the following promissory note to Hal Parker:

PROMISSORY NOTE

$ _450 00/100_   _August 23_   20_00_

60 days   after date _I_   promise to pay to

the order of _Hal Parker_

Four hundred fifty and 00/100   Dollars

at _123 Main Road, Anytown, NY_

Value received   _12%_

No. _31_   Due _October 22, 2000_

76 121   _Frank Cruz_

In this note:

- $450 is the **face value** or **principal.**
- August 23, 2000 is the **date** of the note.
- 60 days are the **terms.**
- Hal Parker is the **payee.**
- Frank Cruz is the **maker.**
- October 22, 2000 is the **due date** or **date of maturity.**
- 12% is the yearly **rate of interest.**

The terms of a promissory note may be a specified number of years, months, or days.

Finding the Maturity Date

Example 1 Find the maturity date of a 3-month note dated July 15.

Solution: Count 3 months forward from July 15: from July 15 to August 15 is 1, to September 15 is 2, to October 15 is 3.

Answer: October 15 is the maturity date.

PROCEDURE: To find the maturity date of a note whose terms are specified *in days:*

1. Write the date of the note (the day, not the month).
2. Add the terms of the note in days.
3. Subtract from that total the number of days in the month of the note's date.
4. Subtract the number of days in each of the following months from each remainder.
5. The day of maturity will be the last remainder that is less than the number of days in that month.

Example 2 Find the maturity date of a 60-day note dated March 9.

STEP 1.	9	Write the date of the note in March.
STEP 2.	$\dfrac{+\ 60}{69}$	Add the terms of the note.
STEP 3.	$\dfrac{-\ 31}{38}$	Subtract the number of days in March.
STEP 4.	$\dfrac{-\ 30}{8}$	Subtract the number of days in April.

Answer: The maturity date is 8 days into the next month, that is, May 8.

HINTS: To find the maturity date, you will have to remember the number of days in each month of the year. Try to memorize the following:

"30 days have September, April, June, and November.
All the rest have 31, except February, which has 28,
and in Leap Year, 29."

Another method of finding the number of days in each month is to make a fist. The knuckles represent the months that have 31 days (the high months). The spaces between the knuckles represent the months that have 30 days (the low months), with February having 28 or 29 days.

Finding the Maturity Value

The **maturity value** of a promissory note is the face value plus the *interest* for the term of the loan.

Example 3 Find the maturity value of a $600 note at 13% interest for 3 months.

HINT: Maturity value = Face value + Interest. To find the amount of interest, use the basic formula:

$$\text{Interest} = \text{Principal} \times \text{Rate} \times \text{Time}$$

$$I = P \times R \times T$$

STEP 1.　$I = \$600 \times 13\% \times 3 \text{ months}$

$$= \frac{\overset{6}{\cancel{600}}}{1} \times \frac{13}{\underset{1}{\cancel{100}}} \times \frac{\overset{1}{\cancel{3}}}{\underset{4}{\cancel{12}}}$$

$$= \frac{78}{4} = \$19.50 \text{ interest}$$

Use the formula $P \times R \times T$ to find the interest.

STEP 2.　　$600.00 ← face value
　　　　　<u>+ 19.50</u> ← interest
　　　　　$619.50 ← maturity value　*Answer*

Then add the face value and the interest to find the maturity value.

Check:　Maturity value　=　$600 + \left($600 \times 13\% \dfrac{\overset{1}{\cancel{3}}}{\underset{4}{\cancel{12}}}\right)

$$= \quad 600 \boxplus \boxed{(} (600 \boxtimes 0 \underset{\cdot}{\boxdot} 13 \boxtimes 1 \boxdiv 4 \boxed{)} \boxed{=} 619.5$$

$$= \quad \$619.50 \; \surd$$

Example 4　Find the maturity value of a $550 note at 12% interest for 45 days.

Maturity value = Face value + Interest

STEP 1.　　$I = P \times R \times T$

　　　　　$= \$550 \times 12\% \times 45 \text{ days}$

$$= \frac{\overset{5.50}{\cancel{550}}}{1} \times \frac{\overset{1}{\cancel{12}}}{\underset{1}{\cancel{100}}} \times \frac{\overset{3}{\cancel{45}}}{\underset{\underset{2}{\cancel{30}}}{\cancel{360}}} = \frac{16.50}{2} = \$8.25 \text{ interest}$$

STEP 2.　　$550.00
　　　　　<u>+　8.25</u>
　　　　　$558.25 maturity value　*Answer*

Check:　Maturity value　=　$550 + \left(550 \times 12\% \times \dfrac{45}{360}\right)$

$$= \quad 550 \boxplus \boxed{(} (550 \boxtimes 0 \underset{\cdot}{\boxdot} 12 \boxtimes 45 \boxdiv 360 \boxed{)} \boxed{=} 558.25$$

$$= \quad \$558.25 \; \surd$$

Note:　To simplify the calculation of interest, it is common practice to use a 360-day year. The 360-day year, known as the **commercial year,** consists of 12 months of 30 days each.

Exercises

Exercise A Find the maturity date for each of the following promissory notes:

	Date of Note	Terms	Maturity Date
1.	September 19	3 months	_____
2.	May 3	60 days	_____
3.	August 12	20 days	_____
4.	February 8	90 days	_____
5.	January 21	30 days	_____
6.	December 7	20 days	_____
7.	June 16	8 months	_____
8.	November 28	6 months	_____
9.	July 10	60 days	_____
10.	October 5	45 days	_____
11.	March 9	45 days	_____
12.	February 8	3 months	_____
13.	June 16	90 days	_____
14.	July 10	60 days	_____
15.	December 18	2 months	_____
16.	April 15	120 days	_____
17.	August 28	6 months	_____
18.	January 14	180 days	_____
19.	May 20	90 days	_____
20.	September 21	60 days	_____

Find the maturity date, interest, and maturity value of each of the following promissory notes:

	Face Value	Date of Note	Rate	Terms	Due Date	Interest	Maturity Value
21.	$ 790	July 3	13%	90 days	_____	____ __	_____ __
22.	850	Sept. 11	9	45 days	_____	____ __	_____ __
23.	475	Nov. 12	8.5	3 years	_____	____ __	_____ __
24.	1,250	Dec. 18	10	4 months	_____	____ __	_____ __
25.	950	Oct. 1	12	120 days	_____	____ __	_____ __
26.	2,450	May 27	14	60 days	_____	____ __	_____ __
27.	565	June 8	$10\frac{1}{2}$	40 days	_____	____ __	_____ __
28.	1,875	Feb. 17	11.75	6 months	_____	____ __	_____ __
29.	765	Mar. 12	$9\frac{3}{4}$	90 days	_____	____ __	_____ __
30.	1,550	Apr. 9	2.75	3 months	_____	____ __	_____ __

Word Problems

Exercise B   Solve the following problems:

31.   Find the due date and maturity value of a promissory note for $675 dated March 9, for 90 days at 14% interest.

32.   Find the due date of a promissory note dated June 16, for 120 days.

33.   On July 11 Jim borrowed $1,575 at 12% interest for 75 days and signed a promissory note. When will the note become due, and how much will he have to pay back?

34.   How much is the interest on a $950 note at 13% for 9 months?

35.   Find the face value of a note for 1 year at 9% if the amount of interest is $108.

UNIT **2** Borrowing from a Bank

You may need to borrow from a bank to pay college tuition, purchase a car, finance a vacation, or make home improvements. The bank will make a loan based on the **credit standing** of the individual, that is, his or her ability to repay the loan. Sometimes the bank will require either a **cosigner,** another person who will guarantee the repaying of the loan, or **collateral,** the temporary transfer of a possession to the bank to guarantee the loan.

If your loan is from a bank or some other lending institution, you will have to sign an agreement, similar to a promissory note, which states the amount of money borrowed, the rate of interest, the time or duration of the loan, and the details of repayment.

Calculating Interest

PROCEDURE: To calculate interest, multiply the **principal,** the amount of the loan, by the **rate of interest** and by the **time** (the duration) of the loan. The formula is

$$I = P \times R \times T$$

Example 1   Find the interest on a loan of $1,200 at 12% interest for 2 years.

STEP 1. $I = P \times R \times T$ Write the formula.

STEP 2. $I = \dfrac{\$1,200}{1} \times \dfrac{12}{100} \times \dfrac{2}{1}$ Substitute the given facts in the formula.

STEP 3. $I = \dfrac{\$1,\cancel{200}}{1} \times \dfrac{12}{\cancel{100}} \times \dfrac{2}{1} = 288$ Solve for interest.

$\quad = \dfrac{12}{1} \times \dfrac{12}{1} \times \dfrac{2}{1} = 288$

$\quad = \$288$ interest for 2 years *Answer*

Check: Interest for 2 years $= \$1,200 \times 12\% \times 2$
$= 1200 \boxtimes 0 \boxdot 12 \boxtimes 2 \boxminus 288 \checkmark$
$= \$288$

Example 2   Find the interest on a loan of $2,250 at 10% interest for 120 days.

STEP 1. $I = \quad P \quad \times \quad R \quad \times \quad T$

STEP 2. $I = \$2,250 \times \dfrac{10}{100} \times \dfrac{120}{360}$

STEP 3. $I = \dfrac{\overset{22.50}{\cancel{2250}}}{1} \times \dfrac{\cancel{10}}{\underset{10}{\cancel{100}}} \times \dfrac{\overset{1}{\cancel{120}}}{\underset{3}{\cancel{360}}} \dfrac{225}{3} = 75$

$\quad = \$75$ interest for 120 days   *Answer*

Check: Interest for 2 years $= 2250 \boxtimes \boxdot 1 \boxtimes 120 \boxdiv 360 \boxminus 75 \checkmark$

Calculating the Net Amount and Monthly Payments of Loans

On most personal loans, the bank will **discount** the loan; that is, it will deduct the amount of interest from the principal and give the borrower the **net amount.** The principal is paid back in monthly payments for the duration of the loan.

PROCEDURE: To find the net amount of a loan, subtract the interest from the amount of the loan.

Example 3   John borrows $3,750 at 13% for 2 years. The interest is discounted, and he has to pay back the loan in 24 payments. Find the net amount that John will receive and the amount of his monthly payment.

STEP 1. $I = \quad P \quad \times \quad R \quad \times \quad T$

STEP 2. $I = \$3,750 \times \dfrac{13}{100} \times \dfrac{2}{1}$

STEP 3. $I = \dfrac{\overset{37.50}{\cancel{3750}}}{1} \times \dfrac{13}{\underset{1}{\cancel{100}}} \times \dfrac{2}{1} = \quad = 975$

$\quad = \$975$ interest

STEP 4. $3,750 ← principal
            − 975 ← interest
            $2,775 ← net amount   *Answer*

Check: Net amount = $3,750 − (3,750 × 0.13 × 2)
                      =   3750 ⊟ ⦅ 3750 ⊠ 0 ⊡ 13 ⊠ 2 ⦆ ⊟ 2775 √

PROCEDURE: To find the monthly payment, divide the principal by the num-
             ber of payments.

STEP 5. $3,750 ÷ 24 = $156.25 monthly payment   *Answer*

The net amount of the loan is $2,775; the monthly payment is $156.25.

The 12%-30 Days Method

For short-term loans, it may be convenient to use the 12%-30 days method of calculating interest. This method can also be applied to other periods of days or
months.

One month, or 30 days, is $\frac{1}{12}$ of a 360-day (commercial) year. If the interest
rate is 12% per year, then the rate for 30 days is $\frac{1}{12}$ of 12%, or 1%.

PROCEDURE: To find the interest on a sum of money for 30 days at 12%,
             multiply the principal by 1% (0.01) by moving the decimal
             point in the principal two places to the left.

Example 4   Find the interest on a loan of $750 at 12% interest for 30 days.

Multiply $750 × 0.01 by moving the decimal point in the principal two places
to the left:

$$\$750 \times 0.01 = \$7.50 \text{ interest} \quad \textit{Answer}$$

Example 5   Find the interest on $865.85 at 12% interest for 30 days.

Multiply $865.85 × 0.01 by moving the decimal point in the principal two
places to the left:

$$\$865.85 \times 0.01 = \$8.65(85) = \$8.66 \text{ interest} \quad \textit{Answer}$$

Using Parts and Combinations of 30 Days

Bearing in mind that 12% for 30 days is equal to 1% of the principal, you can
make further application of this method.

HINT: If the period of time is 15 days, use the 30-day method and multiply the
       interest for 30 days by $\frac{1}{2}$, the fraction that 15 days is of 30 days $\left(\frac{15}{30} = \frac{1}{2}\right)$.

Example 6 Find the interest on $4,550 at 12% for 15 days.

STEP 1. $4,550 × 0.01 = $45.50 interest for 30 days

STEP 2. $\dfrac{\overset{22.75}{\cancel{\$45.50}}}{1} \times \dfrac{1}{\underset{1}{\cancel{2}}} = \$22.75$ interest for 15 days   *Answer*

Example 7 Find the interest on a loan of $1,800 at 12% for 45 days.

$$\$1,800 \times 0.01 = \$18$$

HINT: Interest for 30 days = $18.

Interest for 45 days = $18 × $1\dfrac{1}{2}\left(\dfrac{45}{30} = 1\dfrac{1}{2}\right).$

$$\dfrac{\overset{9}{\cancel{18}}}{1} \times \dfrac{3}{\underset{1}{\cancel{2}}} = \$27 \text{ interest for 45 days} \quad \textit{Answer}$$

Example 8 Find the interest on $1,350 at 12% interest for 120 days.

HINT: Interest for 30 days   = $13.50.

Interest for 120 days = $13.50 × 4 $\left(\dfrac{120}{30} = 4\right).$

$13.50 × 4 = $54 interest for 120 days   *Answer*

The following are the most commonly used parts and combinations of 30 days:

Using Parts and Combinations of 30 Days

Parts	Combinations
5 days = $\dfrac{1}{6}$	35 days = $1\dfrac{1}{6}$
6 days = $\dfrac{1}{5}$	40 days = $1\dfrac{1}{3}$
10 days = $\dfrac{1}{3}$	45 days = $1\dfrac{1}{2}$
15 days = $\dfrac{1}{2}$	60 days = 2
20 days = $\dfrac{2}{3}$	90 days = 3
25 days = $\dfrac{5}{6}$	120 days = 4
	150 days = 5
	180 days = 6
	210 days = 7
	240 days = 8
	300 days = 10

Exercises

Exercise A Find the interest and the net amount on each of the following discounted loans:

	Principal	Rate	Time	Amount of Interest		Net Amount	
1.	$1,285	10%	2 years	____	__	____	__
2.	1,500	$12\frac{1}{2}$	90 days	____	__	____	__
3.	2,350	13	60 days	____	__	____	__
4.	3,475	11.5	120 days	____	__	____	__
5.	5,425	$10\frac{1}{2}$	4 years	____	__	____	__
6.	3,215	$12\frac{1}{4}$	3 years	____	__	____	__
7.	2,875	8.75	$1\frac{1}{2}$ years	____	__	____	__
8.	4,365	11.5	36 months	____	__	____	__
9.	2,575	$9\frac{1}{4}$	9 months	____	__	____	__
10.	3,570	13	3 months	____	__	____	__

Find the interest, the net amount, and the monthly payment on each of the following discounted loans:

	Principal	Rate	Time	Amount of Interest		Net Amount		Monthly Payment	
11.	$1,875	13%	18 months	____	__	____	__	____	__
12.	2,325	14.5	12 months	____	__	____	__	____	__
13.	4,560	$11\frac{1}{2}$	36 months	____	__	____	__	____	__
14.	3,480	10	48 months	____	__	____	__	____	__
15.	2,750	13	24 months	____	__	____	__	____	__
16.	4,375	$10\frac{1}{4}$	48 months	____	__	____	__	____	__
17.	2,575	15	18 months	____	__	____	__	____	__
18.	3,200	12	36 months	____	__	____	__	____	__
19.	4,500	11.75	48 months	____	__	____	__	____	__
20.	5,250	11	48 months	____	__	____	__	____	__

Without using written calculations, find the interest at 12% on the following loans:

21. $685 for 60 days

22. $1,950.70 for 60 days

23. $2,400 for 30 days

24. $7,500 for 120 days

25. $5,260.75 for 60 days

26. $4,000 for 15 days

27. $3,237.80 for 60 days

28. $1,200 for 180 days

29. $5,000 for 240 days

30. $3,600 for 40 days

Find the interest and the total amount due on each of the following loans at 12% interest:

	Principal	Time	Interest		Amount Due	
31.	$3,475	60 days	____	__	____	__
32.	5,315	40 days	____	__	____	__
33.	2,463	150 days	____	__	____	__
34.	6,853	210 days	____	__	____	__
35.	4,295	10 days	____	__	____	__
36.	3,985	15 days	____	__	____	__
37.	2,560	75 days	____	__	____	__
38.	3,375	120 days	____	__	____	__
39.	4,290	90 days	____	__	____	__
40.	5,325	180 days	____	__	____	__

Word Problems

Exercise B Solve the following problems:

41. Sandy plans to borrow $1,250 to pay for a vacation. The bank charges 16% interest. Sandy expects to repay the loan in 18 months. If the bank discounts the interest, what is the net amount she will receive from the bank?

42. Bob took out a car loan from the bank. The loan was for $9,285 at 15%, to be paid back in 3 years. How much was each monthly payment?

43. John needs $1,800 to pay his college tuition. If the bank charges 11% and he plans to pay off the loan in 1 year, how much should the amount of the loan be?

44. Angelo repaid a 9% loan in 2 years. If the amount of interest was $122.50, what was the amount of the loan?

45. Jim took out a loan of $4,320 at 13% for 4 years. What was the net amount of the loan?

46. Jane borrowed $1,875 for 90 days at 12% interest. How much interest did she pay?

47. What is the total amount due the bank on a $1,370 loan at 12% for 45 days?

48. Jose borrowed $2,325 at 12% for 180 days. What was the net amount of the loan?

49. Find the interest on a $1,765 loan at 12% for 40 days.

50. What is the cost of borrowing $2,350 at 12% for 210 days?

UNIT **3** Credit Buying

Buying on credit has become a way of life in many American households. Department stores offer their own credit cards, and banks and other companies market major credit cards.

There are two main approaches to credit purchases: the use of a **credit card** and the use of an **installment plan.**

Credit cards typically are offered to an individual who has passed a credit search. These cards can then be used in stores or businesses accepting the card up to the credit limit set by the credit company. There are a number of different systems, but most provide a revolving line of credit to the cardholder and will add an interest charge on the unpaid balance.

Installment Buying

Expensive items such as furniture, home appliances, televisions, cars, and carpeting are often purchased on a time-payment or **installment plan.** Instead of paying cash or using a credit card, the buyer must make a **down payment** of part of the purchase price and sign an agreement to *pay the balance* in *equal monthly payments* for a specified period of time.

Total payments with an installment plan are usually higher than the cash price. The difference is called the **carrying charge.** The carrying charge is higher than the interest charged by a bank for a comparable loan because the retailer also adds to the interest the clerical cost of maintaining the installment sales.

Calculating the Carrying Charge

HINT: The carrying charge is the difference between the cash price and the installment price of an item.

Example 1   The cash price of a freezer is $525. The installment terms for the freezer specify a $75 down payment and 12 monthly payments of $42.50. Find (a) the total cost and (b) the carrying charge.

(a) Total cost = Down payment + Monthly payments
          = $75   + $510 (12 × $42.50)
          = $585 total cost   *Answer*

(b) Carrying charge = Total cost − Cash price
              = $585   − $525
              = $60 carrying charge   *Answer*

Some retailers will display the installment price of the item (including the carrying charges, the required down payment, and the number of monthly payments). To find the amount of each payment, subtract the down payment from the installment price and divide the difference by the number of payments to be made.

Example 2   The installment price of a piano is $2,890, the down payment is $250, and the balance is to be paid in 48 months. How much will each monthly payment be?

STEP 1. $2,890 − $250 = $2,640   Subtract the down payment from the price to find the balance.

STEP 2. $\dfrac{\$2,640}{48}$ = $55.00 per month   *Answer*   Divide the balance by the number of payments to find the amount of each payment.

Calculating the True Rate of Interest

The advantage of installment buying is that you can enjoy items you cannot immediately afford. The disadvantage is that carrying charges and interest can be very expensive.

Until recently, the cost of borrowing money was not easy to determine, as different firms used different methods to calculate the rate of interest. Then the Truth-in-Lending Law was passed, making the public aware of these rates, which are now calculated uniformly.

To verify the true interest rate, you may use the following formula:

$$R = \frac{2YC}{B(N+1)}$$

where R = true rate of interest
     Y = 12 months
     C = carrying charge
     B = balance of cash price minus down payment
     N = number of installments

Example 3 Mario purchased a stereo for $120 cash, or $15 down and 8 payments of $15 each. Find the true interest rate.

STEP 1. $15 + ($15 × 8) = $15 + $120 = $135   Find the installment price.

STEP 2. $135 − $120 = $15   Subtract to find the carrying charge.

STEP 3. $R = \dfrac{2YC}{B(N+1)}$ Substitute the figures from Steps 1 and 2 in the formula, and complete the problem.

$$= \frac{2 \times 12 \times 15}{105(8+1)} = \frac{2 \times \overset{4}{\cancel{12}} \times \overset{1}{\cancel{15}}}{\underset{7}{\cancel{105}} \times \underset{3}{\cancel{9}}}$$

$$= \frac{8}{21} = 0.381$$

```
        0.380 ⑨
21)8.000 0
    6 3
    1 70
    1 68
       20 0
       18 9
        1 1
```

$= 38.1\%$ *Answer*

Exercises

Exercise A Find the carrying charge for each of the following installment purchases:

	Item	Cash Price	Down Payment	No. of Payments	Monthly Payments	Carrying Charge	
1.	Carpeting	$ 775	$110	24	$33	____	__
2.	Color TV	590	75	12	53	____	__
3.	Washer	245	65	18	12	____	__
4.	Dryer	285	75	18	18	____	__
5.	Piano	1,250	225	36	45	____	__
6.	Refrigerator	465	120	18	25	____	__
7.	Diamond ring	525	85	24	27	____	__
8.	Freezer	615	90	24	30	____	__
9.	Dishwasher	185	45	18	13	____	__

Find the amount of each payment for the following installment purchases:

	Item	Installment Price		Down Payment	Number of Payments	Amount of Each Payment	
10.	A	$535	50	$ 75	18	___	___
11.	B	248	95	53	12	___	___
12.	C	627	80	95	24	___	___
13.	D	428	65	85	36	___	___
14.	E	347	80	72	12	___	___
15.	F	753	60	115	36	___	___
16.	G	757	90	53	24	___	___
17.	H	438	65	85	18	___	___
18.	I	235	19	64	12	___	___
19.	J	463	85	82	18	___	___

Find the true rate of interest on each of the following installment purchases:

	Item	Cash Price	Down Payment	Number of Payments	Monthly Payments	True Rate of Interest
20.	K	$ 550	$ 90	24	$28	___
21.	L	750	130	24	35	___
22.	M	610	85	12	54	___
23.	N	255	75	18	12	___
24.	O	275	70	18	18	___
25.	P	1,375	250	36	48	___
26.	Q	475	125	18	24	___
27.	R	650	110	24	30	___
28.	S	210	55	18	14	___
29.	T	510	75	24	26	___

Word Problems

Exercise B   Solve the following problems:

30.   The Wilsons bought a dining room set on the installment plan. The price of the set was $763.75. They made a down payment of $150 with the balance to be paid in 18 months. How much will each payment be?

31. A TV set can be bought for $465 cash or on the installment plan with a $50 down payment and 12 payments of $38 each. Find the carrying charges if the set is purchased on the installment plan.

32. Bill can buy a camera for $268 cash or with a down payment of $35 and 18 payments of $15 each. What is the true interest rate of the installment plan purchase?

33. The installment price of a freezer is $685. If the down payment is $75 and the balance is to be paid in 24 equal installments, how much will each installment be?

34. Tina bought a washing machine with a down payment of $45 and will make payments of $20 each. Find the true interest rate if the cash price for the washing machine is $350.

35. Alfredo bought a radio for $138.95. He made a down payment of $35 and will pay off the balance in 1 year. If the finance charge is $18.65, what will be the total balance to be paid?

UNIT **4** Review of Chapter Ten

HINTS:
- "30 days have September, April, June, and November. All the rest have 31, except February, which has 28, and in Leap Year, 29."
- The 12%-30 days method: 12% interest for 1 year is equivalent to 1% interest for 30 days.

Find the maturity date for each of the following promissory notes:

	Date of Note	Terms	Maturity Date
1.	February 15	4 months	_____
2.	January 28	60 days	_____
3.	April 20	90 days	_____
4.	July 17	120 days	_____
5.	December 18	45 days	_____

Find the maturity date, interest, and maturity value of each of the following promissory notes:

	Face Value	Date of Note	Rate	Terms	Due Date	Interest		Maturity Value	
6.	$1,460	Nov. 8	14.5%	180 days	_____	_____	_____	_____	_____
7.	2,575	Aug. 25	13	3 months	_____	_____	_____	_____	_____
8.	979	Mar. 15	$12\frac{1}{2}$	90 days	_____	_____	_____	_____	_____
9.	1,500	May 21	$15\frac{1}{4}$	45 days	_____	_____	_____	_____	_____
10.	3,125	Feb. 8	$11\frac{3}{4}$	60 days	_____	_____	_____	_____	_____

Find the interest and the total debt on each of the following loans:

	Principal	Rate	Time	Interest		Total Debt	
11.	$1,350	12.25%	3 years	_____	_____	_____	_____
12.	2,400	$13\frac{1}{4}$	180 days	_____	_____	_____	_____
13.	3,875	14.5	18 months	_____	_____	_____	_____
14.	2,670	11.75	24 months	_____	_____	_____	_____
15.	4,125	$14\frac{3}{4}$	$1\frac{1}{2}$ years	_____	_____	_____	_____

Find the interest, net amount, and monthly payment on each of the following loans:

	Principal	Rate	Time	Interest		Net Amount		Monthly Payment	
16.	$4,650	$14\frac{1}{2}$%	18 months	_____	_____	_____	_____	_____	_____
17.	5,690	13.25	24 months	_____	_____	_____	_____	_____	_____
18.	3,875	15.125	36 months	_____	_____	_____	_____	_____	_____
19.	6,540	13	48 months	_____	_____	_____	_____	_____	_____

Find the carrying charge for each of the following installment purchases:

	Item	Cash Price	Down Payment	Number of Payments	Monthly Payments	Carrying Charge	
20.	A	$ 875	$135	24	$40	____	____
21.	B	1,475	245	36	45	____	____
22.	C	1,175	225	18	65	____	____

Find the amount of each payment on each of the following installment purchases:

	Item	Installment Price		Down Payment	Number of Payments	Amount of Each Payment	
23.	1	$1,342	75	$325	36	____	____
24.	2	2,563	90	415	24	____	____
25.	3	1,168	85	285	18	____	____

CHAPTER **ELEVEN**

Home, Car, and Insurance Expenditures

UNIT **1** Home Ownership

With the continuing shift in population to the suburbs, more and more families are becoming homeowners instead of apartment dwellers.

The apartment dweller runs the risk that his or her rent will be increased over the years to the point where the rent will be equal to or more than the cost of maintaining a home. Also, the rent goes to the landlord, and the apartment dweller derives few benefits from the rent payments.

The homeowner's monthly mortgage payments to the bank remain relatively constant for the duration of the mortgage, with some increases if the real estate tax in the community is increased. The homeowner may look forward to paying off the mortgage and owning the home, or building up equity (part ownership) over the years.

In addition to the down payment, owning a home involves many expenses, such as interest on the mortgage, real estate taxes, insurance, and repairs.

Computing Mortgage Payments

When buying a house, the purchaser makes a down payment, which is usually between 10% and 20% of the cost of the house, and borrows the balance from a bank. He or she agrees to pay to the bank monthly payments that include the interest on the loan and a part of the principal.

The agreement the purchaser signs, called a **mortgage,** specifies the amount of principal, the rate of interest, and the number of years of the loan. Mortgages are usually made for periods ranging from 15 to 30 years. The rate of interest has varied over recent years from as low as 9% to as high as 16% or 17%. The rate will also vary from state to state during any one period. During the last few years, in addition to the conventional fixed rate mortgages, different types of mortgages have been introduced, including the variable rate mortgage.

A mortgage also serves as security for the loan. It gives the lender the right to take possession of the property if the borrower fails to pay the interest and principal in accordance with the agreement.

To help determine the monthly payments on mortgages, **amortization tables** are used to give the amount of the monthly payment needed to pay the principal and interest in the specified number of years.

The following table is based on each $1,000 of the mortgage for the number of years indicated:

TABLE 1. Monthly Payment Schedule for Each $1,000 of a Mortgage

Duration of Mortgage (years)	Interest Rate (%)							
	10	$10\frac{1}{2}$	11	$11\frac{1}{2}$	12	$12\frac{1}{2}$	13	$13\frac{1}{2}$
15	$10.75	$11.06	$11.37	$11.69	$12.01	$12.33	$12.66	$12.99
20	9.66	9.99	10.33	10.67	11.02	11.37	11.72	12.08
25	9.09	9.45	9.81	10.17	10.54	10.91	11.28	11.66
30	8.78	9.15	9.53	9.91	10.29	10.68	11.07	11.46

PROCEDURE: To find monthly mortgage payments:

1. Find the number of thousands in the amount of the mortgage by dividing by 1,000.
2. In Table 1, find the monthly payment per thousand dollars at the given mortgage rate for the duration of the mortgage.
3. Multiply the number from Step 1 by the amount in Step 2 to find the monthly payment.

Example 1   In purchasing her home, Martha Agnew was granted a mortgage of $22,350 at $11\frac{1}{2}\%$ for 30 years. How much will her monthly payments be?

STEP 1. $22,350 ÷ 1,000 = 22.35   First find the number of thousands in $22,350 by dividing by 1,000.

STEP 2.   Monthly payment = $9.91   In Table 1, find the monthly payment per $1,000 for 30 years at $11\frac{1}{2}\%$.

STEP 3.   22.35 × $9.91 = $221.49   Multiply to find the monthly payment.
monthly payment   *Answer*

In Example 1 you have calculated only the monthly payment needed to pay back the principal and interest on the loan for 30 years. However, the monthly payment to the bank will also include real estate taxes and insurance costs.

Real Estate Taxes

A major source of income for towns and cities to help pay for services such as schools, a police force, a fire department, and water supply is a **real estate tax** levied on buildings, homes, and land.

The amount of tax is based on the **assessed value** of the property. This value is determined by local tax assessors and is usually lower than the market value of the property.

The Tax Rate

The method of expressing the tax rate varies in different localities. The tax may be expressed as an amount in dollars for each $100 or $1,000 of assessed valuation, such as $6.486 per $100 or $64.86 per $1,000.

Example 2   Darryl Vukovich's home is assessed at $14,500. If the real estate tax rate is $5.863 per $100, how much real estate tax will he pay a year?

STEP 1. $14,500 ÷ 100 = 145   Divide by 100 to find the number of $100 units in $14,500.

STEP 2.   145 × $5.863 = $850.14 yearly tax   *Answer*   Then multiply 145 by $5.863, the rate per $100.

Example 3   Find the real estate tax on property assessed at $18,000, if the rate is $63.45 per $1,000.

STEP 1. $18,000 ÷ 1,000 = 18   Divide by 1,000 to find the number of $1,000 units in $18,000.

STEP 2.   18 × $63.45 = $1,142.10 tax   *Answer*   Multiply the result by $63.45, the rate per $1,000.

Some localities may express the real estate tax in *mills* per $1 or *cents* per $1 or as a *percent* of the assessed value.

PROCEDURE: To find the tax when the rate is expressed as mills or cents per $1:

1. Change the mills or cents to an equivalent number in dollars.
2. Multiply the result by the assessed valuation of the property.

HINT: There are 1,000 mills in 1 dollar. Therefore, to change mills to dollars, divide the number of mills by 1,000 and prefix the dollar sign to the result.

Similarly, there are 100 cents in 1 dollar. To change cents to dollars, divide the number of cents by 100 and prefix the dollar sign to the result.

Example 4   What will the tax be on a home assessed at $14,900 if the rate is 52 mills per $1?

STEP 1.   52 ÷ 1,000 = $0.052

Divide by 1,000 to change mills to an equivalent amount in dollars.

STEP 2. $14,900 × $0.052 = $774.80 tax   *Answer*

To find the tax, multiply the assessed valuation by $0.052.

Example 5   Mrs. Gerena's property is assessed at $17,500. How much tax will she pay if the rate is 5.25 cents per $1?

STEP 1.   5.25 ÷ 100 = $0.0525

Divide by 100 to change the cents to an equivalent amount in dollars.

STEP 2. $17,500 × $0.0525 = $918.75 tax   *Answer*

Multiply the assessed valuation by $0.0525 to find the tax.

Exercises

Exercise A Using the monthly payment schedule (Table 1) on page 265, find the monthly and yearly payments for each of the following mortgages:

	Mortgage	Rate	Period of Years	Monthly Payments		Yearly Payments	
1.	$45,350	$12\frac{1}{2}$ %	30	———	——	———	——
2.	28,790	13	20	———	——	———	——
3.	55,675	$10\frac{1}{2}$	25	———	——	———	——
4.	42,950	11	30	———	——	———	——
5.	64,500	$13\frac{1}{2}$	25	———	——	———	——
6.	48,350	$10\frac{1}{2}$	30	———	——	———	——
7.	51,570	$10\frac{1}{2}$	25	———	——	———	——
8.	48,650	12	30	———	——	———	——
9.	32,410	$11\frac{1}{2}$	25	———	——	———	——
10.	47,850	12	30	———	——	———	——

Find the real estate tax on each of the following properties:

	Assessed Valuation	Tax Rate	Amount of Tax	
11.	$12,500	$7.45 per $100	_____	___
12.	19,250	5.53 cents per $1	_____	___
13.	16,000	$62.35 per $1,000	_____	___
14.	15,750	73 mills per $1	_____	___
15.	21,500	7.23 cents per $1	_____	___
16.	14,250	$53.35 per $1,000	_____	___
17.	17,500	$6.28 per $1,000	_____	___
18.	18,250	54 mills per $1	_____	___
19.	9,500	$6.43 per $100	_____	___
20.	15,500	4.35 cents per $1	_____	___

Word Problems

Exercise B   Use the monthly payment schedule (Table 1) on page 265 in solving the following problems:

21.   Mr. Carlsen bought a $78,750 house. He made a 15% down payment and was granted a 30-year mortgage at $13\frac{1}{2}\%$ for the remainder. Find his monthly payments.

22.   Find the yearly cost of a $63,500 mortgage at $12\frac{1}{2}\%$ for 25 years.

23.   A house sells for $93,750. If the purchaser is required to make a 20% down payment and pay the remainder with a 30-year mortgage at $11\frac{1}{2}\%$, how much will the monthly payments be?

24.   Ana Lahti has a $13\frac{1}{2}\%$ mortgage. If $7,357.32 is her payment for the year for *interest only*, find the amount of her mortgage.

25.   A real estate agent offers a house for $48,950. If this includes a 15% commission for the agent, what would be the price of the house if bought directly from the seller?

26.   Mr. Morton paid $54,800 for his home. If it is assessed at 45% of the market value, how much tax will he pay if the tax rate is $6.85 per $100?

27. Mr. Bondi owns two pieces of property assessed at $9,500 and $7,250. What will be his tax for this year if the rate is 7.15% of the assessed value?

28. Last year, Ms. Fisher paid $816 in real estate tax. If the tax rate is 6.4% of assessed value, what is the assessed value of her property?

29. If the tax rate is 53 mills per $1, how much will the tax be on property assessed at $19,650?

30. Find the tax on a piece of property assessed at $16,500, if the rate is $74.50 per $1,000.

UNIT **2** Home Insurance

The homeowner, as well as the businessperson, needs protection against financial losses caused by fire, storms, water, smoke, falling aircraft, and explosion. Protection against loss by fire can be purchased from insurance companies at a nominal cost, and for a small additional charge **extended coverage** may be obtained for the other hazards.

The company selling the insurance is called the **insurer,** and the individual or company buying the protection is referred to as the **insured.** The contract between the insurance company and the insured is known as the **policy.** The amount of insurance covered by the policy is referred to as the **face** of the policy. The amount of money paid to the insurance company for the protection is called the **premium.**

Premium Rates

Premium rates are usually based on $100 units of insurance for 1 year. Insurance companies classify homes and buildings according to risk factors, such as construction, location, and use of the building, with higher rates charged when the risk of fire is greater.

To encourage homeowners to insure their property for periods longer than 1 year, insurance companies offer **term rates** as shown in Table 2.

TABLE 2   Term Rates

Period	Term Rate
2 years	1.85 times annual rate
3 years	2.7 times annual rate
4 years	3.55 times annual rate
5 years	4.4 times annual rate

Thus, if the annual rate is $0.26 per $100, a 3-year policy would be 2.7 × $0.26, or $0.702 per $100.

Example 1   A house is insured for $42,500. What is the annual premium if the rate is $0.28 per $100?

STEP 1. $42,500 ÷ $100 = 425

Divide by 100 to find the number of $100 units in $42,500.

STEP 2.   425 × $0.28 = $119 annual premium   *Answer*

Multiply the result by $0.28 to find the annual premium.

Example 2   Find the total premium for a 5-year policy on a home insured for $54,000 if the annual rate is $0.25 per $100 of insurance.

STEP 1.   4.4 × $0.25 = $1.10

Table 2 indicates that the term rate for a 5-year policy is 4.4 times the annual rate.

STEP 2. $54,000 ÷ $100 – 540

Divide by 100 to find the number of $100 units in $54,000.

STEP 3.   540 × $1.10 = $594 total premium   *Answer*

Multiply the result by $1.10.

Canceling a Policy

Seldom does a homeowner sell his or her house at the exact time the insurance expires. When a policy is canceled, the insurance company will refund part of the premium in proportion to the unexpired time of the life of the policy, on a **pro rata basis.**

Example 3   A fire insurance policy was canceled at the end of 125 days. If the yearly premium was $163, how much was refunded for the unexpired time of the policy?

HINT: The unexpired time is 365 days – 125 days, or 240 days. To find the amount of refund, multiply $\frac{240}{365} \times \$163$:

$$\frac{\overset{48}{\cancel{240}}}{\underset{73}{\cancel{365}}} \times \frac{163}{1} = \frac{7,824}{73} = 7824 \boxed{÷} 73 \boxed{=} 107.178$$

$$= \$107.18$$

$$= \$107.18 \text{ amount of refund}   \textit{Answer}$$

Exercises

Exercise A   Find the premium for 1 year on each of the following policies:

	Face Value of Policy	Annual Rate per $100	Annual Premium	
1.	$68,500	$ 0.35	_____	_____
2.	53,000	0.34	_____	_____
3.	61,750	0.29	_____	_____
4.	45,750	0.32	_____	_____
5.	54,000	0.36	_____	_____

Find the total premium on each of the following policies for the terms indicated:

	Face Value of Policy	Annual Rate per $100	Term of Policy	Total Premium	
6.	$57,500	$ 0.33	2 years	_____	_____
7.	69,750	0.36	4 years	_____	_____
8.	73,500	0.35	3 years	_____	_____
9.	68,750	0.32	5 years	_____	_____
10.	74,500	0.34	4 years	_____	_____

Find the unexpired days and the amount of refund on each of the following canceled yearly policies.

	Annual Premium	Policy in Force	Unexpired Days	Amount of Refund
11.	$186	75 days	_____	_____
12.	210	115 days	_____	_____
13.	224	235 days	_____	_____
14.	193	175 days	_____	_____
15.	215	180 days	_____	_____

Word Problems

Exercise B   Solve the following problems:

16. Mr. Sakata has insured his home for $98,000. If the rate is $0.53 per $100, how much will the annual premium be?

17. Jennifer Lodge insured her house, which is valued at $53,000, for 3 years. The annual rate is $0.55 per $100. If the 3-year term rate is 2.7 times the annual rate, how much is the total premium for the 3-year policy?

18. A fire insurance policy was canceled after 210 days. If the yearly premium was $235, how much was refunded by the company for the unexpired time of the policy?

19. Ben Singer wants to insure his home, which is valued at $63,000. The annual rate is $0.56 per $100, and the term rate for 5 years is 4.4 times the annual rate. How much would Mr. Singer save by insuring his home under the 5-year term rate?

20. Alec Theissen insured his home, which is valued at $78,000. If the annual rate is $0.64 per $100, how much is his premium?

UNIT 3 Car Ownership

There are two expense factors to consider when purchasing a car. One is the purchase expense, such as the down payment and the monthly payments to repay the balance plus finance charges. The other factor is the annual operating cost, which includes expenses such as license fees, insurance, parking, gasoline, oil, tires, repairs, general upkeep, and the annual depreciation of the car.

The largest single expense in owning a car is the annual depreciation of the car. The **depreciation** is the loss in value of the car through use and the passage of time. Thus, if you buy a car for $9,000 and 5 years later the car is worth $4,000, the value of the car has depreciated $5,000 over the 5 years.

Computing the Annual Depreciation

The greatest depreciation on a car occurs during the first year; depreciation decreases in the succeeding years. It is therefore most economical for the car owner to keep a car for as many years as possible, provided that the repair bills do not become too high.

The best method to estimate the annual depreciation is the **straight-line method,** in which the total depreciation is spread out evenly over the service life of the car.

Example 1   Athena bought a car for $9,200 and 5 years later traded it in for $900. How much was the average annual depreciation?

STEP 1.   Total depreciation   = $9,200 – $900
                                = $8,300

STEP 2.   Average annual   = Total depreciation ÷ Number of years
          depreciation

                               = $8,300   ÷ 5
                               = $1,660 average annual depreciation   *Answer*

Example 2   The original cost of a car was $8,000. If the average annual depreciation is $800, find the rate of depreciation.

Method 1: Fraction method

To find the annual rate of depreciation, write a fraction comparing the average annual depreciation to the original cost of the car. Carry out the division to the nearest hundredth, and change the decimal to a percent.

$$\frac{\$800}{\$8,000} = \frac{\overset{1}{\cancel{8}}}{\underset{10}{\cancel{80}}} = 0.10 = 10\% \text{ rate of depreciation}\quad Answer$$

Method 2: $\dfrac{\text{IS}}{\text{OF}}$ method

The facts in Example 2 can be restated as "$800 is what percent of $8,000."

$$\frac{\text{IS}}{\text{OF}} = \frac{800}{8,000} = \frac{\overset{1}{\cancel{8}}}{\underset{10}{\cancel{80}}} = 0.10 = 10\%$$

Use the proportion method to check the solution.

Method 3: Proportion method

$$Check: \frac{x}{100} = \frac{800}{8,000}$$

$$\frac{80x}{80} = \frac{\overset{10}{\cancel{800}}}{\underset{1}{\cancel{80}}} = 10$$

$$x = 10\%$$

Exercises

Exercise A   Find the annual depreciation in each of the following:

	Original Cost	Trade-In Value		Annual Depreciation	
		At the End of	Amount		
1.	$6,800	4 years	$1,300	_____	____
2.	8,400	5 years	900	_____	____
3.	9,800	6 years	1,100	_____	____
4.	7,500	6 years	800	_____	____
5.	8,650	5 years	900	_____	____

Find the annual depreciation and the rate of depreciation to the nearest percent in each of the following:

	Original Cost	Trade-In Value		Annual Depreciation	Rate of Depreciation
		At the End of	Amount		
6.	$8,350	5 years	$1,200	_____	____
7.	9,600	4 years	1,500	_____	____
8.	6,900	6 years	800	_____	____
9.	7,800	6 years	900	_____	____
10.	9,900	5 years	1,100	_____	____

Word Problems

Exercise B   Solve the following problems:

11.   Todd bought a car for $9,350. Six years later he sold it for $1,150. How much was the annual depreciation of the car?

12.   Harriette bought a car for $7,800. The trade-in value of the car after 3 years was $2,250 and after 5 years was $1,350. What was the average annual depreciation: (a) after 3 years? (b) after 5 years?

13.   Floyd bought a car for $9,500. Five years later he was allowed $1,150 for it toward the purchase of a new car. Find, to the nearest percent, the annual rate of depreciation.

14. A car cost $8,950. Find the annual cost of operating the car if the annual rate of depreciation is 23%, the cost of insurance is $287, expenses for gas and oil are $678, and the cost of general upkeep for the year is $235.

15. After keeping his car for 4 years, Marty sold it for $2,150. If he originally paid $7,275, what was the annual depreciation of the car?

UNIT **4** Automobile Insurance

A major expense in owning a car is the cost of insurance to protect the car owner against financial losses caused by car accidents.

There are four types of insurance that can be purchased to protect the car owner: **bodily injury, property damage, collision,** and **comprehensive.**

Bodily Injury Insurance

The greatest financial losses result from injuring other people. Many states make insurance mandatory for every car registered in these states. The basic bodily injury policy may be the $10,000/$20,000 or the **10/20 policy.** Under this policy the insurance company will pay any one person up to $10,000 for injuries caused in an accident, and a *total* of $20,000 to all people injured in the same accident.

Suppose you were involved in an accident that injured three people. One of the injured persons sues you and is awarded $12,500 by court action. The other two are awarded amounts of $3,500 and $2,500. The insurance company will pay the person who was awarded $12,500 only $10,000, because that is the maximum limit of the $10,000/$20,000 policy to any one person injured in the accident. You will have to pay the injured person $2,500 (the difference between the $12,500 award and the maximum $10,000 limit set by the policy). The insurance company will pay the full amounts to the other two persons, because the total of $3,500 and $2,500 added to the $10,000 paid the first person does not exceed the $20,000 maximum limit set by the policy.

For better protection, it is desirable for a car owner to purchase insurance having higher maximum limits. A $25,000/$50,000 policy will insure against losses of up to $25,000 for any one injured person and a maximum of $50,000 for all persons injured in the same accident. Frequently, policies of $50,000/$100,000, $100,000/$300,000, or higher are available to car owners.

Property Damage Insurance

This type of insurance protects you from financial losses in the event you damage someone else's property, such as a car, a house, a storefront, a lawn, a bicycle, or anything else of value. The basic property damage policy is for $5,000 and goes up to $50,000. If you have a $10,000 property damage policy and cause damage to property in the amount of $11,000, the company will pay only $10,000 and you will pay $1,000.

Rates for bodily injury and property damage insurance are based on four considerations:

1. The frequency with which accidents occur in the territory in which the insured lives.
2. The age of the principal driver.
3. The purpose for which the car is used.
4. The number of accidents the insured has had in the last 3 years.

Each state is divided into territories, with higher base premiums charged in territories with a higher frequency of car accidents. The person who lives in a busy city area will pay a higher base premium for the same coverage than the person who lives in a suburban or country area.

Following is a sample base premium table:

TABLE 3 Base Premiums for Private Passenger Automobiles

Type and Amount of Policy	Territory					
	01	02	03	04	05	06
Bodily Injury						
$ 10,000/$20,000	$84	$76	$63	$49	$32	$28
25,000/50,000	86	77	66	52	35	31
50,000/100,000	93	81	70	56	39	35
100,000/300,000	98	84	74	59	43	39
Property Damage						
$ 5,000	$36	$31	$28	$24	$20	$18
10,000	38	34	30	26	22	20
25,000	41	37	33	29	25	23
50,000	45	40	37	33	28	27

The next three tables—Age, Use of Car, and Driving Record—are called **factor tables.** The **factor** is a number by which the base premium is multiplied in order to find the cost of the insurance.

The age factor table takes into consideration the age of the principal driver. Statistical studies have found that the unmarried young male under the age of 21 has the most accidents. Therefore, he is assigned a higher cost factor until he reaches age 30. The male driver at age 30 and the female driver at age 21 will pay the base premium.

TABLE 4   Age Factor Table

Male		Female	
Age	*Factor*	*Age*	*Factor*
Under 21	2.50	Under 21	1.65
21–24	1.60	21–up	1.00
25–29	1.50		
30–up	1.00		

The next table is based on the use of the car and the distances driven.

TABLE 5   Use of Car Factor Table

Pleasure	Business	Work Less than 20 Miles	Work 20 Miles or More
1.00	1.75	1.15	1.55

The last consideration in figuring premiums is the number of accidents the insured has had in the last 3 years.

TABLE 6   Driving Record Factor Table

Number of Accidents	0	1	2	3	4
Factor	0.00	0.25	0.65	1.40	1.75

PROCEDURE: To find the cost of bodily injury and property damage insurance:

1. Check the three factor tables and add the appropriate factors from each table that apply to the insured.
2. Multiply the total factor by the base premium and round to the nearest dollar, because all premiums are charged to the nearest dollar.
3. Add the premium for each type of coverage to get the total premium.

Example   John Dale, age 23, purchased an insurance policy with $50,000/$100,000 bodily injury coverage and $25,000 property damage coverage. He lives in territory 04, had one accident last year, and uses the car for pleasure. Find the total premium for his insurance.

STEP 1.	Age factor	= 1.60	Check the three
	Use of car factor	= 1.00	factor tables to
	Driving record factor	= 0.25	find the total
	Total factor	= 2.85	factor.

STEP 2. Bodily injury premium = $56 × 2.85
$$= \$159.60$$
$$= \$160 \text{ (rounded off)}$$

Property damage premium = $29 × 2.85
$$= \$82.65$$
$$= \$83 \text{ (rounded off)}$$

Multiply the total factor by the base premium and round to the nearest dollar.

STEP 3. Total premium = $160 + $83 = $243   *Answer*

Add both premiums to get the total premium.

Collision Insurance

Collision insurance insures you against damages to your car as a result of collision caused by an accident with another car or any other object, a blowout, skidding, overturning, or any similar mishap. The damages paid by the insurance company will depend on the type of coverage you have. The types of policies are *$100 deductible*, *$200 deductible*, and *$500 deductible*.

With a $100-deductible policy, the insurance company will pay only for the part of the damages to your car that exceeds $100, because the first $100 is deductible. If you suffer damage to your car for $265, the company will pay only $165. If the damage is $95, the company will not pay, because the first $100 of damage is deductible.

Comprehensive Insurance

Comprehensive insurance protects you against any type of damage to your car through causes other than collision. In the case of fire or theft, the insurance company will pay the replacement value of the car at the time the car was destroyed by fire or stolen.

Exercises

Exercise A Using Tables 3 to 6, find the premium for each of the following bodily injury insurance coverages:

	Coverage	Territory	Sex	Age	Use	Number of Accidents	Premium	
1.	10/20	06	F	19	Pleasure	1	___	___
2.	50/100	04	M	18	Pleasure	2	___	___
3.	25/50	01	M	26	Business	0	___	___
4.	100/300	03	F	21	Over 20 miles	3	___	___
5.	50/100	05	F	30	Under 20 miles	0	___	___

Find the premium for each of the following property damage insurance coverages:

	Coverage	Territory	Sex	Age	Use	Number of Accidents	Premium	
6.	$10,000	03	M	23	Business	1	___	___
7.	5,000	06	F	20	Pleasure	0	___	___
8.	50,000	01	F	19	Under 20 miles	2	___	___
9.	25,000	04	M	26	Over 20 miles	0	___	___
10.	50,000	05	M	34	Pleasure	3	___	___

Word Problems

Exercise B Solve the following problems:

11. Arthur Wilson carries $100,000/$300,000 bodily injury coverage and $25,000 property damage coverage. He is 27 years old, lives in territory 02, and drives to work a distance of 17 miles. He had one accident 2 years ago. What are his yearly premiums for both coverages?

12. Wanda Gould was involved in an accident that injured five persons. Through court action she was required to pay the five persons the following amounts: $28,000; $16,000; $8,000; $7,000; and $4,000.

      (a) If her coverage for bodily injury was $50,000/$100,000, did the insurance company pay the full amounts awarded each person?

      (b) If her coverage had been $25,000/$50,000, how much would she have had to pay the injured persons?

13. During a rainstorm Luis skidded off the road and hit a tree. Repairs on his car amounted to $348.75. If he carried $50-deductible collision insurance coverage, how much did the insurance company pay for the damages?

14. Norma, age 18, lives in territory 04, uses her car for pleasure, and has had no accidents. She has bodily injury coverage of $50,000/$100,000 and property damage coverage of $25,000. Find the yearly premium for both coverages.

15. Evelyn is 20 years old, lives in territory 03, and drives to work a distance of 23 miles. She had one accident 2 years ago. Her coverage is $100,000/$300,000 for bodily injury and $50,000 for property damage.

      (a) Find the yearly premium for both coverages.

      (b) When she renews her policy next year, she will be over 21. What will her premium be then?

UNIT **5** Life Insurance

The purpose of life insurance is to protect families against financial hardship in the event the head of a family or other wage earner dies.

All insurance is based on the fact that, if a large number of people each contribute an amount of money, a fund is built up that enables a payment in the event of something adverse happening—a fire, an accident, or, in the case of life insurance, a death. The company or organization that administers the fund is called the **insurer.** The person whose life is insured is the **policyholder** or, simply, the *insured*. The details of the agreement between them is written in a contract called the **policy.** The money paid for this protection is the **premium.** The premium can be paid annually, semiannually, quarterly, or monthly, and is usually paid in advance. Upon the death of the insured, the amount of insurance purchased (the **face value** of the policy) is paid to a person or persons named in the policy. These payees are known as **beneficiaries.** There are four major types of life insurance: **term, straight life, limited-payment life,** and **endowment.**

Term Insurance

Term insurance provides protection for a limited period of years and is the least expensive form of life insurance. Term insurance may be purchased for limited periods of time, such as 5, 10, or 15 years. This type of insurance is usually purchased by young people when their financial responsibilities are greatest. For example, when purchasing a home, the purchaser will want to buy term insurance equal to the amount of the mortgage and for the same time period as the mortgage.

When purchasing a 15-year term policy with a face value of $15,000, the insured agrees to pay premiums for 15 years or until his or her death, whichever occurs first. The insurance coverage ceases at the end of the 15-year period. Should the insured die before the 15-year period ends, the beneficiary will receive $15,000. (As with all life insurance policies, the beneficiary will receive the full face value of the policy even though the insured may die after having made just one premium payment on the policy.)

Straight Life Insurance

Under a straight life insurance policy, the insured agrees to pay premiums for his or her entire life. At the time of the insured's death, the beneficiary will receive the face value of the policy.

Limited-Payment Life Insurance

With this type of policy, premiums are paid for a fixed period, such as 20 or 30 years. At the end of the fixed period, the insured stops paying premiums but is insured for the remainder of his or her life. The face value plus dividends, if any, are paid to the beneficiary at the time of the insured's death.

Endowment Insurance

This form of insurance is similar to the limited-payment life insurance policy. Premiums are paid for a fixed period of time. If the insured is still alive at the end of this period, he or she receives the face value of the policy and is no longer insured.

Table 7 shows sample annual rates for each $1,000 of insurance. These rates may differ somewhat from company to company and also may vary according to the health and occupation of the insured.

TABLE 7   Annual Premiums per $1,000 of Life Insurance

Age at Issue	Term		Straight Life	Limited-Payment Life		Endowment	
	10 Years	15 Years		20 Years	30 Years	20 Years	30 Years
20–24	$ 8.44	$ 9.21	$19.72	$34.63	$26.82	$57.42	$46.72
25–29	9.33	10.05	22.68	38.24	31.24	58.92	48.32
30–34	10.42	11.78	25.35	42.38	35.62	61.42	51.60
35–39	12.73	14.61	29.30	46.71	39.80	63.19	53.90
40–44	15.82	18.19	35.84	50.28	44.21	65.38	55.34
45–49	20.47	23.68	39.95	55.65	49.62	68.17	57.43
50–54	27.38	32.28	49.10	62.28	56.34	71.24	____
55–59	38.64	____	60.18	69.08	63.19	73.82	____
60+	____	____	75.72	81.54	73.34	74.15	____

Example   Find the annual premium of a straight life policy with a face value of $12,500, issued at age 27.

STEP 1. $12,500 ÷ 1,000 = 12.5

Find the number of 1,000's in $12,500 by moving the decimal point three places to the left.

STEP 2.   12.5 × $22.68 = $283.50 annual premium

Answer

Using Table 7, find the annual premium rate per $1,000 of straight life insurance at age 27 ($22.68). Then multiply by 12.5.

Exercises

Exercise A   Using Table 7, find the annual premium for each of the following policies:

	Policy	Age at Issue	Face Value	Premium per $1,000		Number of 1,000's in Face Value	Annual Premium	
1.	15-year term	22	$22,500	___	___	___	___	___
2.	30-year payment	43	35,000	___	___	___	___	___
3.	Straight life	28	24,500	___	___	___	___	___
4.	30-year endowment	33	25,000	___	___	___	___	___
5.	10-year term	26	19,500	___	___	___	___	___
6.	20-year payment	54	33,500	___	___	___	___	___
7.	Straight life	33	40,000	___	___	___	___	___
8.	20-year endowment	41	38,500	___	___	___	___	___
9.	10-year term	31	29,000	___	___	___	___	___
10.	Straight life	57	42,500	___	___	___	___	___

Word Problems

Exercise B Solve the following problems:

11. How much will the annual premium be on a 15-year term policy with a face value of $28,500, issued at age 26?

12. Find the annual premium on a 20-year payment policy for $35,000 issued at age 40.

13. At age 40, Gus Hartman purchased a 30-year endowment policy with a face value of $25,500. How much less would his annual premiums have been if he had purchased the policy at age 30?

14. Ernesto Hernandez purchased a $32,500 20-year payment policy at age 34. How much will he have paid in premiums for the 20-year period?

15. In Problem 14, if Mr. Hernandez had bought a 20-year endowment policy for the same face value, how much more would his yearly premium have been?

UNIT **6** Review of Chapter Eleven

Using Table 1, find the monthly and yearly payments for each of the following 30-year mortgages:

	Mortgage	Rate	Monthly Payment		Yearly Payment	
1.	$46,750	$10\frac{1}{2}\%$	_____	___	_____	___
2.	54,500	12	_____	___	_____	___
3.	53,250	$11\frac{1}{2}$	_____	___	_____	___
4.	49,990	$12\frac{1}{2}$	_____	___	_____	___

Find the real estate tax on each of the following properties:

	Assessed Valuation	Tax Rate	Amount of Tax	
5.	$24,700	$8.63 per $100	_____	____
6.	26,250	9.75 cents per $1	_____	____
7.	23,500	$11.25 per $1,000	_____	____
8.	31,450	87 mills per $1	_____	____

Find the premiums for 1 year in each of the following policies:

	Face Value of Policy	Annual Rate per $100	Annual Premium	
9.	$27,850	$0.47	_____	____
10.	34,500	0.43	_____	____
11.	39,250	0.48	_____	____

Find the total premium on each of the following home insurance policies for the term indicated. (Use Table 2 on page 270.)

	Face Value of Policy	Annual Rate per $100	Term of Policy	Total Premium	
12.	$42,500	$0.43	3 years	_____	____
13.	37,750	0.46	5 years	_____	____
14.	48,250	0.49	4 years	_____	____

Find the number of unexpired days and the amount of refund on the following canceled yearly policies:

	Annual Premium	Policy in Force	Unexpired Days	Amount of Refund	
15.	$235	113 days	_____	_____	____
16.	247	243 days	_____	_____	____
17.	253	195 days	_____	_____	____

Find the annual depreciation for each of the following cars:

	Original Cost	Trade-In Value		Annual Depreciation	
		At the End of	Amount		
18.	$9,575	5 years	$2,450	_____	____
19.	7,990	6 years	1,950	_____	____
20.	8,790	4 years	2,460	_____	____

Find the annual depreciation and the rate of depreciation to the nearest percent in each of the following:

	Original Cost	Trade-In Value		Annual Depreciation	Rate of Depreciation
		At the End of	Amount		
21.	$9,890	5 years	$2,725	_____	____
22.	8,950	6 years	1,850	_____	____
23.	9,745	5 years	2,650	_____	____

Find the premium for each of the following car insurance coverages:

	Coverage	Territory	Sex	Age	Use	Number of Accidents	Premium	
24.	Bodily injury 50/100	03	F	23	Business	2	_____	____
25.	Bodily injury 100/300	05	M	28	Over 20 miles	3	_____	____
26.	Property damage $50,000	02	F	19	Pleasure	0	_____	____
27.	Property damage $25,000	04	M	32	Under 20 miles	2	_____	____

Find the annual premiums on each of the following life insurance policies:

	Policy	Age at Issue	Face Value	Premium per $1,000		Number of 1,000's in Face Value	Annual Premium	
28.	30-year payment	35	$43,600	___	___	___	___	___
29.	15-year term	24	52,750	___	___	___	___	___
30.	Straight life	31	65,000	___	___	___	___	___
31.	30-year endowment	34	70,000	___	___	___	___	___

Word Problems

Solve the following problems:

32. The Harringtons can afford a monthly mortgage payment of $550. If their bank charges $11\frac{1}{2}\%$ on a 30-year mortgage loan, what should be the limit of their mortgage loan?

33. Adrienne Ganz bought a condominium for $66,250. She made a down payment of 20% and secured a 30-year mortgage for the balance at $13\frac{1}{2}\%$ interest.

    (a) How much will her monthly payments be?
    (b) How much less money will she pay for the same mortgage over a period of 25 years instead of 30 years?

34. Mr. Mendez bought a house for $87,950. His assessment for real estate taxes is 40% of the purchase price. If his tax rate is $11.95 per $100, how much will his monthly tax bill be?

35. Howard paid $67,500 for his house. His tax rate is $95.25 per $1,000, and his house is assessed at 50% of the purchase price.

    (a) How much will he pay per year in real estate taxes?
    (b) If he sold his house for $105,500 ten years later, how much will the new buyer pay a year in real estate taxes?

PART III

APPLICATIONS
OF MATHEMATICS
TO BUSINESS

CHAPTER **TWELVE**

Mathematics of Retailing

UNIT **1**   Sales Slips

In business, whenever a purchase is made, it is customary for a written record to be made. This enables both the businessperson and the customer to keep track of the details of the transaction. In a retail store, this written record usually takes the form of a **sales slip.** Your copy of the sales slip is not only proof that you paid for the purchase but is also usually required for return of an item or for service under a warranty.

Sometimes these sales slips are written by hand, but they are often generated by the cash register (today, a computer) and hence are called **cash register receipts** or simply **register tapes,** such as those that are seen in supermarkets.

The following information should be included on a sales slip:

1. The name, address, and telephone number of the store. This is usually preprinted so it need not be written in.

2. The date of the purchase and the name and address of the purchaser.

3. The quantity of items purchased, a description of the items, the unit price of each, and the amount. This amount, sometimes called the extension total, is found by multiplying the number of items by the cost of each.

4. The total amount of the purchase, which is found by adding all of the extensions and the appropriate sales tax.

5. The exchange policy of the store, which spells out the terms under which merchandise can be exchanged or returned.

Example   Following is a properly completed sales slip. Next to it is a cash register receipt for the same purchase.

<table>
<tr><td colspan="4">

G & G CLOTHING CO.
372 Elm Street
Baltimore, MD 21204

Aug. 3, 20 ___

SOLD TO   A. Borden

ADDRESS   475 Macon Street

Baltimore, MD 21204
</td></tr>
<tr><td>Quantity</td><td>Description</td><td>Unit Price</td><td>Amount</td></tr>
<tr><td>4</td><td>Shirts</td><td>5 75</td><td>23 00</td></tr>
<tr><td>2 pr.</td><td>Slacks</td><td>18 50</td><td>37 00</td></tr>
<tr><td>4 pr.</td><td>Socks</td><td>1 50</td><td>6 00</td></tr>
<tr><td colspan="3"></td><td>66 00</td></tr>
<tr><td colspan="3" align="right">Sales tax</td><td>5 28</td></tr>
<tr><td colspan="3" align="right">Total</td><td>71 28</td></tr>
<tr><td colspan="4" align="center">REFUNDS AND EXCHANGES MADE WITHIN
7 DAYS FROM DATE OF PURCHASE.</td></tr>
</table>

G & G CLOTHING CO.	
Aug. 03, 20–	
	5.75
	5.75
	5.75
	5.75
	18.50
	18.50
	1.50
	1.50
	1.50
	1.50
Subtotal	66.00
Tax	5.28
Total	71.28

Exercises

Exercise A   Find the total amount of each of the following sales. (The symbol @ means "each." Thus, "3 shirts @ $5.95" means that each shirt costs $5.95.)

1.   3 White shirts @ $5.95   _____

    2 pr. Slacks @ $17.50   _____

    1 Sport jacket @ $39.75   _____

                                 _____

         8% Sales tax →   _____

            Total   _____

2. 2 Blouses @ $8.95   _____

    2 Skirts @ $15.65   _____

    1 Sweater @ $11.75   _____

                          _____

        5% Sales tax →   _____

        Total   _____

3. 3 pr. Jeans @ $12.50   _____

    2 pr. Shoes @ $14.95   _____

    5 pr. Socks @ $1.95   _____

    1 pr. Sneakers @ $11.80   _____

                          _____

        7% Sales tax →   _____

        Total   _____

4. 4 Bed sheets @ $7.95   _____

    2 Bed covers @ $22.75   _____

    6 Pillow cases @ $2.50   _____

                          _____

        4% Sales tax →   _____

        Total   _____

5. 4 Window shades @ $6.25   _____

    3 Curtains @ $11.90   _____

    3 Curtain rods @ $3.75   _____

                          _____

        3% Sales tax →   _____

        Total   _____

Exercise B Using the forms provided, write a sales slip for each of the following purchases:

6. 2 pairs of gloves @ $5.95; 3 ties @ $4.35; 2 leather belts @ $3.99; 1 wool hat @ $9.49. The sales tax is 8%.

7. 2 bathing suits @ $27.95; 1 beach robe @ $15.50; 2 beach towels @ $3.75; 2 bathing caps @ $4.50. The sales tax is 5%.

8. 1 Instamatic camera @ $63.50; 3 rolls of film @ $2.75; 2 photo albums @ $3.95. The sales tax is 7%.

9. 5 sets of underwear @ $3.50; 8 pairs of socks @ $1.75; 2 pairs of slippers @ $5.95. The sales tax is 3%.

10. 2 pairs of shoes @ $22.95; 3 pairs of slacks @ $19.50; 2 sport shirts @ $11.75. The sales tax is 8%.

6.

```
                                    _____ 20
SOLD TO _____
ADDRESS _____
CLERK     | DEPT    | AMT REC'D
QUAN.     | DESCRIPTION      | AMOUNT
          |                  |
          |                  |
          |                  |
          |                  |
          | Subtotal         |
          | 8% Sales tax     |
          | Total            |
     POSITIVELY NO EXCHANGES MADE UNLESS
     THIS SLIP IS PRESENTED WITHIN 3 DAYS
```

7.

```
                                    _____ 20
SOLD TO _____
ADDRESS _____
CLERK     | DEPT    | AMT REC'D
QUAN.     | DESCRIPTION      | AMOUNT
          |                  |
          |                  |
          |                  |
          |                  |
          | Subtotal         |
          | 8% Sales tax     |
          | Total            |
     POSITIVELY NO EXCHANGES MADE UNLESS
     THIS SLIP IS PRESENTED WITHIN 3 DAYS
```

8.

```
                                    _____ 20
SOLD TO _____
ADDRESS _____
CLERK     | DEPT    | AMT REC'D
QUAN.     | DESCRIPTION      | AMOUNT
          |                  |
          |                  |
          |                  |
          |                  |
          | Subtotal         |
          | 8% Sales tax     |
          | Total            |
     POSITIVELY NO EXCHANGES MADE UNLESS
     THIS SLIP IS PRESENTED WITHIN 3 DAYS
```

9.

```
                                    _____ 20
SOLD TO _____
ADDRESS _____
CLERK     | DEPT    | AMT REC'D
QUAN.     | DESCRIPTION      | AMOUNT
          |                  |
          |                  |
          |                  |
          |                  |
          | Subtotal         |
          | 8% Sales tax     |
          | Total            |
     POSITIVELY NO EXCHANGES MADE UNLESS
     THIS SLIP IS PRESENTED WITHIN 3 DAYS
```

10.

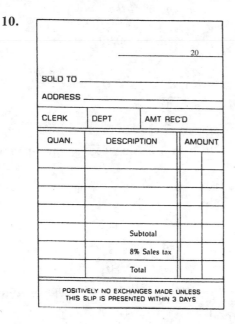

		20

SOLD TO _____

ADDRESS _____

CLERK	DEPT	AMT REC'D

QUAN.	DESCRIPTION	AMOUNT
	Subtotal	
	8% Sales tax	
	Total	

POSITIVELY NO EXCHANGES MADE UNLESS
THIS SLIP IS PRESENTED WITHIN 3 DAYS

UNIT **2** Unit Pricing and Pricing Fractional Parts

Finding the Unit Price

A supermarket shopper is confronted with a bewildering array of sizes, types, and prices of goods. Since it is extremely difficult to determine whether a 13-oz. can for $0.98 is a better buy than a 1-lb. 2-oz. can for $1.25, many stores have adopted a policy of **unit pricing.** In fact, unit pricing is required by law in some areas. When unit pricing is used, two prices are posted: one is the price of the item, and the other is the price per unit (per pound, per quart, etc.). Thus, if a can of vegetables is priced at $0.29 for an 8-oz. can, the unit price of "$0.58 per pound" would also be displayed.

PROCEDURE: To find the unit price of a given fractional part, divide the cost of the fractional part by the fraction of the unit. In the above example about the can of vegetables, 8 oz. $\left(\frac{1}{2} \text{ lb.}\right)$ was multiplied by the price per pound (unknown) to give the price of the can, $0.29. Writing these facts as an equation, you have

Check: $\frac{1}{2}$ lb. $\times u = \$0.29$

Proportion Method	*Equation Method*

$$\frac{1}{2} = \frac{0.29}{x}$$

$$\frac{1}{2} \times u = \$0.29$$

$$x = 0.29 \times 2$$

$$\frac{\frac{1}{2}u}{\frac{1}{2}} = \frac{0.29}{\frac{1}{2}} \qquad \text{Divide both sides by } \frac{1}{2}.$$

$$= 0.58$$

$$= \$0.58 \ \checkmark$$

$$u = 0.29 \times \frac{2}{1} \quad \text{Multiply by the}$$
$$\text{reciprocal of } \frac{1}{2}.$$

$$u = 0.58$$

$$= \$0.58$$

Answer: The price per pound is $0.58.

Example 1 What is the price per pound of a 4-oz. jar of instant coffee selling for $2.45?

Method 1: Equation Method

$$\left(4 \text{ oz.} = \frac{4}{16} \text{ lb.} = \frac{1}{4} \text{ lb.}\right)$$

$$\frac{1}{4} \text{ lb.} \times u = \$2.45$$

$$\frac{\frac{1}{4}u}{\frac{1}{4}} = \frac{2.45}{\frac{1}{4}} \qquad \text{Divide both sides by } \frac{1}{4}.$$

$$u = 2.45 \div \frac{1}{4}$$

$$= 2.45 \times \frac{4}{1} \qquad \text{The reciprocal of } \frac{1}{4} \text{ is } \frac{4}{1}.$$

$$= 2.45 \times 4 = 9.80$$

$$u = 9.80$$

$$= \$9.80$$

Method 2: Proportion Method

$$\frac{1}{4} = \frac{2.45}{x}$$

$$x = 4 \times 2.45$$

$$= 9.80$$

$$= \$9.80$$

Answer: The price per pound is $9.80.

Check: Use the $\dfrac{\text{IS}}{\text{OF}}$ fraction to solve this problem.

$$\frac{\text{IS}}{\text{OF}} = \frac{\$2.45}{\frac{4}{16}} = \frac{2.45}{1} \div \frac{\overset{1}{\cancel{4}}}{\underset{4}{\cancel{16}}} = 2.45 \div \frac{1}{4} = \frac{2.45}{1} \times \frac{4}{1} = 2 \boxed{.} 45 \boxed{\times} 4 \boxed{=} 9.8$$

$$= \$9.80 \text{ per pound}$$

Standard Units of Measure

Weight	Units
1 pound = 16 ounces	1 dozen = 12 items
1 ton = 2,000 pounds	1 gross = 144 items (12 dozen)
Distance	**Liquids**
1 foot = 12 inches	1 pint = 16 ounces
1 yard = 3 feet (36 inches)	1 quart = 2 pints (32 ounces)
	1 gallon = 4 quarts

Example 2   What is the unit price per gallon of a pint of cream marked $.49? 1 pint is $\frac{1}{8}$ of a gallon. There are 8 pints in 1 gallon.

$$\textit{Proportion Method}$$

$$\frac{1}{8} = \frac{0.49}{x}$$

$$x = 8 \times 0.49$$

$$= 8 \boxtimes 0 \boxdot 49 \boxminus 3.92$$

$$= \$3.92$$

Answer: The unit price per gallon is $3.92.

Example 3   Which package of green beans is more expensive, $6\frac{1}{2}$ oz. at $.49 or 18 oz. at $1.32?

Package 1. *Proportion Method*

$$6\frac{1}{2} \text{ oz. package}$$

$$\frac{6.5}{16} = \frac{\$.49}{x}$$

$$\frac{\cancel{6.5}x}{\cancel{6.5}} = \frac{7.84}{\cancel{6.5}}$$

$$x = \frac{7.84}{6.5}$$

$$= 7 \boxdot 84 \boxdiv 6 \boxdot 5 \boxminus 1.21 \boxdot$$

$$= 1.21$$

$$= \$1.21 \text{ per pound}$$

Package 2. *18 oz. package*

$$\frac{18}{16} = \frac{\$1.32}{x}$$

$$\frac{\cancel{18}x}{\cancel{18}} = \frac{21.12}{\cancel{18}}$$

$$x = \frac{21.12}{\cancel{18}}$$

$$= 21 \boxed{.} 12 \boxed{\div} 18 \boxed{=} 1.17 \underline{|3...}$$

$$= 1.17$$

$$= \$1.17 \text{ per pound}$$

Answer: The $6\frac{1}{2}$ oz. package is more expensive

Pricing Fractional Parts of Units

There are times when a customer will buy fractional parts of units of weights or measures, such as 6 ounces of ham priced at $3.75 per pound or 16 inches of ribbon priced at $1.79 per yard.

PROCEDURE: To find the cost of a fraction of a unit:

1. Change the units you bought to the fractional part of the unit in the price.
2. Multiply the fractional part of the unit by the price per whole unit. Note that any fraction of a cent is considered an additional cent.

Example 4 Find the cost of 6 oz. of ham priced at $3.75 per pound.

Caution: In this example, you bought 6 *ounces* and the price is given per *pound:*

STEP 1. 6 oz. $= \dfrac{6}{16}$ lb.

6 oz. is to 16 oz. as $x is to $3.75

Change the ounces to a fractional part of a pound.

STEP 2. $\dfrac{6}{16} = \dfrac{x}{\$3.75}$

$$\frac{\cancel{16}x}{\cancel{16}} = \frac{22.50}{16}$$

$$= 22.5 \boxed{\div} 16 \boxed{=} 1.40 \underline{|6....}$$

$$= 1.41$$

$$= \$1.41 \text{ for 6 oz.} \quad Answer$$

Remember: When setting up the proportion, establish it so that *the fractional units bought must be the same units as the units in the price:*

- If you bought 5 items and the price is per dozen, change the 5 items to $\frac{5}{12}$ of a dozen.
- If you bought 5 feet and the price is per yard, change the 5 feet to $\frac{5}{3}$ of a yard.

Exercises

Exercise A   From the information given, find the unit price of each of the following items:

	Item	Fractional Weight or Measure	Cost of Fractional Unit	Unit	Price per Unit	
1.	Candy	8-oz. bag	89¢	Pound	___	___
2.	Bologna	6-oz. pkg.	75¢	Pound	___	___
3.	Ribbon	2 ft.	62¢	Yard	___	___
4.	Velvet	24 in.	$ 3.75	Yard	___	___
5.	Pencils	36 doz.	2.75	Gross	___	___
6.	Coffee	12-oz. jar	4.25	Pound	___	___
7.	Wine	3 qt.	6.75	Gallon	___	___
8.	Tomato juice	8-oz. can	.25	Quart	___	___
9.	Socks	8 pr.	10.40	Dozen	___	___
10.	Underwear	5 pr.	12.75	Dozen	___	___

For each of the following items, from the information given, find the fractional part and its cost.

	Item	Price per Unit	Quantity Purchased	Fractional Part	Cost of Fractional Part	
11.	Coffee	$ 5.35 per pound	12 oz.	——	——	——
12.	Socks	14.75 per dozen	5 pr.	——	——	——
13.	Gingham	3.49 per yard	28 in.	——	——	——
14.	Oranges	1.05 per dozen	16	——	——	——
15.	Ribbon	2.15 per yard	2 ft.	——	——	——
16.	Paint	7.98 per gallon	3 qt.	——	——	——
17.	Velvet	6.25 per yard	48 in.	——	——	——
18.	Lamb chops	3.69 per pound	13 oz.	——	——	——
19.	Steak	2.85 per pound	25 oz.	——	——	——
20.	Candy	1.10 per pound	11 oz.	——	——	——

Word Problems

Exercise B   Solve the following problems:

21.   Mr. Welk bought a 6-oz. bag of candy for $1.45.

(a) What fraction of a pound did he buy?
(b) What is the price per pound?

22.   Carmen bought 7 handkerchiefs for $8.95. What is the price of the handkerchiefs per dozen?

23.   Mrs. Acosta bought $\frac{2}{3}$ yard of satin for $2.49. What is the price per yard?

24.   Mr. Lesbourne paid $163.50 for 1,500 pounds of coal. How much will a ton of coal cost?

25.   Mr. Goldberg bought 48 dozen wood screws for $12.75. What is the price per gross?

26.   Fran Greco bought 30 inches of linen priced at $3.85 per yard.

(a) What fraction of a yard did she buy?
(b) How much did she pay?

27.   How much would 14 oz. of cheese cost if the price was $2.69 per pound?

28. Instant coffee sells for $8.75 per pound. How much does a 4-oz. jar cost?

29. Geraldine bought 18 hair rollers priced at $4.89 per dozen. How much did she pay?

30. Gene bought 9 oz. of bologna priced at $2.75 per pound. How much did he pay?

UNIT **3** Sale Items

Goods offered for sale in retail stores usually have the prices written on price tags or tickets attached to the items. The price that the consumer pays for an article is called the **marked price, selling price,** or **list price.**

There are times when the retailer will reduce the price on some articles. The amount of reduction is called the **discount** or **markdown,** and the price the consumer pays is called the **sale price.** The reason for these reductions may be to sell slow-moving merchandise, to hold seasonal clearance sales, or to dispose of floor samples. The reduction in price may be in the form of either a discount percent to be deducted from the marked price or a new sale price written on the price tag with the original price crossed out.

Finding the Discount Amount

PROCEDURE: 1. To find the *discount amount,* multiply the original price by the discount percent.

2. To find the *sale price,* subtract the discount amount from the original price.

Example 1 During a clearance sale, a coat originally selling for $135 was marked down 30%.

(a) What is the discount amount?

(b) What is the sale price of the coat?

(a) Discount = Original price × Discount percent   To find the
amount   discount amount,
= $135   × 30%   multiply the
= 135   × 0.30   original price by
135   ☒ 0 ⊡ 30 ⊟ 40.5   the discount percent.
= $40.50

Proportion Method

$$\frac{0.30}{100} = \frac{x}{135}$$

$$x = 135 \times 0.30$$

$$135 \times 0.30 = 40.5$$

$$= \$40.50$$

Answer: Discount amount = $40.50

(b) Sale price = Original price − Discount amount

= $135 − $40.50

= $94.50

To find the sale price, subtract the discount amount from the original price.

Answer: Sale price = $94.50

In Example 1 you had to find the discount amount and the sale price. If you have to find the *sale price only,* you can use a more direct method. Since the discount percent is based on the original price, the original price is 100% of itself. If 30% is discounted from the original price, 100%, then the remaining percent, 70%, is the sale price percent. (100% minus 30% equals 70%.)

PROCEDURE: To find the sale price only:

1. Subtract the discount percent from 100%.
2. Multiply the original price by the remaining percent.

Example 2 What is the sale price of a camera originally priced at $235.95 and now marked 25% off?

STEP 1. Sale percent = 100% − Discount percent

= 100% − 25%

= 75%

STEP 2. Sale price = Original price × Sale percent

= $235.95 × 75%

= $176.96 *Answer*

Check:

$$\frac{0.75}{100} = \frac{x}{235.95}$$

$$x = 0 \boxed{.}\, 75 \boxed{\times}\, 235 \boxed{.}\, 95 \boxed{=}\ 176.962$$

$$= \$176.96\ \checkmark$$

Alternative Solution: To find the sale price only, rewrite the facts in the problem as an equation, and solve the equation.

$$\text{Sale price} = \$235.95 - (\$235.95 \times 25\%)$$
$$= 235.95 - (235.95 \times 0.25)$$
$$= 235 \boxed{.} 95 \boxed{-} \boxed{(} 235 \boxed{.} 95 \boxed{\times} 0 \boxed{.} 25 \boxed{)} \boxed{=} 176.96 \lfloor 2 \ldots$$
$$= \$176.9$$

$$= \$176.96 \quad \textit{Answer}$$

Some retail stores will advertise discounts as common fractions, such as "$\frac{1}{3}$ off original price." Since some of these fractions do not convert evenly to percents, it is often easier to use common fractions when calculating discounts or sale prices.

Example 3   What is the sale price of a TV set selling for \$465.99 during a $\frac{1}{3}$ off sale?

STEP 1.   Sale fraction $= \dfrac{3}{3} -$ Discount fraction

$$= \frac{3}{3} - \frac{1}{3}$$

$$= \frac{2}{3}$$

STEP 2.   Sale price $=$ Original price $\times$ Remaining fraction

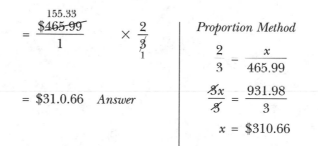

$$= \frac{\overset{155.33}{\cancel{\$465.99}}}{1} \times \frac{2}{\underset{1}{\cancel{3}}}$$

$$= \$31.0.66 \quad \textit{Answer}$$

Proportion Method

$$\frac{2}{3} = \frac{x}{465.99}$$

$$\frac{\cancel{3}x}{\cancel{3}} = \frac{931.98}{3}$$

$$x = \$310.66$$

Exercises

Exercise A Complete the following tables:

	Item	Original Price		Discount Percent	Discount Amount		Sale Price	
1.	Coat	$125	90	35%	——	—	——	—
2.	Jacket	63	75	$\frac{1}{3}$ off	——	—	——	—
3.	TV	169	50	25%	——	—	——	—
4.	Dress	73	25	15%	——	—	——	—
5.	Desk	87	50	$\frac{2}{3}$ off	——	—	——	—

	Item	Original Price		Discount Percent	Remaining Percent	Sale Price	
6.	Stereo	$237	00	$\frac{1}{3}$ off	——	——	——
7.	Chair	115	75	30%	——	——	——
8.	Radio	83	90	35%	——	——	——
9.	Typewriter	147	50	$\frac{2}{3}$ off	——	——	——
10.	Suit	125	50	45%	——	——	——

Word Problems

Exercise B Solve the following problems:

11. A refrigerator selling for $265.75 is marked down 25%. What is the sale price?

12. Carmen bought a coat during a "35% off" sale. The marked price of the coat was $89.50. How much did she pay for the coat?

13. A kitchen set selling for $342 is marked down 25%. What is the selling price of the set?

14. Thomas bought a record player that was selling for $142.90 less 35%. How much money did he save?

15. A lamp selling for $72 was marked down to sell for $54. Find the discount percent.

UNIT **4** Review of Chapter Twelve

Find the total amounts of each of the following sales:

Sample Solution:

1. 4 Shirts @ $9.95 $39.80

     2 Ties @ $6.75   13.50

     1 Sweater @ $15.90   15.90

                        69.20   69 ☐ . ☐ 20 ☒ 0 ☐ . ☐ 095 ☐ = ☐ 6.57 |4

                                            = $6.57

     $9\frac{1}{2}$% Sales tax (9.5%)   6.57

     Total $75.77

2. 3 Blouses @ $14.50   _____

     2 Skirts @ $27.95   _____

     1 Jacket @ $48.95   _____

                             _____

     8% Sales tax   _____

     Total   _____

3. 5 gal. White paint @ $8.85   _____

     6 rolls Wallpaper @ $15.95   _____

     1 Roller/pan set @ $5.35   _____

     2 Brushes @ $8.25   _____

                             _____

     $7\frac{1}{2}$% Sales tax   _____

     Total   _____

From the given information, find the unit price of each of the following items:

	Item	Fractional Weight or Measure	Cost of Fractional Unit		Unit	Price per Unit	
4. **5.**							
6.	Tuna	6 oz. can	$1	05	Pound	____	____
7.	Steak	13.4 oz.	2	68	Pound	____	____
	Fabric	$\frac{3}{4}$ yd.	5	25	Yard	____	____
	Ribbon	28 in.	3	60	Yard	____	____

Find the fractional part and the cost of the fractional part for each of the following items:

	Item	Price per Unit	Quantity Purchased	Fractional Part	Cost of Fractional Part	
8.	Candy	$4 75/lb.	11.25 oz.	____	____	____
9.	Veal	3 85/lb.	$14\frac{1}{2}$ oz.	____	____	____
10.	Satin	5 60/yd.	48 in.	____	____	____
11.	Wine	6 95/gal.	7 qt.	____	____	____

Find the discount amount and the sale price of each of the following items:

	Item	Original Price	Discount Percent	Discount Amount		Sale Price	
12.	A	$235 65	40%	____	____	____	____
13.	B	178 95	$\frac{1}{3}$ off	____	____	____	____
14.	C	141 85	30%	____	____	____	____

Find the remaining percent and the sale price of each of the following items. (Subtract the discount percent from 100%.)

	Item	Original Price	Discount Percent	Remaining Percent	Sale Price	
15.	A	$342 85	45%	____	____	____
16.	B	216 45	$37\frac{1}{2}$	____	____	____
17.	C	169 95	$12\frac{1}{2}$	____	____	____

Word Problems

Solve the following problems:

18. A 5-oz. jar of instant coffee sells for $4.85. How much is the price per pound?

19. If ham sells at $4.65 per pound, how much will 6 ounces cost?

20. A lamp selling for $165.95 is reduced by 45%.

    (a) What is the amount of reduction?
    (b) What is the sale price of the lamp?

21. A piano originally selling for $1,245.75 is on sale at 40% off. What is the sale price of the piano?

CHAPTER **THIRTEEN**

Mathematics of Purchasing

UNIT **1** Purchasing Goods

The Purchase Order

When a manufacturing or other business concern purchases merchandise, raw materials, or other items from a supplier, it will send a purchase order to the supplier.

The **purchase order** is a formal request to sell to the purchaser the items described at the prices indicated. Other important information on the purchase order includes how the merchandise is to be shipped, in some instances what the last date is for shipping the order, and how and when the invoice is to be paid (the **terms of purchase**).

In the purchase order that follows, the terms of purchase are *2/10 n 30*. This means that the purchaser may pay the invoice in one of two ways. He or she can deduct a 2% cash discount if the invoice is paid within 10 days from the date of the invoice, or he or she can pay the full amount within 30 days.

The Invoice

When the merchandise is shipped, the supplier will send an invoice to the purchaser indicating the goods ordered and shipped and the amount owed the supplier. The invoice and the goods received are usually compared to the original purchase order as a check that the prices and goods are exactly as ordered. At times, the quantities received will be less than the quantities ordered because the supplier may be out of stock on certain items and may ship only part of the original order.

AJAX BOX CORPORATION
243 East Willowdale Avenue
Santa Monica, VT 05040

INVOICE NO. **24749**

DATE March 25, 20 -

S
O   Acme Manufacturing Corporation
L   1775 Patriot Way
D   Burlington, Vt 05401
T
O

S
H
I
P
T
O

CUST. ORDER NO.	ORDER DATE	SALESMAN	F.O.B.	TERMS		SHIP VIA
127356	Mar. 3, 20--	Mail		2/10 n 30		Truck

NO. OF CASES	PACK	DESCRIPTION	CODE	PRICE	AMOUNT	
10	500	#170 Corrugated cartons	17356-X	0.0375	$187	50
		10% Trade discount			- 18	75
					$168	75
		Transportation			+ 14	63
				TOTAL AMOUNT ⟶	$183	38

INVOICE

ACME MANUFACTURING COMPANY
1775 Patriot Way
Burlington, VT 05401

To:
Ajax Box Corporation
243 E Willowdale Ave
Santa Monica, Vt 05040

PURCHASE ORDER

No.   127356
Date   March 3, 20-
Ship via   Truck
Terms   2/10 N30

Quantity	Description	Unit Price	Amount
5000	#170 Corrugated Cartons	0.0375	$187.50
	Discount	10%	- 18.75
	Net		$168.75
	Not for resale		
	Tax exempt No. 12374-36		

An **invoice** is an itemized statement informing the purchaser of the quantity, description, and unit and total prices of the items shipped. Additional invoice information includes the purchase order and invoice numbers; the date, cost, and method of shipment; and the terms of purchase.

The **terms of purchase** include a discount given to the purchaser to encourage the paying of the invoice within a specified number of days.

The term "2/10 n 30" means that the purchaser may deduct a *2% discount* if the invoice is paid within *10 days from the date of the invoice*. No discount may be taken after the 10th day, and the *full amount of the invoice is due in 30 days*.

To find the **discount date** (the last date on which the cash discount can be taken) and the **due date** (the last date on which the full amount of the invoice becomes due), you must know the number of days in each month of the year.

If you cannot remember that "30 days have September, April, June, and November. All the rest have 31, except February, which has 28 and, in leap year, 29," perhaps the "fist" method of checking the number of days in a particular month, as explained in Chapter Ten, Unit 1, will help.

Example 1 Find (a) the discount date and (b) the due date of an invoice dated January 19. The terms are 2/10 n 45.

(a) To find the *discount date,* add 10 days to the date of the invoice:

Jan. 19
+   10
———
Jan. 29   Discount date   *Answer*

According to the terms, if the invoice is paid on or before January 29, the 2% cash discount may be taken.

(b) To find the *due date,* follow the procedure you learned in Chapter 10, Unit 1:

1. Write the date of the invoice (January 19).
2. Add the number of days when the full amount becomes due (45).
3. Subtract the number of days in the month of the invoice date (January has 31 days).
4. Subtract the number of days in each of the following months until you get a remainder that is less than the number of days in a month. The last remainder will be the due date.

①		January 19	Invoice date
②		+ 45	Days in terms
		64	Total
③	(January)	– 31	Days in month of invoice date
		33	Remainder
④	(February)	– 28	Days in February
		March 5	Due date *Answer*

Example 2   An invoice in the amount of $347.75 is dated October 18 and the terms are 2/10 n 30. The invoice was paid on October 26. Find:

(a) The discount date.
(b) The due date of the full amount.
(c) The cash discount amount if paid within the discount date.
(d) The net amount paid if the cash discount is taken.

(a)   October 18
            +   10
      October 28   Discount date   *Answer*

(b)   October   18
            +   30
                      48
(October)   −   31
      November   17   Due date   *Answer*

(c) $3 47.75
      ×   0.02
      $6.95 50 = $6.96 Cash discount   *Answer*

(d) $347.75
      − 6.96
      $340.79   Net amount   *Answer*

Exercises

Exercise A   Find the discount date and the due date in each of the following:

	Invoice Date	Terms	Discount Date	Due Date
1.	April 5	2/10 n 30	———	———
2.	December 15	2/10 n 60	———	———
3.	April 25	2/10 n 45	———	———
4.	September 19	3/10 n 90	———	———
5.	February 11	2/10 n 60	———	———
6.	May 16	2/10 n 45	———	———
7.	August 23	2/15 n 60	———	———
8.	November 8	2/15 n 90	———	———
9.	January 13	2/10 n 30	———	———
10.	July 7	2/10 n 60	———	———

Find the discount date, the due date, and the net amount *or* the full amount as required in each of the following invoices:

	Invoice Date	Terms	Amount of Invoice		Discount Date	Due Date	Invoice Paid	Net Amount		Full Amount	
11.	9/10	2/10 n 45	$ 467	50	_____	_____	9/18	_____		_____	_____
12.	3/29	3/10 n 30	680	25	_____	_____	4/15	_____		_____	_____
13.	7/15	3/15 n 60	392	70	_____	_____	7/30	_____		_____	_____
14.	11/17	3/10 n 90	563	74	_____	_____	11/25	_____		_____	_____
15.	10/8	2/10 n 45	963	85	_____	_____	11/25	_____		_____	_____
16.	8/15	3/15 n 60	761	92	_____	_____	8/29	_____		_____	_____
17.	2/8	2/10 n 90	1,242	50	_____	_____	2/15	_____		_____	_____
18.	1/25	2/10 n 45	875	60	_____	_____	2/4	_____		_____	_____
19.	6/16	3/10 n 60	372	45	_____	_____	6/25	_____		_____	_____
20.	5/27	3/10 n 90	630	75	_____	_____	7/15	_____		_____	_____

Word Problems

Exercise B   Solve the following problems:

21. An invoice in the amount of $827.50 is dated 3/9. The terms are 3/15 n 60.

(a) What is the last day for the discount?
(b) When does the invoice become due?
(c) What is the net amount of the invoice, if paid within the discount date?

22. An invoice dated 5/11 in the amount of $863.70 was paid on 5/20. If the terms are 2/10 n 30, what should be the amount of the payment?

23. On 7/21 merchandise was shipped for $639.75, terms 3/10 n 45.

(a) Up to what date may the discount be taken?
(b) What is the last date for payment to become due?
(c) What is the net amount paid if the discount is taken?

24. An invoice is dated 3/12 in the amount of $735.65. The terms are 3/15 n 60.

(a) What is the discount date of the invoice?
(b) What is the due date of the invoice?
(c) What is the net amount if the invoice is paid within the discount date?

25. The Lace Novelty Company received an invoice dated 5/23 for $863.75. The terms are 3/10 n 45.

(a) Up to what date may the discount be taken?
(b) When is the full amount due?
(c) How much will the discount be?

UNIT **2** Calculating Trade Discounts

Some manufacturers and wholesalers sell their merchandise to retailers on the basis of a **suggested retail price** or **list price,** less a **trade discount.** The trade discount serves as a margin of profit for the retailer. The consumer will pay the suggested retail price, while the retailer will pay the manufacturer the **net price,** or **invoice price.**

The practice of giving trade discounts is generally used by manufacturers of standard items such as electrical appliances, cameras and photo equipment, and cars. In almost all cases, the trade discount is given as a rate of percent to be discounted from the list price.

PROCEDURE: To find the trade discount amount and the invoice price:

1. Multiply the list price by the rate of discount to find the amount of discount.
2. Subtract the amount of discount from the list price to find the invoice price, or net price.

Example 1   A refrigerator is listed in a catalog for $345 less a trade discount of 45%. Find the amount of discount and the cost of the refrigerator to the retailer (the invoice price).

STEP 1. $345   Multiply the list price by the
          $\times\ \ 0.45$ discount rate.
          ‾‾‾‾‾‾‾‾
            17 25
           138 0
          ‾‾‾‾‾‾‾‾
          $155.25   Amount of discount   *Answer*

Check: $\dfrac{45.}{100} = \dfrac{x}{345}$

$\dfrac{0.45}{100} = \dfrac{x}{345}$

$x = 155.25$

$= \$155.25\ \checkmark$

STEP 2. $345.00   Subtract the discount from the
        $-\ \ 155.25$ list price.
        ‾‾‾‾‾‾‾‾‾
        $189.75   Invoice price   *Answer*

In Example 1 you were asked to find the amount of discount *and* the invoice price. If the problem asks you to find the invoice price *only,* you may use the more direct method of finding the list price in one calculation. (This is the same direct method you learned in finding the sales price only in Chapter 12, Unit 3.)

PROCEDURE: To find the *invoice price only:*

1. Subtract the discount percent from 100%.
2. Multiply the remaining percent by the list price.

What you are really doing is subtracting the *percent values*— an operation that can be done without pencil and paper—instead of subtracting the *dollar values*—an operation that requires an additional calculation.

STEP 1.

100%	List price percent	Subtract the discount percent from 100%.
− 45%	Discount percent	
55%	Invoice percent	

STEP 2.

$$\begin{array}{r} \$345 \\ \times\ 0.55 \\ \hline 17\ 25 \\ 172\ 5 \\ \hline \$189.75 \end{array}$$ Invoice price   *Answer*

Multiply the remaining percent by the list price.

Check: $\dfrac{0.55}{100} = \dfrac{x}{345}$

$$x\ =\ 189.75$$
$$=\ \$189.75\ \checkmark$$

Alternative Solution: Rewrite the problem as an equation and solve the equation.

Invoice price = $345 − ($345 × 45%)

=   345 − (345 × 0.45)

=   345 $\boxed{-}$ $\boxed{(}$ $\boxed{(}$345 $\boxed{\times}$ 0$\boxed{.}$45$\boxed{)}$ $\boxed{=}$ 189.75

= $189.75 *Answer*

Calculating a Series of Discounts

Additional trade discounts are sometimes offered by manufacturers as an incentive to the retailer to buy in larger quantities. These manufacturers will offer a trade discount, plus additional discounts called **quantity discounts,** when the purchaser orders larger quantities. For example, an additional discount of 10% may be offered on purchases of more than 24 items, and an additional 5% on purchases of more than 48 items.

When two or more discounts are offered, the invoice price is found by *deducting each discount separately.* Each discount is figured on the *remaining balance after the previous discount has been deducted.*

There are several methods of solving problems dealing with a series of discounts. The method used should be the one best suited to the type of problem with which you will be working.

Example 2   A manufacturer lists a radio at $73.50. The trade discount is 40% and the quantity discounts are 10% and 5%.

Method 1   To find the amount of each discount and the invoice price.

If you are asked to find the *amount of each discount* and the *invoice price,* you will have to find each discount amount and subtract it from the remaining balance. The last balance will be the invoice price.

$73.50	List price	$73.50	
−29.40		× 0.40	
$44.10	First balance	$29.4000 First discount	*Answer*
− 4.41			
$39.69	Second balance	$44.10	
− 1.98		× 0.10	
$37.71	Invoice price *Answer*	$4.4100 Second discount *Answer*	

$39.69
× 0.05
$1.9845 Third discount   *Answer*

Method 2   To find the invoice price only.

If you are asked to find the *invoice price only,* multiply the *list price* by the *first remaining percent* and each *remaining balance* by each of the *remaining percents.*

$73.50
× 0.60   (100% − 40% = 60%)
$44.1000
× 0.90   (100% − 10% = 90%)
$39.6900
× 0.95   (100% − 5% = 95%)
19845
35721
$37.7055 = $37.71 Invoice price   *Answer*

Method 3   To find a single discount percent that is equivalent to a series of discount percents.

You may save time in calculating the invoice price by finding a *single discount percent* that is equal to a series of discount percents. To find a single discount percent that is equal to a series of discount percents:

1. Multiply the *remaining percents* by *each other.*
2. Subtract the product from 100%.

STEP 1. $60\% \times 90\% \times 95\% = 0.60 \times 0.90 \times 0.95$
$= 0.513$
$= 51.3\%$

STEP 2. $100\% - 51.3\% = 1.000 - 0.513$
$= 0.487$
$= 48.7\%$ Equivalent single discount percent   *Answer*

Check: $73.50 × 48.7\% = 35.79
$73.50 − $35.79 = 37.71 Invoice price $\checkmark$

Exercises

Exercise A Find the amount of discount and the invoice price for each of the following:

	List Price		Trade Discount Percent	Amount of Discount		Invoice Price	
1.	$245	50	35%	___	___	___	___
2.	363	75	40	___	___	___	___
3.	135	60	50	___	___	___	___
4.	475	40	30	___	___	___	___
5.	316	75	45	___	___	___	___
6.	507	35	40	___	___	___	___
7.	233	50	55	___	___	___	___
8.	382	70	35	___	___	___	___
9.	693	80	30	___	___	___	___
10.	582	25	45	___	___	___	___

Find the amounts of the discounts and the invoice price for each of the following:

	List Price		Trade Discount Percents	First Discount		Second Discount		Third Discount		Invoice Price	
11.	$ 87	50	35%, 10%, 5%	___	___	___	___	___	___	___	___
12.	53	70	40%, 5%, 5%	___	___	___	___	___	___	___	___
13.	135	80	50%, 5%, 3%	___	___	___	___	___	___	___	___
14.	163	40	25%, 15%, 10%	___	___	___	___	___	___	___	___
15.	140	25	30%, 10%, 5%	___	___	___	___	___	___	___	___
16.	270	10	40%, 15%, 5%	___	___	___	___	___	___	___	___
17.	248	65	30%, 20%, 5%	___	___	___	___	___	___	___	___
18.	315	90	45%, 20%, 10%	___	___	___	___	___	___	___	___
19.	363	70	35%, 15%, 10%	___	___	___	___	___	___	___	___
20.	453	80	50%, 10%, 5%	___	___	___	___	___	___	___	___

Find the invoice price on each of the following items. (Use the direct method of subtracting from 100%.)

	List Price		Trade Discount Percent	Invoice Price	
21.	$462	90	45%	_____	____
22.	528	70	40	_____	____
23.	649	25	50	_____	____
24.	247	75	35	_____	____
25.	761	35	55	_____	____
26.	803	50	35	_____	____
27.	638	25	30	_____	____
28.	961	20	45	_____	____
29.	730	50	40	_____	____
30.	819	35	55	_____	____

Find the single discount percent that is equal to the series of discounts in each of the following problems:

	Trade Discount Percents	Single Discount Percent			Trade Discount Percents	Single Discount Percent
31.	45%, 15%	____		36.	40%, 5%, 5%	____
32.	40%, 10%, 5%	____		37.	45%, 10%, 5%	____
33.	35%, 20%, 5%	____		38.	35%, 10%, 5%	____
34.	50%, 10%, 5%	____		39.	50%, 5%, 5%	____
35.	25%, 75%, 60%	____		40.	25%, 20%, 5%	____

Find the single percent that is equal to each series of discounts; then find the invoice price.

	List Price		Trade Discount Percents	Single Equivalent Percent	Invoice Price	
41.	$ 72	60	40%, 10%	____	_____	____
42.	115	50	35%, 10%, 5%	____	_____	____
43.	241	65	40%, 10%, 5%	____	_____	____
44.	263	30	50%, 5%, 5%	____	_____	____
45.	281	70	35%, 10%, 5%	____	_____	____

	List Price		Trade Discount Percents	Single Equivalent Percent	Invoice Price	
46.	$245	50	45%, 5%, 5%	____	____	____
47.	317	45	25%, 20%, 10%	____	____	____
48.	342	20	50%, 10%, 5%	____	____	____
49.	473	90	40%, 5%, 5%	____	____	____
50.	428	30	45%, 15%, 5%	____	____	____

Word Problems

Exercise B   Solve the following problems:

51.   A color TV set is listed in a catalog for $395.75 less 40% trade discount.

(a) What is the amount of discount?
(b) What is the invoice price of the TV?

52.   The list price of a camera is $375.75 less 45% trade discount. What is the cost of the camera to the retailer?

53.   A retailer purchased six watches listed in the catalog for $87.50 and four watches listed for $125.75. If the trade discount is 45%, how much did he pay for all the watches?

54.   A hardware store received an invoice in the amount of $861.35. The trade discount is 35% and the terms of the invoice are 3/15 n 45. If the invoice is paid within the cash discount period, what is the net amount of the payment?

55.   An appliance store bought a washing machine listed at $285.75 and four dryers listed at $245.80. If the trade discount is 40%, what is the net amount of the invoice?

56.   A furniture manufacturer offers a bedroom set at $1,865.50 less trade discounts of 50%, 10%, and 5%. Find the amount of each discount and the invoice price of the set.

57.   Wholesaler A offers merchandise with trade discounts of 35%, 5%, and 5%. Wholesaler B offers the exact same merchandise with trade discounts of 30%, 10%, and 5%.

(a) What is the single equivalent discount for each series of discounts?
(b) Which wholesaler offers a better buy?

58.   What should the net payment be on an invoice for $1,250.70 less discounts of 40% and 15%?

59.   An invoice dated 4/10 for $875.60 less 45%, 5%, and 5% is paid on 4/24. If the terms are 3/15 n 30, what should the payment be?

60.   A bedroom set is listed at $1,275 less trade discounts of 35%, 10%, and 5%.

(a) What is the single discount equal to the series of discounts?
(b) What is the invoice price of the bedroom set?

UNIT **3** Pricing Goods on the Basis of Selling Price

Retailers purchase their merchandise from manufacturers or wholesalers. The price that they pay for each article is called the **cost.**

To cover his or her operating expenses and provide a profit, the retailer must sell the item for more than it cost. The amount that a retailer adds is called the **markup,** or **gross profit.** Markup is the difference between the retailer's original cost and the *selling price.*

The general practice in retailing is to calculate the markup amount as a markup percent of the selling price or a markup percent of the cost price. Most retailers prefer to base their markup on a percent of selling price, because retail establishments calculate their profits on total sales.

From past records and experience, retailers determine *a given markup rate based on selling price* that will give them the gross profit necessary to meet their operating expenses and earn a reasonable net profit.

The mathematics of pricing retail goods can be expressed by the following three formulas:

1. Selling price = Cost + Markup.

2. Markup = Selling price − Cost.

3. Cost = Selling price − Markup.

Thus, if a retailer pays $60 for a coat and sells it for $90, the markup amount is $30.

Finding the Amount of Markup

The basic formula for finding the amount of markup based on the selling price is

$$\text{Selling price} \times \text{Markup percent} = \text{Markup amount}$$

Example 1 A retailer sells a coat for $135. If the markup rate is 40%, find the markup amount and the actual cost of the coat.

STEP 1.

$$\begin{array}{r} \$135 \\ \times\ 0.40 \\ \hline \$54.00 \end{array} \quad \text{Markup amount} \quad \textit{Answer}$$

Using the basic formula, multiply $135 × 40%.

Proportion Method

$$\frac{0.40}{100} = \frac{x}{135}$$

$$x = \$54$$

STEP 2. Cost = Selling price – Markup   To find the actual cost,
         = \$135   – \$54   substitute in formula 3.
         = \$81 Cost   *Answer*

To find the actual cost only, a more direct method is used.
Actual cost = \$135 – (\$135 × 40%)
         = 135 – (135 × 0.40)
         = 135 $\boxed{-}$ $\boxed{(}$135 $\boxed{\times}$ 0$\boxed{.}$40 $\boxed{)}$ $\boxed{=}$ 81
         = \$81

Finding the Rate of Markup

In some problems you will be given the selling price and the markup amount of an item and you will have to find the rate of markup.

Example 2   A jeweler sells a watch for \$78.50. The markup amount is \$31.40. Find the markup percent.

Method 1: Equation method

The basic formula is:

Selling price × Markup percent = Markup amount

$$\$78.50u = \$31.40$$

$$78.50u = 31.40$$

$$\frac{78.50u}{78.50} = \frac{31.40}{78.50}$$

$$u = \frac{31.40}{78.50}$$

$$= 0.40 = 40\% \text{ Markup rate} \quad Answer$$

Method 2: $\dfrac{\text{IS}}{\text{OF}}$ method

The facts in Example 2 can be restated as "($31.40 is) what percent of \$78.50?"

$$\frac{\text{IS}}{\text{OF}} = \frac{\$31.40}{\$78.50} = 0.40 = 40\%$$

Check: $$\frac{x}{100} = \frac{31.40}{78.50}$$

$$\frac{78.50x}{78.50} = \frac{3,140}{78.50}$$

$$x = 40\% \checkmark$$

When you are given the *cost* and the *selling price* of an article and you have to find the *markup percent,* you will have to use two steps:

Step 1. Find the markup amount:

$$\text{Markup amount} = \text{Selling price} - \text{Cost}$$

Step 2. Find the markup percent:

$$\text{Selling price} \times \text{Markup percent} = \text{Markup amount}$$

Example 3   A TV set sells for $138.90. The retailer paid $72.23 for the TV. Find the markup percent.

Step 1.   Markup amount = Selling price − Cost
                            = $138.90   − $72.23
                            = $66.67

Step 2. Selling price × Markup percent = Markup amount

Method 1: Equation method

$$\$138.90u = \$66.67$$

$$138.90u = 66.67$$

$$\frac{\cancel{138.90}u}{\cancel{138.90}} = \frac{66.67}{138.90}$$

$$u = \frac{66.67}{138.90}$$

$$= 0.479 = 48\% \text{ Markup percent}\quad \textit{Answer}$$

Method 2: $\dfrac{\text{IS}}{\text{OF}}$ method

The facts in Example 3 can be restated as "The markup amount, $66.67, is what percent of $138.90?"

$$\frac{\text{IS}}{\text{OF}} = \frac{66.67}{138.90} = 0.48 = 48\%$$

Check: $$\frac{x}{100} = \frac{66.75}{138.90}$$

$$\frac{\cancel{138.90}x}{\cancel{138.90}} = \frac{6675}{138.90}$$

$$x = 48\% \;\checkmark$$

Finding a Selling Price That Will Yield a Given Rate of Markup

Retailers determine the rate of markup that will give them their desired gross profit, and they know the cost price of each item of merchandise they buy. On the basis of these two known factors, retailers have to calculate what the selling price of their merchandise should be.

Example 4 A jeweler marks up all her merchandise 45% of the selling price. If the cost price of a ring is $66, what should the selling price be?

Since the selling price is used as the base, it can be expressed as *100%* of itself. If *45%* of the selling price is the markup percent, then the remaining *55%* of the selling price is the *equivalent percent of the cost of the merchandise.*

STEP 1. Cost percent = Sales price percent – Markup percent
$$= 100\% \qquad\qquad - 45\%$$
$$= 55\%$$

STEP 2. Since 55% of the selling price is equal to $66, you can write the problem as follows:

Method 1: Equation method

$$\text{Selling price} \times \text{Cost percent} = \text{Cost}$$

$$0.55u = \$66$$

$$\frac{0.55u}{0.55} = \frac{66}{0.55}$$

$$u = \frac{66}{0.55} = \$120 \text{ Selling price} \quad \textit{Answer}$$

Check:

$$\begin{array}{r} \$120 \\ \times\, 0.45 \\ \hline 6\,00 \\ 48\,0 \\ \hline \$54.00 \end{array} \text{ Markup amount}$$

$$\begin{array}{r} \$120 \text{ Selling price} \\ -\ 54 \text{ Markup amount} \\ \hline \$\ 66 \text{ Cost price } \surd \end{array}$$

Method 2: $\dfrac{\text{IS}}{\text{OF}}$ method

The facts in Example 4 can be restated as " $\$66$ is 55% of what number?"

$$\frac{\text{IS}}{\text{OF}} = \frac{\$66}{55\%} = \frac{66}{0.55} = \$120$$

Check:

$$\frac{0.55}{100} = \frac{66}{x}$$

$$\frac{.55x}{0.55} = \frac{66}{0.55}$$

$$x = \$120 \ \surd$$

Example 5 A retailer paid $37.40 for a dress. If he marks up the dress 35% of the selling price, what should the dress sell for?

STEP 1. Cost percent + Markup percent = 100%
Cost percent = 100% − Markup percent
= 100% − 35%
= 65%

STEP 2. Selling price × Cost percent = Cost

Method 1: Equation method

$$0.65u = \$37.40$$

$$\frac{0.65u}{0.65} = \frac{37.40}{0.65}$$

$$u = \frac{37.40}{0.65} = \$57.54 \text{ Selling price} \quad Answer$$

Check:

$57.54
×0.35
2 8770
17 262
20.1390 = $20.14 Markup amount

$57.54 Selling price
−20.14 Markup amount
$37.40 Cost price √

Method 2: $\dfrac{IS}{OF}$ method

The facts in Example 5 can be rephrased as " $37.40 is 65% of what number?"

$$\frac{IS}{OF} = \frac{\$37.40}{65\%} = \frac{37.40}{0.65} = \$57.54$$

Check:

$$\frac{0.65}{100} = \frac{37.40}{x}$$

$$\frac{.65x}{0.65} = \frac{37.40}{0.65}$$

$$x = \$57.54 \ \checkmark$$

Exercises

Exercise A   Find the markup amount and the cost price for each of the following:

	Selling Price		Markup Percent	Markup Amount		Cost Price	
1.	$135	00	35%	____	____	____	____
2.	73	50	40	____	____	____	____
3.	37	85	45	____	____	____	____
4.	175	50	30	____	____	____	____
5.	87	50	45	____	____	____	____
6.	235	90	40	____	____	____	____
7.	120	75	35	____	____	____	____
8.	247	35	40	____	____	____	____
9.	163	80	45	____	____	____	____
10.	198	90	30	____	____	____	____

Complete the following table, supplying the cost *or* markup amount *and* the markup percent for each item. (Markup percent is based on selling price.)

	Selling Price		Cost Price		Markup Amount		Markup Percent
11.	$106	25	____	____	$ 38	50	____
12.	255	43	____	____	114	94	____
13.	63	90	$ 42	60	____	____	____
14.	135	75	84	85	____	____	____
15.	138	90	93	95	____	____	____
16.	152	95	____	____	73	50	____
17.	319	25	143	65	____	____	____
18.	524	50	251	75	____	____	____
19.	191	45	____	____	85	75	____
20.	299	90	____	____	145	60	____

Find the equivalent cost percent and the selling price in each of the following. (Markup percent is based on selling price.)

	Cost Price		Markup Percent	Equivalent Cost Percent	Selling Price	
21.	$ 93	65	45%	—	—	—
22.	132	90	33	—	—	—
23.	68	75	40	—	—	—
24.	109	30	35	—	—	—
25.	365	50	55	—	—	—
26.	47	75	45	—	—	—
27.	86	35	30	—	—	—
28.	216	45	40	—	—	—
29.	188	25	25	—	—	—
30.	137	50	35	—	—	—

Word Problems

Exercise B   Solve the following problems:

31. A jeweler pays $95.75 for a ring and sells it for $185.

    (a) What is the markup amount?
    (b) What is the markup percent based on the selling price?

32. An appliance store sells a refrigerator for $568.90. If the markup amount is $256:

    (a) What is the markup percent based on the selling price?
    (b) What is the cost of the refrigerator?

33. A camera store marks up all its merchandise 40% of the selling price. If the cost of a 35 mm camera is $175.50:

    (a) What should the selling price of the camera be?
    (b) What is the markup amount?

34. A dress shop sells a line of dresses for $38.98 each. If the markup rate is 35% of the selling price:

    (a) What should be the cost price of each dress?
    (b) What is the markup amount of each dress?

35. A shoe store operates on a markup of 45% of the selling price. What is the cost of a pair of shoes that sells for $34.95?

UNIT **4** Pricing Goods on the Basis of Cost

While most retailers calculate their markup on a percent of the selling price, some retailers base their markup on a percent of the cost price.

This method of pricing goods is similar to what you learned in Unit 3. The only difference is that the *cost price* is used as the base instead of the selling price.

Finding the Amount of Markup

The formula for finding the amount of markup based on cost is

$$\text{Cost} \times \text{Markup percent} = \text{Markup amount}$$

Example 1   A retailer pays $87 for a radio. If her markup is 45% of the cost price, find (a) the markup amount and (b) the selling price of the radio.

    (a) Markup amount $=$ Cost $\times$ Markup percent

                  $= \$87 \ \times 45\%$

                  $= 87 \ \ \times 0.45$

                  $= \$39.15$ Markup amount   *Answer*

Proportion Method

$$\frac{0.45}{100} = \frac{x}{87}$$

$$x = \$39.15$$

    (b) Selling price $=$ Cost $+$ Markup

                 $= \$87 \ + \$39.15$

                 $= \$126.15$ Selling price   *Answer*

Check: $\$87 \times 145\% = 87 \times 1.45 = \$126.15 \ \checkmark$

Alternative Solution:

    Selling price $=$ $\$87 + (45\% \text{ of } \$87)$

                $= \ \ 87 \ \ + (0.45 \times 87)$

                $= \ \ 87 \ \boxed{+} \ \boxed{(} \boxed{0} \boxed{.} 45 \boxed{\times} 87 \boxed{)} \ \boxed{=} \ 126.15$

                $= \ \ \$126.15$

Finding the Rate of Markup

When you are given the cost of an item and the markup amount, you can use the formula to find the rate of markup.

Example 2 A retailer pays $380.75 for a piano and marks it up $285.56. What is the rate of markup based on cost?

Method 1: Equation Method

$$\text{Cost} \times \text{Markup percent} = \text{Markup amount}$$

$$\$380.75u = \$285.56$$

$$380.75u = 285.56$$

$$\frac{\cancel{380.75}u}{\cancel{380.75}} = \frac{285.56}{380.75}$$

$$u = \frac{285.56}{380.75}$$

$$= 0.749 = 0.75 = 75\% \quad \text{Markup rate} \quad \textit{Answer}$$

Method 2: $\dfrac{\text{IS}}{\text{OF}}$ method

The facts in Example 2 can be restated as " $\boxed{\$285.56 \text{ is}}$ what percent $\boxed{\text{of } \$380.75}$?"

$$\frac{\text{IS}}{\text{OF}} = \frac{285.56}{380.75} = 0.749 = 75\%$$

Check:
$$\frac{x}{100} = \frac{285.56}{380.75}$$

$$\frac{380.75x}{380.75} = \frac{\cancel{2,856}}{\cancel{380.75}}$$

$$x = 75\% \checkmark$$

If you are given the *selling price* of an article and the *markup amount* and you have to find the *rate of markup* based on cost, you will have to use the two-step method as you did in Unit 3:

STEP 1. Find the cost price.

STEP 2. Find the rate of markup.

Example 3 A retailer sells a desk for $345.50. If the markup amount is $153.75, what is the rate of markup based on cost?

STEP 1. Cost = Selling price − Markup amount
          = $345.50   − $153.75
          = $191.75 Cost price

STEP 2. Cost × Markup percent = Markup amount

Method 1: Equation method

$$\$191.75u = \$153.75$$

$$191.75u = 153.75$$

$$\frac{\overset{1}{\cancel{191.75}u}}{\underset{1}{\cancel{191.75}}} = \frac{153.75}{191.75} \qquad \text{Divide both sides by 191.75}$$

$$u = \frac{153.75}{191.75}$$

$$= 153 \boxed{.} 75 \boxed{\div} 191 \boxed{.} 75 \boxed{=} 0.80\underline{|0}$$

$$= 0.80 = 80\% \text{ Markup percent} \quad \textit{Answer}$$

Method 2: $\dfrac{\text{IS}}{\text{OF}}$ method

The facts in Example 3 can be rephrased as " $\boxed{\$153.75 \text{ is}}$ what percent $\boxed{\text{of } \$191.75}$?"

$$\frac{\text{IS}}{\text{OF}} = \frac{153.75}{191.75} = 0.801 = 0.80 = 80\%$$

$$= 153 \boxed{.} 75 \boxed{\div} 191 \boxed{.} 75 \boxed{=} 0.80\underline{|0}$$

$$= 0.80$$

Check:
$$\frac{x}{100} = \frac{153.75}{191.75}$$

$$\frac{\overset{1}{\cancel{191.75}x}}{\underset{1}{\cancel{191.75}}} = \frac{153.75}{191.75} \qquad \text{Divide both sides by 191.75.}$$

$$= 153 \boxed{.} 75 \boxed{\div} 191 \boxed{.} 75 \boxed{=} 0.80\underline{|0}$$

$$= 0.80$$

$$x = 80\% \ \checkmark$$

Finding a Cost Price That Will Yield a Given Rate of Markup

Many retailers will offer a line of merchandise that sells at a specific price. This practice is known as **price-lining.**

Example 4   A retailer sells a line of sport jackets for $49.95 each. If his markup rate is 65% of the cost price, what should the cost price of a jacket be?

STEP 1. Since the cost is used as the base, it can be expressed as 100% of itself. If the markup rate is 65% of the cost, then the selling price is equal to 165%.

$$\text{Cost} + \text{Markup} = \text{Selling price}$$
$$100\% + 65\% = 165\%$$

STEP 2. The selling price percent, 165%, is the equivalent percent of the selling price, $49.95. The selling price, $49.95, is the product of multiplying the cost price (unknown) by 165%, so you can write the problem as follows:

Method 1: Equation method

$$u165\% = \$49.95$$

$$1.65u = 49.95$$

$$\frac{\overset{1}{\cancel{1.65}}u}{\underset{1}{\cancel{1.65}}} = \frac{49.95}{1.65}$$

$$u = \frac{49.95}{1.65}$$
$$= 49\boxed{.}95 \boxed{\div} 1\boxed{.}65 \boxed{=} 30.27\lfloor 2...$$
$$= 30.27$$

$$= 30.27 = \$30.27 \quad \text{Cost price} \quad \textit{Answer}$$

Check:

$30.27		
× 0.65		Cost price
1 51 35	$30.27	Cost price
18 16 2	+ 19.68	Markup amount
$19.67 55 = $19.68	$49.95	Selling price √

Method 2: $\dfrac{IS}{OF}$ method

The facts in Example 4 can be restated as " $49.95 is 165% of what number?"

$$\frac{IS}{OF} = \frac{\$49.95}{165\%} = \frac{\$49.95}{1.65} = \$30.27$$

Check:

$$\frac{1.65}{100} = \frac{49.95}{x}$$

$$\frac{\overset{1}{\cancel{1.65}}x}{\underset{1}{\cancel{1.65}}} = \frac{49.95}{1.65} \qquad \text{Divide both sides by 1.65.}$$

$$= 49\boxed{.}95 \boxed{\div} 1\boxed{.}65 \boxed{=} 30.27\lfloor 2...$$
$$= 30.27$$
$$x = \$30.27 \ \sqrt{}$$

Exercises

Exercise A   Complete the following tables. The markup is based on the cost price.

	Cost Price		Markup Percent	Markup Amount		Selling Price	
1.	$ 48	75	75%	——	——	——	——
2.	142	50	60	——	——	——	——
3.	93	80	55	——	——	——	——
4.	247	30	80	——	——	——	——
5.	123	25	65	——	——	——	——
6.	83	60	80	——	——	——	——
7.	110	90	75	——	——	——	——
8.	45	50	65	——	——	——	——
9.	165	45	55	——	——	——	——
10.	210	20	60	——	——	——	——

	Cost Price		Markup Amount		Selling Price		Markup Rate Based on Cost
11.	$137	50	$ 69	38	——	——	——
12.	53	75	43	00	——	——	——
13.	215	35	——	——	$355	50	——
14.	161	40	——	——	250	20	——
15.	——	——	51	40	144	85	——
16.	——	——	47	88	127	68	——
17.	263	50	171	28	——	——	——
18.	55	75	——	——	103	15	——
19.	125	90	88	15	——	——	——
20.	137	85	89	60	——	——	——

	Selling Price		Markup Rate Based on Cost	Selling Price Equivalent Percent	Cost Price	
21.	$180	75	73%	——	——	——
22.	235	90	65	——	——	——
23.	432	90	80	——	——	——
24.	89	90	75	——	——	——
25.	58	25	82	——	——	——
26.	135	50	70	——	——	——
27.	105	45	65	——	——	——
28.	238	65	75	——	——	——
29.	117	50	85	——	——	——
30.	250	50	70	——	——	——

Word Problems

Exercise B   Solve the following problems:

31.   A furniture store paid $465.75 for a sofa. The store's markup rate is 65% of the cost price.

(a) Find the markup amount.
(b) Find the selling price of the sofa.

32.   A retailer sells a dishwasher for $265.95. The markup amount is $193.50.

(a) What is the price of the dishwasher?
(b) What is the markup percent based on the cost?

33.   A TV set sells for $380.75. The cost price is $235.50.

(a) Find the markup amount.
(b) Find the rate of markup based on the cost.

34.   A retailer sells a line of shoes for $28.75 each. The rate of markup based on the cost is 70%.

(a) Find the equivalent selling price percent.
(b) Find the cost price of a pair of shoes.

35.   A retailer marks up all his merchandise 75% of the cost price. He sells a line of dresses at $39.95 each.

(a) Find the equivalent selling price percent.
(b) What should be the cost price of the dresses?

UNIT **5** Review of Chapter Thirteen

Find the discount date and the due date for each of the following:

	Invoice Date	Terms	Discount Date	Due Date
1.	February 19	2/10 n 60	————	————
2.	September 28	3/15 n 45	————	————
3.	December 5	2/10 n 90	————	————
4.	July 22	2/15 n 60	————	————

Fill in the discount date and the due date. Then find the net amount *or* full amount, as required for each of the following invoices:

	Invoice Date	Terms	Amount of Invoice	Discount Date	Due Date	Invoice Paid	Net Amount	Full Amount
5.	8/15	2/10 n 45	$ 875 48	————	————	8/23	—— ——	—— ——
6.	3/28	3/10 n 90	953 79	————	————	4/8	—— ——	—— ——
7.	11/17	3/15 n 60	1,673 88	————	————	12/1	—— ——	—— ——
8.	4/4	2/15 n 45	793 28	————	————	4/19	—— ——	—— ——

Find the trade discount and the invoice price for each of the following:

	List Price	Trade Discount Percent	Trade Discount	Invoice Price
9.	$628 75	45%	—— ——	—— ——
10.	435 95	55	—— ——	—— ——
11.	357 45	40	—— ——	—— ——

Find the invoice price for each of the following. (Use the direct method of subtracting from 100%.)

	List Price	Trade Discount Percent	Invoice Price
12.	$955 65	40%	—— ——
13.	675 95	55	—— ——
14.	863 50	45	—— ——

Find the amounts of discounts and the invoice price for each of the following:

	List Price		Trade Discount Percents	First Discount		Second Discount		Third Discount	
15.	$142	95	40%, 10%, 5%	___	___	___	___	___	___
16.	287	75	50%, 10%, 5%	___	___	___	___	___	___
17.	493	65	45%, 8%, 4%	___	___	___	___	___	___

Find the invoice price for each of the following:

	List Price		Trade Discount Percents	Invoice Price	
18.	$125	95	45%, 10%, 5%	___	___
19.	237	50	50%, 5%, 5%	___	___
20.	317	95	35%, 15%, 5%	___	___

Find the single discount percent that is equal to the series of discounts for each of the following:

	Trade Discount Percents	Single Discount Percent
21.	55%, 10%, 5%	___
22.	35%, 15%, 10%	___
23.	40%, 5%, 3%	___

Find the markup amount and the cost price on each of the following items:

	Selling Price		Markup Percent	Markup Amount		Cost Price	
24.	$263	95	45%	___	___	___	___
25.	183	75	35	___	___	___	___
26.	364	50	40	___	___	___	___

Find the cost price *or* markup amount, *and* the markup percent based on the selling price on each of the following items:

	Selling Price		Cost Price		Markup Amount		Markup Percent
27.	$232	75	___	___	$104	75	___
28.	421	80	$247	17	___	___	___
29.	399	95	___	___	149	98	___

Find the equivalent cost percent and the selling price on each of the following items. (Markup percent is based on selling price.)

	Cost Price		Markup Percent	Equivalent Cost Percent	Selling Price	
30.	$185	45	55%	___	___	___
31.	247	95	45	___	___	___
32.	139	50	35	___	___	___

Find the markup amount (based on cost price) and the selling price on each of the following items:

	Cost Price		Markup Percent	Markup Amount		Selling Price	
33.	$ 98	75	60%	___	___	___	___
34.	105	45	70	___	___	___	___
35.	289	90	65	___	___	___	___

Find the cost price, markup amount, *or* selling price, *and* the markup rate based on the cost price on each of the following items:

	Cost Price		Markup Amount		Selling Price		Markup Rate
36.	$161	75	$ 89	39	___	___	___
37.	228	25	___	___	$351	50	___
38.	___	___	104	64	227	75	___

39. An invoice dated 5/15 for the amount of $575.65 was paid on 6/1. If the terms were 3/15 n 30, what was the amount of the payment?

40. A refrigerator lists for $635.95 less a trade discount of 45%. What is the invoice price of the refrigerator?

41. The list price of a TV set is $329.75 less 30%, 50%, and 10%.

    (a)   Find the single discount percent.
    (b)   Find the invoice price of the TV.

42. The cost of a coat is $68.90. If the markup is 45% of the selling price, what is the selling price of the coat?

43. The markup amount of a dress is $23.75. If the markup based on cost is 60%, what is the selling price of the dress?

CHAPTER **FOURTEEN**

Mathematics of Management and Finance

UNIT **1** Calculating Payroll Costs

Employees are paid in many different ways, depending upon the nature of the work and the size and type of company.

- **Salaried employees** earn an annual income, regardless of the hours expended or the output generated.

- **Hourly employees,** on the other hand, are paid for the amount of time spent on the job and often receive an overtime bonus.

- **Piece-work employees** are paid by output, receiving a specified amount of money for each unit produced.

- **Commission employees** are paid a specified percent of the sales generated by them.

Salaried Employees

Salaried employees earn an annual wage regardless of the hours spent or the output at the office. They do not receive additional compensation for extra hours worked at the office or at home during busy times or to meet deadlines. Similarly, there is no loss of salary if the employee misses a reasonable number of days from work as sick days or for personal business.

Example 1 A salaried employee's annual salary is $22,500. What is his monthly income?

$$\frac{\$22,500}{12} = \$1,875 \quad \textit{Answer:} \quad \text{Salary remains constant regardless of extra time worked or time lost from work.}$$

Hourly Employees

Salaried employees earn an annual wage, regardless of the hours spent or the output at the office. *Hourly workers* are paid for the *number of hours worked* during the week. Such an employee is paid on an hourly basis for a 35- or 40-hour week, and any hours worked beyond that are called **overtime.**

Overtime is often paid at *one and one-half times the regular hourly rate,* referred to as *time and a half.* In some industries, overtime is paid at twice the regular rate, referred to as *double time.* It is possible for an employee to be paid some of his or her overtime at one rate (for extra hours during the week) and the rest at a higher rate (for weekend or holiday work).

Example 2   Jack Green is paid $7.25 an hour for a 40-hour week plus time and a half for overtime. Last week he worked 45 hours. How much was his gross pay? Green worked 40 hours of regular time plus 5 hours of overtime.

Regular time pay = 40 × $7.25
= 40 ⊠ 7 ⊡ 25 ⊟ 290
= $290

Overtime pay = 5 × (7.25 × 1.5)
= 5 ⊠ (7 ⊡ 25 ⊠ 1.5) ⊟ 54.37 5
= 54.38
= $54.38

Gross pay = Regular pay + Overtime pay
= $290   + $54.38
= $344.38   *Answer*

Example 3   Juan Rodriguez is paid $8.50 an hour with time and a half paid for any hours worked beyond 8 hours a day. Last week he worked the following hours: Monday, 9 hours; Tuesday, 6 hours; Wednesday, 10 hours; Thursday, 7 hours; Friday, $10\frac{1}{2}$ hours. What were his total earnings for the week?

HINT: Rodriguez is paid overtime for any hours worked beyond 8 hours on each workday. In checking the daily hours he worked, you will note that he worked overtime on Monday, Wednesday, and Friday. His schedule of hours will look like this:

Monday		Tuesday		Wednesday		Thursday		Friday		Totals	
R	OT	R	OT	R	OT	R	OT	R	OT	R	OT
8	1	6	–	8	2	7	–	8	$2\frac{1}{2}$	37	$5\frac{1}{2}$

R = regular hours worked
OT = overtime

STEP 1.   Regular-time rate   = $37 \times \$8.50$
    = 37 ⊠ 8 ⊡ 5 ⊟ 314.50
    = $314.50

STEP 2.   Overtime rate   = $1\frac{1}{2} \times \$8.50$
    = 1 ⊡ 5 ⊠ 8 ⊡ 5 ⊟ 12.75
    = $12.75

STEP 3.   Overtime pay   = $5\frac{1}{2} \times \$12.75$
    = 5 ⊡ 5 ⊠ 12 ⊡ 75 ⊟ 70.12 $\underline{5}$
    = 70.13
    = $70.13

STEP 4.   Total earnings   = $314.50 + $70.13
    = $384.63   *Answer*

Piece-Work Employees

In many industries employees are paid **piece-work wages.** The employee receives a specified amount of money for each article or unit produced. The articles or units are called **pieces,** and the amount received for each piece is called the **piece rate.**

PROCEDURE: To find the total piece-work wages, multiply the total number of *pieces* by the *piece rate*.

Example 4   For the week ending August 12, Lucy Sanchez completed the following numbers of pieces: Monday, 53; Tuesday, 49; Wednesday, 56; Thursday, 52; and Friday, 54. The piece rate is $0.75. Find her total wages.

STEP 1.   53 ⊞ 49 ⊞ 56 ⊞ 52 ⊞ 54 ⊟ 264   Add the number of pieces completed daily.

STEP 2.

$$\begin{array}{r} 264 \\ \times\, 0.75 \\ \hline 13\ 20 \\ 184\ 8 \\ \hline \$198.00 \end{array} \text{ Total wages}$$ OR $264 \times \$\frac{3}{4} = \$198$

264 ⊠ 0 ⊡ 75 ⊟ 198

Answer

Multiply the total number of pieces by the piece rate, $0.75 $\left(\text{or } \$\frac{3}{4}\right)$.

Commission Employees

Most salespeople earn all or part of their wages from commissions. A **commission** is a percent of the dollar value of sales.

When a salesperson earns a commission only, he or she is said to be working on a **straight commission** basis.

In many instances, a salesperson receives a weekly salary, called a **base salary,** plus a commission on his or her sales, or on sales above a fixed amount called a **quota.** This arrangement is called a **salary plus commission basis.**

PROCEDURE: To calculate earnings when a person is on a straight commission basis, multiply the total sales by the rate of commission.

Example 5   Dennis earns a straight commission of 15%. If his sales for the month of August were $12,650, how much commission did he earn?

$$\text{Commission} = \text{Total sales} \times \text{Rate of commission}$$
$$= \$12{,}650 \quad \times 15\%$$
$$= \$12{,}650 \quad \times 0.15$$
$$= 12650 \boxed{\times} 0 \boxed{.} 15 \boxed{=} 1897.5$$
$$= \$1{,}897.50 \quad \textit{Answer}$$

Check: $\dfrac{0.15}{100} = \dfrac{x}{\$12{,}650}$

$x = \$1{,}897.50 \checkmark$

PROCEDURE: To calculate earnings when a person earns a weekly salary:

1. Write the base salary.
2. Find the commission on sales above the given quota.
3. Add the base salary to the commission earned to find the total wages.

Example 6   Felicia is paid a base salary of $85 a week plus a commission of 7% on sales above $850. Her last week's sales totaled $3,989.75. What were her total earnings for the week?

$$\text{Total income} = \text{Base salary} + \text{Commission}$$

STEP 1.   Base salary $= \$85$

STEP 2.   Commission $= 7\% \times (\$3{,}989.75 - \$850)$
$$= 0.07 \times \$3{,}139.75$$
$$= \$219.78$$

Proportion Method

$$\dfrac{7}{100} = \dfrac{x}{3{,}139.75}$$

$$100x = 21{,}978.25$$

$$x = 219.78$$

STEP 3.   Total income $= \$85 + \$219.78$
$$= \$304.78 \quad \textit{Answer}$$

Alternative Solution

You can find the total earnings (and also check the solution) by *writing the facts in the problem as a one-sentence statement, translating* the sentence into a single *equation,* and *solving* the equation.

Total income (earnings) is the *base salary,* $85, *plus* 7% *of total sales,* $3,989.75, *minus* $850.

$$\text{Total earnings} = \$85 + 7\% \text{ of } (\$3{,}989.75 - \$850)$$
$$= 85 \boxed{+} 0 \boxed{.} 07 \boxed{\times} \boxed{(} 3989 \boxed{.} 75 \boxed{-} 850 \boxed{)} \boxed{=} 304.78 | 25$$
$$= \$304.78 \checkmark$$

Exercises

Exercise A Complete the following partial payroll record based on a 40-hour week, with time and a half for overtime:

TRIANGLE MANUFACTURING COMPANY

Payroll for Week Ending April 8 20—

	Employee	M	T	W	Th	F	Regular Hours	Regular Rate	Total Regular Amount	Overtime Hours	Overtime Rate	Total Overtime Amount	Gross Pay
1.	A	9	$8\frac{1}{2}$	6	$10\frac{1}{2}$	9	——	$5 75		——	——		
2.	B	$9\frac{1}{4}$	$8\frac{1}{4}$	8	$10\frac{1}{2}$	10	——	4 10					
3.	C	8	7	$10\frac{1}{2}$	$9\frac{1}{2}$	6	——	4 50					
4.	D	$8\frac{1}{2}$	9	$10\frac{1}{2}$	8	$9\frac{1}{2}$	——	6 80					
5.	E	$9\frac{1}{4}$	$10\frac{1}{2}$	$8\frac{1}{4}$	$9\frac{1}{4}$	10	——	4 25					
6.	F	8	10	$9\frac{1}{2}$	$10\frac{1}{4}$	7	——	5 50					
7.	G	6	10	$8\frac{1}{2}$	$9\frac{1}{4}$	9	——	6 20					
8.	H	7	$10\frac{1}{2}$	$9\frac{1}{2}$	7	10	——	7 35					
9.	I	$9\frac{1}{4}$	$10\frac{1}{2}$	9	$8\frac{1}{4}$	9	——	5 00					
10.	J	10	$9\frac{1}{2}$	$8\frac{1}{4}$	$10\frac{1}{4}$	9	——	6 15					

Complete the following partial payroll record, with overtime paid for hours worked beyond 8 hours each day:

DURABLE PICTURE FRAME COMPANY

Payroll for Week Ending April 15 20—

	Employee	M	T	W	Th	F	Regular Hours	Regular Rate	Total Regular Amount	Overtime Hours	Overtime Rate	Total Overtime Amount	Gross Pay
11.	A	9	6	$8\frac{1}{2}$	7	8	——	$5 35	——	——	——		
12.	B	8	$9\frac{1}{2}$	7	10	6	——	6 75					
13.	C	10	8	7	9	$8\frac{1}{2}$	——	7 80					
14.	D	7	$9\frac{1}{2}$	8	$10\frac{1}{4}$	$8\frac{1}{4}$	——	4 50					
15.	E	8	$9\frac{1}{2}$	$10\frac{1}{2}$	7	6	——	5 20					
16.	F	9	$8\frac{1}{2}$	7	8	10	——	6 90					
17.	G	8	$10\frac{1}{2}$	6	$9\frac{1}{2}$	9	——	7 80					
18.	H	7	$9\frac{1}{2}$	8	$10\frac{1}{2}$	$8\frac{1}{4}$	——	6 25					
19.	I	9	6	7	$10\frac{1}{2}$	12	——	4 75					
20.	J	8	$9\frac{1}{2}$	10	7	$8\frac{1}{4}$	——	4 60					

Exercise B   Using a calculator, find the total wages for each employee. Add horizontally and use equivalent parts of $1 where possible. Multiply by the decimal value of the rate or the equivalent fraction.

		Number of Pieces					Total Pieces	Piece Rate	Total Wages	
	Employee	M	T	W	Th	F				
21.	Allen, J.	105	115	125	118	126	___	$0.40	___	___
22.	Acosta, B.	112	119	121	117	115	___	$0.37\frac{1}{2}$ (0.375)	___	___
23.	Bauer, S.	119	121	116	124	118	___	$0.33\frac{1}{3}$ $(\frac{1}{3})$	___	___
24.	Beam, A.	120	115	113	119	114	___	0.50	___	___
25.	Berg, M.	100	112	117	114	109	___	0.45	___	___
26.	Deluca, C.	114	121	120	113	116	___	$0.62\frac{1}{2}$ (0.625)	___	___
27.	Diaz, J.	118	122	104	123	113	___	0.35	___	___
28.	Eng, M.	121	106	113	119	112	___	$0.66\frac{2}{3}$ $(\frac{2}{3})$	___	___
29.	Wilson, J.	118	121	117	114	119	___	0.75	___	___
30.	Woug, C.	120	118	124	113	117	___	0.60	___	___

Find the total wages for each employee.

		Number of Dozens					Total Dozens	Piece Rate		Total Wages	
	Employee	M	T	W	Th	F					
31.	Adams, C.	13	$11\frac{1}{2}$	$12\frac{1}{4}$	$10\frac{1}{2}$	12	___	$2	95	___	___
32.	Ames, J.	$14\frac{1}{2}$	13	$12\frac{1}{4}$	14	$12\frac{1}{2}$	___	2	80	___	___
33.	Bond, J.	15	$12\frac{1}{4}$	$14\frac{1}{2}$	13	$15\frac{1}{2}$	___	2	78	___	___
34.	Cantor, S.	14	$13\frac{1}{2}$	$14\frac{1}{4}$	15	13	___	2	98	___	___
35.	Crane, V.	$13\frac{1}{2}$	15	$12\frac{1}{4}$	$11\frac{1}{2}$	14	___	2	92	___	___
36.	Dell, M.	$13\frac{1}{2}$	15	$11\frac{1}{4}$	12	$14\frac{1}{2}$	___	3	10	___	___
37.	Dean, J.	14	$13\frac{1}{4}$	$15\frac{1}{2}$	13	12	___	3	05	___	___
38.	Toms, V.	13	$14\frac{1}{2}$	$15\frac{1}{4}$	12	$15\frac{1}{4}$	___	2	87	___	___
39.	Watts, M.	$14\frac{1}{4}$	$13\frac{1}{2}$	15	12	$13\frac{1}{4}$	___	2	92	___	___
40.	Whitt, A.	15	$14\frac{1}{2}$	$13\frac{1}{4}$	$12\frac{1}{4}$	14	___	2	86	___	___

Find the total earnings for each of the following salespersons:

	Salesperson	Salary	Weekly Sales		Sales Quota	Net Sales		Commission	Total Earnings	
41.	Edwards, G.	$85	$ 2,185	60	None	————	——	13%	————	——
42.	Egbert, F.	None	9,640	85	$1,500	————	——	$6\frac{1}{2}$	————	——
43.	Ehlers, M.	None	6,524	00	None	————	——	5	————	——
44.	Farin, M.	$90	8,674	90	$800	————	——	3	————	——
45.	Farrel, S.	$75	3,478	50	None	————	——	8	————	——
46.	Fay, L.	None	24,675	00	$2,500	————	——	$2\frac{1}{2}$	————	——
47.	Lopez, J.	$95	7,460	00	$2,000	————	——	4	————	——
48.	Lowe, S.	None	6,893	00	None	————	——	$5\frac{1}{4}$	————	——
49.	Lucas, B.	None	18,260	00	$5,500	————	——	3	————	——
50.	Lund, C.	$75	6,324	00	None	————	——	6	————	——

Word Problems

Exercise C   Solve the following problems:

51. Richie worked the following hours for the week ending August 15: 9, $9\frac{1}{2}$, 10, $8\frac{3}{4}$, and 9 hours. His hourly rate is $6.75, with time and a half for hours worked beyond 40 hours. What was his gross pay for the week?

52. Sylvia works a 40-hour week, with time and a half for hours worked beyond 8 hours a day. Her hourly rate is $9.25. Find her gross pay if she worked the following hours: Monday, 9; Tuesday, $8\frac{3}{4}$; Wednesday, 8; Thursday, 10; and Friday, $9\frac{1}{2}$.

53. Marvin works a 35-hour week, with time and a half for hours worked over 35 hours and double time for hours worked on Saturday. Last week he worked $8\frac{1}{2}$ hours on Monday, $7\frac{1}{2}$ on Tuesday, 9 on Wednesday, 8 on Thursday, $9\frac{1}{2}$ on Friday, and 4 on Saturday. If his hourly rate is $7.65, how much was his gross pay?

54. Kelly worked the following hours for the week ending July 28: 9, $8\frac{3}{4}$, 10, 8, and $9\frac{1}{2}$. Her hourly rate is $8.48, with time and a half for hours worked beyond 40 hours. How much was her gross pay?

55. Albert's hourly rate is $6.75, with time and a half for hours worked beyond 8 hours a day. Last week he worked the following hours: Monday, $8\frac{1}{2}$; Tuesday, $9\frac{3}{4}$; Wednesday, 8; and Thursday, 10. Friday was a legal holiday with pay. Find his gross pay for the week.

56. Elizabeth's gross pay for the week ending July 21 was $210.50. If she worked 40 hours straight time and 6 hours overtime, what is her hourly rate? (HINT: How many hours of pay are the 6 hours of overtime equal to?)

57. An office employs six clerks earning the following weekly salaries: $285, $315, $265, $247, $348, and $465. What is the total yearly payroll for all the clerks?

58. Mel assembles transistor radios and is paid $1.25 for each radio assembled. Last week he assembled the following numbers of radios: 29, 32, 34, 28, and 33. What were his earnings for the week?

59. Mary is a sewing machine operator and is paid on a piece-work basis. For the week ending July 8, she completed the following number of blouses: Monday, 215; Tuesday, 235; Wednesday, 225; Thursday, 240; and Friday, 228. If she is paid 45¢ for each completed blouse, how much did she earn for the week?

60. Jim is paid $6.68 for each dozen slacks he hems. How much did he earn last week if he completed the following dozens of slacks: $13\frac{3}{4}$, 15, $14\frac{1}{2}$, $13\frac{1}{2}$, and $15\frac{1}{4}$?

61. Jean is paid 75¢ for every toaster she assembles. Last week she assembled the following numbers of toasters: 58, 53, 61, 57, and 56. Find her earnings for the week.

62. Mindy is paid $9.25 for every dozen shirts she completes. If she completed $12\frac{1}{2}$ dozen on Monday, $14\frac{1}{4}$ dozen on Tuesday, 13 dozen on Wednesday, $15\frac{3}{4}$ dozen on Thursday, and $14\frac{1}{2}$ dozen on Friday, how much did she earn for the week?

63. Sarah is paid $5\frac{1}{2}$% commission on sales. Last week her sales for each day were as follows: $345.75, $298.50, $363.85, $363.80, and $375.90. How much commission did she earn for the week?

64. James Badaglio is paid a base salary of $95 a week plus a commission of 12% on total sales. If his sales last week were $2,325.60, what were his total earnings?

65. Greta earns $65 on each vacuum cleaner she sells. If the price of the vacuum cleaner is $285.75, find the rate of commission.

UNIT **2** Calculating Payroll Deductions

All employers are required to make tax deductions from the weekly pay of each employee. These deductions include federal income taxes, FICA (Social Security), and state or local taxes. In addition, deductions are often made for selected benefit packages (such as health or dental insurance) and for optional savings plans (savings bonds, credit unions, pension plans, and the like).

Federal Income Tax

The federal income withholding tax is based on the employee's gross income and the number of exemptions he or she claims. A male employee, for example, may claim one exemption for himself, one for his wife, and one for each dependent child. The amount of tax deducted will decrease with each additional exemption.

At the end of each year, and before the deadline of April 15, the taxpayer files a yearly income tax return to determine his or her income tax for the year. If the tax withheld during the year is less, the taxpayer will pay the IRS the difference. If the tax withheld during the year is more, the IRS will send a refund to the taxpayer for the overpayment.

To estimate the amount of federal withholding tax, employers use federal tax tables like Tables 1 and 2 on pages 344 and 345. A single person earning $785/week with 0 (zero) exemptions would have $143 withheld, while a married person with 0 (zero) exemptions would have $99 withheld.

Example 1   What will be the deduction for a married employee with four exemptions, if her weekly pay is $792.50?

STEP 1.   Turn to the table for married persons, Table 2.

TABLE 1   Federal Income Tax Withholding Schedule

SINGLE Persons—WEEKLY Payroll Period

(For Wages Paid in 2000)

If the wages are—		And the number of withholding allowances claimed is—										
At least	But less than	0	1	2	3	4	5	6	7	8	9	10
		The amount of income tax to be withheld is—										
$600	$610	92	77	67	59	51	43	35	27	18	10	2
610	620	95	80	68	60	52	44	36	28	20	12	4
620	630	98	83	70	62	54	46	38	30	21	13	5
630	640	101	85	71	63	55	47	39	31	23	15	7
640	650	103	88	73	65	57	49	41	33	24	16	8
650	660	106	91	76	66	58	50	42	34	26	18	10
660	670	109	94	79	68	60	52	44	36	27	19	11
670	680	112	97	82	69	61	53	45	37	29	21	13
680	690	115	99	84	71	63	55	47	39	30	22	14
690	700	117	102	87	72	64	56	48	40	32	24	16
700	710	120	105	90	75	66	58	50	42	33	25	17
710	720	123	108	93	78	67	59	51	43	35	27	19
720	730	126	111	96	81	69	61	53	45	36	28	20
730	740	129	113	98	83	70	62	54	46	38	30	22
740	750	131	116	101	86	72	64	56	48	39	31	23
750	760	134	119	104	89	74	65	57	49	41	33	25
760	770	137	122	107	92	77	67	59	51	42	34	26
770	780	140	125	110	95	79	68	60	52	44	36	28
780	790	143	127	112	97	82	70	62	54	45	37	29
790	800	145	130	115	100	85	71	63	55	47	39	31
800	810	148	133	118	103	88	73	65	57	48	40	32
810	820	151	136	121	106	91	76	66	58	50	42	34
820	830	154	139	124	109	93	78	68	60	51	43	35
830	840	157	141	126	111	96	81	69	61	53	45	37
840	850	159	144	129	114	99	84	71	63	54	46	38
850	860	162	147	132	117	102	87	72	64	56	48	40
860	870	165	150	135	120	105	90	74	66	57	49	41
870	880	168	153	138	123	107	92	77	67	59	51	43
880	890	171	155	140	125	110	95	80	69	60	52	44
890	900	173	158	143	128	113	98	83	70	62	54	46
900	910	176	161	146	131	116	101	86	72	63	55	47
910	920	179	164	149	134	119	104	88	73	65	57	49
920	930	182	167	152	137	121	106	91	76	66	58	50
930	940	185	169	154	139	124	109	94	79	68	60	52
940	950	187	172	157	142	127	112	97	82	69	61	53
950	960	190	175	160	145	130	115	100	85	71	63	55
960	970	193	178	163	148	133	118	102	87	72	64	56
970	980	196	181	166	151	135	120	105	90	75	66	58
980	990	199	183	168	153	138	123	108	93	78	67	59
990	1,000	201	186	171	156	141	126	111	96	81	69	61
1,000	1,010	204	189	174	159	144	129	114	99	84	70	62
1,010	1,020	207	192	177	162	147	132	116	101	86	72	64
1,020	1,030	210	195	180	165	149	134	119	104	89	74	65
1,030	1,040	213	197	182	167	152	137	122	107	92	77	67
1,040	1,050	215	200	185	170	155	140	125	110	95	80	68
1,050	1,060	218	203	188	173	158	143	128	113	98	82	70
1,060	1,070	221	206	191	176	161	146	130	115	100	85	71
1,070	1,080	224	209	194	179	163	148	133	118	103	88	73
1,080	1,090	227	211	196	181	166	151	136	121	106	91	76
1,090	1,100	229	214	199	184	169	154	139	124	109	94	79
1,100	1,110	232	217	202	187	172	157	142	127	112	96	81
1,110	1,120	235	220	205	190	175	160	144	129	114	99	84
1,120	1,130	238	223	208	193	177	162	147	132	117	102	87
1,130	1,140	241	225	210	195	180	165	150	135	120	105	90
1,140	1,150	243	228	213	198	183	168	153	138	123	108	93
1,150	1,160	246	231	216	201	186	171	156	141	126	110	95
1,160	1,170	249	234	219	204	189	174	158	143	128	113	98
1,170	1,180	252	237	222	207	191	176	161	146	131	116	101
1,180	1,190	256	239	224	209	194	179	164	149	134	119	104
1,190	1,200	259	242	227	212	197	182	167	152	137	122	107
1,200	1,210	262	245	230	215	200	185	170	155	140	124	109
1,210	1,220	265	248	233	218	203	188	172	157	142	127	112
1,220	1,230	268	251	236	221	205	190	175	160	145	130	115
1,230	1,240	271	254	238	223	208	193	178	163	148	133	118
1,240	1,250	274	257	241	226	211	196	181	166	151	136	121

$1,250 and over   Use Table 1(a) for a **SINGLE person** on page 34. Also see the instructions on page 32.

TABLE 2 Federal Income Tax Withholding Schedule

MARRIED Persons—WEEKLY Payroll Period
(For Wages Paid in 2000)

If the wages are—		And the number of withholding allowances claimed is—										
At least	But less than	0	1	2	3	4	5	6	7	8	9	10
		The amount of income tax to be withheld is—										
$740	$750	93	85	77	69	61	53	45	37	29	20	12
750	760	95	87	78	70	62	54	46	38	30	22	14
760	770	96	88	80	72	64	56	48	40	32	23	15
770	780	98	90	81	73	65	57	49	41	33	25	17
780	790	99	91	83	75	67	59	51	43	35	26	18
790	800	101	93	84	76	68	60	52	44	36	28	20
800	810	102	94	86	78	70	62	54	46	38	29	21
810	820	104	96	87	79	71	63	55	47	39	31	23
820	830	105	97	89	81	73	65	57	49	41	32	24
830	840	107	99	90	82	74	66	58	50	42	34	26
840	850	108	100	92	84	76	68	60	52	44	35	27
850	860	110	102	93	85	77	69	61	53	45	37	29
860	870	111	103	95	87	79	71	63	55	47	38	30
870	880	113	105	96	88	80	72	64	56	48	40	32
880	890	114	106	98	90	82	74	66	58	50	41	33
890	900	116	108	99	91	83	75	67	59	51	43	35
900	910	117	109	101	93	85	77	69	61	53	44	36
910	920	119	111	102	94	86	78	70	62	54	46	38
920	930	120	112	104	96	88	80	72	64	56	47	39
930	940	122	114	105	97	89	81	73	65	57	49	41
940	950	125	115	107	99	91	83	75	67	59	50	42
950	960	128	117	108	100	92	84	76	68	60	52	44
960	970	131	118	110	102	94	86	78	70	62	53	45
970	980	133	120	111	103	95	87	79	71	63	55	47
980	990	136	121	113	105	97	89	81	73	65	56	48
990	1,000	139	124	114	106	98	90	82	74	66	58	50
1,000	1,010	142	127	116	108	100	92	84	76	68	59	51
1,010	1,020	145	130	117	109	101	93	85	77	69	61	53
1,020	1,030	147	132	119	111	103	95	87	79	71	62	54
1,030	1,040	150	135	120	112	104	96	88	80	72	64	56
1,040	1,050	153	138	123	114	106	98	90	82	74	65	57
1,050	1,060	156	141	126	115	107	99	91	83	75	67	59
1,060	1,070	159	144	128	117	109	101	93	85	77	68	60
1,070	1,080	161	146	131	118	110	102	94	86	78	70	62
1,080	1,090	164	149	134	120	112	104	96	88	80	71	63
1,090	1,100	167	152	137	122	113	105	97	89	81	73	65
1,100	1,110	170	155	140	125	115	107	99	91	83	74	66
1,110	1,120	173	158	142	127	116	108	100	92	84	76	68
1,120	1,130	175	160	145	130	118	110	102	94	86	77	69
1,130	1,140	178	163	148	133	119	111	103	95	87	79	71
1,140	1,150	181	166	151	136	121	113	105	97	89	80	72
1,150	1,160	184	169	154	139	123	114	106	98	90	82	74
1,160	1,170	187	172	156	141	126	116	108	100	92	83	75
1,170	1,180	189	174	159	144	129	117	109	101	93	85	77
1,180	1,190	192	177	162	147	132	119	111	103	95	86	78
1,190	1,200	195	180	165	150	135	120	112	104	96	88	80
1,200	1,210	198	183	168	153	137	122	114	106	98	89	81
1,210	1,220	201	186	170	155	140	125	115	107	99	91	83
1,220	1,230	203	188	173	158	143	128	117	109	101	92	84
1,230	1,240	206	191	176	161	146	131	118	110	102	94	86
1,240	1,250	209	194	179	164	149	134	120	112	104	95	87
1,250	1,260	212	197	182	167	151	136	121	113	105	97	89
1,260	1,270	215	200	184	169	154	139	124	115	107	98	90
1,270	1,280	217	202	187	172	157	142	127	116	108	100	92
1,280	1,290	220	205	190	175	160	145	130	118	110	101	93
1,290	1,300	223	208	193	178	163	148	133	119	111	103	95
1,300	1,310	226	211	196	181	165	150	135	121	113	104	96
1,310	1,320	229	214	198	183	168	153	138	123	114	106	98
1,320	1,330	231	216	201	186	171	156	141	126	116	107	99
1,330	1,340	234	219	204	189	174	159	144	129	117	109	101
1,340	1,350	237	222	207	192	177	162	147	131	119	110	102
1,350	1,360	240	225	210	195	179	164	149	134	120	112	104
1,360	1,370	243	228	212	197	182	167	152	137	122	113	105
1,370	1,380	245	230	215	200	185	170	155	140	125	115	107
1,380	1,390	248	233	218	203	188	173	158	143	128	116	108

$1,390 and over   Use Table 1(b) for a MARRIED person on page 34. Also see the instructions on page 32.

STEP 2. Go down the left-hand column until you find weekly incomes bracketing $792.50.

MARRIED Persons—WEEKLY Payroll Period
(For Wages Paid in 2000)

If the wages are—		And the number of withholding allowances claimed is—										
At least	But less than	0	1	2	3	4	5	6	7	8	9	10
		The amount of income tax to be withheld is—										
$740	$750	93	85	77	69	61	53	45	37	29	20	12
750	760	95	87	78	70	62	54	46	38	30	22	14
760	770	96	88	80	72	64	56	48	40	32	23	15
770	780	98	90	81	73	65	57	49	41	33	25	17
780	790	99	91	83	75	67	59	51	43	35	26	18
790	800	101	93	84	76	68	60	52	44	36	28	20
800	810	102	94	86	78	70	62	54	46	38	29	21
810	820	104	96	87	79	71	63	55	47	39	31	23
820	830	105	97	89	81	73	65	57	49	41	32	24
830	840	107	99	90	82	74	66	58	50	42	34	26
840	850	108	100	92	84	76	68	60	52	44	35	27
850	860	110	102	93	85	77	69	61	53	45	37	29
860	870	111	103	95	87	79	71	63	55	47	38	30
870	880	113	105	96	88	80	72	64	56	48	40	32
880	890	114	106	98	90	82	74	66	58	50	41	33

STEP 3. Go across that line until you reach the column for four exemptions.

MARRIED Persons—WEEKLY Payroll Period
(For Wages Paid in 2000)

If the wages are—		And the number of withholding allowances claimed is—										
At least	But less than	0	1	2	3	4	5	6	7	8	9	10
		The amount of income tax to be withheld is—										
$740	$750	93	85	77	69	61	53	45	37	29	20	12
750	760	95	87	78	70	62	54	46	38	30	22	14
760	770	96	88	80	72	64	56	48	40	32	23	15
770	780	98	90	81	73	65	57	49	41	33	25	17
780	790	99	91	83	75	67	59	51	43	35	26	18
790	800	101	93	84	76	68	60	52	44	36	28	20
800	810	102	94	86	78	70	62	54	46	38	29	21
810	820	104	96	87	79	71	63	55	47	39	31	23
820	830	105	97	89	81	73	65	57	49	41	32	24
830	840	107	99	90	82	74	66	58	50	42	34	26
840	850	108	100	92	84	76	68	60	52	44	35	27
850	860	110	102	93	85	77	69	61	53	45	37	29
860	870	111	103	95	87	79	71	63	55	47	38	30
870	880	113	105	96	88	80	72	64	56	48	40	32
880	890	114	106	98	90	82	74	66	58	50	41	33

The tax to be withheld is $68.   *Answer*

Social Security and Medicare (FICA) Taxes

The other federal tax deducted from weekly income under the Federal Insurance Contributions Act is the FICA tax. Commonly known as the Social Security tax, this tax provides retirement income, disability, and survivors' benefits. It also includes the Medicare program, which provides partial benefits on medical expenses for people 65 years of age or over.

For 2000, the rate of the social security tax was 6.20% on the first $76,200 of income, or a maximum of $4,724.40. No social security tax is paid on income beyond the first $76,200. The rate of medicare tax was 1.45% with no wage limit. The combined FICA tax was 7.65%.

Under this Act, the employer must contribute an amount equal to the amount contributed by the employee, which is credited at the Social Security Administration for the employee under his or her Social Security number.

For the employee who earns more than $76,200, the FICA deduction will stop that week of the year when his or her earnings reach the taxable amount of $76,200. On the following week, the take-home pay will be increased by the FICA tax amount usually deducted from his or her salary.

Example 2 Brad earns $1,500 a week, or $78,000 a year. How much FICA tax will be deducted each week?

$$\begin{aligned} \text{FICA tax} &= \text{Weekly salary} \times \text{FICA rate} \\ &= \$1,500 \qquad \times 7.65\% \\ &= \$1,500 \qquad \times 0.0765 \\ &= \$114.75 \quad \textit{Answer} \end{aligned}$$

Example 3 Use the facts from Example 2 and determine during what week of the year the FICA tax from John's salary will not be deducted, resulting in an increase in his take-home pay.

HINT: The number of weeks of deduction is found by dividing the taxable part of the yearly income, $76,200, by $1,500, the weekly salary.

$$\begin{aligned} \text{Taxable weeks} &= \$76,200 \div \$1,500 \\ &= 50.8 \end{aligned}$$

Answer: John's take-home pay will increase in the 51st week, and no FICA tax will be deducted the last week of the year.

Exercises

Exercise A Find the FICA tax deduction for each of the following weekly wages. The rate is 7.65%.

	Weekly Salary		FICA Tax				Weekly Salary		FICA Tax	
1.	$475	50	___	___	6.	$527	50	___	___
2.	580	75	___	___	7.	385	75	___	___
3.	453	45	___	___	8.	460	50	___	___
4.	610	15	___	___	9.	575	80	___	___
5.	463	70	___	___	10.	485	90	___	___

Find the week in which no FICA tax will be deducted from the following weekly salaries:

	Weekly Salary	Week
11.	$ 985	——
12.	995	——
13.	1,005	——
14.	1,250	——
15.	1,670	——

	Weekly Salary	Week
16.	$1,840	——
17.	2,000	——
18.	1,050	——
19.	2,400	——
20.	1,775	——

Exercise B   Complete the following table, using the federal income tax tables on pages 344–345. Remember that the FICA tax rate is 7.65%.

SANDS ELECTRONIC COMPANY

Week Ending   July 10   20—

	Employee	Number of Exemptions	Weekly Salary		Income Tax		FICA Tax		Take-Home Pay	
21.	A: married	3	$767	50	——	——	——	——	——	——
22.	B: single	0	674	80	——	——	——	——	——	——
23.	C: married	4	793	75	——	——	——	——	——	——
24.	D: single	2	674	50	——	——	——	——	——	——
25.	E: single	1	785	50	——	——	——	——	——	——
26.	F: married	5	685	60	——	——	——	——	——	——
27.	G: married	6	873	45	——	——	——	——	——	——
28.	H: married	7	875	75	——	——	——	——	——	——
29.	I: single	4	680	75	——	——	——	——	——	——
30.	J: married	5	987	90	——	——	——	——	——	——

Word Problems

Exercise C   Use the tax tables on pages 344–345 to solve the following problems:

31.   Sandra is single and earns $685.50 a week. If she claims no dependents, what will be her take-home pay?

32. Tom earns $79,500 a year. During what week of the year will the FICA tax not be deducted?

33. Henry earns $66,500 a year. He is married and claims three dependents. How much will his take-home pay be?

34. Andrea earns $34,180 a year, is single, and claims two dependents. What will her weekly net pay be?

35. William earns $880 a week. He is married and claims five exemptions. How much will his net pay be?

UNIT **3** Review of Chapter Fourteen

SUMMARY OF KEY POINTS

- *Regular work week:*   35- or 40-hour work week.
- *Overtime hours:*   Hours worked beyond a 35- or 40-hour week, or beyond an 8-hour day.
- *Overtime rate:*   Two times or one and a half times the regular rate.
- *Piece-work employee:*   Employee paid a specified amount for each unit produced.
- *Commission employee:*   Employee paid a specified percentage of sales.

Complete the following partial payroll record based on a 40-hour week, with time and a half for overtime:

	Employee	M	T	W	Th	F	Hourly Rate	Regular Pay	Overtime Pay	Gross Pay
1.	A	$9\frac{1}{2}$	8	$10\frac{3}{4}$	$9\frac{1}{4}$	$8\frac{1}{2}$	$7 75	___	___	___
2.	B	8	$11\frac{1}{4}$	$9\frac{1}{2}$	$12\frac{3}{4}$	10	8 50	___	___	___
3.	C	9	$10\frac{3}{4}$	$12\frac{1}{2}$	8	$11\frac{3}{4}$	6 85	___	___	___

Complete the following partial payroll record, with overtime paid for hours worked beyond 8 hours each day:

	Employee	M	T	W	Th	F	Hourly Rate	Regular Pay	Overtime Pay	Gross Pay
4.	A	8	$9\frac{1}{2}$	$8\frac{3}{4}$	$10\frac{1}{4}$	$11\frac{1}{2}$	$8 45	___	___	___
5.	B	9	$8\frac{3}{4}$	$10\frac{1}{2}$	$9\frac{1}{2}$	10	7 65	___	___	___
6.	C	$8\frac{1}{4}$	$9\frac{1}{2}$	10	$11\frac{3}{4}$	$9\frac{1}{4}$	6 95	___	___	___

Find the total wages for each employee in Problems 7 through 12.

	Employee	Number of Pieces					Total Pieces	Piece Rate	Total Wages	
		M	T	W	Th	F				
7.	A	85	92	89	98	95	___	$0.60	___	___
8.	B	110	105	108	112	115	___	0.50	___	___
9.	C	225	230	227	236	228	___	0.35	___	___

	Employee	Number of Dozens					Total Dozens	Piece Rate		Total Wages	
		M	T	W	Th	F					
10.	A	28	24	23	26	27	___	$2	48	___	___
11.	B	23	26	27	24	25	___	2	53	___	___
12.	C	26	24	28	29	31	___	2	53	___	___

Find the FICA tax deductions for each of the following weekly wages. The rate is 7.65%.

	Weekly Salary		FICA Tax				Weekly Salary		FICA Tax	
13.	$463	85	___	___		**14.**	$621	50	___	___
15.	568	70	___	___		**16.**	637	90	___	___

Find the week in which no FICA tax will be deducted from the following weekly salaries:

	Weekly Salary		Week		Weekly Salary		Week
17.	$1,538	46	___	**18.**	$2,200	25	___
19.	1,778	85	___	**20.**	1,865	32	___

Using the income tax tables on pages 344–345, complete the following partial payroll. The FICA tax rate is 7.65%.

	Employee	Exemptions	Weekly Salary		Income Tax		FICA Tax		Take-Home Pay	
21.	A: married	4	$763	37	___	___	___	___	___	___
22.	B: single	0	853	95	___	___	___	___	___	___
23.	C: married	5	897	42	___	___	___	___	___	___

Solve the following problems:

24. Ruth earned $585 in commissions last week. If she is paid a 12% commission on all sales above $3,000, what were her total sales last week?

25. Victor's total earnings last week were $468.50. If his sales were $6,790.90 and his rate of commission is $5\frac{1}{2}\%$, find his base salary.

26. Charless Gales is paid 6% commission on sales up to $7,500 and 8% commission on the amount of sales in excess of $7,500. If his sales for July were $23,675, find his total commissions earned for the month.

27. Mary Johnson earns a base salary of $75 plus a commission of $12\frac{1}{2}\%$ on sales over $1,500. Last week her total sales were $3,967.80. How much was her total salary for the week?

28. Andre earned $375 in commissions. If his rate of commission is 15%, what were his total sales?

Answers to Odd-Numbered Problems

Chapter One, Unit 1

Exercise A   **1.** $201.19   **3.** $1,595.53   **5.** $1,178.60   **7.** $3,119.20
9. $9,305.80   **11.** $5,588.77   **13.** $17,099.30   **15.** $40,199.27
17. $66,394.53   **19.** $57,409.36

Exercise B   **21.** $391.24   **23.** $406.55
25. Sales: $78,442.30;   Commission: $7,844.24
27. 546   **29.** 17,908
31. Subtotal: $93.50;   Total: $100.98

Exercise C   **33.** $5,211.60   **35.** $1,622.93   **37.** $80.50   **39.** $364.68
41. $312.09

Chapter One, Unit 2

Exercise A   **1.** 35   **3.** 225   **5.** 323   **7.** 21,962   **9.** 88,065
11. 130,935   **13.** 175,968   **17.** 91,277
19. 150,720

Exercise B   **21.** Adams: 50;   Adman: 45;   Burke: 41;   Curtis: 44;   Dellman: 44;
Evans: 44
Mon.: 53;   Tues.: 49;   Wed.: 61;   Thurs.: 52;   Fri.: 53;   Grand Total:
268
23. 01: $70.87;   02: $83.70;   03: $84.93;   04: $77.01;   05: $105.84;
06: $102.90;   07: $88.23;   08: $111.78;   09: $77.51;   10: $106.85
Fed. Tax: $462.26;   FICA Tax: $158.35;   State Tax: $106.15;   City
Tax: $67.94;   Pension: $83.75;   Health Plan: $31.17;   Grand
Total: $909.62
25. Grocery: $13,556.32;   Produce: $6,248.82;   Dairy: $10,080.39;
Meat: $8,688.70;   Deli: $5,339.13;   Nonfood: $4,625.11
Mon.: $7,631.68;   Tues.: $7,477.31;   Wed.: $6,905.38;
Thurs.: $7,162.70;   Fri.: $6,848.84;   Sat.: $6,371.98;   Sun.: $6,140.58;
Grand Total: $48,538.47
27. Ladies' Wear: $9,220.01;   Men's Wear: $7,088.14;   Children's
Wear: $3,838.75;   Appliances: $10,960.37;   Furniture: $13,891.69;
Toys: $3,819.78
Cash: $15,840.78;   Charge: $16,595.11;   C.O.D.: $16,382.85;   Grand
Total: $48,818.74

Exercise C   **29.** $2,785.09   **31.** $4,501.02   **33.** $2,445.37   **35.** $547.93
37. $220.34   **39.** $199.52   **41.** $195.52

Chapter One, Unit 3

1. $1,019.85   **3.** $1,632.93
5. Cash Sales: $137,950.02;   Charge Sales: $149,928.06
7. Sales: $116,850.54;   Commissions: $8,179.53
9. $206.67   **11.** $6,050.52

Chapter Two, Unit 1

Exercise A   **1.** 42   **3.** 43   **5.** 20   **7.** 49   **9.** 57   **11.** 79   **13.** 89
15. $228.35   **17.** $67.19   **19.** $278.07   **21.** $78.79   **23.** 983
25. 4,924   **27.** $1,890.88   **29.** $19,217.08   **31.** $8,918.93
33. 18,717   **35.** 7,926   **37.** 9,086   **39.** 39,065   **41.** 958
43. 235   **45.** 68   **47.** 1,266   **49.** 42,957   **51.** 17,838

Exercise B   **53.** $172.98   **55.** $194.95   **57.** $219.07   **59.** $216.07
61. $334.13   **63.** $280.75   **65.** $201.28   **67.** $316.25
69. $1,964.89   **71.** $808.84   **73.** $953.71   **75.** $2,094.52
77. $1,790.70   **79.** $215.85   **81.** $207.92

Exercise C   **83.** 247   **85.** $1,853   **87.** $118.88   **89.** $194   **91.** $30,292.81

Chapter Two, Unit 2

Exercise A   **1.** $24.95   **3.** $30.87   **5.** $87.30   **7.** 14,165   **9.** $3.94
11. $4.38   **13.** 3,085   **15.** 27,892   **17.** $463.60   **19.** .982
21. 12,105,081   **23.** $3,793.76

Exercise B   **25.** Suits: 440;   Slacks: 207;   Sports Jackets: 292;   Coats: 263;
Sweaters: 269;   Sport Shirts: 283
Stock: 2,686;   Sold: 932;   Grand Total: 1,754
27. Appliances: $4,763.80;   Furniture: $18,530.14;   Lamps: $3,213.79
Sales: $29,376.18;   Returns: $2,868.45;   Grand Total: $26,507.73
29. A: $5,589.85;   B: $1,369.25;   C: $871.86;   D: $2,772.22;
E: $3,203.95;   F: $3,857.55;   G: $2,106.90
Original Price: $30,515.00;   Amount of Reduction: $10,743.42;   Grand
Total: $19,771.58
31. Alan: $168.52;   Ambrose: $196.39;   Baker: $164.47;   Buntel: $158.62;
Campbell: $183.79;   Chisholm: $169.55;   Fulton: $167.72
Gross Pay: $1,466.28;   Deductions: $257.22;   Grand Total: $1,209.06
33. A: $207.23;   B: $282.85;   C: $260.03;   D: $214.18;   E: $270.52;
F: $241.65;   G: $244.43;   H: $283.53
Gross Pay: $2,681.51;   Deductions: $677.09;   Grand Total: $2,004.42
35. Grocery: $2,183.95;   Vegetables: $1,715.47;   Dairy: $1,180.80;
Delicatessen: $1,111.16;   Nonfood: $893.29;   Meat: $1,887.93
Gross Profit: $13,953.21;   Overhead: $4,980.61;   Grand Total: $8,972.60

Chapter Two, Unit 3

1. A: $56.85; B: $167.55; C: $178.05; D: $74.74; E: $120.17;
   F: $201.25; G: $190.95
   Original Price: $3,794.95; Sales Price: $2,805.39; Grand Total: $989.56
3. A: $149.00; B: $143.01; C: $46.00; D: $206.00; E: $290.00;
   F: $62.98; G: $96.05
   List Price: $1,306.68; Discount: $313.64; Grand Total: $993.04
5. $274.24   7. $6,851.99
9. 4137: $1,255.91; 4332: $3,449.04; 4253: $12,610.07;
   4315: $13,341.97; 4528: $14,882.88
   Amount: $46,514.27; Cash Discount: $974.40; Grand Total: $45,539.87

		Total Deductions	Net Pay		Deductions	Net Pay
11.	101	$190.25	$275.60	104	$167.49	$230.93
	102	177.60	255.10	105	182.82	263.54
	103	200.06	278.42	106	175.09	305.61

13. $14,736.15   15. $228.30

Chapter Three, Unit 1

Exercise A 1. 12,964 3. 19,278 5. 1,695,421 7. 8,154.12 9. 254.8
11. 163.552 13. 79,130 15. 2,656.5625 17. 639.5175
19. 100.4523 21. 169.158 23. 10.515875 25. 1,886.34375

Exercise B 27. #1302: $330.30; #1567: $1,107.84; #158: $1,290.60; #758: $229.14;
Total: $2,957.88
29. #1728: $474.00; #2071: $621.00; #509: $448.20; #1249: $137.90;
#1415: $334.80; Total: $2,015.90
31. #1106: $228.20; #1108: $937.50; Tiles, Yellow: $1,433.44; Tiles,
Blue: $960.75; #708: $1,072.50; #710: $731.25; Total: $5,363.64
33. #307: $1,754.55; #461: $7,792.05; #107: $3,043.25;
#423: $7,175.00; #613: $6,526.05; #707: $8,788.50; #321: $723.20;
Total: $35,802.60
35. White: $1,923.25; Pink: $1,723.75; Blue: $2,912.50;
Green: $1,487.50; Sage: $1,633.25; Orange: $2,583.75;
Total: $12,264
37. $12,600

Exercise C 39. $613.80 41. $2,227.50 43. $282.50
45. $21,506.25

Chapter Three, Unit 2

Exercise A 1. $84.86 3. $10 5. $21.96 7. $23 9. $110.90
11. 3,000 13. $15.25 15. $229.31 17. $42.90 19. $8,976.79

Exercise B 21. Alcohol, Wood: $291.94; Thinner: $422.63; Solvent #5: $721.21;
Solvent #8: $710.72; Alcohol, Denatured: $777.95;
Lacquer: $817.88; Total: $3,742.33
23. Potassium: $97.30; Magnesium: $108.86; Sulfur: $169.20;
Total: $375.36
25. Wheat: $1,624.35; Rice: $1,369.77; Soya Bean: $1,349.93;
Corn: $1,161.53; Oat: $1,089.92; Total: $6,595.50

27.

$1	$100	$1,000	$10,000	$100,000
$ 356,248	$ 356,200	$ 356,000	$ 360,000	$ 400,000
474,563	474,600	475,000	470,000	500,000
1,263,438	1,263,400	1,263,000	1,260,000	1,300,000
835,726	835,700	836,000	840,000	800,000
452,375	452,400	452,000	450,000	500,000
168,935	168,900	169,000	170,000	200,000
244,569	244,600	245,000	240,000	200,000

Exercise C 29. $272.21
31. $411.45

Chapter Three, Unit 3

Exercise A 1. 4.27 3. 53.4 5. $5,150 7. $2,800 9 $9.00
11. $2.50 13. $9,045 15. $3,150 17. 90 19. 8,700
21. 4,500 23. 2,700

Exercise B 25. Screwdrivers: $750; #19 Nails: $50; #22 Nails: $530; #15 Nails: $3,900;
Wire: $2,482; Total: $7,712
27. Sweaters: $955; Blouses: $2,475; Short Jackets: $850; Full-length
Jackets: $960; Total: $5,240
29. Pencils: $300; Erasers: $240; Pens: $3,600; 12" Rulers: $1,060; 8"
Rulers: $1,500; Total: $6,700

Chapter Three, Unit 4

1. Rice: $2,256.07; Corn: $2,276.99; Lentil: $1,980.47; Soya Bean:
$2,072.09; Sesame: $1,071.45; Total: $9,657.07
3. Clips: $100; Ribbons: $2,500; Fluid: $1,400; Envelopes: $360;
Pads: $1,460; Total: $5,820
5. $110 7. $1,250 9. $7,780 11. $10,423.40
13. $1,897.20 15. $289.75 17. $44.71

Chapter Four, Unit 1

Exercise A 1. 1186 3. 0.827 5. 15.31238 7. 7 9. 624
11. 1,539.0935 13. 232.1 15. 216.01639 17. 1.5225071
19. 1.721 21. 0.2130963 23. 3,614,899.3 25. 314,132.35
27. .00001

Exercise B **29.** Pencils: $.06; Pads: $1.31; Erasers: $.08; Ribbons: $.65; #10 Envelopes: $9.17; #6 Envelopes: $4.55
  31. Blue: 126; Plum: 132; Gold: 132; Red: 116; Royal Blue: 125
  33. Carpeting: $6; Tiles: $5; Fabric: $5; Wallpaper: $7; Paint: $5
  35. $103.15; $182.53; $104.90; $237.86; $201.58; $135.01; $159.12; $149.12; $157.94; $110.48
  37. 1: $1.22; 2: $3.32; 3: $3.57; 4: $2.88; 5: $3.05; 6: $5.45; 7: $4.48; 8: $3.24; 9: $3.22; 10: $6.31
  39. 1: $4.09; 2: $5.04; 3: $3.57; 4: $2.90; 5: $3.03; 6: $13.91; 7: $10.54; 8: $15.85; 9: $13.89; 10: $15.07

Exercise C **41.** $11 **43.** $5 **45.** $7.25 **47.** $23

Chapter Four, Unit 2

Exercise A **1.** $2.35 **3.** $.06 **5.** 4.21 **7.** $.02 **9.** 82.67 **11.** .063
  13. .35 **15.** $3.24 **17.** $.12 **19.** $5 **21.** $1,800
  23. $13,215 **25.** $51,000

Exercise B **27.** Pens: $45.13; Notebooks: $90.30; Erasers: $29.38; Pencils: $50.10; Pens: $60.63
  29. Rice: $1,577.52; Wheat: $1,503.53; Barley: $1,358.73; Peanuts: $677.56; Walnuts: $2,159.41

Exercise C **31.** $47.50 **33.** $18.56

Chapter Four, Unit 3

  1. 1,562 **3.** 46 **5.** 2.15 **7.** 4,213,000 **9.** $24.61
  11. $22.57 **13.** $135.39 **15.** 505 **17.** 4,003 **19.** 20.004
  21. 630.33 **23.** $.15 **25.** 6 **27.** 20 **29.** 2.467 **31.** 2
  33. $65.91; $76.97; $108.02; $136.91; $206.54
  35. Sugar: $28.01; Coffee: $82.24; Wheat: $1,130.47; Peanuts: $1,996.44
  37. $345.95 **39.** $219.62
  41. $4,500

Chapter Five, Unit 1

Exercise A **1.** $\frac{1}{3}$ **3.** $\frac{3}{10}$ **5.** $\frac{6}{11}$ **7.** $\frac{3}{4}$ **9.** $\frac{3}{7}$ **11.** $\frac{20}{25}$ **13.** $\frac{25}{30}$

  15. $\frac{44}{48}$ **17.** $\frac{28}{60}$ **19.** $\frac{33}{72}$ **21.** $3\frac{4}{5}$ **23.** $3\frac{7}{12}$ **25.** $3\frac{3}{8}$

  27. $1\frac{7}{9}$ **29.** $8\frac{1}{2}$ **31.** $5\frac{5}{8}$ **33.** $1\frac{1}{13}$ **35.** $1\frac{1}{3}$ **37.** $\frac{31}{7}$

  39. $\frac{37}{3}$ **41.** $\frac{47}{3}$ **43.** $\frac{27}{4}$ **45.** $\frac{19}{7}$ **47.** $\frac{47}{6}$ **49.** $\frac{38}{3}$

Exercise B   **51.** 1   **53.** $\frac{15}{20}$ **55.** 60¢   **57.** $\frac{1}{3}$

59. (a) $\frac{1}{3}$ (b) $10,000

61. $\frac{2}{5}$ **63.** (a) $\frac{3}{22}$ (b) $\frac{19}{22}$

65. $\frac{3}{4}$ **67.** $\frac{1}{3}$

Chapter Five, Unit 2

Exercise A   **1.** $1\frac{13}{15}$ **3.** $1\frac{5}{12}$ **5.** $1\frac{3}{4}$ **7.** $37\frac{151}{168}$ **9.** $70\frac{17}{60}$

11. $65\frac{7}{40}$ **13.** $59\frac{3}{10}$ **15.** $52\frac{29}{30}$ **17.** $\frac{1}{20}$ **19.** $\frac{11}{60}$

21. $\frac{1}{12}$ **23.** $15\frac{1}{8}$ **25.** $16\frac{11}{30}$ **27.** $4\frac{17}{24}$ **29.** $8\frac{1}{4}$

Exercise B   **31.** Alvarez: $46\frac{1}{4}$;   Baines: 46;   Belmore: 50;   Caldwell: $48\frac{3}{4}$;

Carter: $48\frac{3}{4}$;   Cortez: $49\frac{3}{4}$;   Elton: $48\frac{3}{4}$

33. Alvarez: $48\frac{3}{4}$;   Baines: $49\frac{1}{2}$;   Belmore: $48\frac{3}{4}$;   Caldwell: 49;

Carter: $50\frac{3}{4}$;   Cortez: $48\frac{3}{4}$;   Elton: $49\frac{3}{4}$

Exercise C   **35.** $20\frac{1}{4}$ **37.** $3\frac{5}{6}$ **39.** $17\frac{13}{48}$ **41.** $\frac{1}{6}$ **43.** $17\frac{5}{6}$

Chapter Five, Unit 3

Exercise A   **1.** $\frac{7}{12}$ **3.** $\frac{7}{54}$ **5.** $\frac{7}{15}$ **7.** $21\frac{2}{3}$ **9.** $13\frac{1}{5}$ **11.** $\frac{5}{6}$

13. $\frac{8}{9}$ **15.** $2\frac{2}{5}$ **17.** $1\frac{64}{77}$ **19.** $2\frac{1}{8}$ **21.** $\frac{19}{22}$ **23.** $10\frac{2}{3}$

25. 4

Exercise B   **27.** $3\frac{3}{4}$ **29.** 588   **31.** 20   **33.** $212.15

35. (a) $83.33   (b) $50   (c) $116.67

Chapter Five, Unit 4

Exercise A   **1.** 0.7   **3.** 0.5   **5.** 0.7   **7.** 0.88   **9.** 0.42   **11.** 0.72
13. 0.529   **15.** 0.278   **17.** 0.721

Exercise B   **19.** 0.656   **21.** 0.047   **23.** 0.8   **25.** 0.667   **27.** 0.20 or 0.2

Chapter Five, Unit 5

Exercise A   **1.** 66   **3.** 75   **5.** 64   **7.** 133   **9.** 260
11. $21; $40; $31; $70; Total: $162
13. $24; $42; $48; $96; Total: $210
15. $12; $21; $270; $360; Total: $663
17. $16; $15; $18; $48; Total: $97
19. $9; $30; $21; $80; Total: $140
21. $30; $156; $216; $65; Total: $467

Exercise B   **23.** $118; $315; $71; $360; Total: $864
25. $267; $1,214; $596; $384; Total: $2,461

Exercise C   **27.** 174   **29.** $375   **31.** $135.42

Chapter Five, Unit 6

1. $\frac{1}{8}$ **3.** $\frac{4}{9}$ **5.** $\frac{1}{10}$ **7.** $\frac{36}{48}$ **9.** $\frac{36}{45}$ **11.** $2\frac{1}{4}$

13. $1\frac{67}{90}$ **15.** $80\frac{7}{8}$ **17.** $\frac{1}{15}$ **19.** $\frac{7}{12}$ **21.** $5\frac{1}{8}$ **23.** $\frac{3}{4}$

25. 176   **27.** 8,319   **29.** $\frac{14}{15}$ **31.** $\frac{22}{43}$ **33.** $\frac{69}{82}$ **35.** 245

37. 138   **39.** 108

41. $12; $3; $24; $60; $65; $420; Total: $584

43. .8   **45.** .8   **47.** .33   **49.** .60   **51.** .438   **53.** .639

55. $125

Chapter Six, Unit 1

Exercise A   **1.** .29   **3.** .375   **5.** 1.00   **7.** .0798   **9.** .0001   **11.** .0675
13. 25%   **15.** 6%   **17.** 8,750%   **19.** 200%   **21.** 215%
23. 20%   **25.** .0825   **27.** .125   **29.** $254.80   **31.** $204.75
33. $180   **35.** $42.56   **37.** $13.90   **39.** $7.53

Exercise B   **41.** Subtotal: $1,167.00;   Sales tax: $93.36;   Total: $1,260.36

Exercise C   **43.** 40¢   **45.** $33\frac{1}{3}\%$ **47.** 7.50%   **49.** $39,192   **51.** $763.75
53. $379.50

Chapter Six, Unit 2

Exercise A   **1.** 87.5%   **3.** 19.2%   **5.** 25%   **7.** 55.6%   **9.** 20%
11. 37.5%   **13.** 16.7%   **15.** 147%   **17.** 50%   **19.** 58.4%
21. 39.4%   **23.** 5.3%   **25.** 57.4%   **27.** 23.1%   **29.** 20.6%
31. 153.9%   **33.** 21.1%   **35.** 21.2%   **37.** 42.7%
39. 176.6%   **41.** 30.9%   **43.** 34.3%   **45.** $205.71
47. $877.78   **49.** $1,107   **51.** 587.5   **53.** 9,840   **55.** $225.45
57. 448   **59.** $2,833.73   **61.** $72.86   **63.** 2,425.93

Exercise B   **65.** Sale Price: $153.17;   Reduction Percent: 35%
Reduction Amount: $132.13;   Reduction Percent: 40%
Sale Price: $114.30;   Reduction Amount: $61.55
Reduction Amount: $259.18;   Reduction Percent: 45%
Sale Price: $285.25;   Reduction Percent: 33%
Reduction Amount: $182.52;   Reduction Percent: 48%
Reduction Amount: $104.63;   Reduction Percent: 35%
Sale Price: $436.21;   Reduction Amount: $169.64
67. Amount of Sale: $80.92;   Sales Tax Amount: $4.86
Sales Tax Rate: 8%;   Sales Tax Amount: $9.53
Amount of Sale: $233.36;   Sales Tax Amount: $12.83
Amount of Sale: $178.61;   Sales Tax Amount: $14.74
Sales Tax Rate: 5%;   Amount of Sale: $206.17
Amount of Sale: $329.14;   Sales Tax Amount: $13.17
Sales Tax Rate: 4.5%;   Sales Tax Amount: $11.16
Amount of Sale: $321.31;   Sales Tax Amount: $20.89

Exercise C   **69.** 17.9%   **71.** 21.2%   **73.** 19.8%   **75.** 22.6%   **77.** 48.8%
79. $193.08   **81.** $356,666.67   **83.** $13,260

Chapter Six, Unit 3

1. $758.96   **3.** $425   **5.** $590.56   **7.** 75%   **9.** $790
11. $835.16   **13.** 30.3%   **15.** $65,990

Chapter Six, Unit 4

1. $\frac{3}{4}$ **3.** $\frac{3}{1}$ **5.** $\frac{8}{1}$ **7.** $\frac{6}{25}$ **9.** $\frac{9}{1}$ **11.** $\frac{1.20}{1}$ **13.** $\frac{.1}{1}$

15. $\frac{.58}{1}$ **17.** $40   **19.** 108

Chapter Six, Unit 5

1. 5 **3.** 30 **5.** 5 **7.** 32 **9.** .17 **11.** 315 **13.** 3,552
15. $35.25 **17.** $520 **19.** $3,275 **21.** $250

Chapter Six, Unit 6

		Amount of Discount	Net Price
1.	A	$ 50.80	$ 76.20
	B	73.35	89.65
	C	149.60	122.40
	D	85.75	159.25
	E	122.98	163.02
	F	177.84	164.16
	G	318.66	359.34

	Amount of Interest	New Balance
3.	$108.41	$1,347.06
	153.90	1,732.32
	193.86	2,609.56
	248.18	2,819.99
	369.45	4,052.00
	410.22	3,930.82

5. $280 **7.** $413.17 **9.** (a) $10,909.25 (b) 20%
11. $11,207.69 **13.** $5,566.84

Chapter Seven, Unit 1

Exercise A **1.** 32 **3.** 320.8 **5.** 253.2 **7.** 458 **9.** 20.1

	Median	Mode		Median	Mode
11.	70	70	**17.**	47.5	40
13.	25	32	**19.**	180	170
15.	170	191			

Exercise B **21.** $302.89
23. (a) $10,466.67 (b) $10,175
25. $195

Chapter Seven, Unit 2

Exercise A **1.** Sales for Appliance Department **3.** $5,000
5. (a) August (b) $37,000
7. May and September **9.** February, March, May, July, August, and November
11. (a) July (b) $35,000
13. October **15.** July

Exercise B 17.

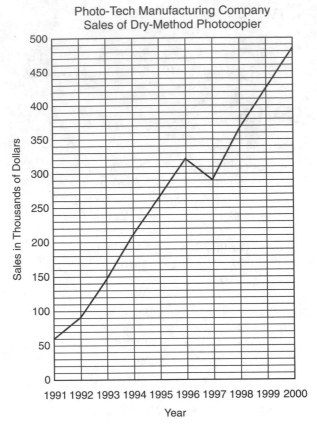

Photo-Tech Manufacturing Company
Sales of Dry-Method Photocopier

Chapter Seven, Unit 3

Exercise A 1. Thrifty Supermarket Sales by Department 3. $10,000
5. (a) Grocery   (b) $88,000
7. $42,000   9. Nonfood and Deli   11. Deli and Grocery
13. 22.9%
15. Grocery, Meat, Dairy, Produce, Nonfood, Deli   (a) Deli
(b) Grocery and Dairy

Exercise B 17. 1995   19. 450   21. 350   23. 36%

Exercise C **25.**

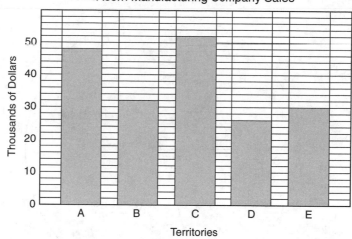

Acorn Manufacturing Company Sales

27.

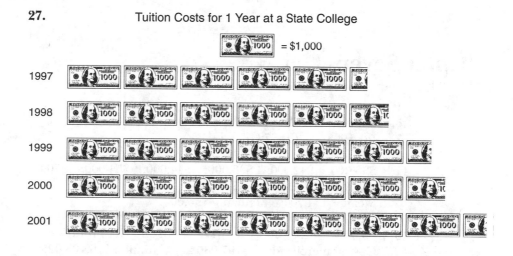

Tuition Costs for 1 Year at a State College

Chapter Seven, Unit 4

Exercise A   **1.** Distribution of the Fernandez Income of $28,500   **3.** 100%
5. Charity   **7.** 59%   **9.** $6,270   **11.** $570

Exercise B **13.**

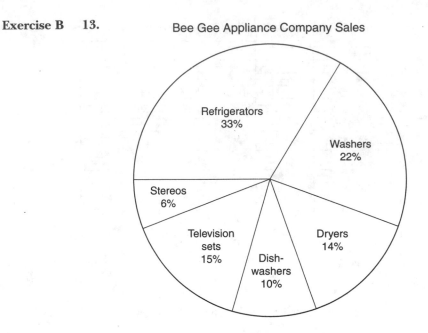

Bee Gee Appliance Company Sales

Refrigerators 33%

Washers 22%

Stereos 6%

Television sets 15%

Dish-washers 10%

Dryers 14%

Chapter Seven, Unit 5

1. 38   **3.** 347.2

5. Median: 75;   Mode: 70

7. (a) 1998   (b) $78,000

9. 1995

11. $36,000; $42,000; $38,000; $44,000; $54,000; $70,000; $58,000; $78,000; $64,000; $58,000;
Mean = $54,200;   Median = $56,000;
Mode = $58,000

13. 15,000   **15.** 20.7%   **17.** Rent and Net profit

19. Cost of merchandise: $797,080.20;   Utilities: $79,708.02;
Rent: $119,562.03;   Maintenance: $79,708.02;   Salaries: $185,985.38;
Net profit: $66,423.35

21. $853,894.20   **23.** 30,000

Chapter Eight, Unit 1

Exercise A   **1.** 25 ft. 2 in.   **3.** 26 gross 3 doz.   **5.** 28 gal.   **7.** 35 gal. 1 pt.
9. 42 gal.   **11.** 4 ft. 5 in.   **13.** 6 gross 10 doz.
15. 8 yd. 2 ft. 11 in.   **17.** 2 gross 8 doz. 10 units
19. 4 gross 6 doz. 11 units

Exercise B   **21.** 29 lb. 13 oz.   **23.** $88   **25.** 4 lb. 9 oz.

Chapter Eight, Unit 2

Exercise A
1. 18 ft. 9 in.   3. 38 yd. 2 ft. 8 in.   5. 55 gal.
7. 53 lb. 10 oz.   9. 26 yd. 2 ft.   11. 2 ft.   13. 3 lb. 2 oz.
15. 2 gal. 2 qt.   17. 2 lb. 2 oz.   19. 2 gross 7 doz. 11 units

Exercise B
21. (a) 21 gross 10 doz.   (b) $157.20   23. (a) 83 lb. 4 oz.
(b) $59.70   25. 2 gal. 2 qt.

Chapter Eight, Unit 3

Exercise A
1. 2.40 m   3. 530 mm   5. 0.573 L   7. 0.0415 L   9. 530 mg
11. 4.375 m   13. 600 mg   15. 80 m   17. 2,350 cg
19. 525 cL   21. 23,500 cL   23. 0.00432 kg   25. 50,000 mL
27. 400 m   29. 6,350 mm

Exercise B
31. 2.64 L   33. 50   35. 3

Chapter Eight, Unit 4

Exercise A
1. 66 ft.   3. 81 mi.   5. 1,191 g   7. 71 mi.   9. 17 L
11. 8 lb.   13. 1 metric ton   15. 83 mm   17. 7 dm
19. 2 kg   21. 12.8 in.   23. 1.65 lb.

Exercise B
25. 1.37 in.   27. 4.8 L   29. 11.8 ft. by 21.3 ft.

Chapter Eight, Unit 5

1. 31 yd. 1 ft. 6 in.   3. 9 gross 8 doz. 10 units   5. 112 gal. 1 pt.
7. 2 gross 5 doz. 10 units   9. 800 mg   11. 825 cL   13. 730 m
15. 1,150 mL   17. 1,503 g   19. 26 mi.   21. 29 mm
23. 23.26 sq. yd.

Chapter Nine, Unit 1

Exercise A

	Amount of Interest	New Balance		Amount of Interest	New Balance
1.	$ 924.00	$ 9,324.00	11.	$ 225.00	$15,225.00
3.	605.00	11,605.00	13.	348.15	8,788.15
5.	609.00	6,409.00	15.	1,062.50	19,812.50
7.	3,400.00	13,400.00	17.	288.36	15,013.36
9.	2,176.53	13,941.53	19.	102.50	24,102.50

21. Interest Rate: 6.75%;   New Balance: $6,244.88
23. Interest Rate: 5.25%;   New Balance: $4,920.44
25. Amount: $9,750.04;   New Balance: $10,883.97
27. $3,600   **29.** $1,347.50   **31.** $993.94   **33.** $2,656.25
35. $888.96

	Amount of Interest	New Balance
37.	$ 64.14	$1,529.89
39.	101.47	2,630.27
41.	226.87	4,748.35

Exercise B   **43.** $6,648   **45.** 14.5%   **47.** $17,217.54

Chapter Nine, Unit 2

Exercise A   **1.** Bills: $107:   Coins: $2.77;   Checks: $127.25;   Tot. Deposit: $237.02
3. Bills: $191:   Checks: $215.28;   Total Deposit: $406.28
5. Bills: $137:   Checks: $158.05;   Total Deposit: $295.05

(*Note:* For #s 7–11 follow the model check shown on page 212.)

7. Balance in register: $171.10
9. Balance in register: $357.85
11. Balance in register: $234.07

Exercise B   (*Note:* For #s 13–21 follow the model bank reconciliation statement on page 214.)

13. Adjusted balance: $245.49
15. Adjusted balance: $243.18
17. Adjusted balance: $279.90
19. Adjusted balance: $155.25
21. Adjusted balance: $558.90

Exercise C   **23.** $195.87   **25.** $57.20   **27.** $231.62   **29.** $215.80

Chapter Nine, Unit 3

Exercise A   **1.** $21.25   **3.** $48.375   **5.** $63.625   **7.** $36.875   **9.** $19.75
11. $2,690   **13.** $4,762.50   **15.** $14,450   **17.** $10,462.50
19. $9,428.13   **21.** $18.50   **23.** $63.625   **25.** $41.875
27. $24.625   **29.** $63.125

	Price per Share	Net Total Price
31.	$54.56	$19,096.00
33.	20.25	7,087.50
35.	7.94	2,779.00
37.	27.44	9,604.00
39.	15.25	5,337.50

Exercise B **41.** $58.45 **43.** $19.90 **45.** $147.08 **47.** $82.94 **49.** $20.44

	Selling Price	Brokerage Fee	Total Cost
51.	$6,900.00	$125.70	$7,025.70
53.	4,375.00	116.88	4,491.88
55.	5,332.50	67.99	5,400.49

	Selling Price	Brokerage Fee	Net Proceeds
57.	$ 9,525.00	$151.73	$ 9,373.27
59.	11,400.00	190.60	11,209.40

Exercise C **61.** (a) $10,281.25 (b) $187.50
63. (a) $7,992.19 (b) $68.75
65. $15,268.75
67. (a) $5,225.00 (b) $13,775.00

Chapter Nine, Unit 4

Exercise A **1.** $935 **3.** $853.75 **5.** $1,022.50 **7.** $477.50
9. $1,151.25 **11.** $946.25 **13.** $892.50 **15.** $951.25
17. +$7.50 **19.** −$6.25 **21.** −$21.25 **23.** +$16.25
25. −$17.50

	Interest Rate	Maturity Year
27.	9.0%	2016
29.	7.25%	2045
31.	8.5%	2022
33.	11.75%	2003

	Price per Bond	Total Price
35.	$687.50	$3,437.50
37.	757.50	3,787.50
39.	675.00	8,100.00
41.	588.75	8,831.25

	Price per Bond	Total Price
43.	$480.00	$ 1,440.00
45.	935.00	11,220.00
47.	542.50	8,137.50
49.	940.00	12,220.00

	Price Paid	Annual Interest	Current Yield
51.	$1,022.50	$141.25	13.8%
53.	857.50	130.00	15.2%

Exercise B

	Fee per Bond	Total Fee
55.	$4.25	$21.25
57.	4.25	34.00
59.	2.75	41.25
61.	8.50	51.00
63.	6.75	94.50

	Fee per Bond	Total Fee	Total Cost
65.	$8.50	$42.50	$ 4,817.50
67.	4.25	34.00	5,624.00
69.	6.75	60.75	7,868.25
71.	2.75	41.25	7,260.00
73.	4.25	68.00	10,568.00

Exercise C **75.** (a) $10,380.00 (b) $622.80 (c) 6.9%
77. (a) $11,340.00 (b) $94.50 (c) $11,434.50

Chapter Nine, Unit 5

	Amount of Interest	New Balance
1.	$1,231.88	$7,801.88
3.	2,765.34	11,105.34
5.	992.55	16,592.55
7.	161.92	4,561.92

9. Bills: $377.00; Checks: $660.55; Total Deposit: $1,037.55
11. Bills: $699.00; Checks: $956.54; Total Deposit: $1,655.54
13. Check #143 (follow model on page 212); balance is $369.59
15. Bank reconciliation statement (follow model on page 214), adjusted balance is $877.18
17. $63.125 **19.** $18.875 **21.** $31.625 **23.** $14,090.63
25. $5,443.75 **27.** $39.125 **29.** $47.25
31. Price per Share: $87.00; Net Total Price: $41,325.00
33. $126.19 **35.** $56.03
37. Selling Price: $5,925.00; Brokerage Fee: $149.03; Total Cost: $6,074.03
39. Selling Price: $4,875.00; Brokerage Fee: $99.38; Net Proceeds: $4,775.62
41. Selling Price: $8,787.50; Brokerage Fee: $101.09; Net Proceeds: $8,686.41
43. $1,051.25 **45.** $957.50 **47.** –$12.50 **49.** +$6.25
51. Interest Rate: 7.5%; Maturity Year: 2001
53. Price per Bond: $782.50; Total Price: $6,260.00
55. Price per Bond: $613.75; Total Price: $9,206.25
57. Price Paid: $871.25; Annual Interest: $131.25; Current Yield: 15.1%
59. Fee per Bond: $6.75; Total Fee: $54.00
61. Fee per Bond: $6.75; Total Fee: $101.25
63. Fee per Bond: $8.50; Total Fee: $110.50; Total Cost: $13,094.25
65. $12,153.61 **67.** $32,846.72 **69.** Corrected balance: $16.29

Chapter Ten, Unit 1

Exercise A
1. December 19   3. September 1   5. February 20
7. February 16   9. September 8   11. April 23
13. September 14   15. February 18   17. February 28
19. August 18

	Due Date	Interest	Maturity Value
21.	October 1	$ 25.68	$815.68
23.	November 12	121.13	596.13
25.	January 29	38.00	988.00
27.	July 18	6.59	571.59
29.	June 10	18.65	783.65

Exercise B
31. June 7; $698.63
33. September 24; $1,614.38
35. $1,200

Chapter Ten, Unit 2

Exercise A

	Amount of Interest	Net Amount
1.	$ 257.00	$1,028.00
3.	50.92	2,299.08
5.	2,278.50	3,146.50
7.	377.34	2,497.66
9.	178.64	2,396.36

	Amount of Interest	Net Amount	Monthly Payment
11.	$ 365.63	$1,509.38	$104.17
13.	1,573.20	2,986.80	126.67
15.	715.00	2,035.00	114.58
17.	579.38	1,995.62	143.06
19.	2,115.00	2,385.00	93.75

21. $13.70   23. $24   25. $105.22   27. $64.76   29. $400

	Interest	Amount Due
31.	$ 69.50	$3,544.50
33.	123.15	2,586.15
35.	14.32	4,309.32
37.	64.00	2,624.00
39.	128.70	4,418.70

Exercise B
41. $950   43. $2,022.47   45. $2,073.60   47. $1,390.55
49. $23.53

Chapter Ten, Unit 3

Exercise A
1. $127 3. $36 5. $595 7. $208 9. $94 11. $16.33
13. $9.55 15. $17.74 17. $19.65 19. $21.21 21. 34.1%
23. 25.3% 25. 34.8% 27. 32% 29. 41.7%

Exercise B 31. $41 33. $25.42 35. $122.60

Chapter Ten, Unit 4

1. June 15 3. July 19 5. February 1

	Due Date	Interest	Maturity Value
7.	November 25	$83.69	$2,658.69
9.	July 5	28.59	1,528.59

	Interest	Total Debt
11.	$496.13	$1,846.13
13.	842.81	4,717.81
15.	912.66	5,037.66

	Interest	Net Amount	Monthly Payment
17.	$1,507.85	$4,182.15	$237.08
19.	3,400.80	3,139.20	136.25

21. $390 23. $28.27 25. $49.10

Chapter Eleven, Unit 1

Exercise A

	Monthly Payments	Yearly Payments
1.	$462.98	$5,555.76
3.	526.13	6,313.56
5.	752.07	9,024.84
7.	487.34	5,848.08
9.	329.61	3,955.32

11. $931.25 13. $997.60 15. $1,554.45 17. $109.90
19. $610.85

Exercise B 21. $767.10 23. $743.25 25. $42,565.22 27. $1,197.63
29. $1,041.45

Chapter Eleven, Unit 2

Exercise A   **1.** $239.75   **3.** $179.08   **5.** $194.40   **7.** $891.41   **9.** $968

	Unexpired Days	Amount of Refund
11.	290	$147.78
13.	130	79.78
15.	185	108.97

Exercise B   **17.** $787.05   **19.** $211.68

Chapter Eleven, Unit 3

Exercise A   **1.** $1,375   **3.** $1,450   **5.** $1,550
7. Annual Depreciation: $2,025;   Rate of Depreciation: 21%
9. Annual Depreciation: $1,150;   Rate of Depreciation: 15%

Exercise B   **11.** $1,366.67   **13.** 18%   **15.** $1,281.25

Chapter Eleven, Unit 4

Exercise A   **1.** $81   **3.** $280   **5.** $84   **7.** $48   **9.** $88

Exercise B   **11.** Bodily injury: $244;   Property damage: $107;   Total: $351
13. $298.75
15. (a) $383   (b) $311

Chapter Eleven, Unit 5

Exercise A

	Premium per $1,000	Number of 1,000's in Face Value	Annual Premium
1.	$ 9.21	22.5	$ 207.23
3.	22.68	24.5	555.66
5.	9.33	19.5	181.94
7.	25.35	40	1,014.00
9.	10.42	29	302.18

Exercise B   **11.** $286.43   **13.** $95.37   **15.** $1,996.15

Chapter Eleven, Unit 6

1. Monthly Payment: $427.76;   Yearly Payment: $5,133.12
3. Monthly Payment: $527.71;   Yearly Payment: $6,332.52
5. $2,131.61   **7.** $264.38   **9.** $130.90   **11.** $188.40

13. $764.06
15. Unexpired Days: 252;   Amount of Refund: $162.25
17. Unexpired Days: 170;   Amount of Refund: $117.84
19. $1,006.67
21. Annual Depreciation: $1,433;   Rate of Depreciation: 14%
23. Annual Depreciation: $1,419;   Rate of Depreciation: 15%
25. $191   **27.** $81
29. Premium per $1,000: $9.21;   Number of 1,000's: 52.75;   Annual Premium: $485.83
31. Premium per $1,000: $51.60;   Number of 1,000's: 70;   Annual Premium: $3,612
33. (a) $607.38   (b) $33,262.80
35. (a) $3,214.69   (b) $5,024.44

Chapter Twelve, Unit 1

Exercise A

1.
$ 17.85
35.00
39.75
$ 92.60
Tax 7.41
Total $100.01

3.
$37.50
29.80
9.75
11.80
$88.95
Tax 6.23
Total $95.18

5.
$25.00
35.70
11.25
$71.95
Tax 2.16
Total $74.11

Exercise B

7.
$55.90
15.50
7.50
9.00
$87.90
Tax 4.40
Total $92.30

9.
$17.50
14.00
11.90
$43.40
Tax 1.30
Total $44.70

Chapter Twelve, Unit 2

Exercise A   1. $1.78   **3.** $.93   **5.** $.92   **7.** $9   **9.** $15.60

	Fractional Part	Cost of Frac-tional Part
11.	$\frac{3}{4}$	$4.01
13.	$\frac{7}{9}$	2.71
15.	$\frac{2}{3}$	1.43
17.	$1\frac{1}{3}$	8.33
19.	$1\frac{9}{16}$	4.45

Exercise B **21.** (a) $\frac{3}{8}$ (b) $3.87

23. $3.74 **25.** $3.19 **27.** $2.35 **29.** $7.34

Chapter Twelve, Unit 3

		Discount Amount	Sale Price
Exercise A	**1.**	$44.07	$ 81.83
	3.	42.38	127.12
	5.	58.33	29.17

7. Remaining Percent: 70%;   Sale Price: $81.03

9. Remaining Percent: $33\frac{1}{3}$%;   Sale Price: $49.17

Exercise B **11.** $199.31 **13.** $256.50 **15.** 25%

Chapter Twelve, Unit 4

3.
$$
\begin{array}{r}
\$\ 44.25 \\
95.70 \\
5.35 \\
\underline{16.50} \\
\$161.80 \\
\text{Tax} \quad \underline{12.14} \\
\text{Total} \ \$173.94
\end{array}
$$

5. $3.20 **7.** $4.63

9. Fractional Part: $\frac{29}{32}$;   Cost: $3.49

11. Fractional Part: $1\frac{3}{4}$;   Cost: $12.16

13. Discount Amount: $59.65;   Sale Price: $119.30

15. Remaining Percent: 55%;   Sale Price: $188.57

17. Remaining Percent: $87\frac{1}{2}$%;   Sale Price: $148.71

19. $1.74 **21.** $747.45

Chapter Thirteen, Unit 1

		Discount Date	Due Date
Exercise A	**1.**	April 15	May 5
	3.	May 5	June 9

	Discount Date	Due Date
5.	February 21	April 12
7.	September 7	October 22
9.	January 23	February 12

	Discount Date	Due Date	Net Amount	Full Amount
11.	9/20	10/25	$ 458.15	
13.	7/30	9/13	380.92	
15.	10/18	11/22		$963.85
17.	2/18	5/9	1,217.65	
19.	6/26	8/15	361.28	

Exercise B   **21.**   (a) 3/24   (b) 5/8   (c) $802.68
23.   (a) 7/31   (b) 9/4   (c) $620.56
25.   (a) 6/2   (b) 7/7   (c) $25.91

Chapter Thirteen, Unit 2

	Amount of Discount	Invoice Price
Exercise A **1.**	$ 85.93	$159.57
3.	67.80	67.80
5.	142.54	174.21
7.	128.43	105.07
9.	208.14	485.66

	First Discount	Second Discount	Third Discount	Invoice Price
11.	$ 30.63	$ 5.69	$ 2.56	$ 48.62
13.	67.90	3.40	1.94	62.56
15.	42.08	9.82	4.42	83.93
17.	74.60	34.81	6.96	132.28
19.	127.30	35.46	20.09	180.85

21. $254.60   **23.** $324.63   **25.** $342.61   **27.** $446.78
29. $438.30   **31.** 53.3%   **33.** 50.6%   **35.** 92.5%
37. 53.0%   **39.** 54.9%

	Single Equivalent Percent	Invoice Price
41.	46%	$ 39.20
43.	48.7%	123.97
45.	44.4%	156.63
47.	46%	171.42
49.	45.9%	256.38

Exercise B   **51.**   (a) $158.30   (b) $237.45
53. $565.40   **55.** $761.37
57. (a) A: 41.3%; B: 40.2%   (b) A
59. $421.59

Chapter Thirteen, Unit 3

		Markup Amount	Cost Price
Exercise A	1.	$47.25	$87.75
	3.	17.03	20.82
	5.	39.38	48.12
	7.	42.26	78.49
	9.	73.71	90.09

11. Cost Price: $67.75; Markup Percent: 36.2%

13. Markup Amount: $21.30; Markup Percent: $33\frac{1}{3}\%$

15. Markup Amount: $44.95; Markup Percent: 32.4%

17. Markup Amount: $175.60; Markup Percent: 55%

19. Cost price: $105.70; Markup percent: 44.8%

	Equivalent Cost Percent	Selling Price
21.	55%	$170.27
23.	60%	114.58
25.	45%	812.22
27.	70%	123.36
29.	75%	251.00

Exercise B	31.	(a) $89.25	(b) 48.2%
	33.	(a) $292.50	(b) $117.00
	35.	$19.22	

Chapter Thirteen, Unit 4

		Markup Amount	Selling Price
Exercise A	1.	$36.56	$ 85.31
	3.	51.59	145.39
	5.	80.11	203.36
	7.	83.18	194.08
	9.	91.00	256.45

11. Selling Price: $206.88; Markup Rate: 50.5%
13. Markup Amount: $140.15; Markup Rate: 65.1%
15. Cost Price: $93.45; Markup Rate: 55%
17. Selling Price: $434.78; Markup Rate: 65%
19. Selling Price: $214.05; Markup Rate: 70%

	Equivalent Percent	Cost Price
21.	173%	$104.48
23.	180%	240.50
25.	182%	32.01
27.	165%	63.91
29.	185%	63.51

Exercise B **31.**   (a) $302.74   (b) $768.49
              33.   (a) $145.25   (b) 61.7%
              35.   (a) 175%   (b) $22.83

Chapter Thirteen, Unit 5

1. Discount Date: March 1;   Due Date: April 20
3. Discount Date: December 15;   Due Date: March 5
5. Discount Date: 8/25;   Due Date: 9/29;   Net Amount: $857.97
7. Discount Date: 12/2;   Due Date: 1/16;   Net Amount: $1,623.66
9. Trade Discount: $282.94;   Invoice Price: $345.81
11. Trade Discount: $142.98;   Invoice Price: $214.47
13. $304.18
15. Discounts: (1) $57.18;   (2) $8.58;   (3) $3.86;   Invoice Price: $73.33
17. Discounts: (1) $222.14;   (2) $21.72;   (3) $9.99;   Invoice Price: $239.80
19. $107.17   **21.** 61.5%   **23.** 44.7%
25. Markup Amount: $64.31;   Cost Price: $119.44
27. Cost Price: $128;   Markup Percent: 45%
29. Cost Price: $249.97;   Markup Percent: 37.5%
31. Equivalent Cost Percent: 55%;   Selling Price: $450.82
33. Markup Amount: $59.25;   Selling Price: $158.00
35. Markup Amount: $188.44;   Selling Price: $478.34
37. Markup Amount: $123.25;   Markup Rate: 54%
39. $575.65
41. (a) 68.5%   (b) $103.87
43. $63.33

Chapter Fourteen, Unit 1

Exercise A

	Regular Hours	Total Regular Amount	O/T Hours	O/T Rate	Total O/T Amount	Gross Pay
1.	40	$230.00	3	8.625	$25.88	$255.88
3.	40	180.00	1	6.75	6.75	186.75
5.	40	170.00	$7\frac{1}{4}$	6.375	46.22	216.22
7.	40	248.00	$2\frac{3}{4}$	9.30	25.58	273.58
9.	40	200.00	6	7.50	45.00	245.00
11.	37	197.95	$1\frac{1}{2}$	8.025	12.04	209.99
13.	39	304.20	$3\frac{1}{2}$	11.70	40.95	345.15
15.	37	192.40	4	7.80	31.20	223.60
17.	38	296.40	5	11.70	58.50	354.90
19.	37	175.75	$7\frac{1}{2}$	7.125	53.44	229.19

Exercise B

	Total Pieces	Total Wages
21.	589	$235.60
23.	598	199.33
25.	552	248.40
27.	580	203.00
29.	589	441.75

	Total Dozens	Total Wages
31.	$59\frac{1}{4}$	$174.79
33.	$70\frac{1}{4}$	195.30
35.	$66\frac{1}{4}$	193.45
37.	$67\frac{3}{4}$	206.64
39.	68	198.56

	Net Sales	Total Earnings
41.	$ 2,185.60	$369.13
43.	6,524.00	326.20
45.	3,478.50	353.28
47.	5,460.00	313.40
49.	12,760.00	382.80

Exercise C **51.** $333.28 **53.** $415.01 **55.** $313.03 **57.** $100,100
59. $171.45 **61.** $213.75 **63.** $96.68 **65.** 22.7%

Chapter Fourteen, Unit 2

Exercise A **1.** $36.38 **3.** $34.69 **5.** $35.47 **7.** $29.51 **9.** $44.05
11. none **13.** none **15.** 47 **17.** 40 **19.** 33

Exercise B

	Income Tax	FICA Tax	Take-Home Pay
21.	$72.00	$58.71	$636.79
23.	68.00	60.72	665.03
25.	127.00	60.09	598.41
27.	72.00	66.82	734.63
29.	63.00	52.08	565.67

Exercise C **31.** $518.06
33. $52,469.04
35. $738.68

Chapter Fourteen, Unit 3

	Regular Pay	O/T Pay	Gross Pay
1.	$310.00	$ 69.75	$379.75
3.	274.00	123.30	397.30
5.	306.00	88.93	394.93

7. Total Pieces: 459;   Total Wages: $275.40
9. Total Pieces: 1,146;   Total Wages: $401.10
11. Total Dozens: 125;   Total Wages: $316.25
13. $35.48   **15.** $43.51   **17.** 51   **19.** 44
21. Income Tax: $64.00;   FICA: $58.40;   Take-Home Pay: $640.97
23. Income Tax: $75.00;   FICA: $68.65;   Take-Home Pay: $753.77
25. $95   **27.** $383.48

Index